Inf[a]

Tested

David H.J.Gay

Let us enquire into [infant baptism's] origin. Should it appear to have been devised merely by human rashness, let us abandon it, and regulate the true observance of baptism entirely by the will of the Lord

John Calvin

These were more fair-minded... in that they... searched the Scriptures... to find out whether these things were so

Acts 17:11

BRACHUS

First published by BRACHUS 2009
davidhjgay@googlemail.com

Scripture quotations, unless otherwise stated,
are from the New King James Version

OTHER BOOKS BY THE SAME AUTHOR

UNDER DAVID GAY
Voyage to Freedom
Dutch: Reis naar de vrijheid
Christians Grow Old
Italian: I credenti invecchiano
Battle for the Church (First Edition)

UNDER DAVID H.J.GAY
The Gospel Offer is Free (First and Second Editions)
Particular Redemption and the Free Offer
Septimus Sears: A Victorian Injustice and Its Aftermath
Baptist Sacramentalism: A Warning to Baptists
Battle for the Church (Second Edition)
The Priesthood of All Believers
John Colet: A Preacher to be Reckoned With
The Pastor: Does He Exist?
Christ is All: No Sanctification by the Law

Contents

Preamble

In 1997, I published *Battle for the Church*. It has been put to me that two of its chapters – an examination of infant baptism – would make a separate work, and ought to be published as such, *including footnotes*. In meeting these suggestions,[1] I have also drawn on other material in the book to form Appendix 1 to show that dipping is essential to the ordinance of baptism. Although I have made some changes – not only to enable the two chapters to stand on their own, but to include recently published material, and, of course, the aforesaid footnotes – this work is substantially the same as the original. Indeed, because of those recent developments, my stance has become even more firm. And you will see why, reader, when you read what is being said and written today by some Reformed infant-baptisers.[2] On one point, however – not directly connected with the subject in hand – I have altered my position since 1997. At that time, I had reservations about the usual Reformed view on the law (Calvin's threefold use), but I have now gone further; I am convinced that Christ's law in the new covenant is not the law of Moses. This important topic makes only a

---

[1] Since I want the arguments of infant baptisers fully weighed, I have also supplied generous (some will say over-generous) extracts (in which, if necessary, I have modernised punctuation and the like without altering the sense). Or, to start as I mean to go on, some who object to my copious extracts might use John Milton's words to put it more bluntly and say they find here 'a paroxysm' or 'horse-loads of citations' (Milton pp75,305). However, as I have said in earlier books, I know how much I appreciate extensive quotes; I can only ask the indulgence of readers who do not. And there is a further point. I am conscious that it is altogether too easy to caricature the position of those I disagree with. While the use of extensive extracts will not avoid this danger entirely, it will, at least, allow those I quote a fair crack of the whip, and make it more difficult for me to build a man of straw in order to set fire to him. Finally on this point, perhaps it might not be out of place to repeat the words of J.H.Plumb: 'The most valuable part of [Winston] Churchill's volumes [on his life of Marlborough] lies in [his] extensive quotations' (Plumb p134).
[2] And not only them. To my amazement, there is a sinister development among Baptists. And so serious is this movement, I intend to publish a separate book on it (which I shall denote by *Baptist Sacramentalism*) as a companion volume to this present work.

fleeting appearance in this book, and has no effect on its argument. It will, however, assume a much larger role in a book I hope to publish on the believer and the law.

Some, no doubt, will object to this present publication,[3] both in its content and tone, calling it divisive, far too polemical. Well, there is no point in denying it – this book *is* passionately controversial, and trenchantly so.[4] But lest there should be any misunderstanding, let me say – without any hint of patronisation whatsoever – I wholeheartedly acknowledge that those I have (principally) in my sights,[5] take

---

[3] Some, it seems, want to avoid all discussion of baptism. The InterVarsity Press, for example, 'have generally steered clear of books on baptism since we prefer not to take sides on the issue' (Cross: 'The Evangelical sacrament' p197, quoting from a private letter from the Senior Editor in the USA in 2004), 'though he [the Editor] proceeded to note the occasional recent exceptions'.

[4] As for the work being *too* polemical, so be it! I have not undertaken the work lightly, and I have wrestled with the accusation. While I do not condone Martin Luther's virulent language as he grew older, I empathise with his 'apology' for it: 'I see that that which is treated quietly in our age soon passes into oblivion, no one caring about it' (Mark U.Edwards p214). (This is the only quotation from Mark U.Edwards. When I quote Jonathan Edwards, I will use 'Edwards'). Milton again: On 'a controversy of great importance... I resolved... to stand on that side where I saw... the plain authority of Scripture leading... with this opinion, which esteems it... unlike a Christian to be a cold neuter in the cause of the church... [Speaking of] Luther... his own friends and favourers were many times offended with the fierceness of his spirit; yet... he thought it God's will to have the inventions of men thus laid open, seeing that matters quietly handled were quickly forgot... When God commands to take the trumpet, and blow a dolorous or a jarring blast, it lies not in man's will what he shall say, or what he shall conceal. If he shall think to be silent as Jeremiah did... he would be forced to confess as he confessed: "His word was in my heart as a burning fire shut up in my bones; I was weary with forbearing, and could not stay". Which might teach these times not suddenly to condemn all things that are sharply spoken or vehemently written as proceeding out of stomach [by which I (DG) mean argument for argument's sake], virulence and ill-nature, but to consider rather that... no man can be justly offended with him that shall endeavour to impart and bestow, without any gain to himself, those sharp but saving words which would be a terror and a torment in him to keep back' (Milton pp105-106,128,298-299; see also Milton pp126-129).

[5] As will become clear, these are believers of a Reformed persuasion.

Scripture as seriously as I do, deplore the present state of baptism, and want to reinstate it to its biblical position. I applaud this aim. It is mine.

But even so, I must write this polemical work. Why? The fact is, with the passing of only a few years since the publication of my *Battle for the Church*, there is even more need to stress the New Testament doctrine of baptism – and to fight (spiritually, with words) for it. A sacramental[6] approach to Christ's ordinance is increasingly widespread.[7] I view this development with horror. But it is not enough for me to throw up my hands in revulsion, and walk away; I must do what I can to warn the unwary of the incoming tide.

Not that I want to open old wounds and make divisions in Christ's church! Certainly not! I raise the issue because of its importance.[8] And

---

[6] By a 'sacrament', I mean the idea that grace is conferred by performance of a rite. I will have to use the word; it is in the literature, and many Reformed writers and others more-than-like it. John Calvin had a high view of the word (Calvin: *Institutes* Vol.2 pp491-511). D.Martyn Lloyd-Jones was not so keen: 'It is unfortunate that this word should ever have been used... Personally, I try not to use this term' (Lloyd-Jones: *The Church* pp26-27). It is, to me, an abomination. See Newton pp74-81; and below. To anticipate an objection: No, I am not confusing sacramentalism and sacerdotalism. But they are connected. Both are unbiblical, and the former leads to the latter – whatever the Reformed might say. I will return to the point.

[7] Not least – and this amazes me – among Baptists! This is what I meant when, a few moments ago, I noted recent trends among Baptists. Take Stanley K.Fowler in 2006, summarising the views of those who are involved in this contemporary Baptist development: 'An accurate interpretation of the Bible demands that baptism be viewed as an effective sign; that is, [as] a sacrament... Something is missing when conversion is not sacramentally sealed' (Fowler p155). The Reformed, of course, have long been sacramentalists – but even here it is on the rise. See end note on p7 for excursus: 'The resurgence of sacramentalism'.

[8] I hope I will be allowed Calvin's justification: 'Should anyone think me more prolix than the subject is worth, let him reflect that, in a matter of the greatest moment, so much is due to the peace and purity of the church, that we should not fastidiously object to whatever may be conducive to both'. Furthermore, reader, I hope you will join me as I echo Calvin again: 'Let us enquire into [infant baptism's] origin. Should it appear to have been devised merely by human rashness, let us abandon it, and regulate the true observance of baptism entirely by the will of the Lord' (Calvin: *Institutes* Vol.2 p529).

also because of its relevance. The fact is, not a few erstwhile Baptists are being attracted to infant baptism today because they are impressed with the logic of the covenant theology which buttresses the practice – which, they imagine, is all thoroughly worked out. They are also taken with the household names of leading Reformed theologians who have advocated the practice; surely, so many distinguished and spiritual men can't be wrong, can they? Furthermore, as I have said, there is an increasing interest in sacramentalism – and in the most surprising quarters![9] And sacramentalism and infant baptism have been walking companions for many a long year.[10]

Note Calvin's reference to 'the church'. He was raising a very important point, and I will have much to say about it.

[9] David Wright spoke of what he considered to be 'several signs of hope' 'early in the third millennium'. These include 'the growing evidence of sacramental thinking among Baptist theologians' – which I have already noted and intend to tackle. Wright, Emeritus Professor of Patristic and Reformed Christianity, Edinburgh – a Reformed historian holding to infant baptism – deploring the long history of (as he saw it) the debasing of baptism by the way infant baptism has been practiced (sadly, he did not recognise that baptism has been debased by infant baptism itself – not just by corruptions of it!), wished to see a more sacramental approach to it; in other words, that those who use the term, and argue for the effects of infant baptism, would mean it (Wright: *What...?* pp10-11,87-102). The same goes for the sacramental Baptists he spoke of. For the post-Puritan 'degeneration' or 'deterioration' (as sacramentalists see it) of the supper from Calvin's position to Ulrich Zwingli's, see Davies Vol.2 pp323-325,531. Sacramentalism is the issue. Wright, however, when, a few months after the appearance of his book, he published an article in which he tackled the question of what to do next, failed to mention sacramentalism (Wright: 'Christian' pp163-169). Given his own emphasis in his book, and the emphasis in the articles and advertisements in the edition of the journal which published his article, this omission, when dealing specifically with the way forward, was serious, and failed to convey the full picture. I refer to the *Evangelical Quarterly* April 2006. (Throughout, by 'Wright' I mean David F.Wright. When on occasion I refer to N.T.Wright, I do so in that form; similarly for Shawn D.Wright).

[10] As Rich Lusk, a modern-day advocate, put it: 'The infant-baptism question hangs, at least in part, on the question of baptismal efficacy... Without a robust understanding of what *God* does in baptism, the grounds upon which infant baptism rested became very tenuous... The logic of infant baptism is tied to its efficacy... A sacrament, by definition, includes the bestowal of the thing signified' (Lusk: 'Paedobaptism' pp96-100, emphasis his).

Well, before they adopt infant baptism, I invite those who are contemplating the step to hear what these theologians have said; I encourage them to weigh their 'thoroughly worked out' arguments; I would like them to take a look at their expositions of Scripture; and I ask them to take a glance at what the practice leads to. 'Look before you leap', is my advice. Cultivate the Berean spirit: 'These were more fair-minded... in that they received the word with all readiness, and searched the Scriptures daily to find out whether these things were so' (Acts 17:11). That is all I ask.[11]

I have, therefore, two main purposes in this publication; one negative, the other positive. *First*, I am writing *against* the views of infant baptisers, trying to show that their arguments do not stand up under biblical scrutiny. Of course, I do not pretend that this book exhausts the subject. Much has been written on the question – and written by authors far more able. Even so I want to say something about it, perhaps to supply an introduction for those who may not be aware of the arguments which infant baptisers use – and their consequences. And that leads me to repeat my next reason for writing. *Secondly*, I write *for* those who are contemplating adoption of infant baptism. Before they take the step, I want to warn them of the consequences. 'Look before you leap', I say again.

* * *

So, reader, this is how this book came to see the light of day, this is what it is about, and this is the tone in which it is written. Do you wish to read on? While the responsibility for it is entirely my own, of course, I thank those who were kind enough to read the manuscript and make detailed observations and suggestions – Jon Bevan, Simon Gay, Jack Green, Nigel Pibworth, Andrew Rome and the late David Wright. As always, I thank Nigel for the many books and articles he has plied me with – as good as a library, he is knowledgeable with it! I pay tribute to him yet again. I thank my wife, Mona, who, as before, has given me sterling help with source-checking and proof-reading. Only those who have tried it, know what is involved. My thanks also go to Audrey Broomhall, Margaret Harvey and Carol Saunderson who

---

[11] See end note on p9 for excursus: 'Honest disagreement must be allowed and expressed'.

kindly read the typeset manuscript, and made many helpful comments. The responsibility for every error which remains is, of course, entirely my own.

End notes to Preamble

The resurgence of sacramentalism

A comment on this resurgence of sacramentalism. The Reformers were sacramentalists, as were the Anglicans: 'Anglican teaching, following the tradition of the early [patristic] and Medieval Church, was that the essential benefit of baptism... is regeneration'. The Puritans were sacramentalists. As for the 18th century, 'almost to a man the evangelicals – Anglican, Methodist, Whitefieldian, Moravian and those led by Lady Huntingdon – accepted that regeneration in some sense accompanies infant baptism'. Sacramentalism's virulent growth among Anglicans in the 19th century – the Oxford Movement, the Tractarians – is a byword. Benjamin Wills Newton, a contemporary witness, wrote: 'The doctrines of "sacramentarianism" [sacramentalism leading to sacerdotalism] are being revived in this country in all their deadly energy, and are again leading thousands into perdition' (Holland pp15,43,129; Newton p81; see also pp146-147; Spurgeon: 'Children Brought'; Iain Murray: *Forgotten* pp123-143). And what about the 20th and 21st centuries? As I will show, Reformed sacramentalism – which has always been there – is now on the march. The fact is, you can't have infant baptism without sacramentalism; if infant baptism is not a sacrament, it is nothing. Peter Toon, arguing for baptism to be performed with patristic ritual, claimed that 'an appropriate policy for the baptism of the infant children of committed church members [note the subtle watering-down of infant-baptiser theology – see below] cannot truly be worked out until a deep understanding of the relationship of baptism and regeneration is recovered[!] by the Western churches' (Toon p189). Quite! Therefore sacramentalism is the root of the trouble, and if sacramentalism is wrong, infant baptism *must* fall. But, as I say, there is a growing emphasis upon Reformed sacramentalism at the beginning of the 21st century. And what about Baptists? In the companion book I mentioned, I will show that during the 20th century, sacramentalism reared its head among the Baptists. And, at the start of the 21st century, its promulgation is growing apace – mostly, at the moment, confined to scholars and writers. But, reader, it will soon reach a Bible college, a pulpit, and then a pew, near you. I want to do what I can to prevent this – or at least warn people about it. Hence the book in question, and this present work. I ask the Reformed (Baptists and otherwise) who think me deplorably divisive to bear in mind the weight of evidence which shows this increasing emphasis upon sacramentalism. It has only one terminus. Rome! Read on.

Furthermore, I shall have occasion to refer to the rise and growth of the New Perspective, to which I see a parallel if not a link to the rise and growth of sacramentalism in the 20th century. For now, compare N.T.Wright's summary of 'The Quest for the Historical Jesus'; namely: 'The... New Quest of the 1950s and 1960s... By the mid-1970s there was a sense of stalemate... In the early 1980s... we were witnessing what I [N.T.Wright] called a "third quest" for Jesus' (N.T.Wright pp1,13-14).

To return to the Reformed sacramentalism of the present day. Even as I was drawing my mss. to a close, I came across this highly sacramental language in Daniel R.Hyde's article in the *Banner of Truth*, May 2008, pp1-8: 'The Holy Spirit operates upon men's hearts through the voice of the minister and through the sacramental elements of water, bread and wine... Baptism is no mere symbol... but is a means of the work of the Spirit in our lives... I am washed with [Christ's] blood and Spirit from the pollution of my soul, that is, from all my sins, as certainly as I am washed outwardly with water... The water of baptism is more than mere water... for the water is so bound to the promise of God that the physical cleansing becomes, if not the instrument, at least the occasion for the spiritual cleansing... As the outer self is washed with water by the minister, the inner self is washed with the blood of the Christ by the Holy Spirit... The two events do coincide and are bound together in the relationship between promise and sign... We are as really washed from our sins spiritually as our bodies are washed with water... The Holy Spirit... washes us from our sins, he interchanges the sign and the thing signified'. Such language, I say, in such a source, in 2008, compels me to write. Sadly, I received no reply to my e-mail raising the point with the magazine.

I go back to the extracts from Luther and Milton about avoiding offence. Why is it, as Robert M.Zins noted with proper disapproval, some modern evangelicals are content to call Rome's doctrine of baptismal regeneration a 'difference', but will not call it an 'error'? He rightly pointed out that 'the devastating effect of the Roman Catholic doctrine of baptismal regeneration and *ex opere operato* (the thing itself brings about the thing signified) is dangerously close to the Reformed view of infant baptism', adding that 'it is not uncommon for Roman Catholic exegetes to defend their practice of baptismal regeneration with Reformed Christian logic based upon the Old Testament covenant with Abraham'. Even so, Zins himself confessed he 'felt the difficulty inherent in denying Rome while affirming the Reformed Churches who still practice infant baptism'. Why? Why this reluctance? It arose because he was 'worried about taking out Luther [it is not only Luther!] as well', and in trying not to cause 'offence' (Zins pp90-92).

Reader, although it might not seem like it, as I have already explained, I too have felt the pressure to keep quiet. Certainly I do not want to cause needless offence, but no good will be served by keeping silent on vital issues to avoid stepping on somebody's toes. An ostrich has many admirable qualities no doubt, but its proverbial way of keeping out of trouble is no model for the believer. To use another example from the animal kingdom; a hedgehog may find curling into a ball works well for most problems it has to face, but the technique's patent failure to cope with a 20-ton juggernaut is all-too visible on our roads, I am afraid.

I say it again: You can't be an infant baptiser without being a sacramentalist. And if things go on as at present, many Baptists will end up sacramentalists. There are only two stable positions: The biblical position – symbol; or, the sacramental position – baptismal regeneration. And we have to choose; we cannot dither between the two (Josh. 24:14-15; 1 Kings 18:21).

Honest disagreement must be allowed and expressed

I take full cognisance of Iain Murray's words: 'It is to be regretted that discussion on this question has frequently been marred by bigotry... Some lesser men [have] aggravated the differences... The material extant upon the controversy certainly shows the need for caution and sympathy with the difficulties of others' (Iain Murray: *Reformation* pp381-382). With respect, although I am one of the 'lesser' men, I do not think it is bigoted to quote the words of infant baptisers, seeking to expose what I see as their unbiblical arguments and claims, and to point out the consequences which must inevitably follow from infant baptism. And it is precisely because I feel for others, that I address those who are thinking of adopting the practice, and warn them of just what it involves. I realise there is a very strong desire today, on the part of many, to gloss over differences on this issue, (or, perhaps, to push 1 Cor. 1:13-17 too far – see below), in the hope of presenting a common Reformed front. But I think the practical effects of infant baptism are too far-reaching for silence. As to this last, I must say that, although I cannot claim to have felt exactly as he did, I empathise in general with Gerrard Winstanley when writing to Oliver Cromwell in 1651: 'I laid aside this in silence, and said I would not make it public; but this word was like fire in my bones ever and anon: "You shall not bury your talent [I am taking this to mean in my case: 'God-given opportunity and responsibility' – DG] in the earth". Therefore I was stirred up to give it a resurrection, and to pick together as many of my scattered papers as I could find, and to compile them into this method, which I do here present to you, and do quiet my own spirit. And now I have set the candle at your door... It may be here are some things inserted which you may not like. Therefore I pray you read it, and be as the industrious bee, suck out the honey and cast away the weeds. Though this platform be like a piece of timber rough hewed, yet the discreet workman may take it and frame a handsome building out of it. It is like a poor man that comes clothed to your door in a torn country garment, who is unacquainted with the learnèd citizens' unsettled forms and fashions. Take off the clownish [or, in my case, offensive] language, for under that you may see beauty' (Winstanley in Hamilton p116). Discussion on this subject has been marred not only by bigotry. The full picture has not always been painted. When, for instance, The Banner of Truth Trust, in 1958-1960, reprinted C.H.Spurgeon's 1890 re-publication of Thomas Watson's *A Body of Divinity*, they did not include Spurgeon's Appendix countering Watson's infant baptism. The publishers, however, while failing to mention this omission, stated: 'The unabridged but revised version of

Watson's *Body of Divinity*, published in 1890, has been followed in the reprint. This present edition... a comprehensive work in itself...' As a young believer, in both senses, I bought this at the time – because I knew that Spurgeon was 'kosher' – but I had no inkling of the omission. What is more, the publishers had room to include 8 pages on Jonathan Edwards – which had no connection with the work in hand.

Furthermore, I want to make it clear that, however inconsistent it might seem – given my view of baptism and the church – I am not 'unchristianising' or 'unchurching' those who practice infant baptism in a responsible manner. I think they are mistaken; I think their practice highly dangerous, and I am prepared to say so, and argue my case. But I do not do it to 'slang [them] off' (see Wright: 'Christian' p167). Indeed, they are not my main concern in this book. Hoping I do not sound conceited, if I can help any of them to reconsider their position and return to the (as I see it) biblical pattern – excellent; but primarily, I say again, I am writing for those Baptists who are thinking of taking up infant baptism.

Of course, as John H.Armstrong noted: 'There are godly, faithful and earnest students of the Bible who hold... different views about water baptism'. Nor is 'disagreement about baptism... proof of rebellion, stupidity or immaturity'. Yes, everybody has to answer 'to his own master (Rom. 14:4)' (although on this point, see below), and 'we can, and we must, work at overcoming the disagreements we can overcome. We can, and we must, remove prejudices and fears wherever possible'. True, 'we are finite beings. None of us will ever be able to comprehend all of God's revelation completely or infallibly'. But, having admitted all that, I cannot accept I have to 'attain a deeper experience of unity' with believers when this involves tolerating sacramentalism – which I find abhorrent, however godly and scholarly its advocates. Consequently, I cannot go along with Armstrong's quotation from the Baptist theologian Richard Kidd: 'The world is already too racked with pain and conflict to permit Christians the luxury of adding to its fragmentation by internal arguments about baptism... I [Kidd] can no longer work... with a stark and uncompromising contrast between believer's baptism, which is right, and infant baptism, which is wrong. Rather, I [Kidd] am discovering here two histories of the one sign we call baptism... These histories... cannot be mixed, nor should one be allowed to replace the other; for in both these ways, the proper integrity of each would be destroyed... But I [Kidd] would like to think I [Kidd] can participate in and celebrate the integrity of what is the other, without threat to what is profoundly my own'. As I say, I disagree with this intensely. I think infant baptism is wrong, and some of its consequences catastrophic. I agree with Armstrong: 'Seeking to ignore the problem will not solve it' (John Armstrong pp12-13,20-21). I dare say my approach will not solve it either – but, reader, I have not set out with any such grand idea. Rather, as I have made clear, I am simply issuing a warning to those who are thinking of becoming infant baptisers. And I mean 'warning'.

But before I move on, I want to sound a note of caution about the use of Rom. 14. This in itself begs an important question. Are we really talking about something 'doubtful' in the sense of 'disputable' (Rom. 14:1 NIV)? True, baptism is *disputed* – but dare we call an ordinance of Christ *disputable*? If so, it would be wrong to pass any opinion on, or make any criticism of, the baptismal practice of others – since we are commanded, in such matters, not to 'dispute' or 'judge' (Rom. 14:1,3,4,10,13). This, it seems to me, would take us into nonsense-land. Not discuss baptism? Not weigh the arguments men use to defend their practice? Not pass an opinion on them? Really? For my part, as I have said, I find certain aspects of current teaching on baptism totally unacceptable, matters which to my mind certainly do not fall within the category of Rom. 14. In saying this, as I have stated, I do not 'despise' or 'show contempt for' my brothers (Rom. 14:3,10) who disagree with me about the subject, but I think they are mistaken and that their teaching leads to very serious and dangerous consequences. And I am prepared to say so. Yes, I do accept all believers (Rom. 15:7) – but that does not mean I have to accept their view of baptism. What is more, if baptism does come into the remit of Rom. 14, not only should we not say a word against the practice of others, we should – all of us – virtually abandon baptism altogether. I should give up denying baptism to infants so as to avoid offending my infant-baptising friends; and they should give up baptising infants to avoid offending me (Rom. 14:15,20-22; 15:1-2). In short, it would be far safer if we all joined the Quakers or the Salvation Army and had nothing to do with baptism. And not only baptism; the Lord's supper, too, would have to cease; or else we should, I suppose, have to tolerate, as something indifferent or disputable, if not the Mass itself, then something very like it. Once again, this would make a nonsense of a clear command of Christ, and, for the sake of tolerance, drive us to an intolerable conclusion. I, for my part, cannot go along with it. The only alternative, therefore, is to speak up; in love, yes, but to speak up. I am not seeking 'a deeper experience of unity' with sacramentalists on baptism. I don't think I should. Granted 'the power of symbol and the attendant importance of visual images in the modern world... the developing "spirituality" [the source and end of which is questionable, to say the least] of modern culture... while multitudes are seeking meaning and purpose in life through a myriad of ways', where, to put it mildly, 'the relevant current literature on baptism reveals that the issue of mode and context is one that is plainly in some state of flux', and that this is leading to a desire for, and experience of, greater unity on baptism – granted all this, I say – I know that my book will strike a note altogether out of harmony with this desire. So be it. I could not disagree more with Armstrong in his wish 'that the importance of baptism might be recovered even while we disagree about its exact meaning'. Discordant it may be to say it, but the opposite is the truth. 'The importance of baptism' *cannot possibly* 'be recovered... while we disagree about its exact meaning', even though Armstrong might say it can (John H.Armstrong pp20-

22,162). Its *meaning* is the heart of its *importance*. What is more, the call for unity over baptism is but the tip of the ice-berg. See below for extracts from *Act 3 Review*, the quarterly of which Armstrong is the editor-in-chief, where I trace the accelerating Romeward movement amongst evangelicals, *not excluding the Reformed*. There is a pig hidden at the bottom of the poke [sack] of infant baptism, and I want to do what I can to let prospective purchasers know what they are getting.

I sum up my position in James Haldane's words: 'There is no danger of the interests of religion suffering by discussion. It may indeed be conducted in an improper spirit, and much sin may be committed while we are attempting to vindicate the truth; but this is the abuse of the apostolic precept, that we should earnestly contend for the faith once delivered to the saints... It appears to [me] perfectly lawful and proper to point out any perversion of the gospel, and to show how it subverts the truth, while [I] do not presume to judge another man's servant, more especially as to his state before God... I [do not] unchristianise... any other man for differing from the view I take of the [subject], but I have not the smallest doubt of his being in error on this subject' (Haldane xi, pp121,330). See Fuller: *Essays* pp858-859.

Part One

Introduction

In which I:

1. Say why it is important that we consider baptism

2. Point out three mistakes which are often made about the subject

3. Introduce the question of infant baptism

4. Note some dangerous statements by infant baptisers

Baptism: Its Importance

Before I look at the arguments put forward by infant baptisers in support of their practice, I want to stress the importance of baptism itself. Reader, I urge you not to dismiss this subject as of little or no consequence. Do not wave it aside as trivial. Jesus described his baptism as 'fitting... to fulfil all righteousness' (Matt. 3:15). He said it was seemly, fitting, to carry out all God's commands and ordinances. How then can baptism be regarded as a matter indifferent or optional, as some (including evangelicals; especially, of all people, Baptists!) think it is? Christ's words show the importance of the issue. I am not interested in a sterile, hair-splitting quarrel over nothing, striving 'about words to no profit' (2 Tim. 2:14).[1]

Some might dismiss my book as written by one with a very low view of baptism – the inevitable consequence, they might add, of my denial of sacramentalism. Well, let me briefly spell out what I think about baptism. Baptism is a standing command – an ordinance – there is nothing optional about it – an ordinance of Christ, an obligation which he has laid upon all his people throughout this age.[2] It is one of

---

[1] 'Early Christianity... knew nothing of an unbaptised believer' (Wright: *What...?* p36). 'I defy anyone to conduct the basic scrutiny of the baptismal references in the New Testament... and emerge with the conclusion that baptism was a second-order issue in the apostolic churches... It would be a severe affront to the New Testament teaching to reckon baptism itself as anything less than fundamental to the church of Jesus Christ' (Wright: 'Christian' p166). My position precisely.
Since I disagree with much that the Baptist sacramentalist George Beasley-Murray has written on the subject, I am glad to be able to quote him on the question of baptism as an ordinance: 'We should observe that the authority of... baptism is of the weightiest order. It rests on the command of the risen Lord after his achieving redemption and receiving authority over the entire cosmos [Matt. 28:18-20]; it is integrated with the commission to preach the good news to the world, and it is enforced by his own example at the beginning of his messianic ministry. Such a charge is too imperious to be ignored or modified. It behoves us to adhere to it and conform to it as God gives grace' (Beasley-Murray: *Baptism in the New Testament* p92).
[2] Although, according to Mark 16:16, there is nothing saving in baptism, Christ commanded it for believers as the outward testimony of an inward

15

two such ordinances; baptism is experienced but once – upon profession of faith[3] – whereas the Lord's supper is to be regularly repeated throughout the believer's life; while baptism is an individual experience, the supper is a corporate act of the local church, and serves to nourish its unity. Both are symbolic acts. But while the grace represented in the symbols is not conveyed by these symbols,[4] nor in

---

experience. Combining this with Rom. 10:9-10, where we are taught that an outward confession is essential, as Spurgeon said: 'The promise of salvation is not made to a faith which is never avowed'. And: 'God requires [baptism in water], and though men are saved without any [water] baptism... [and] though [water] baptism is not saving, yet, if men would be saved, they must not be disobedient' (Spurgeon: *Early* p147; Grass and Randall p59).

[3] Sacramentalism skews – to put it mildly – the biblical order. The infant baptiser, Oscar Cullmann, argued for baptism before faith. 'But how', asked Fowler, 'does all this correlate with the New Testament passages which call for faith prior to baptism?' Quite. Fowler summarised Cullman's black-is-white argument thus: 'What is demanded by baptism is *subsequent* faith' (Fowler p212, emphasis his). How wrong can you be? As Beasley-Murray said: 'Faith is needful *before* baptism... Baptism is administered to converts. This is commonly recognised now [in 1962. Beasley-Murray cited Roman Catholics, Lutherans, Anglicans, Reformed, Congregationalists, Methodists], though not by all. Cremer has many successors. His statement: "Faith must be the *effect* [emphasis original] of our baptism, if the latter has effected anything at all", is manifestly constructed on the basis of infant baptism as the norm of baptismal practice... [and] is anachronistic in the consideration of New Testament teaching' (Beasley-Murray: *Baptism in the New Testament* p274, emphasis his; see also *Baptism Today and Tomorrow* pp38-41). Beasley-Murray was not quite right. This distortion – the utter turning up-side-down of the New Testament – is not only because of infant baptism. He himself pointed out Cremer's reference to baptism *effecting* something. This is the core of the problem. If it is granted that baptism is a sacrament – that is, it *effects* something, it *produces* something – all sorts of distortions of Scripture follow. Naturally, if baptism effects or produces something, that 'something' must follow baptism. So, if baptism produces faith, baptism must precede faith. But baptism does not produce anything! Sacramentalism is the root of the trouble, as I keep saying, and shall keep saying.

[4] Contrary to Richard Sibbes: 'The sacraments are mysteries, because in the one, under bread and wine, there is conveyed to us the benefits of Christ's body broken and his blood shed' (Sibbes: *Fountain* p462). Certainly not. *Salvation* is not *conveyed* to us by the Lord's supper! And I disagree with Calvin: 'I do not... deny that the grace of Christ is applied to us in the sacraments' (Calvin: *Commentaries* Vol.20 Part 2 p239). I do. Take the

the observance, this does not mean they are pointless. In the physical symbols, the believer sees – represented before his eyes – the spiritual realities of his redemption in Christ, and so finds spiritual instruction, edification and encouragement.[5] There is, furthermore, a massive benefit to be gained by sheer obedience to Christ – 'Whatever he says to you, do it' (John 2:5) – even if this should mean being plunged in water! The ordinances also serve as a kind of physical preaching of the gospel to any unconverted who might observe them.[6] Baptism serves another purpose also – a very important purpose, at that. It leads the believer into local church membership,[7] including the Lord's supper.[8]

---

supper. Christ is *represented*, not *presented*. 'This is my body which is given (broken) *for* you; do this in *remembrance* of me' (Luke 22:19; 1 Cor. 11:24-25). It is **not**: 'This is my body which is given (broken) *to* you; do this to *receive* me'. In saying this, I repeat the above – immense blessing comes by obedience to Christ. But this is a far cry from sacramentalism.

[5] I agree with the Reformed infant-baptiser, Richard L.Pratt, although I would have strengthened his statement: 'The visible rite of baptism is added to the preaching of the word in order to confirm what is preached and what we experience through the inward work of the Holy Spirit in connection with preaching' (John H.Armstrong p62). Quite! No nonsense about conveying grace – it confirms, demonstrates what *has already been experienced*. This is undoubtedly the New Testament position. If it had remained the practice in the churches, my book would never have been written. More important, infant baptism would have never been thought of! See below for my comments on the passages which sacramentalists claim to teach sacramentalism.

[6] But I do not place the ordinances above preaching; nor even equal to it. At least some, if not many, infant baptisers do, as I will show. Furthermore, I think the word should be preached at the ordinances.

[7] For Spurgeon on this, see Spurgeon: *Early* pp125,145-152; Grass and Randall pp60-62. Acts 8:38 could be cited against me; similarly, Acts 9:18. But not every detail in Acts (or the Gospels) should be taken as normative for church practice – the letters are designed for that purpose. Acts records a transition period, a time of explosive spiritual power when extraordinary things were happening – some unique in the history of the church. And I mean unique, never (whatever some may claim) to be repeated. Just as hard cases make bad law, so to use extraordinary – unique – events as normative for the church today, is far from sensible. Consider, for instance, the immediacy of New Testament baptism. If I may speak personally, while I acknowledge that excessive delay of baptism is the mistaken norm in some circles, as one who has had the responsibility for baptising, I have felt the need in our culture, blighted by centuries of Christendom (see below), for more caution than

Whether or not all this is dismissed as a low view of baptism, it is (although I have not stopped to set out the biblical arguments)[9] – as I see it – the biblical position.[10]

---

seems warranted by the practice in Acts – which practice was carried out under very different social and religious conditions to our own. Compare the rapid funeral arrangements in Acts 5:1-11 with ours today. I will return to this point about the extraordinary.

To get back to the two texts in question: As for Acts 8:38, it is hard to see what Philip could have done with an individual convert who was travelling back to North Africa where there was no other believer – let alone a church. If similar circumstances should occur today, no doubt a like-baptism would take place. But we are talking about the other 99.9999% of cases. Let us not legislate for such an isolated instance. As for Acts 9:18, note how, upon baptism, Paul immediately joined the disciples at Damascus, and started preaching there (Acts 9:19-20). As for the connection between baptism and church life as found in the Gospels and Acts, Matt. 28:18-20 is unassailable for the former, and Acts 2:41-42 for the latter. See Fuller: *Essays* p857.

Of course, it is easy to caricature, poke fun at, and dismiss, Baptists for their efforts at regulating church membership and introducing members (Ella pp7-23 and *passim*) – and there is a good deal of serious criticism that needs to be made and acted upon – but what about infant-baptiser churches and their methods and results? I shall have more to say on this, in addition to what I have already said in my *Battle*; which see.

[8] See end note on p23 for excursus: 'Strict communion'.

[9] I emphasise the 'biblical'. If I *was* writing about believer's baptism, I would not depend on history. It would be no part of my case to try to establish an unbroken line of believer's baptism from the apostles to the Anabaptists. I know there is little documentary evidence to support it. But there may be reasons. Leaving to one side – for the moment – the time of the very early Fathers, it is to acknowledge the obvious to say that for at least 1400 years after the apostles, the *biblical* ordinance was carried out only by the minority. Furthermore, it was the practice of a desperately persecuted minority. 'Heretics' on the run – and worse – can hardly be criticised for not retiring to the study (which they did not possess) to set out their case in writing, especially in those days without easy writing-facilities, PCs, CD ROMs, memory sticks, printers (indeed, a printing-press!), internet, e-mails, mobile phones and all the rest. To cap it all, can it really be thought that Rome – who tried to destroy the 'heretics' – would have preserved their writings? In saying all this, however, I am not conceding that there was no witness to believer's baptism in those days. But my case would not depend on it.

[10] I am not setting out what I see as the biblical – the Baptist – position. My purpose in this book is confessedly negative, exposing the errors and dangers,

And baptism goes far deeper than baptism; the truth is, it goes to the very heart of church life.[11] The nature of the church, who its

---

as I see them, of infant baptism – to act as a siren (in the opposite sense to Greek mythology!), warning the unwary of treacherous reefs ahead. In this regard, I make no apology for being strident – mariners kept from foundering on the rocks don't often complain of the clanging bell which disturbed their sleep. As to that, while some want only a positive approach, the Bible shows us how necessary – and God-honouring – a negative course can be. Lloyd-Jones: 'It is the business of a Christian teacher, as I understand it from the New Testament itself, not only to give a positive exposition but also to oppose wrong teaching. The New Testament itself does that, but this approach is not popular today. People say: "Don't be negative, give us the positive truth; don't be controversial". But if error is being taught it must be corrected. Paul does this constantly. He exposes the false, warns against it, urges Christians to avoid it; at the same time he gives the positive truth. So we must of necessity do the same. What we believe is of vital importance, because it is going to affect our whole life and conduct' (Lloyd-Jones: *Sons* pp92-93). And eternity. As I have explained, I aim to speak the truth, albeit trenchantly, in love. If I needlessly offend, I sincerely apologise, and ask those who disagree with my tone, to be kind enough to remember why I have written. *It is the care of souls which moves me.* I dread to have to confess with W.E.Gladstone (in a pamphlet published late in life): 'It has been my misfortune all my life, not to see a question of principle until it is at the door – and then sometimes it is too late!' (A.N.Wilson p474). I quote this with regard both to myself *and those who read what I write.* The same goes for this further piece from Winstanley's address to Cromwell in 1651: 'I must speak plain to you', he said, 'lest my spirit tells me another day: "If you had spoken plain, things might have been amended"' (Hill: *Defeat* p19). I have wrestled over 2 Tim. 2:23-26. But I do not think I have engaged in 'foolish and ignorant disputes'; nor have I set out to 'generate strife'; and I hope I have not been guilty of what Paul meant by 'contention' or 'striving'. John Gill's comments are apt: 'Such an one ought not to strive about words *to no profit*, about *mere* words, and in a litigious, quarrelsome manner, and *for mastery and not truth*; though he may, and ought to strive for the faith of the gospel; and this is praiseworthy in him' (Gill Vol.6 p636, emphasis mine). Calvin, too, I have found helpful, especially when he, even in his comments on the verse, was prepared to call the views of those he opposed, 'silly trifles' (Calvin: *Commentaries* Vol.21 Part 3 p233) – not forgetting, also, his diatribes against the Anabaptists and others. I hope my attitude bears at least some semblance to 2 Cor. 2:3-4. Jude 3 springs to mind, also.

[11] H.M.Carson, when writing about how he came to question his involvement in infant baptism: 'Significantly the question was bubbling in my mind at the

members are, how they become members and what is expected of them – that is what lies at the heart of this subject. The infant-baptiser B.B.Warfield put it this way: 'According as is our doctrine of the church, so will be our doctrine of the subjects of baptism. If we believe... that only those already united to Christ have right within his house and to its privileges... If we are to demand anything like demonstrative evidence of actual participation in Christ before we baptise, no infant, who by reason of years is incapable of affording signs of his union with Christ, can be thought a proper subject of the sacrament'. As just noted, Warfield believed in infant baptism, and therefore he did not demand the evidence he referred to. But even so his statement illustrates the point I am making – baptism and the doctrine of the church are inseparably linked. What we believe about baptism, and what we do about it, will be governed by – and will influence – what we believe concerning the church, because 'as is our doctrine of the church, so will be our doctrine of the subjects of baptism'.[12] I agree with Warfield. Robert L.Dabney made the same point when he said that the doctrine of baptism and the Lord's supper 'is closely dependent on that of the church; and is treated by many authorities, as strictly consequent thereon'.[13]

Let me illustrate what I am trying to say by an example totally unconnected with baptism. Think about the atonement, especially the extent of the atonement. For whom did Christ die? The question of the extent of the atonement is not a barren discussion about mere numbers – the very nature of redemption itself is at stake. Did Christ accomplish a certain redemption for all the sinners for whom he shed his blood? Or did he die for some sinners who will never be saved? In

---

very time as I was facing the fundamental problem of the doctrine of the church. It was the biblical doctrine of the church, as I understood it, that ultimately forced me out of the Church of England. I was now beginning to discover that the two issues were not separate... The biblical doctrine of the church as [at the very least] a company of believers drawn from the world was, in fact, one of the factors leading me towards the acceptance of the baptism of believers as being the only true baptism – just as the Anglican view of the national and comprehensive Church was more consistent with the practice of infant baptism' (Carson: *Farewell* pp64-65).

[12] Warfield p389.

[13] Dabney p726. Note the link Dabney properly made between baptism, the supper and the church.

other words, it is not merely the number of the sinners for whom Christ died, but what did he actually accomplish by his death?[14]

Similarly, in this book I do not consider baptism only. As I said, the issue goes far deeper; the very nature of the church depends on it; and it has no small effect on salvation itself. Indeed, salvation can be jeopardised by a wrong view of baptism. In short, eternity is at stake. *That* is how important it is.[15]

And that leads us to another neglected aspect of the subject – one which strikes me personally as I write about it. As to the place of baptism in addressing sinners, I feel the force of C.H.Spurgeon's comments on Ananias' command to Saul: 'Arise, and be baptised, and wash away your sins':

The tendency with many good evangelists is to say nothing upon that point. The main thing is to get this man to be a believer in the Lord Jesus Christ, but to say: 'Arise, and be baptised', is not that far less important? Brethren, we have nothing to do with altering Christ's message, but are bound to deliver it as a whole, without addition or diminution. The tendency everywhere is to say: 'Baptism should not be mentioned; it is sectarian'. Who said so? If our Lord commanded it, who dares call it sectarian? We are not commanded to preach a part of the gospel, but the whole gospel; and this Ananias did. Is it not written: 'He that believes and is baptised shall be saved'? Why omit one clause? I question whether God's blessing has not been withheld from some teachers and preachers because they have failed to repeat their message in its entirety. A brother will write to me next week and say: 'I am sorry that I cannot circulate your sermon, because you allude to baptism'. My dear brother, if you cannot circulate the sermon, I must be content without your kind help; but I cannot amend the Lord's word to please the best man upon the earth. What prominence is given to baptism here [in Acts 22:16]! We should greatly err if we believed in baptismal regeneration, or even in the efficacy of washing in water for the removal of sin; but, on the other hand, we are not to place in the background an ordinance which, by the language of Scripture, is placed in the forefront. Ananias said to Paul: 'Arise and be baptised, and wash away your sins'. And this tallies with that other text: 'He that believes and is baptised shall be saved'. In both of these passages,

---

[14] See my *Particular*.

[15] For this reason, I do not think I am 'obsessed with disputes and arguments over words, from which come envy, strife, reviling, evil suspicions, useless wranglings' (1 Tim. 6:4-5). If any reader thinks concern for the eternal welfare of souls is described by such words, he and I part company.

the Lord puts a special honour upon baptism, and it would be ill for us to neglect that which he so evidently esteems. Do not make any mistake, and imagine that immersion in water can wash away sin; but do remember that if the Lord puts this outward profession side by side with the washing away of sins, it is not a trifling matter. Remember that other text: 'With the heart man believes unto righteousness, and with the mouth confession is made unto salvation'. Faith must be followed by obedience, or it cannot be sincere; do, then, what Jesus bids you. That is not, however, my point. I want to urge upon you that you should always speak the Lord's word faithfully, and be true to that which the Lord reveals to you, even to the jots and tittles. In these days there is much talk about 'undenominationalism', and in that talk there is much to be admired; but the danger is lest [that?] we should on all hands begin to pare away a little from the word of God for the sake of an imaginary unity. The suggestion is that one is to give up this, and another to give up that; but I say to you – give up nothing which your Lord commands.[16]

Quite!

I leave it there. Whether or not I have succeeded in allaying the fears of any who think I have a low view of baptism, I cannot say. But this is what I think about the ordinance.

Now for a look at infant baptism. But, before getting into the heart of the matter, some cautionary remarks are necessary. They will form the next chapter.

---

[16] Spurgeon: *Metropolitan* Vol.31 pp250-251.

End note to Baptism: Its Importance

Strict communion

J.C.Philpot: 'If strict communion is according to the precept of Christ and the practice of the apostles, no arguments against it, drawn from other sources, are admissible. For if once we admit any reasons to prevail over the testimony of God in his word of truth, we reject divine revelation, we deny that the Scriptures are a perfect rule of faith and practice, we turn our back upon the teachings of the Holy Ghost on that particular point, and we open a wide door for the introduction of every error. If baptism is an ordinance of Christ, it stands upon his authority. It is not to be slighted as unnecessary, still less to be rejected with contempt. Nor can a child of God safely shelter himself under the names of great and good men who have not seen, nor submitted to that ordinance. Highly esteemed though they are to be for their work's sake, they are not our Lord; they did not die for our sins, nor rise again for our justification. They were [as we all are] but men, fallible men, and in many things offending all, though beloved of God, and blessed in their work. If the principles and practice of the churches founded by the apostles were not those of strict communion, let it be unceremoniously discarded; but if, as I fully believe, and as I think I have proved in the following pages [of his book], the churches set up by the Holy Ghost immediately after the day of Pentecost were strict baptist churches, those that reject that order are guilty of [mis-understanding, ignorance or] disobedience. I put the question wholly upon scriptural precept and scriptural practice. Let the practice of strict communion stand or fall by the unerring testimony of God' (Philpot pp3-4). See Fuller: *Essays* pp852-859.

Since I have quoted Spurgeon above, it is only fair to point out that he did not practice a closed table.

Infant Baptism: Three Common Mistakes

As I closed the previous chapter, I said that before we explore the theory and practice of infant baptism, some cautionary remarks are necessary. For a start, the dispute over infant baptism does not concern merely the age of a person to be baptised. No, the controversy is not over *adult* baptism as against *infant* baptism. That is to trivialise the debate. It is *believer's* baptism as against all other sorts of baptism.[1] Having made that important point, I now move on to look at three common but fundamental mistakes in dealing with infant baptism.

1. It is wrong to dismiss the practice of infant baptism on the grounds that it is 'Old Testament teaching'

It is true that infant baptisers make a great deal of the Old Testament in one way or another in the presentation of their case, and they do mistakenly rely heavily on the Old Testament rite of circumcision.[2]

---

[1] Believer's baptism is in fact a tautology, if we are talking in New Testament terms. Only believers were baptised in those days. A baptised unbeliever (Simon in Acts 8, for instance) got short shrift when discovered. The qualifying adjective is needed only because of the invention and predominance of infant baptism. 'Infant baptism took over from believer's baptism', with dreadful consequences for the history of the ordinance (see Wright's entire book, not least its title). What is more, there is a good case for the disuse of 'infant baptism' – except for serious Latinists – and calling it by its proper name, 'baby baptism'. But, for its advocates, as Wright said, the former 'retains a certain gravity', whereas the latter 'seems disrespectful, even flippant' (Wright: *What...?* pp35,47). So it does, but it is the truth, all the same.

[2] In the 1640s, at the Westminster Assembly, Lord Say 'complained that it was not very helpful to take their examples for the church (as the divines often did) from the Old Testament' (Paul p236). Quite right, too! However, it has taken a long time, it seems, for such a self-evident comment to sink in, but I am pleased to record that Wright could properly speak with approval of infant baptisers who are now 'taking with greater seriousness the New Testament, rather than the Old Testament, in considering a theology of baptism, since traditional defences of infant baptism have leaned heavily on the [so-called] parallel with circumcision' (Wright: *What...?* p15). I will return to the misuse

Having said that, it is too easy – and it is totally wrong – to dismiss their arguments as 'merely Old Testament teaching'. It is a terrible error to dismiss the Old Testament. In this book I say some strong things about its misuse, and the misguided application of it to church life, but this must not be taken to mean that I dismiss the Old Testament itself. Let me say it – and say it loud and clear – the Old Testament is a part of the infallible word of God, and it must be treated as such. However, there are substantial differences between the two Testaments, and it is vital to give these their proper weight.[3] Nevertheless, this must never degenerate into dismissing the Old Testament. It is sometimes done, and it is wrong.

2. It is also wrong to regard every reference to baptism in the Bible as meaning water baptism

It is not so. In some passages of Scripture, the baptism involved cannot possibly refer to water baptism.[4] Baptists sometimes – perhaps frequently – mistakenly take these particular verses as referring to water baptism, and then qualify the biblical statements by introducing the idea of faith and/or 'representation'.[5] This is wrong. The truth is,

---

of the Levitical order. In passing, I note infant baptisers feel the need to 'defend' their practice. As one who baptises believers only, I have no sense that I need to 'defend' my practice. Spurgeon saw no need to defend the Bible any more than he would a lion. Open the cage and let it out! Believer's baptism is written plainly upon the pages of the New Testament. Evidently, as infant baptisers themselves admit (I will provide plenty of evidence), the same cannot be said for infant baptism.

[3] I will go more fully into the continuity/discontinuity debate in my forthcoming book on the law. The continuity/discontinuity question is vital; it is *the* doctrinal issue which must be settled right from the start. A mistake here casts a long shadow, as we shall see.

[4] Indeed, I think the only major passage in Paul's letters (and the major only passage in the letters as a whole) which does refer to water baptism is 1 Cor. 1:13-17. I will argue my case as we go on.

[5] Both Reformed and Baptist confuse water and spiritual baptism. See, for instance, John H.Armstrong, Thomas J.Nettles and Richard L.Pratt in John H.Armstrong pp16-18,31-33,36-38,60-61,80-81. Take one example from Nettles. He claimed that in 1 Pet. 3:21 the apostle says: 'Baptism represents the confident reliance on the judgement Christ took for us, which judgement

the Bible speaks of both water baptism and spiritual baptism. These must always be distinguished. The New Testament does, and in no uncertain terms. I must spend just a little time on the differences between the two.

One baptism is a physical act to do with water; the other is at least regeneration by the Holy Spirit, a baptism which unites the person to Christ (1 Cor. 12:13; 1 Pet. 3:21).[6] In Matthew 3:11, Mark 1:7-8, Luke 3:16 and John 1:33, a clear distinction is drawn between these two baptisms.[7] John baptised with water; Jesus baptises with the Holy

---

becomes our salvation' (John H.Armstrong p38). With respect, Peter does not. He speaks of a baptism 'which now saves us', not which *represents* our salvation. I will have more to say on the verse, but the question – 'Which baptism is he talking about?' – is always *the* question. Always!

Those who do introduce water baptism where it has no place have also to introduce qualifiers or glosses to avoid disastrous consequences. Take, for instance, Hendriksen on: 'As many of you as were baptised into Christ have put on Christ' (Gal. 3:27; see also Rom. 6:3). Paul does *not* mean that all who, in addition to being baptised in water, have been truly baptised by the Spirit into Christ, have put on Christ. Not at all. As I have said, water baptism is not in the verse or context. What is more, there is not a hint or a qualification in Paul's statement. 'All who are regenerate have put on Christ'. This is what he said and this is what he meant. But note Hendriksen's glosses: 'All those... who by means of their baptism [water baptism, he meant] have truly laid aside, in principle, their garment of sin, and have truly been decked with the robe of Christ's righteousness, having thus been buried with him and raised with him, have put on Christ... In Christ they have risen to newness of life. They have become united with him... And this, let it be stressed once again, is true of them all' (Hendriksen: *Galatians* p149). Note the 'have truly laid aside, in principle... have truly been'. I have no quarrel with the sentiment these words express – if we are talking about inward experience judged by outward profession. *But that is not what Paul is talking about in Gal. 3:27*. Hendriksen had to introduce the glosses because he wrongly brought in the idea of water. This must always be the case – unless those who bring in water baptism are prepared to live with the consequences and say that all who are so baptised are united to Christ – which some do!

[6] See my book on Baptist sacramentalism for the development of 'at least'.

[7] Contrary to Calvin: 'John... did not mean to distinguish the one baptism from the other'. But he did. As Calvin immediately went on: 'But [John] contrasted his own person with the person of Christ, saying, that while he was a minister of water, Christ was the giver of the Holy Spirit... The apostles... and... those who baptise in the present day... are only ministers of the external sign,

Spirit. Both men were baptisers, but they baptised in different realms. Furthermore Jesus is still baptising to this very day, something which is not always appreciated. A comparison – even a contrast – is drawn between John the Baptist and Jesus Christ as to their persons (John 1:19-28; 3:26-36). One was a great prophet; the other is the Son of God. And there is a corresponding contrast drawn between their baptisms. This contrast is not between two water baptisms, but between two baptisms in two totally different realms – baptism in water and baptism in the Spirit. 'John truly baptised with water, but you shall be baptised with the Holy Spirit not many days from now' (Acts 1:5). I repeat, these two baptisms (water baptism and Spirit baptism) must be carefully distinguished. Infant baptisers, as well as Baptists, can confuse them, with disastrous results. I will produce the evidence.[8]

Observe this also: It is Christ who baptises with the Holy Spirit. As just noted, Christ is still a baptiser, and this fact must be given its full weight; he does not delegate it to others. He does not use his ministers (let alone priests) to baptise with the Spirit. Nor does he use his ministers to baptise with water and thereby baptise with the Spirit. No! Jesus himself baptises with the Spirit. Now, Papists believe that when a priest sprinkles an infant, Christ is baptising the infant with the Holy Spirit through and by the ministrations of the priest. And we shall see that Reformed infant-baptisers get dangerously close to saying

---

whereas Christ is the author of internal grace' (Calvin: *Institutes* Vol.2 p517). In other words, John *did* contrast the two baptisms. If Calvin's words here are not self-contradictory, I don't know what is. Whenever John's words are quoted in the New Testament, the contrast between the two baptisms is always made (Matt. 3:11; Mark 1:8; Luke 3:16; John 1:26; Acts 1:5; 11:16).

[8] For now, see Wright: *What...?* pp83-102. Steve Wilkins: 'The Bible teaches us that [water] baptism unites us to Christ and his body by the power of the Holy Spirit (1 Cor. 12:13). Baptism is an act of God (through his ministers) which signifies and seals our initiation into the triune communion (we are baptised *into the name* of the Father, Son, and Holy Spirit). At baptism we are clothed with Christ, united to him and to his church which is his body (Gal. 3:26-28)' (Wilkins: 'Covenant' p55, emphasis his). This is a modern statement. I will provide plenty of evidence to show that Calvin and many others have said the same or similar. And many are still saying it. I will also return to 1 Cor. 12:13.

something similar.[9] Reader, before you throw my book down in disgust at that statement, I ask you to read on. I produce evidence for what I assert. But whoever says it and for whatever motive, I contend that when men say that Christ baptises with his Spirit as ministers baptise with water, they are grievously in error. Jesus is the only minister who baptises with the Spirit, and he does not delegate this work to any man. He does it himself; he does it directly. Who regenerates and renews by the Holy Spirit? Is it ministers? No! it is not. Is it Christ through ministers? No! It is '*God* our Saviour... according to his mercy *he* saved us, through the washing of regeneration and renewing of the Holy Spirit, whom *he* poured out on us abundantly through Jesus Christ our Saviour' (Tit. 3:4-6). God our Saviour baptises with the Spirit through Jesus Christ. God does not do it through his ministers by water baptism. It is Christ who does the work, he is the minister who spiritually baptises.

What is more, water baptism is not only different to spiritual baptism, the one has no cause-effect connection with the other – none whatsoever. 'Ah', says an objector, 'but what about those verses which speak of water or washing?' Now it is true that water or washing is mentioned in John 3:5, 1 Corinthians 6:11, Ephesians 5:26, Titus 3:4-6 and Hebrews 10:22, for instance, but this does not refer to water baptism; the water, the washing, is figurative, in exactly the same way as the fire in Matthew 3:11 is figurative – 'he will baptise you with the Holy Spirit and fire'. Just because water is mentioned, we must not leap to the conclusion that we are talking about baptism. Those who think the water is literal, must be consistent and in addition to sprinkling infants they should roast them! But the water and the fire are both figurative; they are figures of the purifying, cleansing, renewing power of the Spirit of God in regeneration,[10] in which he

---

[9] Why is it that although 'the Protestant Reformers had their quarrels with the Roman Catholic Church over the import and minor aspects of the practice of infant baptism... these were scarcely comparable in magnitude to their polemic against the Mass as a wholesale perversion of Christ's supper' (Wright: *What...?* p3)? And why, on baptism, are many of the Reformed so close to Rome today?

[10] Not excluding, of course, those repeated cleansings necessary in all our approaches to God.

gives a new, clean heart (Ps. 51:10; Ezek. 18:31; 36:25-27; Mal. 3:1-3; Heb. 10:22), nothing to do with water baptism.[11]

---

[11] Take John 3:5. 'Most assuredly, I say to you, unless one is born of water and the Spirit, he cannot enter the kingdom of God'. Continuing what I say above about the difference between water baptism and Spirit baptism, and that just because water or washing is mentioned in a text, it does not mean that we are talking about baptism. Note, as Robert Anderson observed, in John 3:5, Christ did not say a man has to be born of water and be born of the Spirit. Christ was not speaking of two births or two baptisms, one baptism by water and the other baptism by the Spirit. In other words, the truths I set out above have little or no relevance to John 3:5. Christ was speaking of only one baptism – baptism by the Spirit – and one birth – new birth by the Spirit, contrasting it with the old birth by the flesh, the baptism by the Spirit and regeneration by the Spirit being one and the same thing. See Anderson p222. Although water is in the passage, it does not refer to water baptism. Consequently, John 3:5 fails to establish sacramental baptism, simply because the verse does not speak of water baptism in the first place.

But, of course, Christ did bring water into the discussion. Now, whatever the water speaks of, unless he has experienced the washing it speaks of, no one will enter the kingdom; he will not be saved. Consequently, if the sacramentalist still wants to insist that the water refers to baptism, then no unbaptised person can be regenerated and saved; in particular, the thief on the cross. Rome ridiculously argues that he was baptised – by the spurting blood of Christ! Such an argument proves the paucity of the case. (See Beasley-Murray: *Baptism Today and Tomorrow* p40 for his extract from H.J.Wotherspoon on martyrdom being the spiritual equivalent of baptism). Now who will say that no one can be saved without baptism? In asking this, I am not minimising baptism, but circumstances can easily be envisaged where someone is converted, and baptism is simply not possible. The fact is, the water in John 3:5 does *not* speak of baptism. If it does, as Calvin said: 'Then... by baptism we enter into the kingdom of God, because in baptism we are regenerated by the Spirit of God. Hence arose the belief of the absolute necessity of baptism, in order to the hope of eternal life... But it is absurd to speak of the hope of salvation as confined to the sign. So far as relates to this passage, I cannot bring myself to believe that Christ speaks of baptism... "Water" or "fire" [express the Spirit's] power... By "water"... is meant nothing more than the inward purification and invigoration which is produced by the Holy Spirit' (Calvin: *Commentaries* Vol.17 Part 2 pp110-111). See Newton p27.

Moreover, if John 3:5 does teach that water baptism regenerates, when an adult is baptised (to regenerate him), is he willing or unwilling? If he is willing, how does he (an unregenerate man) have the will to be baptised in

To return to the main point: There are two baptisms, which must be differentiated. Peter, when he dealt with Cornelius, distinguished the two baptisms – by the Spirit and by water; he only thought of water baptism *after* the people had been spiritually baptised and the evidences of it were clearly visible (Acts 10:44-48). Peter later explained that when he saw these evidences which demonstrated that his hearers had been spiritually baptised, then he 'remembered the word of the Lord' that 'John indeed baptised you with water, but you shall be baptised with the Holy Spirit' (Acts 11:15-16). As Peter said: 'God gave them the same gift' (Acts 11:17). Notice that – God gave the gift. They were spiritually baptised by God *directly*; it did not involve water at the hands of a minister. God baptised the people with the Spirit, he gave them the gift of the Spirit – and he did so directly, without water. Likewise it was Christ, said Peter, who had poured out the Holy Spirit at Pentecost (Acts 2:33) with no reference to water baptism.

Water baptism is a symbol of spiritual baptism, yes, but the two are clearly differentiated in Scripture. We know that water baptism is a baptism which is to take place at (after) conversion; in other words, leaving aside the extraordinary circumstances of the apostolic era, in New Testament terms water baptism takes place only and always after a person has been baptised with the Holy Spirit. It is true that in one or two verses spiritual and water baptism appear to be telescoped together – as in Acts 2:38 and 22:16 – but even in those verses there is no warrant to think that the water baptism produced the spiritual baptism, or that the two were identical.[12] The New Testament makes a clear distinction between the two. This distinction must not be blurred. To do so is to make a great mistake, with massive consequences. But it is done.[13]

---

order to be regenerated? A spiritual will can be found only in one who is regenerate (1 Cor. 2:14), surely?

[12] See end note on p33 for excursus: 'Water baptism in Acts'.

[13] The baptism of Rom. 6:1-11, for instance, is spiritual baptism. See Lloyd-Jones: *Romans 6* pp29-147. Paul does not here call baptism *a picture of* or *a symbol of* union with Christ; he says that baptism *unites* to Christ. Evangelicals who argue that Paul is speaking of water baptism, have to fight tooth and nail to avoid baptismal regeneration. But they fight in vain; *if* Paul was speaking of water baptism, he *was* teaching baptismal regeneration. The

Nor must it be forgotten, the concept of washing, cleansing and sprinkling is common in the New Testament (John 13:8; 15:3; Acts 18:6; 2 Cor. 7:1; Heb. 12:24; Jas. 4:8; 1 Pet. 1:2; 1 John 1:7,9; Rev 1:5; 7:14), without any suggestion of baptism. All the references are figurative. All!

3. It is also wrong to regard every biblical reference to circumcision as meaning the physical rite in the flesh

This cannot be right.[14] After all, there is the circumcision of the heart, for example (Deut. 10:16; 30:6; Rom. 2:29), and this does not mean open-heart surgery! While there is a physical circumcision 'made in the flesh by hands' (Eph. 2:11), 'outward in the flesh' (Rom. 2:28), there is also a spiritual circumcision which is regeneration by the Holy Spirit (Col. 2:11), 'of the heart, in the Spirit' (Rom. 2:29). These two circumcisions, like the two baptisms, must always be distinguished. Christ is the only one who can spiritually circumcise. Only he can circumcise 'without hands, by [better, in] putting off the body of the

---

fact is, however, he was speaking of spiritual baptism – regeneration by the Spirit of God. Wright, it appears, taking the baptism as water baptism, did not fight against the logical conclusion of regeneration in that baptism (Wright: *What...?* pp88-102). Unfortunately, despite the above, Lloyd-Jones was obscure (or worse): 'The sacraments are not only signs, but are also seals of grace. They confirm the grace that we have already received. Yes, but shall we go further? They even *exhibit* it... in a sense they *convey* it'. Citing Acts 2:37-38; 22:16; Rom. 6:3-6; 1 Cor. 6:11; 12:13; Gal. 3:27; Col. 2:12; Tit. 3:5; 1 Pet. 3:21, he said: 'In baptism' – and he meant water baptism – 'in baptism we are cleansed from the guilt of sin... "washing" does partly refer to baptism... it puts us into this position of union', but went on to distance himself from baptismal regeneration. However, more clarity than this is wanted. As he himself said: 'Care is needed' (Lloyd-Jones: *The Church* pp30,37-39, emphasis his). Sadly, he failed to show enough of it here. Because of their importance, I will return to these verses, and Lloyd-Jones' comments. I agree with John H.Armstrong: 'How we understand the biblical-theological argument of texts such as Rom. 6:3-4; Col. 2:11-12; Gal. 3:26-29, will ultimately determine how we relate to a host of other questions regarding baptism' (John H.Armstrong p163).

[14] 'Circumcision... is [sometimes] spiritualised as rebirth' (Wright: 'Children' p29).

sins of the flesh, by the circumcision of Christ' (Col. 2:11).[15] It is a great mistake not to differentiate between physical and spiritual circumcision.

In both cases, baptism and circumcision, if the physical and spiritual are confused, the most appalling price will have to be paid. Yet this is done very frequently – especially by infant baptisers.

* * *

So much for my cautionary remarks of introduction to the subject. I now move on briefly to account for the rise of infant baptism, and what it has led to.

---

[15] 'In him you were also circumcised, in the putting off of the flesh, not with a circumcision done by the hands of men but with the circumcision done by Christ' (NIV).

End note to Baptism: Three Common Mistakes

Water baptism in Acts

Regarding Acts 2:38, 10:47-48; 19:5-6, as Wright said, 'no tidy schema can be constructed out of these divergent experiences in Acts'. But was he right to go on: 'But the bond between baptism and the receiving of the Spirit remains clear throughout' (Wright: *What...?* p91)? Does it? Let me grasp the nettle. Consider every reference to water baptism in Acts; 'divergent' is the word. Baptism is linked with the forgiveness of sins and the gift of the Spirit in Acts 2:38; with the forgiveness of sins, but no mention of the Spirit, in Acts 22:16; with neither forgiveness nor the Spirit in Acts 8:12-17,38; 9:18; 16:15,33; 18:8; it follows the (independent) gift of the Spirit, and is clearly distinguished from it, in Acts 10:44-48; 11:15-17; it precedes the (independent) gift of the Spirit, and is clearly distinguished from it – coming, as it does, with the laying on of hands, not baptism – in Acts 8:12-17; 19:5-6; and Paul's baptism is described in different terms in Acts 9:18; 22:16. Note also, baptism is linked with the gift of the Spirit only in Acts 2:38, and with the forgiveness of sins only in Acts 2:38; 22:16, and this last is Paul's testimony about his experience in Acts 9. The gift of the Spirit is linked with faith with no mention of baptism in Acts 11:17, and even when it is remotely connected with baptism in Acts, the gift of the Spirit refers to the extraordinary (Acts 2:1-33; 10:45-46; 11:15-17; 19:6; and, so I think, Acts 2:38; 8:15-17; 9:17), not to be repeated in these days. In the 'extraordinary', I include events, circumstances (take Acts 19:3-5, for instance; who else was re-baptised following John's baptism?) and gifts. Indeed, the extraordinary is characteristic of most of the history of Acts, as I have already noted. As for the 'extraordinary' baptisms, they occurred at specific and significant times for the gospel advance – Pentecost, Samaria, Cornelius and the Ephesian disciples – Acts 1:4-8 having set the scene for the entire book. See Donald Macleod pp11-18,29-38. These events, therefore, (for the moment adopting J.I.Packer's illustration) are to be seen as 'milestones' in the history of the church, not 'models' of church practice to be copied today; so much so, 'I guess Luke would have been both startled and distressed had he foreseen how some of his latter-day readers would misconstrue him in these matters' (Packer p205).

But Packer's milestone-illustration is too placid, conjuring up, as it does, the present-day church (at least for many of us in the UK), plodding on its weary way. Acts reads very differently. Far from being a 'normal' history, some events are given much space, while several months or even years are telescoped into a few words, according to their importance in Luke's overall scheme. Note, perhaps in particular, the way the history tails off with Paul in Rome. Luke, it is clear, did not intend to give a sedate history, a measured account, rounded and nicely balanced – as editors and publishers would demand today. Rather, recording volcanic events, he did not concern himself with the precise order within each eruption, nor did he stand back and formulate a theology for church practice, but left that for others (for example, Acts 6:1-6 is probably best expounded in 1 Tim. 3:8-16, while Acts 1:15-26; 14:23 are best expounded in Eph. 4:7-16; 1 Thess. 5:12-13; 1 Tim. 3:1-7,14-16; 5:17-20; 2 Tim. 2:2; Tit. 1:5-9, and so on). The baptismal passages in question, therefore, are not germane to the regular and ordinary practice of baptism – which is what I am concerned with in this book.

Putting all this together, it is not wise to erect a massive building on so fragmented and varied a foundation, and to extrapolate from these (obviously) special and isolated events to set up a norm of such importance for the rest of the history of the church. In any case, the overwhelming evidence, *even in Acts*, is that water baptism generally had no link with the gift of the Spirit and/or forgiveness of sins.

Finally, if baptism *is* the means of grace claimed for it, why did Paul treat it the way he did in 1 Cor. 1:13-17? This is a vital statement by the apostle. Whatever it teaches in its own right, the context is conclusive. The entire section 1 Cor. 1:17 – 4:21 is probably the greatest passage in the entire Bible for the priority of gospel preaching in the calling of sinners. Now for 1 Cor. 1:13-17. Fee, with consummate understatement: 'It seems clear from this passage that Paul does not understand baptism to effect salvation' (Fee: *1 Corinthians* p63). Indeed, he 'deliberately subordinates baptism to the proclamation of the gospel. This does not mean he minimises baptism; what he will not allow is that it holds the same level of significance as the preaching of Christ... He specifically associates the reception of the Spirit with his proclamation of the gospel, not with baptism. In Paul's mind, baptism stands on a different level... as [a] response to [the] grace received through the Spirit's coming in connection with the hearing of faith at the time of proclamation. It is nearly unthinkable that Paul could speak so casually of baptism and of his having baptised only two of them (plus one household that he had to be reminded of!), if, in fact, he understood the Spirit to come at their baptism. [What is more,] in [1 Cor.] 2:1-5, he insists that the Spirit came on them precisely at the point of his ministry, through proclamation, which would hardly be true if [the Spirit] came during baptism, since [the apostle] baptised so few of them, one of whom he had actually forgotten about... One can scarcely imagine Paul to have argued the way he does in 1 Cor. 1:13 – 2:5, if, in fact, the Spirit came on believers at baptism... [Take] Gal. 3:2-5... nothing in this text even remotely suggests that Paul presupposes this reception to have taken place at baptism; indeed, his argument loses its point if the reception of the Spirit were simply being transferred from one rite (circumcision) to another (baptism). [Paul, of course, was not saying the Spirit came through circumcision]. This could perhaps look like an inconclusive argument from silence were it not for the several texts in which Paul ties his converts' reception of the Spirit directly to his own proclamation of the gospel. For Paul, the Spirit came in the context of his preaching and of their hearing of the gospel (1 Thess. 1:5; Rom. 15:16,18-19). By his own admission he rarely engaged in the actual baptising of converts. Thus, it seems scarcely possible that Paul himself understood the reception of the Spirit to be in response to their baptism in water. For him it would have been exactly the opposite... What... this evidence... suggest[s] is that the close tie [made by many; see my note below] of water baptism to the Spirit does not come from a close reading of Paul, but stems from reading back into Paul the later experience of the church' (Fee: *God's* pp862-863).

Fee was not quite strong enough here. 'It seems scarcely possible that Paul himself understood the reception of the Spirit to be in response to their baptism in water... What... this evidence... suggest[s]...' We can put it more dogmatically than that. The passage utterly rules out the notion that water baptism conveys the Spirit. The evidence is incontrovertible.

Preaching, then, not baptism, was Paul's emphasis when, in the very same context, he said: 'It pleased God through the foolishness of the message *preached* to save those who believe. For Jews request a sign, and Greeks seek after wisdom' – and, I cannot help observing, sacramentalists demand baptism – 'but we *preach* Christ crucified' (1 Cor. 1:21-23). In all his instructions to Timothy and Titus, not once did the apostle mention baptism, but repeatedly referred to preaching and teaching (1 Tim. 1:3; 2:7; 3:2; 4:6,11,13,16; 5:1,17; 6:2-5,17; 2 Tim. 1:11; 2:2,14-15,25; 3:10,16; 4:2,17; Tit. 1:3,9,13; 2:1-10,12, 15; 3:1,8-9); see also 1 Thess. 2, for instance. I repeat the sentiment already expressed: I do not suggest for a minute that the apostle minimised baptism, nor am I going back on the earlier quotation from Spurgeon's preaching on Ananias in Acts 9:10, but all this is a warning to those who give baptism a place not warranted by Scripture. 'The apostle's manner of speaking of baptism in this connection as subordinate to preaching is, therefore, a wonder to those who are disposed unduly to exalt the sacraments' (Charles Hodge: *1 Corinthians* p17), the very thing many Reformed infant-baptisers do. Although, no doubt, hands will shoot up in horror at the suggestion, it is an inevitable consequence of the principles of infant baptism. But even if not, many Reformed teachers do 'unduly exalt' what they call 'the sacrament' of baptism. Read on! See Lusk for a modern call for emphasis upon the sacraments at the expense of preaching, and for his reasons: 'Preservation of sacramental efficacy was part and parcel of the preservation of Calvinism... The early Reformers... had insisted the sacraments were mighty actions of God through which he applied Christ's redemption to his people, forming them into a Spirit-filled community. They were not efficacious in themselves, of course, nor did they derive their efficacy from the human officiant. But they were regarded as effective because God had promised in his word to be active in them, making them genuine means of grace. There was nothing odd or impossible in suggesting that God used creaturely means to accomplish and apply his supernatural salvation. In the sacraments, God's role was to give and man's was to receive. In fact, it was precisely because the Reformers insisted on the gracious saving activity of God in the sacraments that they rejected the

Baptism: Three Common Mistakes

various other rituals regarded by Rome as sacraments' (Lusk: 'Paedobaptism' pp77-83).
Finally, if Paul argued so vehemently against circumcision making any contribution to salvation (Gal. 3:1-5; 5:1-6), how could 'believe and be baptised' mean that baptism does make a contribution? And how is it possible that infant baptisers should talk, as they must, of 'be baptised and believe'? And if baptism *is* a part of the saving experience, how, I ask again, could the apostle make the statement to the Corinthians (1 Cor. 1:13-17) – which we have looked at – when we know he had baptised so few of them, yet had been used to bring many of them to faith (1 Cor. 4:15), they being baptised only *after* they had heard the apostle and believed (Acts 18:8)? See Nettles in John H.Armstrong pp32-33.
In all this, I see a huge, unbridgeable difference between Paul and sacramentalists (Reformed, Baptist and Romanist). On the relative importance of the ordinances (sacraments, as they see them) and preaching, sacramentalists are clearly out of step with the apostle. See below. For now, let Leonard Verduin close this note by setting the point in its historical context: 'It was... inevitable that with the coming of "Christian sacralism" [Christendom based on sacramentalism – see below], preaching was crowded aside by act. In the place of salvation by a believing response to the preached word came salvation by act, by sacramental manipulation. The two have been in competition with each other ever since... In sacramental-churches, preaching atrophies; in preaching-churches, the sacraments [ordinances] are secondary. Attempts have been made to combine the two "means of grace", but one or the other is always *primus inter pares* [top dog]. No church has been able to achieve in practice the equality to which it in theory holds. As the one increases the other decreases. Just now [1964-1980] we witness a heightening of sacrament in many Protestant churches; this could be illustrative of what we say; the word has been discredited (we do not say rightly discredited); hence the sacrament receives the attention which once went to the word' (Verduin p136).

Infant Baptism: An Introduction

Where did infant baptism come from? Who started it? Very briefly, the details are as follows. The apostolic practice of baptising only believers[1] was soon corrupted by the Fathers.[2] What did the

---

[1] 'The universal baptising of babies... took place under Christendom and supplanted the practice of believer's baptism'; the Anabaptists were 'the first significant modern advocates of long-lost dimensions of New Testament baptism'; 'the norm of baptism is faith baptism... shorthand... for baptism on personal profession of faith... which is in good measure a summary [more, it is *the* summary, the only summary] of the New Testament witness to baptism'; 'baptism upon personal profession of faith is the most clearly attested [more, it is the *only*] pattern in the New Testament' (Wright: *What...?* vii, pp4,6,14,15,36). Bearing in mind Wright's standpoint, this testimony, albeit too cautious in places, cannot be ignored. See also Bradshaw pp101-115; Lane pp139-145; Tidball pp157,159. Lloyd-Jones put it more simply and directly: 'The teaching of the New Testament is that the people who are to be baptised are those who have already given evidence that they are regenerate; it is believers who are baptised in the New Testament' (Lloyd-Jones: *Romans* 6 p31). Yes, and only believers. 'I only have a right to be baptised because I am regenerate... Those who are to be baptised should be adult believers. I cannot see the case... for infant baptism' (Lloyd-Jones: *The Church* pp38,46). Sadly, Lloyd-Jones contradicted this clear-cut statement by what he said in the same context: 'In the New Testament there is no clear evidence that children were ever baptised. I cannot prove that they were not, but I am certain that there is no evidence that they were; it is inconclusive. The statements are such that you cannot make a dogmatic pronouncement' (Lloyd-Jones: *The Church* p41). I object to the 'clear'; as he himself recognised, there is no evidence at all that infants were baptised. What is more, since the unmistakeable teaching of the New Testament means that only believers can be baptised, a dogmatic statement can be made, and ought to be made.
James Bannerman admitted: 'An examination in detail of Scripture practice... will sufficiently bear out the conclusion... that at least a profession of faith is necessary as a prerequisite to the scriptural administration of the ordinance... The ordinance ought to be dispensed to those alone who "profess their faith in Christ, and their obedience to him"... That a profession of faith is required, both by the scriptural commission given to the apostles to baptise, and by the apostolic examples in this matter, on the part of the person to be baptised... there is no room for doubt'. The only way Bannerman could still argue for infant baptism, was to say this New Testament doctrine, practice and

Infant Baptism: An Introduction

introduction of infant baptism lead to? It was not long before the Papists developed a full-blown doctrine of baptismal regeneration through the sprinkling of infants at the hands of a priest, so that these infants became members of the Catholic Church and, supposedly, members of Christ.[3] The Church of England preserved – and continues to hold[4] – this wicked notion of baptismal regeneration. 'Seeing now... this child is regenerate, and grafted into the body of Christ's Church', are words in the Church of England *Book of Common Prayer*, words which are regularly repeated to this day over sprinkled infants who will prove that they are anything but regenerate.

And what about the Reformers? François Wendel's testimony concerning Calvin, the prince of Reformed teachers, should not be forgotten:

Throughout [his] reasoning [on infant baptism in his *Institutes*], Calvin is following Bucer's line of argument... Most probably... it was in reliance upon the patristic evidences adduced by Bucer... Since it was not possible for him [Calvin] to adduce a single New Testament passage containing a

---

'language applies primarily to the ordinary case of adults, and not to the exceptional case of infants' (Bannerman pp64-66,104-105). This is nothing but special pleading, begging the question. Primarily? Ordinary? Exceptional? Adult? We are talking about the New Testament doctrine and practice of baptism, about which there is no question of such qualifiers as 'primarily, ordinary, exceptional or adult'. The New Testament knows only the baptism of believers. Full stop! So, although I am glad to be able to repeat Wright's testimony of 'the widespread and still spreading recognition' by infant baptisers in recent years that 'faith in Jesus Christ' is 'the norm... of Christian baptism, both in theology and in practice' (Wright: 'Christian' p163), I baulk at 'norm' – if this is taken to mean 'custom' or 'usual'; it is *the* practice in the New Testament, the *only* practice. Furthermore, I baulk also at Wright's softening even of 'norm'; namely, 'the norm, in an appropriately qualified sense'.
[2] See end note on p43 for excursus: 'History of infant baptism'.
[3] See Wright: *What...?* for the most damning account of the history of infant baptism I know, and that in short compass. Tidball, speaking of Wright's book: 'At long last a responsible scholar outside the Baptist tradition has had the courage to say what many have thought: "When it comes to infant baptism, the Emperor has no clothes"' (Tidball p157).
[4] Though changes in the ritual are afoot, the situation is still 'bizarre', and 'perpetuates... incongruity'. Other Churches are changing, too, sometimes for the oddest reason or 'strange notion' (Wright: *What...?* pp57-62).

38

clear allusion to infant baptism, he had to be content with indirect inferences and analogies drawn from circumcision and Christ's blessing of the children. Calvin has been much reproached for the weakness of this reasoning... and he himself seems to have been aware of the defects of his exegesis upon this point. He was debarred, however, from using any other, from the moment when he undertook to defend, on scriptural grounds, an institution of later date than the New Testament writings, and to [try to] justify an ecclesiastical tradition after having proclaimed that all tradition, to be valid, must be based upon certain scriptural proof... [If he had taken his own medicine, it] would have enabled him to come to the [right] conclusion... frankly acknowledging that one cannot find an acceptable basis for it [infant baptism] in the Scriptures.[5]

Things did not get any better. The Reformers, *including the men at Westminster*, not only kept the practice of infant baptism by sprinkling, but made statements which, as I shall show, get very close to baptismal regeneration. Indeed, they taught it.[6] It stands today in the Westminster Confession.[7]

Infant baptism – is it easy to explain and understand? Certainly not! Indeed, at this point, I must offer an apology. I am truly sorry this book is as complicated as it is.[8] I try to write in a way which is easy to understand, but this time I am bound to fail to a certain extent. I have to wrestle with involved arguments and complex reasonings. Why? It is inevitable; and the responsibility for it lies at the door of infant baptisers. The truth is, some of their defences of infant baptism are tortuous, and their invented concepts are very difficult for non-experts

---

[5] Wendel pp326,328-329. While I will have more to say on some of these themes, see end note on p44 for excursus: 'The leading Reformers and baptism'.

[6] See end note on p48 for excursus: 'The Reformed, their Confessions, and baptismal regeneration'.

[7] See end note on p51 for excursus: 'The Reformed, their Confessions, and the weight they place on them in defending infant baptism'.

[8] Castelein: 'Reformed and Presbyterian theologies approach baptism and salvation within the framework of an incredibly complex system of Calvinistic theological beliefs [that is, their own invented covenant theology – DG]' (John H.Armstrong pp83-84). I agree. In my book, therefore, I cannot avoid trying to follow this 'complex system'. There is also some repetition, but my purpose is polemical not academic. What is more, some repetition is inevitable – rising out of the way certain arguments recur across the range of infant-baptiser claims.

to follow. One needs to be a first-rate metaphysicist to unravel the fine detail. I really do wonder how many parents who baptise their infants have actually sorted out all the essential ramifications of the logic required for what they consider to be a proper use of their system. To my mind at least, it is all very far removed from the simple directness of the New Testament, where baptism is a perfectly straightforward matter. So how does the complication arise? Not only do Reformed infant-baptisers badly expound various passages of Scripture, they get the debate about the continuity/discontinuity of the Testaments wrong, and lean heavily upon their invented covenant theology, thus erroneously forcing the Old Testament into the New. In this way, they produce complex arguments which, in this book, I am duty bound to try to follow, if I am to expose their unbiblical nature.[9] My wish, however, is that we might get back to that simplicity where we do not need to be academic theologians to understand all the niceties concerning infant baptism. The Christian religion in general, and church life in particular, are designed for those who are best described by 1 Corinthians 1:26-27.

Some infant baptisers, however, do not like the suggestion that their practice needs complicated reasoning to support it. John Legg, for instance, asserted: 'This is not, as is often alleged, a complicated belief'.[10] In flat contradiction we have the words of another infant baptiser, James Bannerman. He admitted that 'the subject is a delicate and a difficult one, and demands a more than usually earnest investigation... The difficulty that stands in the way of infant baptism lies on the very surface of the question; and [those who oppose infant baptism] have the advantage of an argument on their side which is both popular and plausible'.[11] Just so! This is why my book is as difficult as it is – infant baptisers have made it so. Some of them, at least, admit it.

A similar testimony came from William Cunningham who, in his defence of the practice of infant baptism, wrote:

---

[9] In my forthcoming book on the law, I will examine covenant theology more fully. For a very brief overview, see Davies Vol.2 pp311-313.

[10] Legg p2.

[11] Bannerman p67. I dissent, however, from Bannerman's 'plausible'. The biblical argument for believer's baptism does not merely *seem* reasonable and persuasive. It is both – because it is biblical.

There are undoubtedly some difficulties in the way of applying fully to the baptism of infants the definition usually given of a sacrament, and the general account commonly set forth of the objects and ends of baptism – we are very apt to be led to form insensibly very erroneous and defective views of the nature and effects of baptism, as an ordinance instituted by Christ in his church, or rather, to rest contented with scarcely any distinct or definite conception upon the subject.

With friends to write like this, infant baptism hardly needs opponents! Cunningham went on to speak of the need to modify the subject to accommodate infants, and to say that this necessity leads to disastrous consequences unless the modifications and limitations are fully understood by those who practise infant baptism. The upshot is to 'leave the whole subject in a very obscure and confused condition in their minds', he admitted. Quite! He went on to observe that infant baptisers 'are apt to rest contented with very obscure and defective notions of the import and objects of baptism'. No wonder! What is more, he pinpointed the source of the complication. Cunningham had to confess that 'minute and detailed expositions of the reasons and the effects of infant baptism are unwarranted by Scripture'. He acknowledged that it is impossible to explain the 'bearing and effect of baptism' in relation to infants. 'Scripture really affords no adequate materials for doing this', he said. Exactly! As soon as we stray from Scripture we move into error, and make things very complicated.

Cunningham concluded his arguments for infant baptism by speaking of 'the difficulties which undoubtedly attach to it, and with the obscurity in which some points connected with it are involved'.[12] Here we have it. The explanation of infant baptism is acknowledged to be difficult and obscure, and this is admitted by those who advocate it. I wonder, once again, since those who are expert in infant baptism find it as difficult and obscure as this, what is the average parent in the pew supposed to make of it?

As examples of the non-scriptural complications and obscurities which infant baptisers introduce, what do 'federal holiness', 'presumptive regeneration', 'elect or church' seed, 'internal, external or organic' covenant, mean to the average Christian? Very little I suspect. I think I have been fair in saying that the arguments for infant baptism are tortuous. 'Out of their own mouths'.

---

[12] Cunningham pp145-146,148,150,154.

But the arguments are not only elaborate and difficult – far worse, they are downright dangerous! In the next chapter, I will prove it!

End notes to *Infant Baptism: An Introduction*

History of infant baptism

I have no intention of stumbling very far into the minefield of who started the business of infant baptism and when. Sufficient to say, infant baptisers have abused the history of the Fathers in their eagerness to justify their practice, to try to make out it arose as early as possible. But it will not do! While it is undeniable that the baptism of the New Testament was corrupted some time during the 2nd to 4th centuries, the facts, in brief, seem as follows: Symbol was gradually replaced by sacrament, so that by the time of Irenaeus (about 200AD) it was believed that both remission of sins and regeneration were produced by baptism. This was the first and biggest mistake! As for infant baptism, possible traces can be found in Hippolytus (first half of the 3rd century), but definitely in Origen (about 240AD), though its acceptance made only slow progress – believer's baptism still being the overwhelming norm. Pressure for infant baptism came from those who, since baptism was thought to effect the forgiveness of sins, wanted the rite as early as possible. Others, because of their view that sin after baptism is unforgivable, argued the reverse, and wanted it as late as possible. Views on original sin also affected the practice (Stander and Louw; Wright: *What...?*). In short: 'The patristic literature of the first four centuries clearly shows how infant baptism developed. Probably the first instances known, occurred in the latter part of the 3rd century, mostly in North Africa, but during the 4th century, infant baptism became more and more accepted... While the 3rd century voiced objections against what appears to have been a growth in the number of infants being baptised, the 4th century seems to have accepted these baptisms along with adult [believer's] baptism which was still performed on a regular scale. It may, however, be said that since the 4th century, infant baptism began to develop into a generally accepted custom' (Stander and Louw p184). And as for the 4th century, 'all historians of the development of early Christian baptism are agreed that for a period of several decades in the 4th century the children of most Christian parents were not baptised in infancy'. Augustine, himself, (*the* theologian of infant baptism) was not baptised as an infant (Wright: 'Infant' pp352-355). This, and similar testimony, from such sources, ought to put an end to the abuse of history indulged in by many infant baptisers in their attempt to foist the myth of infant baptism on the very early days of the church, not excluding the New Testament itself.

There is another point. Infant baptisers often draw attention to the fact that the introduction of infant baptism seems to have caused little fuss. This, it is argued, shows that few if any in those early centuries were sticklers for believer's baptism. In reply, I note there was *some* objection. In addition, I point out, infant baptisers hereby admit that infant baptism is an introduction – it is not in the New Testament. Furthermore, once men were persuaded that baptism accomplishes what it symbolises (symbol gives way to sacrament), the next downward step – putting babies through the rite – was easy. The protest should have come at the first false step – from symbol to sacrament. 'Infant baptism seems an almost necessary adjunct to the doctrine that the waters of baptism have in themselves a mystic efficacy; and that [particular] doctrine was early welcomed' (Newton pp36-37; see also Newton pp53-56,134-147). So the real question is not: 'Why so little fuss about infant baptism among the Fathers?'; but: 'Why so little fuss about sacramentalism?' Sacramentalism was *the* issue *then* – as it is *now*.

One of Luther's reasons for infant baptism was bizarre. Jaroslav Pelikan set out Luther's 'reasoning': 'The continuity of the Church had been preserved in spite of the Papacy, but because of infant baptism. Thus it was evidence for the correctness of infant baptism... "Our baptism has been of this sort from the beginning of Christianity, and the custom has been to baptise children", Luther asserted. "Infant baptism derives from the apostles and has been practiced since the days of the apostles". At that point', said Pelikan, 'he did not supply any evidence in support of the claim, and was even compelled to admit that "from Scripture we cannot clearly conclude that you could establish infant baptism as a practice among the first Christians after the apostles"'. In trying to establish the impossible, Luther's exegesis, following Augustine, was risible – from 1 John 2:14 of all places. All he could do with such a desperate argument was to conclude 'even in the absence of explicit scriptural warrant for the practice, "you can well conclude that in our day no one may reject or neglect the practice of infant baptism which has so long a tradition, since God has actually not only permitted it, but from the beginning so ordained that it has not yet disappeared"' (Pelikan pp90,92-93). On such a ridiculous argument, murder could be justified – after all, it has a much longer traditional pedigree than infant baptism. As for Augustine, since he has played such an important and disastrous part in the Reformed view of baptism, I have set out extensive extracts from his works – see Appendix 2 – so that you, reader, can judge them for yourself.

The leading Reformers and baptism

Calvin allowed his judgement to be badly warped by his inordinate zeal against the Anabaptists. We will meet this again. Shawn D.Wright (p217) noted David Wright's observation on the change in Calvin's *Institutes* where, in the early section he 'defines baptism in such terms that it might almost have been written of believer's baptism only', and how this leads to 'the huge problem in relating' this to his practice of infant baptism as set out in the later section. Let me explore this a little. At the start, when confronting the errors of Rome, Calvin held the biblical essence of believer's baptism; faith must precede it. In the earlier section of the *Institutes*, note the frequency of 'faith' and the like – 'support our faith', 'confirm our faith', 'believed', 'believers'; the sacraments are 'added' to 'faith'; 'they... sustain, nourish, confirm and increase our faith'; and so on and on; in short, the Lord's 'mercy and... pledge of his grace... is not apprehended save by those who receive the word and sacraments with firm faith'; 'for what is a sacrament received without faith, but most certain destruction to the church?'; 'they [sacraments] confer nothing, and avail nothing, if not received in faith... we gain nothing unless insofar as we receive in faith'. But after the spread of the radicals, though he let this stand, things changed. See David Wright: *What...?* pp19-20; Calvin: *Institutes* Vol.2 pp491-554; Wendel pp318-329; Lane p143; Shawn D.Wright. And not only Calvin. David Wright again: 'The invocation of circumcision with its covenantal context was generally not an original feature in [the] Reformers' baptismal teaching. It emerges in general terms when, having nailed their colours to the mast of *sola Scriptura* [Scripture only], they had to row back from an initial emphasis on the necessity of faith for beneficial reception of baptism. This re-positioning occurred when the opposition against whom this emphasis was directed, the old Roman Church, was supplanted by the new foe of Anabaptism. We should not underestimate the seriousness of the challenge posed by Anabaptist radicals. More than one of the magisterial Reformers had to overcome early doubts about infant baptism, independently of Anabaptist protests. It can be seriously argued that the baptism of babies was the single most significant constitutive element of church order that the Reformers preserved [from Rome] without explicit biblical warrant'. Wright proceeded, minutely and precisely, to detail these changes in Luther and Calvin – changes which culminated in contradictions between 4:15 and 4.16 in Calvin's *Institutes* from 1536 to 1559. 'The impression [it is more than an 'impression'!] is given that there is [for Calvin] one theology of [believer's – biblical!] baptism and another of infant baptism. Too much of the later [Reformed] tradition has either lost sight of the former, or simply collapsed it into the latter, and hence worked with a doctrine of baptism that, to all intents and purposes, has been a doctrine of infant baptism alone' (Wright: 'Children' pp30-37).

Yet Calvin, even as late as 1555, could still declare, albeit somewhat weakly, when commenting on Matt. 28:19; Mark 16:15-16: 'The meaning amounts to this, that by proclaiming the gospel everywhere, they should bring all nations to the obedience of the faith, and next, that they should... ratify their doctrine by the sign of the gospel. In Matthew, they are first taught simply to teach; but Mark [16:15] expresses... that they should preach the gospel... Christ enjoins that those who have submitted to the gospel, and professed to be his disciples, shall be baptised; partly that their baptism may be a pledge of eternal life before God, and partly that it may be an outward sign of faith before men. For we know that God testifies [note, testifies – not conveys] to us the grace of adoption by this sign, because he engrafts us into the body of his Son, so as to reckon us among his flock; and, therefore, not only our spiritual washing, by which he reconciles us to himself, but likewise our new righteousness, are represented by it... All who present themselves for baptism do, as it were, by their own signature, ratify their faith... But as Christ enjoins them [the preachers] to teach before baptising, and desires that none but believers shall be admitted to baptism, it would appear [it most definitely is the fact!] that baptism is not properly administered unless when it is preceded by faith... Baptism is enjoined to the faith of the gospel, in order to inform us that the mark of our salvation is engraven on it; for had it not served to testify [note, testify – not convey!] the grace of God, it would have been improper [for] Christ to have said that they who shall believe and be baptised shall be saved [Mark 16:16]'. Excellent! Even so, despite what he rightly said about faith before baptism, this did not stop Calvin immediately launching a lengthy tirade against the Anabaptists, using the old arguments to come to the self-contradicting conclusion that though faith is essential, and 'though infants are not yet of such an age as to be capable of receiving the grace of God by faith', nevertheless 'it is not rash to administer baptism to infants' (Calvin: *Commentaries* Vol.16 Part 1 xxxiii; Vol.17 Part 1 pp383-388). If Calvin's logic were to be used by a defendant today, is there any doubt what the magistrate would say? 'My son was too young to have a driving licence, too young to be insured, too young to be capable of passing the driving test, but I assured him that it wasn't rash of me to compel him to drive on the motorway', would get short shrift, would it not? Incidentally, Matthew Poole took a similar line to Calvin: 'I cannot be of their mind who think that persons may be baptised before they are taught; we want precedents of any such baptism in Scripture, though indeed we find precedents of persons baptised who had but a small degree of the knowledge of the gospel; but it should seem that they were all first taught that Jesus Christ was the Son of God, and were not baptised till they professed such belief (Acts 8:37)' (Poole Vol.3 p146). Very good! However, like Calvin, this did not stop Poole arguing black is white. Since 'children are a great part of any nation, if not the greatest part... infants are capable of the obligations of baptism, for obligation arises from the equity of the thing, not from the understanding and capacity of the person'. Of this, as much as is comprehensible is ludicrous.

Calvin had not been alone in his change of views when challenged by the Anabaptists. Earlier, Luther had done the same. 'Luther... in his early Reformation years placed such a conspicuous emphasis on faith in relation to baptism' (Friesen p118). Between 1520 and 1528, however, he radically changed tack. Jonathan H.Rainbow: 'When facing Roman Catholic sacramental objectivity [in the early 1520s], Luther had been at pains to emphasise the necessity of personal faith... Now [in the late 1520s], facing a perceived Anabaptist subjectivity (that is, the insistence on personal faith and intelligent confession of faith as a prerequisite to baptism), Luther emphasised the objectivity of baptism'. In 1520, Luther could say: 'Unless faith is present, or comes to life in baptism[!], the ceremony is of no avail'. Yet in 1528, amazingly he could declare: 'Whoever bases baptism on the faith of the one to be baptised can never baptise anyone... Even if they could establish that children are without faith, it would make no difference to me... Since there is no difference in baptism whether faith precedes or follows, baptism does not depend on faith... We are not to base baptism on faith' (Rainbow p195). Pelikan commented: 'Luther's elevation of spirit over structure and his stress on faith made it even more essential that the baptismal vow be taken freely and consciously... It was reasonable in the light of this for many of his contemporaries to conclude that Luther's position, consistently carried out, [there's the key!] would undercut the traditional doctrine and practice of the Church regarding infant baptism... but when it came to the relation between faith and the means of grace, or at any rate to the relation between faith and infant baptism, he did not assign the decisive importance to faith, but gave it to the structured mediation of divine grace in baptism... He declared: "Anyone who wants to use the faith of the person to be baptised as the basis for baptism may never baptise anyone; for even if you were to baptise the same man a hundred times in one day, you would not know a single one of those times whether he believes". Theologian of faith though he quite self-consciously was, Luther would not make infant faith the determinative issue in his defence of infant baptism... The defence of infant baptism, then, could not be based solely on the assertion that infants could have faith... Neither the faith of the priest nor that of the candidate could affect the objective validity of the sacrament of baptism... The covenant of God was a stronger and surer foundation for baptism than the faith of the individual, for faith, too, was a sometime thing. How could one be sure, even in the case of an adult, that his faith was authentic and sincere'. I pause. Apparently, because of this difficulty, it is better to baptise unbelievers! For the same on Zwingli, see Verduin p201. Pelikan again, summarising Luther: 'The covenant... to this, Abraham and his descendants were to look, not to their subjective state' (Pelikan pp77,82-83,94-95). In other words, sinners are to be encouraged to think about their physical ancestors – and not look to Christ in faith and repentance. And not only for baptism – but salvation! Really? Luther said of the Waldensians: 'These brethren hold to the idea that every man must believe for himself and on the basis of his own faith receive baptism, and that otherwise baptism... is useless. So far they believe and speak correctly'. Nevertheless, even though 'there is not sufficient evidence from Scripture that one might justify the introduction of infant baptism at the time of the early Christians after the apostolic period [that is, in the time of the Fathers]... but so much is evident that no one may venture with a good conscience to reject or abandon infant baptism, which has for so long a time been practiced' (Verduin pp196,203-204). Amazing! By such an argument, one could 'prove' anything!

Zwingli, too, in his early days actually denied infant baptism, but drew back. And how! Zwingli: 'Nothing grieves me more than that at the present I have to baptise children, for I know it ought not to be done'. 'If we were to baptise as Christ instituted it then we would not baptise any person until he has reached the years of discretion; for I find it nowhere written that infant baptism is to be practiced'. 'However, one must practice infant baptism so as not to offend our fellow men' (Verduin pp198-199). Zwingli actually 'severed baptism from faith... Zwingli cut baptism loose from faith': One covenant, one covenant people; therefore circumcision and baptism 'must be... identical in meaning'. Although Zwingli was not the first to argue for infant baptism on the basis of circumcision, it was he who made it the central plank in the infant baptiser's argument. See Rainbow pp196-200.

Bucer wrote to Luther in 1524: 'Although the baptism of [believing] adults alone would probably be far more in accord with the practice of the early church, and also with the teachings of Scripture which *order* that those who know Christ should be baptised, confessing Christ in baptism after they have been taught the doctrine of godliness; and by baptising [believing] adults only would also be destroyed a deceptive trust in baptism [what an important observation – DG]... nevertheless...'. Bucer then proceeded to speak up for infant baptism! Abraham Friesen listed Oecolampadius, Bucer, Capito, Vadian, Ulrich Hugwald and Sebastian Hoffmeister as all 'early opposed to infant baptism... It was political opposition that turned Reformers against believer's baptism. When that happened, "magisterial Reformers" were forced to find reasons to oppose it' (Friesen pp82,89, emphasis his).

In short, Calvin's settled position was, as Wendel said: 'In everything concerning baptism, Calvin limited himself, in a general way, to harmonising as well as he could the ideas and the reasoning that he had found in... Augustine, in Luther and in Bucer, the last of whom had reproduced Zwingli's argument in all essentials, at least in so far as the main problem was how to refute the Anabaptists' (Wendel p329). Friesen: 'Catholic polemicists of the 16th century were quick to point out that the Anabaptists had out-principled the Reformers on the matter of *sola Scriptura*. John Eck [observed]... that when the Anabaptists appeared on the scene the Reformers "could not refute them, [so] they had to depart from their fundamental principle and [in order to maintain their system] concede that many things were to be believed and observed which had not been written [in Scripture], as Zwingli has pointed out with regard to... infant baptism"' (Friesen p142).

If this does not give the game away, I don't know what does. The right way to approach this subject, of course, is the same as every other: What does the Bible teach? Not: How can we stop the Anabaptists?

The Reformed, their Confessions, and baptismal regeneration

The Reformed Confessions teach baptismal regeneration. 'The divines who laboured so long and hard on the Westminster Assembly benches clearly held to regeneration as God's normal baptismal gift. The erosion of such full-bodied teaching about infant baptism among Protestant evangelicals in modern times distances them from the Reformers more markedly than on almost any other topic... The Westminster Confession teaches baptismal regeneration of infants and older persons. Just as [the usual] qualifications are commonplace among the Reformers, so also the generality of their baptismal theology conveys a decisively realist message: baptism is God's normal channel for imparting his gifts... to his children' (Wright: *What...?* pp24,99). Lusk: 'The Reformed Confessions clearly teach that a sacrament includes *both* the sign *and* the thing signified. Sacraments are not merely signs; they are signs *conjoined* with the gracious work of Christ and the Spirit'. In this, the Reformed Confessions were following 'Calvin [who] repeatedly claimed the sacraments perform what they picture; that in them, God accomplishes what he signifies' (Lusk: 'Paedobaptism' pp96-102, emphasis his). See also Wilkins: 'Introduction' pp12-13. All advocates – and would-be advocates – of the Westminster Confession, and the like, particularly over infant baptism, need to take full account of these testimonies. See below.

Calvin certainly gave the impression that he believed in baptismal regeneration. He made this plain enough when rightly arguing that the regenerate are not entirely free of sin: 'By regeneration, the children of God are delivered from the bondage of sin, but not as if they had already obtained full possession of freedom, and no longer felt any annoyance from the flesh... When it is said that God purifies his church so as to be "holy and without blemish" (Eph. 5:26-27), that he promises this cleansing... and performs it in his elect, I understand that reference is made to the guilt rather than to the matter of sin. In regenerating his people, God indeed accomplishes this much for them; he destroys the dominion of sin, by supplying the agency of the Spirit, which enables them to come off victorious from the contest. Sin, however, though it ceases to reign, does not cease to dwell in them... The remains of sin survive, not to have dominion, but to humble them under a consciousness of their infirmity'. So far, so good. But what of Calvin's words in between these last two sections (from 'by regeneration' to 'in regenerating')? How does God regenerate his elect? 'When it is said that God purifies his church so as to be "holy and without blemish" (Eph. 5:26-27)... he promises this cleansing *by means of baptism*' (Calvin: *Institutes* Vol.1 pp516-517, emphasis mine). In other words, baptismal regeneration.

In his *Commentaries*, I admit, he rowed back – employing the usual qualifiers just mentioned – double-speak, I call it – but before I quote him there, we must not forget his own stated position; namely, that his *Institutes* represent his definitive position: 'I have endeavoured [here in the *Institutes*] to give such a summary of religion in all its parts... Having thus... paved the way, I shall not feel it necessary, in any Commentaries on Scripture which I may afterwards publish, to enter into long discussions of doctrine... In this way, the pious reader will be saved much trouble and weariness, provided he comes furnished with a knowledge of the [*Institutes*] as an essential prerequisite... seeing that I have in a manner deduced at length all the articles which pertain to Christianity' (*Institutes* Vol.1 pp21,23, in his prefixed explanations for the work dated 1539 and 1545).

Now for what he said on 'washing of water' (Eph. 5:26) in his *Commentaries*: 'Having mentioned the inward and hidden sanctification, [the apostle] now adds the outward symbol, by which it is visibly confirmed; as if he had said that a pledge of that sanctification is held out to us by baptism'. I pause. Note, reader, the glosses. Who said anything about baptism? who said anything about symbol? who said anything about adding the symbol? Baptism is not even mentioned in Eph. 5:26. Note also Calvin's subtle watering down of his *Institutes*. In the latter, baptism wrought regeneration; in the *Commentaries*, sanctification is held out to us by baptism. Which is it? To let Calvin go on: 'Here it is necessary to guard against unsound interpretation [quite – DG], lest the wicked superstition of men, as has frequently happened, change a sacrament into an idol. When Paul says that we are washed by baptism [he doesn't – DG], his meaning is that God employs it for declaring to us that we are washed, and at the same time performs what it represents [in other words, baptismal regeneration – DG]. If the truth – or, which is the same thing, the exhibition of the truth – were not connected with baptism, it would be improper to say that baptism is the washing of the soul [which it is not – DG]. At the same time, we must beware of ascribing to the sign, or to the minister, what belongs to God alone. We must not imagine that washing is performed by the minister [but it is; he baptises the infant, does he not, and Calvin said baptism is the washing – DG], or that water cleanses the pollution of the soul, which nothing but the blood of Christ can accomplish [quite – DG]. In short, we must beware of giving any portion of our confidence to the element or to man; for the true and proper use of the sacrament is to lead us directly to Christ, and to place all our dependence upon him. Others again suppose that too much importance is given to the sign, by saying [that is, when we – Calvin – say] that baptism is the washing of the soul. Under the influence of this fear, they labour exceedingly to lessen the force of the eulogium [high praise] which is here pronounced on baptism [by Calvin – not Paul – DG]. But they are manifestly wrong; for, in the first place, the apostle does not say that it is the sign which washes, but declares it to be exclusively the work of God. It is God who washes, and the honour of performing it cannot lawfully be taken from its Author and given to the sign. But there is no absurdity in saying that God employs a sign as the outward means. Not that the power of God is limited by the sign, but this assistance is accommodated to the weakness of our capacity. Some are offended at this view, imagining that it takes from the Holy Spirit a work which is peculiarly his own, and which is everywhere ascribed to him in Scripture. But they are mistaken; for God acts by the sign in such a manner, that its whole efficacy depends upon his Spirit. Nothing more is attributed to the sign than to be an inferior organ, utterly useless in itself, except so far as it derives its power from another source. Equally groundless is their fear, that by this interpretation the freedom of God will be restrained. The grace of God is not confined to the sign; so that God may not, if he pleases, bestow it without the aid of the sign. Besides, many receive the sign who are not made partakers of grace; for the sign is common to all [infants who are baptised under Calvin's system – DG], to the good and the bad alike; but the Spirit is bestowed on none but the elect, and the sign, as we have said, has no efficacy without the Spirit' (Calvin: *Commentaries* Vol.21 Part 1 pp319-320).

As I say, this is full of the double-speak so beloved of the Reformed – we shall meet it time and again. By this, Calvin certainly has given me the impression that he was only too well aware of the weakness of his position, and tried to stifle nagging doubt (in himself and others) by sheer weight of words. Methinks he protested too much. He certainly professed too much for baptism.

The Reformed, their Confessions, and the weight they place on them in defending infant baptism

I draw your attention, reader, to the weight the Reformed place upon their Confessions when trying to defend infant baptism. As I will show, they openly turn to man-made Confessions in preference to Scripture. Take Pratt: 'To understand how baptism relates to covenant, we must delve further into'... Into what? Scripture? No! 'We must delve further into Westminster's theology' (John H.Armstrong p64). A brief glance at all Pratt's contributions in the book in question will confirm the point.

This present-day appeal to the Confession – above Scripture – is nothing new. Without, at this point, deciding on the rights and wrongs of the verdict, see George M.Tuttle's account of the way in which, in 1831, the Church of Scotland tried, found guilty and deposed John Mcleod Campbell for heresy on the atonement. 'At the beginning each party claimed to base its case on both the Scriptures and the Confession. By the climax of the trial for heresy, Campbell's opponents were standing firmly on the Confession as such, interpreting the Scriptures on its terms. To counter this, Campbell was resting his case on the Bible, and was even beginning to question the Confession's compatibility with the Bible... [His] accusers... were disposed... to turn away from Scripture to found their accusation on the Confession of Faith. This was evident very early in the proceedings... when a certain Mr George, agent for the [prosecution], declared... "I am persuaded that the Presbytery will consider any detailed reference to the Scriptures altogether unnecessary". This mood was underlined by a minister... "We are far from appealing to the word of God on this ground; it is by the Confession of Faith that we must stand; by it we hold our livings"'. After Campbell had argued his case, in part by citing other Confessions, he was told: 'We must not go back to any Confession before the Westminster, for to it we must bow'. Tuttle observed: 'Even the Bible, apparently, was to come under the authority of the Confession, for the same gentleman continued: "By my subscription, I am bound to receive the Bible in the sense of the Westminster Confession"' (Tuttle pp40-54). This illuminating comment had, at least, the merit of honesty.

Dangerous Statements
by Infant Baptisers

Let me illustrate my claim that some of the statements of infant baptisers are highly dangerous.[1] More, they are frankly unbiblical. As I have already noted, some of their statements give the impression (to put it no stronger) that they believe in baptismal regeneration; their Confessions teach it! This can have a devastating – even disastrous – effect on those who take the statements at face value. I realise and acknowledge that Reformed infant-baptisers say other things to contradict these statements – their usual 'qualifiers' – but that does not alter the fact that they did – and still do – make these dangerous assertions in the first place.

Martin Luther, for example, commenting on: 'For as many of you as were baptised into Christ have put on Christ' (Gal. 3:27):

Putting on of Christ... consists... in a new birth and a new creation... which is done in baptism... They which are baptised, are regenerated and renewed by the Holy Ghost... There rises in them... new and holy affections, [such] as the fear of God, true faith and assured hope... There begins in them also a new will.

---

[1] Let me explain my use of 'dangerous'. When I wrote *Battle*, I felt that the things I had read in Luther, Calvin, the Puritans and their followers, ought not to be read as they appear; that the caveats the theologians introduced blunted or sanitised their claims, assertions and promises. I judged, however, such statements to be 'dangerous' in that those who read or heard the claims, and who did not fully grasp the nuances of the caveats, might actually believe what (it appeared) they were being told. That was how I felt about these things. But I have now come to a firmer, more sinister conclusion. I have allowed the word 'dangerous' to stand, but I am now convinced that these statements – for all their qualifiers – were intended to mean what they seem to mean. What is more, many who follow the Reformers and their Confessions take them to mean what they seem to mean; and increasingly so. I will provide plenty of evidence in addition to what I have already produced. In short, I would now say the statements are not merely dangerous; they are (and I use the word advisedly) diabolical.

He attacked the Anabaptists,[2] saying they were:

Fond and fantastical spirits, which go about to deface the majesty of baptism, and speak wickedly of it. Paul contrariwise commends and sets it forth with honourable titles, calling it 'the washing of the new birth, the renewing of the Holy Ghost' (Tit. 3:5). And here also he says, that all they which are baptised, have put on Christ. As if he said: You have not received through baptism a mere token whereby you are enrolled in the number of the Christians, as in our time many fantastical heads have supposed, which have made of baptism a token only, that is to say, a bare and empty sign. But as many (says he) as have been baptised, have put on Christ: that is, you have been carried out of the law into a new birth, which is wrought in baptism... Paul therefore teaches that baptism is not a sign, but the garment of Christ... Wherefore baptism is a thing of great force and efficacy.[3]

---

[2] Luther marked out the path – which many Reformers followed: When in a tight corner, attack the Anabaptists. It reminds me of the preacher's notes: 'Argument weak here. Shout!' Interestingly, as Pelikan pointed out: 'Despite his many [caustic] references to the Anabaptists throughout the last two decades of his life, Luther knew very little about the group who drew such a radical conclusion from his thought. It seems clear that he probably never saw a genuine Anabaptist face-to-face. Moreover, he persisted in his identification of the Anabaptists with other opponents who had no direct connection with them, even when he had the opportunity to become more precisely informed about the differences... Luther seems to have been content with the rumours he got from others, and the suspicions he had within himself, and on this basis he formed his judgements' (Pelikan p78). As I will show, because of their detestation of the Anabaptists, the Reformers (including Calvin), instead of going for a full biblical reformation on issues such as baptism, showed that they would rather cling to Rome, and try to invent ways out of the corrupting morass this led them into. As the infant baptiser, J.M.Ross, observed, blinded by their prejudice, 'the Reformers felt that they must continue to baptise children, and find non-Roman reasons for doing so. Some[!] of these reasons will not bear examination' (Ross p111).

[3] Luther pp340-341. 'If any man... denies (as the fantastical spirits [Anabaptists] do) that righteousness and salvation is given unto an infant when first it is baptised... such a one utterly takes away salvation from baptism' (Luther pp234-235). Well, I for one, 'fantastical spirit' or not, deny it! I certainly take away salvation from baptism (or, rather, refuse to give it to baptism). As for the attack on the Anabaptists by Luther, Calvin and all the rest, at long last the Reformed are admitting the dreadful treatment their ancestors meted out to them. Of course, as I made clear in my *Battle*, I am not defending the Anabaptists on every issue; indeed, there is no such body as *the*

Paul, of course, did not say what Luther tried to make him say. Luther confused water baptism with spiritual baptism. Paul was not speaking of water baptism at all in Galatians 3:27. It was spiritual baptism he was writing about. Luther's comments are highly dangerous and wrong; they boil down to the doctrine of baptismal regeneration. He

---

Anabaptists – they formed a disparate and scattered group of persecuted believers with widely differing views on many subjects. Nevertheless, on the issue in hand – baptism – we owe a massive debt to those we call the Anabaptists, and I am glad to be able to quote the following, and I pay tribute to Wright's frankness: 'When the Anabaptist protest emerged... the new [that is, the Reformed] Papalism alongside the old, as the Anabaptists [rightly] read it – joined ranks in suppressing the dissenters. The contemporary church still waits for the appropriate acknowledgement by the Vatican and the worldwide Anglican and Reformed communions (the Lutherans of Germany have in good measure led the way, and the Swiss Reformed churches have followed more recently) of their forbears' scandalous mistreatment of the first significant modern advocates of long-lost dimensions of New Testament baptism. One legacy of the baptismal breach of the 16th century... has been the stubborn hauteur displayed towards Baptists and believer's baptism by infant-baptist churches and theologians... The obscuring [by infant baptisers] of a truer picture [of the history of baptism] derives ultimately from 16th-century apologetic, both Catholic and Protestant, against the Anabaptists'. It was their reaction 'against 16th-century Anabaptists' and 'later Baptists', which drove infant baptisers to skew their theology and make 'exaggerated historical claims, especially about the New Testament era and the next centuries'. See my earlier note on this warping of history by the advocates of infant baptism. 'The Anabaptists... opposed... infant baptism, including fundamentally the Church-State alliance and the use of the coercive powers of State authorities in defence of the new Protestantism... Rejection of infant baptism not only set the radicals against both the Old Church and the new evangelical Churches, but also put in jeopardy their belonging to the civil community [that is, they were to be – literally – exterminated!], co-terminus as it was with the infant-baptised Church of the city or the region. Religious dissent had inseparable social and political implications, and the Anabaptists suffered repression in many places. They interpreted their persecutions as a baptism of blood in which they were identified with the sufferings of Christ. Their afflictions were a further confirmation, a further seal, of their being members of Christ's body' (Wright: *What...?* pp4-6,18-20,29). The fact is, 'one of the interesting [grievous, sad] aspects of Reformation polemics is that Medieval heretics – as earlier opponents of the Papacy – have been much more favourably treated by church historians than have the Anabaptists, even though they may have shared ideas in common with the latter' (Friesen p143).

clearly stated that the 'new birth... is done in baptism', the 'new birth... is wrought in baptism', and he meant water baptism. This is Popery! It is an entirely false assertion.[4] What the verse actually teaches is that all who are baptised by the Spirit into Christ – that is, all who are spiritually baptised – that is, all who are regenerated – that they, and only they – are true Christians, having put on Christ. Water baptism is *not* the washing of regeneration. Spiritual baptism is. Water baptism, following faith, symbolises it, yes. But water baptism is not in view in the verse at all. Even though Luther derided them, the Anabaptists in 1525 saw this distinction clearly. Luther did not. He did not understand Galatians 3:27. He did not understand baptism. What he said was wrong; and it was dangerous.

As another example of dangerous statements made by infant baptisers, listen to John Calvin. He, like Luther, also said things which tended (to say the least) towards baptismal regeneration, confusing spiritual and water baptism:

Our children, before they are born, God declares that he adopts for his own when he promises that he will be a God to us, and to our seed after us... As soon as infants are born among them, the Lord signs them with the sacred symbol of baptism; they are therefore, in some sense, the people of God... The offspring of believers are born holy... included in the covenant of eternal life... admitted into the church by baptism... they belonged to the body of Christ before they were born... The children of the godly are born the children of the church and... they are accounted members of Christ from the womb... Children derive some benefit from their baptism... being ingrafted into the body of the church.[5]

This is confused. Infants, by baptism are 'ingrafted into the body of the church', even though 'they belonged to the body of Christ before they were born'. Which is it?[6] Even so, according to Calvin, infants born to

---

[4] The New Testament demands baptism *after* the Spirit has given repentance and faith (Matt. 28:19; Mark 16:16; Acts 2:38; 8:12-13,36-37; 16:30-33), whereas Luther spoke of the gift of the Spirit, and his work in repentance and faith, *being produced by* baptism.

[5] Calvin: *Institutes* Vol.2 pp525,535. See Graham Miller p16; Boorman p77.

[6] 'The children of believers are not baptised in order that though formerly aliens from the church they may then, for the first time, become children of God, but rather are received into the church by a formal sign, because, in virtue of the promise, they previously belonged to the body of Christ'. Those who disagreed with him, Calvin dismissed as 'frenzied spirits', 'furious

56

Christians are in some sense the people of God and holy. They belong to the body of Christ, are accounted members of Christ, and by their baptism are ingrafted into the church. This is a dreadful statement. This is Popery! While it is readily granted that infant baptism may make infants into members of the Roman Catholic Church, the Presbyterian Church, the Church of England, or whatever, it will never – never – make them members of the church of Christ.[7] When Calvin said that baptised infants are 'in some sense the people of God', in what sense, exactly, did he mean? No child is born holy, in the sense Calvin implied. All are born in sin and are the children of wrath (Ps. 51:5; 58:3; Eph. 2:1-3).

As another example of a dangerous statement by infant baptisers, consider the Presbyterian Westminster Confession:

Baptism... is for the solemn admission of the party baptised into the visible church...[8] Not only those that do actually profess faith in and obedience unto Christ, but also the infants of one, or both, believing parents, are to be baptised... The grace promised is not only offered, but

---

madmen' (Calvin: *Institutes* Vol.2 pp526,529,535). Well, I for one, 'madman' or not, disagree with him! I find *his* contradictions quite 'mad' enough. Why *did* Calvin baptise infants? Does anybody *know*? According to Wright, Calvin baptised infants because he thought 'they were already regenerate' (Wright: *What...?* p100). But, according to Lusk: 'For Calvin, regeneration began at the font' (Lusk: 'Paedobaptism' p89). For more on Calvin's and other Reformers' view of baptism, see Lusk: 'Paedobaptism' pp89-102. As Lusk showed, Bucer developed an even stronger sacramentalism than Calvin (who, as I have noted, was influenced by Bucer – Wendel pp324,326); nor were John Knox and Cornelius Burges laggards. See below for more on the confusing (contradictory) reasons given by infant baptisers for their practice.

[7] Wright ironically pointed out the opposite in Scottish *Book of Common Order* (1994). The baptised baby is received 'as a member of the one, holy, catholic and apostolic Church', but 'oddly enough', said Wright, 'the service is not so explicit about the child's becoming a member of the Church of Scotland! The lesser does not seem to follow from the greater – or is it encompassed within the greater?' he asked (Wright: *What...?* p84).

[8] I will have much to say on the 'visible church' – which is an unscriptural term. Those who use it do so to describe what they think is the biblical norm; namely, a church composed of the regenerate and unregenerate. It is, I say, unscriptural both as a term and concept.

really exhibited, and conferred, by the Holy Ghost, to such (whether of age or infants) as that grace belongs unto.[9]

The Independent or Congregational Savoy Declaration of 1658 repeated this terrifying assertion. Note the word *conferred*. What a word! Do those who hold to these statements today really believe that grace is actually *conferred* to elect infants in their baptism? Where do infant baptisers find any scriptural justification for this? Are infant baptisers prepared to assert, categorically, that every one of the elect who is baptised as an infant is regenerated at the time of their baptism? Those who hold to the Westminster Confession say it is so.[10]

Again, consider the words of J.W.Alexander, who encouraged infant baptisers to think of their children as Christians, even to say to them: 'You are Christian children – you are Christ's – you ought to think and feel and act as such!'[11] What an alarming statement. Where do infant baptisers find this parental attitude in the New Testament? Is this the way preachers ought to speak to unregenerate children (and, eventually, unregenerate adults) simply because they were baptised as infants? Where do infant baptisers find the scriptural justification for it? Immense dangers attend the notion.

Listen to the words of Charles Hodge who pleaded with parents to baptise their infants, saying: 'Do let the little ones have their names written in the Lamb's book of life, even if they afterwards choose to erase them; being thus enrolled may be the means of their salvation'.[12] Did Hodge really believe this? Can an infant's name be written in the book of God's decrees by baptism? Can the growing infant then choose to erase it? Was Hodge an Arminian or a Calvinist at this

---

[9] Westminster pp114-116.

[10] What about the elect who are *not* baptised as infants? And what about the *non*-elect who *are* baptised as infants? And notice the 'whether of age or infants'. Does this mean that baptism confers saving grace on all the elect irrespective of their age when baptised? But if the adult was a believer when baptised, didn't he have saving grace before his baptism?

[11] Kingdon p63.

[12] Kingdon p65. Some modern-day infant baptisers regard Charles Hodge as weak in this area. Commenting on Hodge's 'distress over the loss of infant baptism' in America in the first half of the 19th century, according to Lusk, Hodge himself 'proved to be part of the problem'. And Lusk had no doubt as to the reason: 'Hodge failed to develop a robust sacramental theology' (Lusk: 'Paedobaptism' pp71,83).

point? It seems that some infant baptisers, when they speak of baptism, can forget the doctrines of grace. How do Hodge's words square with election? On what do infant baptisers base these opinions?

Another infant baptiser, Archibald Alexander, said:

How solicitous should parents be for their children, that God would bestow his grace upon them, even before they know their right hand from their left; and, when about to dedicate them to God in holy baptism, how earnestly should they pray that they might be baptised with the Holy Ghost – that while their bodies are washed in the emblematical laver of regeneration, their souls may experience the renewing of the Holy Ghost, and the sprinkling of the blood of Jesus. If the sentiments expressed above be correct, then there may be such a thing as baptismal regeneration; not that the mere external application of water can have any effect to purify the soul; nor that internal grace uniformly or generally accompanies this external washing, but that God, who works when and by what means he pleases, may regenerate by his Spirit the soul of the infant, while in his sacred name, water is applied to the body. And what time in infancy is more likely to be the period of spiritual quickening, than the moment when that sacred rite is performed which is strikingly emblematical of this change? Whether it be proper to say that baptism may be the *means* of regeneration depends on the sense in which the word *means* is used.[13]

Reader, I remind you, I am presenting you with what I call dangerous statements by infant baptisers. I deliberately restrain my reaction to these words just quoted – words which tend to Papistry. I content myself to wonder that, however much Alexander tried to guard his assertions, is there any danger that some parents baptising their infant according to this system, might really believe that their child is actually regenerate in and through their baptism? Have any parents actually believed Alexander's words that 'there may be such a thing as baptismal regeneration'? Whether or not they understand the ins-and-outs of baptismal regeneration, and all the theological niceties surrounding the word 'means', I suggest that some parents might, in practical terms, take their child away from 'the emblematical laver of regeneration', as Alexander put it, with their heads and hearts filled with the diabolical and Papist notion of baptismal regeneration. They might well think that their baby is now regenerate, their baby 'is now all right if anything should happen'. I say it is a very real possibility

---

[13] Archibald Alexander: *Thoughts* pp12-13, emphasis his.

and danger, and one which arises out of Alexander's words. If I am right, or if there is any chance that I might be right, all infant baptisers ought to think about it very seriously. Those who teach this kind of thing carry an enormous weight of responsibility – the full extent of which will not be known until the day of judgement.

As another example of a dangerous statement by an infant baptiser, take the words of A.A.Hodge: 'In the baptism of every infant there are four parties present and concerned in the transaction – God, the church, the parents, and the child. The first three are conscious and active, the fourth is for the time unconscious and passive'.[14] I ask: What – precisely – is God doing in 'the baptism of every infant'? In particular: What is he doing in the baptism of a child who will never be regenerate?

Listen to Calvin again: 'Children are baptised for future repentance and faith. Though these are not yet formed in them, yet the seed of both lies hid in them by the secret operation of the Spirit... Paul... terms it the "washing of regeneration and renewing" (Tit. 3:5)'.[15] Calvin was mistaken. Paul did not call water baptism the washing of regeneration. Do infant baptisers really believe that God's Spirit works in infants, producing the seed of repentance and faith within them by sprinkling? What is the justification for this astounding assertion? And what is 'the *seed* of repentance and faith'? I do not deny that God can regenerate a sinner when he will, but that is very different to what Calvin said.[16] What is more, a literal understanding of his statement leads to only one end – the indiscriminate baptism of all children. All of them – apparently – will have the secret work of the Spirit within them. I realise Calvin did not actually believe this, but that is why I say that the assertions I have quoted are so very dangerous. They tend to baptismal regeneration. Indeed on the plain reading of the words they tend to nothing else. To put it bluntly, they assert it!

As a further example of statements made by infant baptisers which are perilous, not to say downright wrong, consider the words of David J.Engelsma:

---

[14] A. A. Hodge p336.
[15] Calvin: *Institutes* Vol.2 p543.
[16] The question of whether or not infants can be regenerated is a red herring – of course they can – but when such a statement is made in connection with baptism (Calvin: *Institutes* Vol.2 p541), it is loaded beyond description.

The children of believers are included in the covenant *as children*, that is, already at conception and birth. They receive forgiveness of sins through the blood of Jesus, the Holy Spirit of sanctification, and church membership – as children. For they have God as their God, and are his people – as children. Therefore, they have full right to baptism... God does not merely put the children of believers in a more advantageous position [than the children of unbelievers], so as to make it likelier that they will be saved; but he establishes his covenant with them, so as to be their God. God gives to the children the promise of the Holy Spirit of Jesus Christ. Accordingly... the Reformed Church regards them, and must regard them, as those 'sanctified in Christ'... God... gathers his church from age to age from the children of believers... Covenant children are... Jehovah's children (Ezek. 16:20,21). They are not sinful flesh, spiritually like the devil; but they are holy (1 Cor. 7:14). Quite unlike the children of disobedience, who are ruled by the prince of the power of the air so that they have their conversation in the lusts of their flesh (Eph. 2:1-3), the baptised children of believers are in the Lord Jesus.

Engelsma said that he witnessed boldly to God's covenant because, among other things, God, 'looked upon me in my infancy in grace, incorporated me as a baby by his Spirit into his Son, Jesus'.[17] He meant, of course, by infant baptism.

I must be brief in my comments, but these words cannot go unchallenged. First, observe Engelsma's emphasis; God blesses the children of believers *as children*, even from 'conception and birth', he said. He claimed that they receive the forgiveness of their sins as children. But the Scriptures say that we receive the forgiveness of sins through and by faith (Acts 10:43; 13:38-39; Rom. 4:1-13). We are saved through faith (Eph. 2:8). Sinners have to be converted to receive forgiveness of sins (Acts 26:16-18). Sinners have to confess their sins before they are forgiven (1 John 1:9). Do the children of believers stand outside all this? Do the children of believers receive forgiveness of their sins as children, because they are the children of believers? Most definitely not! Does this need to be said? Apparently it does. A man, a woman, a child, can only receive the benefits of salvation through faith – their own personal, saving faith (Rom. 3:21-31; Gal. 3:14,22; Eph. 2:8; Phil. 3:9). They are not saved by proxy. Infant baptisers agree that no infant can exercise saving faith – how then can

---

[17] Engelsma pp9,12-13,17-18,23.

61

he receive the benefits of Christ's redemption? To be saved, a sinner has to believe. No infant can savingly believe.

Reader, please do not allow yourself to be side-tracked at this stage on to the vexed and sad question of infants who die. This red herring is often raised by infant baptisers, but the spiritual condition and fate of such infants is another issue altogether, totally unconnected with the main argument. In the tragic case of infant death, let us rest in the assertion: 'Shall not the judge of all the earth do right?' (Gen. 18:25).[18] He is the gracious God who is 'abundant in mercy, forgiving iniquity and transgression' (Num. 14:18). We may safely leave such infants, along with all those who never develop a sufficient sense of reason to be responsible before God, in the merciful hands of the LORD. But, as I said, none of this is relevant to the debate about infant baptism.[19]

To return to the main point: The plain biblical fact is, no one is saved because his parents are believers. Every sinner must come to Christ by faith in order to be saved, and until he does so come, he is under the wrath of God (Eph. 2:3). We do not become the children of God by being the children of believers, as Engelsma asserted – no! we become the children of God 'through faith in Christ Jesus' (Gal. 3:26).

Further, what of Engelsma's assertion that the children of believers are not merely *more likely* to be saved than the children of unbelievers? What did he intend by that statement? After all, according to his own words, these children already have the Holy Spirit, already are the children of God and have already received the forgiveness of sins. What is left? But taking his words at face value – what, precisely, is the advantage Engelsma referred to? In comparison with the children of unbelievers, they are more than more likely to be saved, he said. How much more? Very likely? Almost certainly? In reality, as I have just said, if Engelsma's words mean anything, these children are

---

[18] And, it must be remembered, Abraham used this argument with God to prevent 'the righteous' minority being caught up in the judgement of 'the wicked' majority. Of course, each of us – every infant born (except Christ) – is a sinner, and God's judgement is just, but, to my mind, Abraham's argument is very powerful. If he felt it would carry weight with God over Lot in Sodom, how much more for us over infants who die before they have reached the age of responsible action! I will return to Gen. 18:25.

[19] As always, it is foolish to legislate on the basis of the exception. Hard cases make bad law.

certain to be saved! They are already saved. If they are incorporated into Jesus in infancy by infant baptism, what remains to be done? If words mean anything at all, it amounts to an assertion that all the children of believers are saved because they are the children of believers and have been sprinkled. Indeed, Engelsma called them Jehovah's children.

What is more, Engelsma declared that the children of believers are not born sinners like others, in that they are not born with the grim consequences of the fall as listed in Ephesians 2:1-3. They are 'quite unlike the children of disobedience', he declared, they do not conduct themselves in the lusts of the flesh, since 'the baptised children of believers are in the Lord Jesus'. Did Engelsma mean to say this? If so, he contradicted himself. In another statement he said that 'our children are by nature dead in sin';[20] that is, of course, they are included in Ephesians 2:1-3, they are among the children of disobedience, and they do conduct themselves in the lusts of the flesh.

I am not interested in merely pointing out the inconsistency of Engelsma's assertions; I am deeply concerned, passionately concerned, lest anyone should believe the totally unscriptural view that any child – any child – is born in a condition not covered by the fall. All the sons of Adam are ruined from conception (Ps. 51:5), contrary to Engelsma's assertion that the children of believers are the children of God from that time. His alarming statement runs directly counter to Scripture. All children, including the children of believers, are born 'dead in trespasses and sins... by nature children of wrath' (Eph. 2:1-3). Paul stated that 'we all' were ruined in Adam – all of us, including the children of believers. Jesus is the only man to have avoided this corruption; are the children of believers free of it? Do they escape this ruin by being conceived of believing parents who sprinkle them in infancy? Is this what the gospel amounts to?

Finally, in contradiction of Engelsma's claim, it is a relief to be able to state that God does not 'gather his church... from the children of believers'.[21] Rather, he gathers his elect from out of the mass of fallen humanity, 'the same lump' (Rom. 9:21). He redeems, calls and saves the ungodly as sinners (Mark 2:17; Rom. 5:6-10; 1 Tim. 1:15). God delights to call sinners as sinners; he does not work among the

---

[20] Engelsma p18.
[21] I am not saying, of course, that God does not call children of believers!

children of believers as such, nor exclusively among them. Indeed, he glories in spreading his arms wide to embrace those who have no connection whatsoever with the covenant people (Rom. 9:24-26; 10:11-21). This is a vital point. There is no distinction whatsoever in the gospel call, neither on the basis of race nor of family connection. God calls sinners *as sinners*.[22] The Spirit is sent to convince men of sin (John 16:8); this is the warrant for faith, since Christ died for sinners. Am I a sinner? Then I am invited to Christ. If it is true that God gathers his elect out of the line and descent of believers, then the Spirit must convince men that their parents were truly the children of God! But we have no promise to say that he does so convince.[23] Reader, do you not see that Engelsma's words are dangerous, as I claimed earlier? They are unscriptural. Their effect is devastating.

Herman Hanko, in his defence of infant baptism, said that 'believers and their seed are saved. And the seed of believers are saved as children'. He also declared that believers have 'the sure knowledge that God's promise is to save them and their children. They instruct covenant children. And their instruction will be fruitful for it falls upon hearts which are regenerated by the Spirit of Christ'. Did Hanko really believe this? Are all the baptised children of believers regenerated? He said they were! If God has given his promise to all believers, as Hanko

---

[22] 'Does not the potter have power over the clay, from the same lump to make one vessel for honour, and another for dishonour?' (Rom. 9:21). It is 'from the same lump', from fallen humanity, that God chooses and forms elect or reprobate vessels. 'Paul is not now dealing with God's sovereign rights over men as men but over men *as sinners*' (John Murray Vol.2 p32, emphasis mine). 'The mass of *fallen men* are in [God's] hands, and it is his right to dispose of them at pleasure' (Charles Hodge: *Romans* p319, emphasis mine). 'The potter does not create the clay; he starts with it, it is there in front of him on the bench... The apostle is not dealing here at all with God's purpose in the original creation of man, or with what God does with human nature as such. He is dealing with God's relationship to *fallen humanity*' (Lloyd-Jones: *Romans 9* pp199-200, emphasis mine). See also editor's notes in Calvin: *Commentaries* Vol.19 Part 2 pp366-367. All humanity, elect and reprobate, are at birth, whether born of believers or not, 'by nature children of wrath' (Eph. 2:3), of 'the same lump'.

[23] Compare the hyper-Calvinist's insistence on a sinner being made 'sensible' before he is invited to Christ (see my *Offer* pp8-10, and my forthcoming book on Septimus Sears).

claimed, that both they and their children are to be saved, why is it sadly undeniable that some children of some believers are not saved? How sure is this 'sure knowledge' which Hanko spoke of? He also said: '[When] believers... instruct their children in the ways of the Lord, they have the sure word of God that they are instructing children of God, God's own elect people'.[24] Well, are the children of believers elect and regenerated by God because their parents are believers? What a breathtaking assertion! Is this the Christian religion? Is this the doctrine of the Bible? Even Papists do not go this far. Dangerous? Statements like these are diabolical.

Finally, as the last in this long catalogue of terrifying assertions by infant baptisers, listen to the horrific *Prayer of Thanksgiving* of the Reformed Church: 'Thou hast forgiven us, and our children, all our sins, through the blood of thy beloved Son Jesus Christ, and received us through thy Holy Spirit as members of thine only begotten Son'.[25] If these words are true – if, and what an 'if' – what is left for the children of believers? They are saved because their parents are believers is the claim! Those who believe these words ought to have as many children as possible in order to populate the world with Christians! But it is not enough for sinners to belong to believing parents. Listen to the words of Christ: 'Most assuredly, I say to you, unless one is born again, he cannot see the kingdom of God... That which is born of flesh is flesh' (John 3:3-8). Yes! And that includes the children of believers – they are born of flesh, are they not? They must be born again. The fact that their parents are believers will never ensure their salvation.

Reader, is my assertion not true? When infant baptisers argue for their practice, they say things which are highly dangerous; and worse.[26]

---

[24] Hanko: *We* pp55,56,89.
[25] Engelsma p11.
[26] Reader, if you need further damning evidence, see Wright: *What...?* pp81-102. Let Lusk sum this up. In furthering his claim that 'a truly Calvinistic soteriology requires a Calvinistic sacramentology and *vice-versa*', his extracts from various writers showed what he meant. Hughes Oliphant Old: 'The Reformers insisted that according to Scripture there was one baptism. To divide the sacrament into a baptism of water and a baptism of the Spirit... was misleading... Reformed churches should not in their liturgical practice give ground to a separation of the baptism with water and the baptism of the Spirit'. James White: 'The traditional Catholic and [please note!] Reformation

Dangerous Statements by Infant Baptisers

* * *

It is high time we examined the so-called biblical basis of infant baptism. What claims do infant baptisers put forward? Naturally, it is impossible to know what every infant baptiser has said. When I assert, therefore, that infant baptisers justify their claims by a certain line of reasoning, I only intend to say that at least some infant baptisers argue in that particular way. With this in mind we shall look at ten classes of argument.

---

view [is] that God acts to accomplish God's purposes through sacraments'. Cornelius Burges: 'Sacred baptism, the laver of regeneration and of the renewing of the Holy Ghost... I do not deny future actual efficacy of baptism after the act of administration, but I only plead for some efficacy when it is administered'. Lusk added that 'Burges claimed Calvin for support of this view'. Lusk also rightly argued that 'the ordinary necessity of baptism for salvation is simply the teaching of the Westminster standards... The Confession teaches that there is no ordinary possibility of salvation outside the visible church and baptism is the mode of entrance into the visible church' (Lusk: 'Paedobaptism' pp97,118,122,124,125; Westminster pp107-108,114).

66

Part Two

Ten Arguments

In this section, I examine ten arguments which are used by infant baptisers to justify their practice:

1. Their children are holy (1 Cor. 7:14)

2. Their children are said to be in the covenant

3. The church is said to be continuous from the Old to the New Testament

4. Circumcision

5. Baptism is said to be a seal (Rom. 4:11)

6. The practice of John the Baptist

7. Household baptism

8. The mothers and their children coming to Jesus

9. Silence

10. Sacraments

Argument 1

Infant Baptisers Claim that the Children of Believers Should be Baptised because They are Holy

This unwarranted claim is based upon a faulty – incredible – interpretation of 1 Corinthians 7:14:

For the unbelieving husband is sanctified by the wife, and the unbelieving wife is sanctified by the husband; otherwise your children would be unclean, but now they are holy.

It is to state the obvious, but the verse does not mention baptism or church membership at all.[1] Nor does the context. This must be borne in mind. *Whatever the verse teaches, its primary application has nothing to do with infant baptism or church membership*. Nothing! Paul wrote these words, not to deal with the baptism of infants, nor to deal with church membership, but to deal with the question of a marriage where one of the partners had been subsequently converted. Any application of the verse to baptism or church membership must be incidental at best, which even some infant baptisers admit. In the light of this plain and indisputable fact, it would seem odd, to say the least, that this verse plays such an important part in the infant-baptiser's case.[2]

The verse teaches that if a woman is converted after marriage, and her husband is not (or *vice-versa*), then the Christian wife can continue with the marriage; she is not sinning by her continuing marriage to a pagan. The believing wife is not tainted by the unbelieving husband. Rather, the reverse; the unbelieving husband is sanctified by the believing wife. This does not mean, however, that he is saved or holy

---

[1] Church membership? I raise the issue only because of what Reformed infant-baptisers say about it based on 1 Cor. 7:14. Otherwise, the notion would not have crossed my mind.

[2] 'One of the curiosities of the use of Scripture in the church has been the use of this text to support infant baptism' (Fee: *1 Corinthians* p301).

or acceptable to God. Nor does it mean he is a member of the church. The word 'sanctified' cannot bear such a meaning in this verse. It means 'clean', being contrasted to that which is unclean, that which must be abstained from in order to avoid impurity. Though the woman is now a Christian, while her husband remains a pagan, the marriage has not broken down, nor is the believer polluted by going on with it. Likewise the children of such a marriage are not polluted by the unbelieving father or mother. If the unbelieving husband did contaminate the believing wife, in the same way he would pollute the children. He does neither. That is what the verse teaches. But to jump from that to a full-blown doctrine of infant baptism, and the incorporation of those infants into the church of Christ, beggars belief. But that is exactly what infant baptisers do. It is amazing. It cannot be justified. It is wrong.[3]

Calvin, commenting on the verse, was spot on in his opening remarks:

A believer [in the circumstances envisaged in the verse] may, with a pure conscience, live with an unbeliever... [who] is sanctified [as defined in the verse], so as not to infect the believing party with his impurity. Meanwhile this [particular] sanctification is of no benefit to the unbelieving party; it only serves thus far, that the believing party is not contaminated by intercourse with him, and the marriage itself is not profaned.

So far so good. Excellent, indeed. But when Calvin reached the part of the verse dealing with children, his tone changed, and how! He wrote:

The passage, then, is a remarkable one, and drawn from the depths of theology; for it teaches that the children of the pious are set apart from

---

[3] In the verse, please note, nothing is done to the children. Nothing! There is not a hint of a suggestion of any baptism. But, allowing for the moment, that infant baptisers are right, and something *is* done to them, notice that the children are holy *before* it is done to them; they are holy by virtue of the believing parent. Therefore, says the infant baptiser, we baptise the children – on the basis of their holiness. But, as I will show, infant baptisers are not always as confident as their trumpeted claims. Sometimes they want to stick to what they say on 1 Cor. 7:14 – that the children are baptised *because* they are holy; at other times, however, they claim that the children receive grace *by* their baptism. It is all a nonsensical interpretation and deduction from the verse, of course, but which do infant baptisers really believe? Is it *because* or *by*? Calvin, for one, couldn't make up his mind.

others by a sort of exclusive privilege, so as to be reckoned holy in the church.

According to Calvin, the sanctifying effect on the unbelieving husband is a relatively small matter, 'of no benefit' as he put it. But when the child comes into view, why, now we plumb 'depths of theology'! This expositional lurch is nothing but special pleading, a most inconsistent piece of work; shoddy, indeed. Rolling up his sleeves, Calvin went on to describe an enormous sanctifying benefit for the children. His words are astonishing. Referring to Ephesians 2:3 and Psalm 51:5, he wrote:

There is a universal propagation of sin and damnation throughout the seed of Adam, and all, therefore, to a man, are included in this curse, whether they are the offspring of believers or of the ungodly; for it is not as regenerated by the Spirit, that believers beget children after the flesh. The natural condition, therefore, of all is alike, so that they are liable equally to sin and to eternal death. As to the apostle's assigning here [1 Cor. 7:14] a peculiar privilege to the children of believers, this flows from the blessing of the covenant, by the intervention of which the curse of nature is removed; and those who were by nature unholy are consecrated to God by grace... But if the children of believers are exempted from the common lot of mankind, so as to be set apart to the Lord, why should we keep them back from the sign? If the Lord admits them into the church by his word, why should we refuse them the sign?[4]

In other words, Calvin asserted that all the children envisaged in 1 Corinthians 7:14 ought to be baptised because they are holy, the curse of nature – the effects of original sin – having been removed because they were born of a believing parent and are, therefore, in 'the covenant', 'in the church'. Did Calvin really intend to say this? It is a shocking statement. He has gone even further than Papists. Are the children of believers free from original sin because they are connected by birth to a believer? Words fail! I repeat my question: Are the children of believers free from original sin because they are connected by birth to a believer? Most definitely they are not! No one is free from the curse of nature because father or mother is a Christian. Does this need to be said? Surely John 1:11-13 is a sufficient statement to the contrary! What is more, if Calvin's claim for the children is true, why does the same not apply to the unbelieving husband? If the godly wife is of so great a benefit to her children, why is her husband

---

[4] Calvin: *Commentaries* Vol.20 Part 1 pp242-243.

likewise not set apart for the Lord, and all the rest of it? A consistent interpretation is needed. There is not the slightest justification for the baptism of infants from this sort of reasoning. Its practical effect is frightening.

Bannerman also wrote on the verse. He said that 'the infants are to be accounted clean, or fit for the service of God and the fellowship of his church. The holiness of the one parent that is a member of the Christian church, communicates a relative holiness to the infant, so that the child also is fitted to be a member of the church, and to be baptised... To translate the phrase into ecclesiastical language, the child is entitled to church membership because the parent is a church member'.[5] This is an amazing and unjustified deduction from a verse which says nothing – nothing at all – about baptism or church membership.

In order to baptise an infant, said Robert Shaw, 'it is sufficient if one of the parents be a member of the visible church'. Not only did he unjustly force baptism into the verse, but in light of what constitutes a member of the visible church according to infant baptisers (see below), Shaw changed Paul's reference to a *believer* in 1 Corinthians 7:14, reducing it to a mere *professor*. This in itself is a reckless exposition. A little later, Shaw wrote:

To be holy, as here used, is the converse of being unclean, and denotes that which may be offered to God. To be sanctified... is to be separated for religious purposes, consecrated to God... or to be in a proper condition to appear before God... The only appointed way in which children may be offered to God is baptism. The children of believing parents are, therefore, to be offered to God in baptism.[6]

Leaving aside the whole ridiculous and unscriptural notion of baptism being an offering to God, my question is: How is the 'sanctified unbelieving husband' to be offered to God? If the 'sanctified' children of a believing mother are to be offered to God in baptism, why is the husband – of that same woman and in that same marriage – why is he not to be offered to God in baptism, along with his children, and for exactly the same reason?

---

[5] Bannerman pp90-91.
[6] Shaw pp288-289.

73

Horace Bushnell argued that although the children envisaged in this verse are not 'actually and inwardly holy persons... [yet they are] Christian children as distinguished from the children of unbelievers'.[7] Charles Hodge went as far as to speak of them as 'Christian children [who] are not made holy by baptism, but... are baptised because they are holy'.[8] The Heidelberg Catechism teaches that infants must be baptised 'since they as well as the adult are included in the covenant and church of God'. *The Form for the Administration of Baptism* insists that 'infants are to be baptised as heirs of the kingdom of God and of his covenant'. The children are said to be 'sanctified in Christ, and therefore, as members of his church, ought to be baptised'.[9] Observe what is claimed. The infants are to be baptised because they are sanctified in Christ, and members of his church. The Church of England baptises infants to make them Christians; the Reformed Church goes further and baptises them because they are! And it all comes from a totally misguided interpretation of 1 Corinthians 7:14.

I have already hinted that one reasonable deduction from these arguments is that not only should the infant be baptised because its mother is a believer, and therefore she has sanctified the child – the unbelieving husband should also be baptised because he likewise is sanctified by his wife. Infant baptisers wriggle at this point, and try to argue that the words 'sanctified' and 'holy', which are used to describe the unbelieving husband, and the unbelieving child, respectively, are different. This will not stand scrutiny. Such cavalier treatment of Scripture is reprehensible. While it is readily agreed that one is a verb, and the other is an adjective, both words have a common root. The lexicon makes it very clear. The husband is sanctified. The verb is ἁγιαζω . The children are holy. The adjective is ἅγιος. It could not be plainer. What is said of the child, is said of the husband. Therefore, on the reasoning of the infant baptisers, if the child can be baptised on the grounds of its holiness, cleanness or sanctification, so can the unbelieving husband (or wife). This is nonsense![10]

---

[7] Kingdon p89.
[8] Charles Hodge: *1 Corinthians* p118.
[9] Engelsma p11. Calvin: 'Baptism... by which we testify that infants are included in the divine covenant' (Calvin: *Institutes* Vol.2 p533).
[10] Although I have already used strong words, perhaps this is the place where I ought to address those who object to my use of 'nonsense', and such like. I

74

Another logical outcome of the infant baptiser's argument is that in all marriages where one partner is converted after marriage, the couple ought to produce as many children as possible, and baptise them as infants. Added to the children of marriages where both husband and wife are Christians, this would rapidly produce a generation of holy children who are members of the church. They, in their turn, would produce another generation of holy children; and so on. Within a few generations, the world would be well on the way to being wholly converted! Come to think of it, if this rigmarole is true, why – after two thousand years of post-Pentecost procreation by men and women 'in the covenant' – are there so few believers in the world today?[11] It is, of course, poppycock from beginning to end!

Furthermore, the pagan husband, according to Charles Hodge, *is* sanctified, by which he meant something more than what 1 Corinthians 7:14 asserts. He said: 'The pagan husband, in virtue of his union with a Christian wife, although he remained a pagan, was sanctified; he assumed a new relation; he was set apart to the service of God'. That is, claimed Hodge, the pagan man is set apart to the service of God by his marriage union with a Christian, even though he remains a pagan. What an astonishing assertion. Hodge also said that the child is clean, holy and sanctified, 'belonging to the church' and to be regarded as 'sacred'.[12] This raises a question of the utmost practical importance. When that clean, sanctified child, who is a member of the church, grows up and has children of his own, are they, on the basis of 1 Corinthians 7:14, sanctified, clean, sacred and members of the church as well? If so, does this continue to apply even if the first child, on

---

ask them to consider Wright's words (which, I admit, I have gathered into one list) as he described the history of infant baptism: 'Scandalous, confusing consequences, incurable antiquarianism or a flight from reality, failure, exaggerated historical claims, grossly misleading, lamentable, strange notion, incongruity, ventriloquist charade, absurdity, half-baked, descent into unreality, ventriloquism' (Wright: *What...?* pp4,8,9,18,20,61,62,71,72,80). He was, I agree, describing what he rightly saw as abuses. But the biggest abuse to me is to take Christ's ordinance for believers and turn it into a ritual for babies! And I find the theology behind this switch 'confusing, a flight from reality, exaggerated, misleading, lamentable, strange, absurd'. In short, nonsense!

[11] See the following chapter for the arithmetic.

[12] Charles Hodge: *I Corinthians* p116.

reaching adult age, never becomes a Christian? This is no idle speculation. It is a very real problem for infant baptisers. Ways have had to be invented down the centuries to cope with this muddle – methods like 'half-way covenant' churches, for example.[13] These mistaken views and practices must inevitably produce church members who are nothing more than nominal Christians. This is admitted by infant baptisers themselves. Indeed, the probability of producing unregenerate churches (what a contradiction!) by this scheme, is simply a question of irresistible arithmetic.

Legg, for example, wrote about some of the problems for infant baptisers as far as church life is concerned. He spoke about the 'malpractice' which has 'prejudiced sincere Christians against infant baptism. They feel that it gives false security to hardened unbelievers', he said. He went on to admit that he had much sympathy with this attitude, and he deplored the 'indiscriminate infant baptism' which was introduced by the Congregationalists in the 19th century. He was scathing of the practice and the way it has degenerated in the 20th century into 'little more than a tribal custom, with evangelicals trying to salve their consciences by making some evangelistic use of the Cradle Roll', as he put it.

But it is not only 'indiscriminate' baptism, nor the 'malpractice' of infant baptism, which is at fault. Infant baptism *per se* tends to produce unbelieving church members, and infant baptisers have always had to try to handle the problem which arises even in their best-regulated churches. Legg spoke about the 'half-way covenant' in the churches of 17th century New England, which I mentioned a moment ago. This device 'allowed baptism to the children of those who had themselves been baptised in infancy, but who, while orthodox and moral, could not satisfy the rigorous New England requirements for communicant church-membership... It must be obvious', he went on, 'that such a practice will end in indiscriminate baptism as the next generation claims the same right on the same ground, a sort of quarter-way covenant!'[14] In other words, indiscriminate infant baptism can arise not only through Liberalism, as in the 1900s, or sheer ineptitude, as in the 20th and 21st centuries, but it can also occur where spiritual,

---

[13] See Boorman pp73-102; see below.
[14] Legg pp6-7. By now, they must be at the 0.00025th-way (or less) covenant! See the following chapter for the arithmetic.

orthodox men try to cope with the muddle and spiritual disarray produced by infant baptism itself. These are serious criticisms from an advocate of the practice!

This aspect of infant baptism is so important, I shall return to it later. It is getting to the heart of the practical problem as far as my book is concerned. The point I have tried to make is, infant baptisers by their practice tend to produce churches which are very different to the New Testament pattern. And they do so as a direct result of their system. I fully acknowledge that many churches which baptise only believers leave a great deal to be desired; a great deal.[15] In some cases, are they churches at all? But the present issue is not whether churches fall short of the standard they set themselves – my claim is that infant baptism *per se* tends to produce churches with non-believing members. In saying this, I simply repeat what the advocates of the practice maintain in their own documents. Infant baptisers really do accept, as the norm, churches made up of the regenerate and the unregenerate.[16] I say this is wrong according to the New Testament, and if there was nothing else against infant baptism, this would be sufficient to stop the practice. And quick!

I close this chapter with two sacramental Baptists who, though I disagree with much they have written on baptism, got this right. Talking about the infant-baptiser's claims from 1 Corinthians 7:14, Neville Clark declared:

---

[15] I admit the force of: 'Let us not beat about the bush... I know that [believer's baptism is] quite capable of leading nowhere in terms of active church membership' (Wright: *What...?* p85).

[16] We have seen the 17th century use of the half-way covenant. In the 20th century, John Murray fell back on the unscriptural invention of two sorts of church members; 'confederate members' – that is, baptised members who are not believers; and 'communicant members' – that is, baptised members 'who exhibit godly lives' and are allowed to take the Lord's supper. Unless the discipline of the church is effective in persuading the 'confederate' members openly to avow and embrace the covenant already 'sealed by their baptism in infancy[!]', said Murray, they will not be 'in a fit state to receive[!] baptism for their children' (see Shawn D.Wright p225). I draw attention to Murray's unscriptural notion of a parent *receiving* baptism for their children. It reminds me of the present practice in the UK of parents receiving a government hand-out – a trust fund – for their new-born baby.

Either we draw the conclusion that such children are, by virtue of birth, made members of the body of Christ, and thus baptism, which [in the sacramentalist view] effects this very thing, is redundant; or else the possession of this holiness involves something other than membership of the new Israel,[17] and is not directly relevant to the initiatory rite of baptism. In the one case, we have proved too much; in the other case, too little.[18]

Let R.E.O.White neatly – and accurately – sum it all up:

The argument has the air of a desperate expedient, and the exegesis is hopelessly inconsistent.[19]

1 Corinthians 7:14 does not provide any basis for infant baptism. None whatsoever.

---

[17] This reference to the new Israel leads us nicely into the next chapter.
[18] Clark p314.
[19] R.E.O.White p213.

Argument 2

Infant Baptisers Claim that the Abrahamic Covenant Applies to Believers and Their Children

In addition to their mistaken view of 1 Corinthians 7:14, infant baptisers support their practice of infant baptism by arguments based on the Old Testament Abrahamic covenant, those promises which God made to Abraham concerning his physical seed. They apply these promises to the church, by which they mean believers and their children. In this way, the circumcision of Israelite boys comes to be replaced by the baptism of infants who are born in families where the father or the mother, or both, are Christians (or nominally so). The promises of the Abrahamic covenant are applied to such children.

This is totally unwarranted. Unwarranted, it may be – it is! – even so, it does not lack, what seems to many, an impressive theology to buttress it. But... let us see how well this 'impressive' theology stands up.

Its fullest formulation comes from covenant theology, that logical system invented by the Reformers,[1] which is built upon the mistaken

---

[1] Although Johann Heinrich Bullinger (1504-1575) was probably the first to publish a work containing the concept of federal salvation, Kaspar Olevianus (1536-1587) 'was the real founder of a well-developed federal theology' (Berkhof pp211-212). This took place in Germany when Olevianus and Zacharias Ursinus (1534-1583) drafted the final version of the Heidelberg Catechism (1562). William Ames (1576-1633) was the leading British exponent of covenant theology, which dominated the Westminster Confession of the Presbyterians (1643-1646) and the Savoy Declaration of the Independents (1661). See Douglas pp36,165,267,729,1005; Kendall pp38-39. Although covenant theology plays an important part in infant baptism today, the dates just cited tell all; it is a relatively recent development. What is more, its introduction did not go uncontested. These facts need wider recognition. The Fathers, when they drifted towards infant baptism, did not argue for it on the basis of the covenant; indeed, by them, 'the Abrahamic covenant is hardly

premise that the two Testaments are continuous,[2] and leads to the application, to the church, of principles which concerned Israel.[3] As

---

ever mentioned'. True, the 4th century laid the foundations for it (Stander and Louw pp37,69,80,185), but it was the Reformers who systematised covenant theology, and the Puritans who took it to its pinnacle. See Davies Vol.2 pp311-313.

So why did the Reformers invent covenant theology? Wright: 'The 16th-century Reformers... were confronted with the urgency of justifying [infant baptism] in the face of Anabaptist protests which took *sola Scriptura* more strictly than did the likes of Luther, Calvin and company. [Supposed] covenantal parallelism [between the covenant with Abraham and the new covenant] proved the most sophisticated and durable of their [attempted] defences, which in turn made the assumption of universal infant baptism (made legally binding in some Reformation strongholds, such as Geneva) a factor in the rise of covenantal theology to prominence in the later 16th and the 17th centuries' (Wright: 'Children' p28). Wright quoted Riggs: 'From a historical perspective, the Reformed use of covenant to interpret Christian baptism first arose, almost always, when arguing for infant baptism. In other words, its origin was not in theological or exegetical reflection on baptism as such, but as a specific response to the [Anabaptist] challenge to a long-held practice of infant baptism' (Riggs p122). In other words, the Reformers began with the practice they had inherited from Rome, and went looking for a theology to support it. But if they had taken Scripture as seriously as did the Anabaptists, they would have started with Scripture, tested their practice against it, and come to the right way to baptise.

[2] I have already noted the significance of this mistake. We have not heard the last of it.

[3] 'For the Reformers, the total Bible was to be taken as one flat book, with every text having the same kind of authority, regardless of its place in the Bible, when it served their purposes' – when it served their purposes! So, for instance, 'the religious government of the Old Testament could be an example for the State Church in the 16th century without reference to what happened to that government under divine providence in the Old Testament or what Jesus did about being a king... The Anabaptists were the only mission group of the Reformation to make clear the fundamental distinction between the Old Testament and the New... Over against the "mainstream magisterial" Reformation for which in all history there has been but one age since the covenant with Abraham... the Anabaptists spoke... of the old covenant and the new... The significance of the relationship between [the] Testaments is enormous in practical consequences' (Yoder pp19-20). 'It would seem that the Reformers, in their haste to find the [Anabaptists] guilty of heresy at this point, were themselves led into error, the error of not appropriating the

Warfield put it, infant baptisers believe that the church 'carried over into itself all that was essentially Israelitish'.[4] But this is wrong; it flies in the face of the New Testament itself.

It is not only wrong, it is complicated. To try to unravel the arguments infant baptisers use, I will look at them under four headings. *First*, I will examine their claims based on the Abrahamic covenant. *Secondly*, I will consider the double aspect of that covenant from Romans 9. *Thirdly*, I will look at the way infant baptisers confuse the Abrahamic covenant with the Mosaic and new covenants. *Finally*, I will consider the new covenant itself.

---

teaching, found so unmistakeably present in the letter to the Hebrews for example [as well as Romans and Galatians], that the Old Testament is superseded by the New. One can go very far indeed in saying that there is a discontinuity between the Old Testament and the New before one lands in error as great as that of the man who refuses to accept the discontinuity that the New Testament plainly teaches' (Verduin pp210-211). Given Verduin's background, these comments cannot be ignored.

Ronald E.Diprose noted how the Presbyterians at the Westminster Assembly argued for their view of the church by what they called 'Jewish subordinations' which, they alleged, 'do, in the moral equity of them, concern us as well as them... We may... urge an argument', they claimed, 'from subordinations in the Jewish Church to prove a subordination still... There should be subordinations now in the Christian Church, that was then in the Jewish'. 'In other words', Diprose observed, 'Israel's Levitical order is seen [by such men] to constitute a model for the church' (Diprose pp137-138). See Newton pp43,48-49,51-52; Stuart Murray: *Biblical* pp97-124; Lusk: 'Paedobaptism' pp106-107; Wellum; Wright: 'Christian' p168. In addition to the ridiculous notion (see below) of a *Jewish* as opposed to a *Christian* church, among the many dreadful consequences which have come from over-emphasising the continuity between the Testaments, Cyprian used it to establish the priesthood; the slaughter of heretics has been justified on its basis; and, principally for my purposes, infant baptism has been built on circumcision. As I have said, I will go into this in more detail in my forthcoming book on the law. Even in this present book, however, I do not ignore the 'sharp questions' about the covenant, which those who, like me, baptise believers need to face (Wright 'Christian' p168). But Reformed infant-baptisers, likewise, cannot duck some 'sharp questions' about the logical system they have foisted upon Scripture.

[4] Warfield p404.

81

1. The Abrahamic covenant

The terms of the Abrahamic covenant are found in Genesis 17:7-8:

And I will establish my covenant between me and you and your descendants after you in their generations, for an everlasting covenant, to be God to you and your descendants after you. Also I give to you and your descendants after you the land in which you are a stranger, all the land of Canaan, as an everlasting possession; and I will be their God.

Before we examine these promises in more detail, some preliminary and obvious remarks are called for. The promises God gave to Abraham applied to the man himself *and to his descendants*. As Warfield's words make clear, infant baptisers take this principle – this Abrahamic, Israelitish principle of physical descent – into the New Testament, into the church. But this is utterly out of order; it is completely misguided; it runs counter to Scripture. We have no need to guess or speculate as to what the New Testament understands by 'the seed of Abraham'; it tells us – and plainly: The children or seed of Abraham in New Testament terms *are believers, all believers, only believers and nothing other than believers*. Most definitely *they are **not** the **children** of believers*.[5] The covenant does not apply to the children of Christians on the basis that they are the physical descendants of believers. In the New Testament it is not a matter of physical descent; it is entirely a question of faith. The issue is not: 'Is my father a believer?' But: 'Am I a believer?' The New Testament is clear. Abraham is:

The father of all those who believe... who also walk in the steps of the faith which our father Abraham had... Abraham... is the father of us [believers] all... Therefore know that only those who are of faith are sons of Abraham... So then those who are of faith are blessed with believing Abraham... For you are all sons of God through faith in Christ Jesus... And if you are Christ's, then are you Abraham's seed, and heirs according to

---

[5] I am not saying, of course, that the children of believers cannot themselves be the spiritual children of Abraham. Rather, that in the New Testament, the *definition* of the seed of Abraham does not include the children of believers. Those who do include such children in the definition of Abraham's seed, fly in the face of Scripture, and confuse the physical and the spiritual. Nowhere is it ever stated that Abraham is the father of believers *and their children*.

the promise... Now we, brethren, as Isaac was, are children of promise (Rom. 4:11-12,16; Gal. 3:7,9,26-29; 4:28).

These verses clearly teach that it is believers – and only believers – who are the seed of Abraham in the language of the New Testament; *not the children of believers.* It is only 'those who are of faith' who are the 'sons of Abraham'. Only believers are in the covenant in the gospel age; not believers and their children. Thus, when infant baptisers contend for infant baptism on the basis of the promises of God to Abraham concerning his physical seed, their argument is utterly false; utterly false, I repeat. But this is just what infant baptisers do. They wrongly apply the terms of the Abrahamic covenant to Christians *and their children.* Where, in the New Testament, are the children of believers told they áre the seed of Abraham? and told it simply because they are the children of believers?[6]

What is more, when they apply the promises of the covenant which God made with Abraham and his physical seed, to Christians and their children, infant baptisers are not only wrong; they prove too much. Let us look at Genesis 17:7-8. By God's promise, since all the descendants of Abraham were in the covenant, then it followed that they all inherited all the promises of the covenant. Once a boy born to an Israelite was circumcised, he himself was an Israelite, one who inherited all the rights and privileges of an Israelite. God established his covenant with that circumcised boy and his descendants for ever through Abraham. That is what God promised in the Abrahamic covenant. He said as much in Genesis 17. The point is, infant baptisers wrongly apply this covenant principle to Christian parents. This must mean – it can only mean – that they think a Christian's children are in the covenant in the same way as – or, at least, parallel to – the terms of Genesis 17. A Hebrew's children were Hebrews; a Christian's children must be Christians! If this passage could be applied to Christians as

---

[6] I invite anybody who suggests Acts 2:39 to read it again. There is no mention of any covenant. If the claim is still maintained, then it follows that not only are the children of believers in the covenant, but everybody is – 'all who are afar off'. If it is then said that the qualifying clause – 'as many as the Lord our God will call' – governs all, I agree entirely. The promise here is to everybody without exception. All who repent (and believe) and are baptised will be saved. If the verse is still applied to the Abrahamic covenant, however, then indiscriminate baptism must be the result. I will return to the verse.

infant baptisers do apply it – a big 'if' – it would mean that all the children of all believers are included in the covenant; and in it for ever. What is more, they all inherit all the promises of the covenant.[7]

---

[7] Calvin, replying to the Anabaptists, declared that they were criticising God, not the Reformers, when they argued against infant baptism: 'The Lord did not anciently bestow circumcision upon [the Israelites] without making them partakers of all the things signified by circumcision... The covenant... is no less applicable to the children of Christians in the present day... If ['since' Calvin meant] [the children] are partakers of the thing signified, how can they be denied the sign? If they obtain the reality, how can they be refused the figure?... Let God, then, be demanded why he ordered circumcision to be performed on the bodies of infants. For baptism and circumcision being here in the same case [Oh? What a begging-of-the-question!], [the Anabaptists] cannot give anything to the latter without conceding it to the former'.
Calvin's argument was both dangerous and puerile. God 'ordered circumcision to be performed' on baby boys under the Abrahamic covenant, yes; he guaranteed – guaranteed – all the promised inheritance to those boys, yes; they were Israelites, with all the benefits attached to being an Israelite. But where did God order believers to baptise their babies, and guarantee them all the inheritance of true believers? Calvin's premise was wrong; 'baptism and circumcision' are not 'in the same case'; in covenant theology, they may be, but not in Scripture. Do the babies of believers 'partake of the thing signified' in baptism? Do they have 'the reality' of the figure? According to Calvin, apparently so: 'The divine symbol communicated to the child, as with the impress of a seal, confirms the promise given to the godly parent, and declares that the Lord will be a God not to him only, but to his seed; not merely visiting him with his grace and goodness, but his posterity also to the thousandth generation'. 'If [since] the children of believers, without the help of understanding, are partakers of the covenant, there is no reason why they should be denied the sign, [just] because they are unable to swear to its stipulations'. Such 'children, deriving their origin from Christians, as [since] they are immediately on their birth received by God as heirs of the covenant, are also to be admitted to baptism... Baptism... is a kind of entrance, and as it were initiation into the church, by which we are ranked among the people of God, a sign of our spiritual regeneration, by which we are again born to be children of God... Wherefore, if we would not maliciously obscure the kindness of God, let us present to him our infants, to whom he has assigned a place among his friends and family; that is, the members of the church' (Calvin: *Institutes* Vol.2 pp531-532,534,542,546,549,554). Phew! If Calvin was only half right, why would Paul have said that Christ had not sent him to baptise (1 Cor. 1:17)? It brings to mind the claims of faith-healers. Why don't they visit the hospitals and empty the wards? Likewise, if baptism carries such

But do infant baptisers really believe that all the children of Christians are Christians? Do they believe that all the baptised children of believers inherit all the covenant promises? Well, do they? Surely it does not need to be pointed out, but the sad fact is, unfortunately, not all the children of believers will be converted, whether or not they are baptised as infants. On the infant baptiser's logic, why is this? They claim that they and their children are in the covenant of Genesis 17. Well then, since God was the covenant God of the seed (or children) of Abraham (Gen. 17:7), is he the God, the covenant God, of the seed (or children) of believers or not? Do infant baptisers really believe that their children are in covenant with God for ever? Furthermore, are the children of *their* children in an everlasting covenant with God likewise? Abraham's descendants were. All of them were. If infant baptisers are right, then a Christian's baptised children are in the covenant, his grandchildren are in the covenant, his great-grandchildren are in the covenant, *ad infinitum*. Really? Infant baptisers claim that the Abrahamic covenant applies to believers and their children. If they are right then all their seed are in the covenant for ever. They are all – all of them – regenerate.

But this is ridiculous. The mistake, of course, is to leap from the physical covenant made with Abraham – and it was physical, 'in your flesh' (Gen. 17:13) – to the spiritual life of the church. This is totally unwarranted, and, as a result, highly dangerous. The truth is, the physical covenant blessings promised to the seed of Abraham have no connection with the church at all. None whatsoever. Physical covenant blessings certainly came through physical descent in the Old Testament, but does grace come through physical descent? It most

---

benefits, why preach? Have as many children as you can, and baptise them all! And why stop at baptism – why not the Lord's supper? Read on!

I have already asked if anybody knows why Calvin baptised infants. May I broaden the question a little? I ask all covenant theologians: Are these particular infants in the covenant by birth, or does baptism bring them into it? A personal note: I was standing with fellow-speakers at a Reformed conference for a group photograph. The birth of my grandson had been announced at the meeting that morning. I felt a nudge in my side. A Reformed minister hissed in my ear: 'Get him under the covenant, brother; get him under the covenant'. As I recall it now, I wish I had asked: 'On your principles, isn't he already under the covenant?' Or is there a difference between being '*in* the covenant' and *under* it?

decidedly does not. It never did. And in New Testament terms it is expressly ruled out. It is not a question of physical descent. This vital point has been made already. Regeneration has nothing to do with human birth ties. Nothing whatever. Let me quote John 1:11-13:

He came to his own, and his own did not receive him. But as many as received him, to them he gave the right to become children of God, even to those who believe in his name: who were born, not of blood, nor of the will of the flesh, nor of the will of man, but of God.

Is it not perfectly clear? Grace does not run in the line of physical descent in the New Testament. As we shall see, it never did, not even in the Old Testament. There never was a time when it did. It never will. Infant baptisers are going further than the Abrahamic covenant itself.

Another of the promises in Genesis 17 concerned the land (Gen. 17:8). Infant baptisers say that to this day the physical seed of believers are included in the covenant. Well then, is the physical land also included? Will the baptised children of believers inherit the promised land? Of course not! What a silly suggestion! But what *will* they inherit? Since the children of Abraham did inherit the land, on the infant baptiser's argument the children of believers must inherit something. They must inherit the promise of God. What promise? What, if not the land? Is it 1 Peter 1:4? Do the children of Christians come into 'an inheritance incorruptible and undefiled and that does not fade away, reserved in heaven'? All believers have this covenant inheritance. God has promised it to them. Do the children of believers come into this, on the basis that their parents are Christians, and consequently they themselves are in the covenant and were baptised? Believers possess an incorruptible inheritance – do their baptised children possess it, too? If not, why not? On the arguments of infant baptisers, children must inherit something from the covenant by virtue of their physical descent from Christians. What, exactly, do the children of believers inherit through the covenant?

Further, must it be an eight-day baptism (Gen. 17:12)? If not, why not? And what about servants in a home where the husband or wife or both are Christians or nominally so? Are they included in the covenant? What about the children of these servants? Are they included in the covenant, likewise? They were in the Abrahamic covenant, with no suggestion that they had adopted Israelite

86

convictions (Gen. 17:12-13). So, to come to a practical case, if a Christian has adult servants, must they be baptised? What if they are not converted, or do not even make a profession, must they be baptised even so? Are they in the covenant? Are they Christians? These are no idle questions. Meredith Kline tried to face up to them, but the consequences proved too much:

Perhaps the complications that can easily be foreseen developing in this area are in themselves sufficient to turn us from further consideration of this approach as a proper interpretation of New Testament directives.[8]

Is this the best that can be said for the practical consequences of the attempt to apply the covenant in the way infant baptisers do? It is more than 'sufficient to turn us from further consideration of this approach'. It is an utter farce. It is nothing less than a frank admission of the failure of their case based upon a most improper interpretation of Scripture. Infant baptism, on the basis of this kind of partial, pick-and-choose application of the Abrahamic covenant, ought to be stopped now!

Again, if an Israelite parent did not circumcise his infant, that boy was to be 'cut off from his people'; he had broken God's covenant (Gen. 17:14). How does this apply to infant baptism? What will infant baptisers do to those persons whose parents were Christians but who did not baptise them as infants? What will they do to the unbaptised infant? How will the child be 'cut off from his people'? What will it mean? My wife and I were such parents; we were believers but we did not baptise our infants. Thus the question is of personal interest to me and millions like me. What happens to those whose parents did not baptise them as infants? Will infant baptisers cut them off from Christ and salvation? What will this mean in down-to-earth terms? Would some infant baptiser spell it out for us?[9]

---

[8] Kingdon pp48-49.

[9] My parents were not believers when I was born. I was not baptised as an infant. In my teens, I was converted and baptised. My parents later professed faith, and were baptised. In time, I married a believer who had been baptised upon profession of faith – her believing parents had not baptised her as an infant. When our children were born, we did not baptise them as infants. On credible profession of faith, in their teens, at their request and after due examination, they were baptised. When, in their turn, in their marriages to believers, they had children, they did not baptise them as babies. But these

Ishmael was circumcised but he was expressly excluded from the covenant (Gen. 17:15-27; Rom. 9:7-8; Gal. 4:22-31). What, exactly, is the spiritual equivalent of this in the baptism of the New Testament? Who are the Christian Ishmaelites?

What is more, why do Reformed infant-baptisers not baptise *all* children? Since the covenant applies for a thousand generations (Deut. 7:9; 1 Chron. 16:15-17; Ps. 105:5-10), once a man is in the covenant, all his descendants are in the covenant, even to a thousand generations. On the principles of infant baptism, once any man is in the covenant, all his descendants must be baptised, even to a thousand generations. Let us pause for a moment and consider this. It is bound to mean virtual indiscriminate baptism in the end.[10] The point is, what happens

---

children are now coming to profess Christ, and those who have so professed him have been baptised. As I say, would some infant baptiser please write to me, and set this in the context of Gen. 17? Who should be 'cut off'? And what will that mean?

[10] The arithmetic is unassailable. In round figures, 2000 years have passed since the New Testament; 70 generations, say. Allowing, for the moment, 2 offspring *per* generation, and no intermarriage, a believer of the New Testament age would now have 2^{70} descendants, approximately 10^{22}, alive today. So the 120 believers at Pentecost would have approximately 10^{24} descendants alive today; a million, million, million, million. Obviously, this figure will be drastically reduced by intermarriage and all the rest, (but it will be increased if more than two offspring are produced and have children in each generation). The point I am making is that when the arithmetic is applied to all the generations since Pentecost, leaving aside isolated tribes, the likelihood of anybody alive today not having at least one believer in his ancestry, is so remote as to be unthinkable. (As I write, the world population is just under a 'mere' 7000 million!) In other words, everybody alive today must be in the covenant. Furthermore, why begin at Pentecost? What about Abraham? He lived 42 generations before the birth of Christ (Matt. 1:17). So we are talking about 110 generations! All this makes the possibility – of anybody alive today *not* being in the covenant – even more remote. Nor must it be forgotten, Ps. 105 speaks of 1000 generations – which Calvin applied to the babies of believers. In short, everybody alive today almost certainly has at least one ancestor who was in the covenant. And this has large consequences for infant baptisers and covenant theologians. Let John Cotton spell it out: 'If you can say, you have known some of your ancestors in this covenant, and you have not refused it, but laid claim to it, when you understand it yourselves, it is certain this covenant reaches to you' (Perry Miller p92). Cotton was stricter than the Bible. A man is in the covenant if but *one* of his

if an infant's father is a rank infidel, but his grandfather is a true believer? Since the grandfather is in the covenant, his son, though an unbeliever, is also in the covenant! But even if he is not, the promise still descends to the infant through his grandfather. Are infants to be baptised because the father is in the covenant, or because the grandfather is, or because the great-grandfather is? Louis Berkhof said that some infant baptisers actually do reason on this basis to the end that 'children whose parents have left the church have not thereby forfeited their privileges as children of the covenant'. In other words, some infant baptisers do argue for the virtual indiscriminate baptism of infants, irrespective of the standing of the parents. 'Covenant theology' has come to a sorry state when this happens.[11]

---

ancestors was. And he is in it, whether or not he knows his ancestor was. And where does this idea of 'refusing the covenant' come from? Can a man, in the covenant by God's decree through birth, refuse it?

By the way, how does Ex. 20:5 effect the infant-baptiser's argument based on the generations in the covenant? 'I, the LORD your God, am a jealous God, visiting the iniquity of the fathers upon the children to the third and fourth generations of those who hate me'. Suppose a man is a believer, but his son, though in the covenant and baptised as an infant, turns out to be a hater of God. Are *his* children in the covenant, or does God visit the iniquity of their father upon them? And so on.

[11] Calvin to John Knox: 'God's promise comprehends not only the offspring of every believer in the first line of descent, but extends to thousands [*sic*] of generations. Whence it has happened that the interruption of piety which has prevailed in Popery has not taken away from baptism its force and efficacy... To us then it is by no means doubtful [a *litotes*; that is, it is certain] that offspring descended from holy and pious ancestors, belong to the body of the church, though their fathers and grandfathers may have been apostates... [Let me suppose a case:] It is unjust, when God, three hundred years ago or more [say], has thought them worthy of adoption [that is, one of their ancestors at that time was a believer], that the subsequent impiety of some of their progenitors should interrupt the course of heavenly grace. In short, as each person is not admitted to baptism from respect or regard to one of his parents alone, but on account of the perpetual covenant of God, so in like manner, no just reason suffers children to be debarred from their initiation into the church in consequence of the bad conduct of only one parent' (Calvin: *Letters* pp215-216). See below for note on Calvin: *Institutes* Vol.2 p521. So much for the children of apostates, according to covenant theology. But a question suggests itself: Were those apostates, themselves, in the covenant or not? After all, they had an ancestor who was.

On the basis of Genesis 17:12, why do infant baptisers not adopt infants, and baptise them? This is no trivial question. Berkhof said it is the principle and practice of some infant baptisers where 'the parents were unfit or unwilling to vouch for the Christian education of their children'. As he put it: 'Others could step in to guarantee this'.[12]

What is more, if a foreigner became an Israelite, his children and slaves had to become – and did become – Israelites, too, by circumcision (Exod. 12:48). Charles Hodge, at least with the merit of consistency, said that the equivalent applies to Christians! Really? He was actually prepared to maintain that 'if the father becomes a citizen of a country he makes his children citizens. In like manner, when a man becomes a Christian, his children are to be regarded as doing the same thing'.[13] This is staggering. It is unbelievable. I agree that if a man takes on English or American nationality, say, his dependent children do,[14] but do infant baptisers really believe that if a man is converted, his children are to be regarded as converted? Apparently they do. Warfield, for instance, said that the parent acts as a representative of his child, and 'that the status of the parent determines the status of the child'. And to remove all misunderstanding, he explained that he meant 'in the church of God... as well as... in the State'.[15] What an incredible claim!

John Murray said that 'baptised infants are to be received as the children of God and treated accordingly'.[16] Surely this must be a gross mistake. But A.A.Hodge was even more frank. He said that the baptised infant should be 'taught from the first to recognise himself as a child of God, with all its privileges and duties; trained to think, feel, and act as a child of God'.[17] What an amazing statement! How terribly misguided. What untold damage this must have done to unregenerate

---

[12] Berkhof p642. What is this talk of 'Christian education'? I am not, of course, implying that parents should not train up their children in the ways of God (Prov. 22:6), but, according to covenant theology, the infant is in the covenant, full stop, by virtue of the faith of its parent, grand-parent or whoever – whether or not the parent gives it a 'Christian education'.

[13] Kingdon p47.

[14] As Paul said: 'I was born a [Roman] citizen' (Acts 22:28). Where in the Bible is anyone said to be 'born a Christian'?

[15] Warfield p403.

[16] Kingdon p47.

[17] A. A. Hodge p337.

children who have been trained, constantly brought up, to look upon themselves as children of God. It is horrific.

I ask again: Since all the children of the Israelites were Israelites by the covenant, are infant baptisers really prepared to say that all the children of Christians are themselves Christians? In their discussion of infant baptism, it is obvious that they get very close to saying it, if not actually committing themselves to the position. And it is totally wrong and a diabolical suggestion. Reader, I can do no better than to refer you to John 1:11-13 once more. In New Testament terms, birth has nothing to do with spiritual life. That there are advantages in being born to Christian parents, no one denies. But this is not the issue.

In the Presbyterian *Directory for the Public Worship of God*, the section on the *Administration of the Sacraments* gives this counsel to a minister when he baptises a child. He is to say:

The promise is made to believers and their seed; and that the seed and posterity of the faithful, born within the church, have, by their birth, interest in the covenant, and right to the seal of it, and to the outward privileges of the church, under the gospel, no less than the children of Abraham in the time of the Old Testament... that children by baptism, are solemnly received into the bosom of the visible church, distinguished from the world, and them that are without, and united with believers... That they are Christians, and federally holy before baptism, and therefore are they baptised.[18]

This is a shocking statement to be found in a Reformed document. As I have indicated, I shall have something more to say about the use of the words 'sacrament' and 'visible church', but for now I call your attention to what is said about children who 'have by their birth' come into all these benefits, including 'that they are Christians'. Christians by their birth? Does the principle of John 1:11-13 not run totally contrary to the *Directory*? How can any non-Papist speak as the *Directory* advises? A child of a Christian is a Christian by means of his birth? Is this what infant baptism comes to?

The arguments for infant baptism based upon the Abrahamic covenant are mistaken, and worse. And the consequences are alarming. But certain questions remain. What of the Abrahamic covenant and the Christian? Is there no connection whatsoever between the two? And

---

[18] Westminster pp382-383.

where does the new covenant (Heb. 8:13) fit into this discussion? We now look into these matters.

2. The double aspect of the Abrahamic covenant

Romans 9:6-8 must be considered at this point. It reads:

But it is not as though the word of God has taken no effect. For they are not all Israel who are of Israel, nor are they all children because they are the seed of Abraham; but: 'In Isaac your seed shall be called'. That is, those who are the children of the flesh, these are not the children of God; but the children of the promise are counted as the seed.

Infant baptisers fail to act on the practical implications of this passage. It is worse; they act against them. The passage teaches that there was a two-fold aspect to the covenant which God made with Abraham; there was a two-fold line of descent. One, physical; the other, spiritual. Abraham's physical descendants were physical Israelites. Isaac was, Esau was, Jacob was, and so on. But within and among the physical descendants there was another line of descent – those who were Abraham's spiritual children. Abraham's physical descendants, or 'the children of the flesh' (Rom. 9:8), were physical Israelites; Abraham's spiritual descendants, or 'the children of the promise' (Rom. 9:8), were spiritual Israelites. All Abraham's descendants were the seed of Abraham, but not all of them were his children, in the terms of the covenant (Rom. 9:7). Jacob was. Esau was not (Rom. 9:10-13).

This is the very point Paul develops in Romans 9:6-8. God declared his mind to Abraham. He gave him his word, he instituted his covenant with him. When Paul wrote to the Romans, this covenant, this word from God, had not failed or collapsed (Rom. 9:6), though it might appear that it had, since not every Israelite was saved. The truth is, God's covenant had not failed, and for this reason – Abraham's descendants were of two sorts, physical and spiritual. 'For they are not all Israel who are of Israel' (Rom. 9:6); that is, just because they were physically descended from Abraham, it did not mean that they were so spiritually. God's word had not failed. All the spiritual Israelites had received the fulfilment of the spiritual promise of the covenant. That is what Paul taught in Romans 9:6. The principle applies today. In particular, all believers – Jew and Gentile – are the spiritual Israelites, and all of them inherit the spiritual promise to Abraham. In addition, the spiritual descendants of Abraham are not only the children of Abraham, they are much more; they are even 'the children of God' (Rom. 9:8). In other words, the spiritual descendants of Abraham are, in New Testament terms, believers. See Galatians 3:7,9,26-29. The physical descendants of Abraham are most decidedly not the children of God simply because they are the physical descendants of Abraham (Rom. 9:8). This double aspect to the Abrahamic covenant is brought out very clearly in various other passages – Luke 3:8; John 1:47; 8:30-32,37-39; Romans 2:28-29; Galatians 4:22-29; 6:16, for instance. If only infant baptisers would act upon this double aspect of the covenant, the discussion would be at an end.

What is more, it is the new covenant which is in force in the New Testament (Heb. 8:13), and it is precisely this covenant which is the continuation of the spiritual aspect of the covenant with Abraham. Moreover, it is through the new covenant that believers during the gospel age are linked to Abraham and all the Old Testament saints in the line of faith and grace. Reformed infant-baptisers go astray at this point. They link believers to the physical aspects of the covenant with Abraham. This is a mistake of immense proportions. For one thing, they do not give sufficient weight to the *newness* of the new covenant. I shall have more to say on this.

The contrast between the two aspects of the Abrahamic covenant is highlighted by the following: How does a man become a physical Israelite? By being born into an Israelite family and then being circumcised. How does a man become a spiritual Israelite? Certainly not in that way. 'For he is not a Jew who is one outwardly, nor is that circumcision which is outward in the flesh; but he is a Jew who is one inwardly, and circumcision is that of the heart, in the spirit, and not in the letter' (Rom. 2:28-29). In other words, a man becomes a true spiritual Jew (that is, a believer) by being spiritually circumcised; that is by being regenerated. Regeneration is the way a man becomes a spiritual Israelite (that is, a child of the promise), a child of God and a child of Abraham. This regeneration shows itself in faith (and repentance), so that Abraham is 'the father of all those who believe, though they are uncircumcised... who also walk in the steps of the faith which our father Abraham had while still uncircumcised' (Rom. 4:11-12). This regeneration, which leads to faith, itself comes about as God works out his purpose and promise according to his electing grace.

Paul developed this argument more fully in the verses which follow on from Romans 9:6-8. He spoke of 'the word of promise... the purpose of God according to election' (Rom. 9:9-11), and he continued in the same vein to the end of chapter 11, saying: 'Israel has not obtained what it seeks; but the elect have obtained it, and the rest were hardened. Just as it is written' (Rom. 11:7-8). Simply because a man is a physical Israelite – that is, because he is in the Abrahamic covenant in its physical aspect – it does not mean he is elect and hence will be regenerated and come to faith. By no means. True spiritual Israelites are those who are believers, and only they; they are believers through their regeneration; and they are regenerated because of the election of God. Timothy's mother is a classic case – she was a 'Jewish woman who believed' (Acts 16:1). She was a daughter of Abraham in a physical sense by her natural birth; she was his spiritual daughter by election and regeneration.[19] The same goes for all the elect, Jew or Gentile. God has determined to save them, he has decreed it, he has promised it, and they all come to faith. Thus it is that his word has not failed (Rom. 9:6). Certainly not! For all the elect (whether Jew or Gentile) will be regenerated, they will all come to faith. The covenant of God stands firm.[20] 'Therefore it is of faith that it might be according to grace, so that the promise might be sure to all the seed, not only to those who are of the law, but also to those who are of the faith of Abraham, who is the father of us all' (Rom. 4:16); that is, the father of us – the believing elect – all – whether Jew or Gentile. Abraham was 'fully convinced that what [God] had promised he was also able to perform' (Rom. 4:21). God's predestination is so powerful, he can even raise up his elect from stones (Luke 3:8).

To summarise all this. There is a descent from Abraham according to the flesh, and there is a descent according to the Spirit. The children of the flesh are the natural children of Abraham, whereas the children of the promise are the spiritual children – they are the children of God,

---

[19] Note the distinction between a Jew and a disciple in the words of Christ: 'As I said to the Jews... so now I say to you' (John 13:33).

[20] 'All Israel will be saved... for the gifts and calling of God are irrevocable' (Rom. 11:25-29). Whether 'all Israel' means 'all elect Jews' or 'all the elect, the new Israel', does not affect the point. All the elect will be saved; God's covenant is absolute.

and they only. The physical promises of the covenant applied to the physical children,[21] but the spiritual promises apply only to the spiritual children.

Reader, you might well ask: What bearing does all this have on the question of infant baptism? As I said earlier, infant baptisers do not act according to the principles of Romans 9:6-8. They take the *physical* promises (or some of them – they are selective!) which were made to Abraham in Genesis 17, and apply them to *spiritual* men – to believers. They confuse the two strands in the line of descent. This is just downright foolishness, and worse. The physical promises and conditions of the covenant (circumcision, the promised land, and so on) applied to the physical descendants of Abraham, and only to them. On the other hand, the spiritual promises apply only to the spiritual children of Abraham, to the elect who prove their election by their saving faith. These two strands must not be mixed up; they must not, under any circumstances, be confused. But this is exactly what infant baptisers do. They try to apply the physical covenant to believers. In particular, they take the terms, conditions and promises involved in physical circumcision, and then apply them to the physical children of believers in baptism. It is an appalling mistake, and one with dire consequences.

But it is not only infant baptisers who mix up the two strands in the Abrahamic covenant. Far from it. In fact they repeat the error of many Jews themselves; as for example the Jews in Luke 3:8. The Jews in question, who had been circumcised, but were not spiritually minded, made exactly the same mistake as can be made by infant baptisers today. Those physical Israelites forgot – or did not understand, or chose to neglect – the distinction between the physical and the spiritual descendants of Abraham. They confused the double aspect of the Abrahamic covenant. And it had disastrous results. They thought that just because they were the children of Abraham they must be the children of God. 'We have Abraham as our father', they protested, they bragged. 'We are Abraham's descendants... Abraham is our father... We have one Father – God... Our father [is] Abraham' (John 8:33,39,41,53). John the Baptist disabused them of this mistaken

---

[21] I will not plunge into an examination of prophecy to look at the future (if any) of physical Israel and the land *etc*. It is not relevant to the work in hand.

notion in no uncertain terms (Luke 3:8); as did Christ (John 8:37-47,53-55). They were most definitely not the children of God, even though they were Abraham's physical children. Yes, they had descended from Abraham and had been circumcised, but that did not make them the true sons of Abraham, the children of God.

William Hendriksen justly commented on Luke 3:8:

The reason why these people were headed for damnation was that for their eternal security they were relying on their descent from Abraham... John the Baptist was fully aware of the fact that physical descent from Abraham did not guarantee being a true son of Abraham.[22]

The application of this to the present discussion of infant baptism lies in this: Those who have been brought up under the infant baptism system stand exposed to precisely the same dangerous assumption as the Jews of Luke 3:8, and over exactly the same issue. What about those who were baptised as infants, but are never regenerated? If they have been baptised as infants on the basis of the covenant, but they are not regenerate, they can plead – falsely like the Jews – that since their father is in the covenant, and they were dealt with as infants in accordance with the covenant, then it follows they are in the covenant themselves. I do not say that all who were baptised as infants, but who are never regenerated, do argue this way. I say it is a possibility. And a completely understandable possibility from their point of view. It is possible that they might claim that they are in the covenant, when they are not. They might claim they are Christians, when they are nothing of the sort – just like the physical Jews tried to claim they were spiritual Jews, when they were not. To use Hendriksen's words – they can make the mistake of 'relying on their descent' from a man who is in the covenant. If so, they are 'headed for damnation'.

I go further. I say that if those who were baptised as infants actually believe what they have been told times without number by their teachers, it is likely they will argue this way, even if they are not regenerated. Why? Those who have been baptised as infants can very easily make the mistaken claim that they are Christians, when they are not, because – after all – from their earliest days they have been assured by the teaching of many – if not all – of their elders, their catechisms and the Confessions under which they have been reared,

---

[22] Hendriksen: *Luke* p205.

that they are Christians. Since they have been treated and regarded as Christians from childhood, it cannot be wondered-at if they actually do believe their teachers and parents, and think they are saved! They have been 'received as children of God', they have been told that they are 'in some sense the children of God, accounted members of Christ from the womb, ingrafted into the church, and have put on Christ'. They have been 'taught from the first to recognise themselves as children of God'. They have been told they are in the covenant.

What if they actually do believe such horrific and erroneous statements? It would not be at all surprising if they did. What if they act upon them?[23] What if they die relying upon them? What will the minister who baptised an infant – an infant who never was regenerated – say to the unregenerate but professing Christian on the day of judgement? What will the minister say to him just before he is cast into hell? It will not do, it will be no comfort on that awful day – it will be no excuse – to try to explain at that frightful moment that the Confession said that not 'all who are baptised are undoubtedly regenerated'. It will be cold comfort to say that the unregenerate professor ought to have listened more carefully to the qualifying statements of the theologians who warned him that not all baptised children would definitely become believers. An apt reply suggests itself – which end of the dog was I supposed to believe – his wagging tail or his slavering jaws?[24] You told me I was a Christian! I believed it. I was mistaken. You were mistaken. Now what...?

Reader, please do not run away with the idea that I pretend that all those baptised as believers are truly regenerate. In the day of judgement, we shall have many surprises – and some shocks – no doubt. And all those responsible for baptising believers will have to answer for what they have done. If they have been lax or corrupt, the

---

[23] I have not moved much in infant-baptist circles, but when preaching in one of their strongholds, I had a new experience. I met an unbeliever (aged about 60) who thus far had been impervious to the gospel, precisely on this basis: 'My father was in the covenant!' was his reply to all offers of mercy and the direst of warnings. Indeed, so I was told, he liked nothing better than a strong sermon on judgement! His believing son, rightly, was seriously concerned about it. This experience, as I say, was new to me. I ask those who do move among infant-baptisers: 'Is it an isolated case?'

[24] See end note on p109 for excursus: 'Reformed double-speak'.

burden of their responsibility will be great. But if they have sincerely and honourably applied the tests of Scripture to those they baptised, and if they have been honest in saying that they have no right or power to guarantee that the candidate is truly believing – not being able to read men's hearts – no more can be asked of them.

My point about infant baptisers is that the infant was told two directly contradictory things. Which was he supposed to believe? True, he was warned that not all baptised infants are regenerated. But nevertheless he was also treated and addressed as a Christian. Above all, he was *assured* that he is regenerate, when he was not. For my own part, if I may be forgiven for the introduction of another personal note, I never assure anyone whom I baptise that he is a believer. I say that I baptise on the best evidence I have before me, and on the basis of the most searching tests I can apply. But only God knows the truth. I sincerely aim to act now so that no one on the day of judgement will be able to say that I told him he was a Christian.[25] This is the point I

---

[25] Speaking for myself, Lloyd-Jones posed a man of straw: 'There are people who seem to think that they can solve this problem very simply. They say infant baptism must be wrong because baptism is the seal and sign of regeneration, and we do not as yet know whether a child will be regenerate or not. But that is a very dangerous argument, surely, because are you certain that the adult is regenerate? Someone may certainly say that he believes in the Lord Jesus Christ, but does that prove that he is regenerate? If you say that you are sure he is, because he has said that he believes, then what do you say later on when he denies the faith entirely, as many have done? No, we cannot be certain that anybody is regenerate. It is not for us to decide who is born again and who is not... Similarly, people often say something like this: "Look at the thousands of children who were baptised when they were infants. They were accepted into the Christian Church but subsequently they lapsed, proving that they were never really Christians at all". The answer again, of course, is exactly the same' (Lloyd-Jones: *The Church* pp42-43).
With respect, no, it is not! There are several mistakes here. As I will explain, baptism is not a seal of anything; it is a sign. As to the practice of baptising believers, I apologise once again for the personal note, but since I do not know what everyone else does, I can only speak for myself. I do not baptise anybody assuring him he is definitely regenerate. If he later proves apostate, I admit, as it turns out, I had made a mistake – even though I did my best at the time to find out if he was truly converted – but he can never say I deceived him by giving him a false assurance. Above all, there is a vast difference between baptising an adult who voluntarily confesses Christ – and I look for

have tried to raise here. I say, with respect and a sense of horror and sadness, that some – if not many – infant baptisers will have to face those whom they assured that they were regenerate, when they were not.

No wonder the term 'lapsed Christians' has to be invented to cope with this body of so-called 'unregenerate Christians'. What is an unregenerate Christian? Lapsed? They never were Christians in the first place! But they have been repeatedly assured throughout their childhood that they are. They have been received and regarded as such. And all the time they were anything but. This dreadful – literally, full of dread – possibility is reason enough to abandon the practice of infant baptism. To build its practice on the covenant is fallacious. It arises out of a confusion of the two strands of the Abrahamic covenant.

3. Confusion of the Abrahamic, Mosaic and new covenants

Some infant baptisers muddle the various covenants in Scripture, virtually boiling them down into one.[26] For instance, they believe that the Abrahamic and Mosaic covenants are 'essentially the same', to use Berkhof's words. Then they say that these two covenants are the same as the new covenant. Berkhof stated that the covenant 'is essentially the same in all dispensations'. In particular, he alleged that 'the covenant of Sinai was *essentially* the same as that established with Abraham... Little need be said respecting the New Testament dispensation of the covenant', he went on. 'The covenant of grace, as it is revealed in the New Testament, is essentially the same as that which governed the relation of Old Testament believers to God', he maintained.[27]

---

more than a mere verbal testimony – and taking a baby and telling everybody that it is being baptised because it is regenerate, or because we presume it is regenerate, or will be regenerate, and that it is in the covenant, that it is holy, and so on. If tragic disappointment comes after baptism – and, sadly, it is not unknown – someone is responsible. In the case of believer's baptism, if the baptiser has dealt faithfully with the person being baptised, the responsibility falls squarely on the professing believer. Who carries the can for the baby who is baptised but proves to be finally unregenerate? The baby, the parent, the minister, the theologian, or...?

[26] See my forthcoming book on the law for more on this.

[27] Berkhof pp279,297,299.

This last statement of Berkhof's is perfectly correct as it stands – the Old Testament saints, along with the New Testament saints, are in the new covenant, which is the spiritual aspect of the Abrahamic covenant. However, that is not all that Berkhof meant, as can be readily seen. He said that the Abrahamic covenant, the Mosaic covenant and the new covenant are all essentially the same covenant.

Yet this is manifestly not true, and his statement confuses the issue terribly. Berkhof failed to distinguish the twofold aspect of the Abrahamic covenant at this point. If only infant baptisers would agree that the essential unity and continuance of the covenant between the two Testaments consists of that oneness between the new covenant and the spiritual aspect of the Abrahamic covenant, the debate would be over. Berkhof certainly kept to his assertion that he thought little need be said about the new covenant, since his subsequent explanation of the glorious changes under that covenant was woefully inadequate. What a mistake, seeing that these glorious changes found in the new covenant lie at the very heart of the gospel!

It is clear that other infant baptisers – besides Berkhof – also fail to distinguish between the covenants when they claim that the Abrahamic covenant, the Mosaic covenant and the new covenant are virtually one and the same. Engelsma, for instance, wrote of *the* covenant. He referred to Genesis 17:7, Jeremiah 31:31-34, Ezekiel 16:20-21 and Exodus 4:22 applying all the references to *the* covenant, as he called it.[28] Reader, this is clearly wrong. How can references to the Abrahamic covenant, the Mosaic covenant and the new covenant all apply to *the* covenant? After all, the Jeremiah passage could not be plainer. The new covenant is the *new* covenant, and it is expressly said to be 'not according to' the Mosaic covenant. It must be different. It cannot be the same covenant, can it?

Nevertheless, Calvin certainly thought the various covenants were one covenant. He went even further when he attacked 'some madmen of the sect of the Anabaptists', as he called them, for daring to express their views on the differences between the old and new covenants. He declared that 'the covenant made with all the fathers in so far from differing from ours in reality and substance, that it is altogether one

---

[28] Engelsma pp4-5.

and the same'. To say anything to the contrary was, according to Calvin, a 'pestilential error'.[29]

But risking Calvin's strictures, are we not told very plainly and bluntly that the old covenant has been abolished and the new has come? (See Rom. 6:14-15; 7:1-6; 8:2-11; 2 Cor. 3:7-11; Heb. 7:11-19; 8:6-13; 9:15; 10:16-20). We know that the Mosaic covenant has been abolished (2 Cor. 3:7-11).[30] What is more, as the old covenant was abolished and the new covenant came in, a comparison, even a stark contrast, was drawn between the two. Far from being 'altogether one and the same' covenant, as Calvin put it, they are very, very different. How different can be easily seen in Paul's words. He said: 'God... made us... ministers of the new covenant, not of the letter but of the Spirit; for the letter kills, but the Spirit gives life. But if the ministry of death, written and engraved on stones, was glorious... which glory was passing away, how will the ministry of the Spirit not be more glorious? For if the ministry of condemnation had glory, the ministry of righteousness exceeds much more in glory. For even what was made glorious had no glory in this respect, because of the glory that excels. For if what is passing away was glorious, what remains is much more glorious' (2 Cor. 3:5-11).

This is a vital point. The Bible contrasts the two covenants, the old and the new, and contrasts them very sharply indeed. In the following quotations, please observe the use of the words *but*, *yet* and *on the other hand*. They are words of contrast. Two covenants are clearly contrasted in the following passages:

For the law was given through Moses, but grace and truth came through Jesus Christ (John 1:17).
You are not under law but under grace (Rom. 6:14).
For Christ is the end of the law for righteousness to everyone who believes. For Moses writes about the righteousness which is of the law, 'The man who does those things shall live by them'. But the righteousness of faith speaks in this way... if you confess with your mouth the Lord

---

[29] Calvin: *Institutes* Vol.1 pp369-370. Calvin, as I have explained, allowed his judgement to be badly warped by his inordinate zeal against the Anabaptists. We will meet this again.
[30] I link the physical aspect of the Abrahamic covenant with the Mosaic covenant, and take the two to be the old covenant. See John 7:22.

Jesus and believe in your heart that God has raised him from the dead, you will be saved (Rom. 10:4-9).

For as many as are of the works of the law are under the curse; for it is written, 'Cursed is everyone who does not continue in all things which are written in the book of the law, to do them'. But that no one is justified by the law in the sight of God is evident, for 'The just shall live by faith'. Yet the law is not of faith, but 'The man who does them shall live by them'. Christ has redeemed us from the curse of the law, having become a curse for us... that the blessing of Abraham might come upon the Gentiles in Christ Jesus, that we might receive the promise of the Spirit through faith (Gal. 3:10-14).

For these are the two covenants: the one from Mount Sinai which gives birth to bondage, which is Hagar – for this Hagar is Mount Sinai in Arabia, and corresponds to Jerusalem which now is, and is in bondage with her children – but the Jerusalem above is free (Gal. 4:24-26).

For on the one hand there is an annulling of the former commandment because of its weakness and unprofitableness, for the law made nothing perfect; on the other hand, there is a bringing in of a better hope, through which we draw near to God (Heb. 7:18-19).

But now he has obtained a more excellent ministry, inasmuch as he is also the mediator of a better covenant, which was established on better promises. For if the first covenant had been faultless, then no place would have been sought for a second (Heb. 8:6-7).

Are these quotations not sufficient to prove that the old and new covenants are very different? Do they not show that the new is far superior to the old? How can anyone maintain that they are 'essentially the same', or 'altogether the same', as infant baptisers do? Rather, we must stand with Paul in Romans 8:2-3: 'For the law of the Spirit of life in Christ Jesus has made me free from the law of sin and death. For what the law could not do in that it was weak through the flesh, God did by sending his own Son in the likeness of sinful flesh...'. There it is – two laws, two systems, two economies, two covenants. The old, the law of sin and death; the new, the law of the Spirit of life in Christ Jesus. The contrast, I say again, could not be greater. The old was a covenant of death, the new is a covenant of life. There is no greater contrast than between death and life! No wonder Hebrews 8:13 declares: 'In that he says: "A new covenant", he has made the first obsolete'. Christ has taken 'away the first that he may establish the second' (Heb. 10:9).

Think of the highly significant words of Christ in Mark 2:18-22. Infant baptisers like Calvin, Matthew Henry and Hendriksen prove woefully inadequate in their comments on the passage, a passage in which Christ draws a very clear contrast between the old and the new covenants. He illustrates this in two ways: It is futile both to sew a piece of new cloth onto an old garment, and to put new wine in old wineskins. The lesson? The two covenants are very different; they cannot be cobbled together.

The same point is made in Hebrews 2:1-4, which reads:

Therefore we must give the more earnest heed to the things we have heard, lest we drift away. For if the word spoken through angels proved steadfast, and every transgression and disobedience received a just reward, how shall we escape if we neglect so great a salvation, which at the first began to be spoken by the Lord, and was confirmed to us by those who heard him...?

The contrast is drawn, as before, between two covenants, and once again the contrast is stark. One covenant is 'the word spoken through angels', which is the law (Acts 7:53; Gal. 3:19); the other covenant is 'the things which we have heard... so great a salvation', which is the gospel. In other words, a clear contrast is marked out between the law and the gospel, between the old and the new covenants. The old covenant was concerned with 'transgression and disobedience', in that every sin 'received a just reward', retribution or penalty; the new covenant is also concerned with sin, but instead of bringing punishment it brings salvation. As before, the contrast could not be more sharply made. The new covenant, of course, is far superior to the old, and that is why 'we must give the more earnest heed to the things we have heard'. These things are so much better than what was heard under the Mosaic covenant.

John Brown commented on the passage, justly saying that 'there is a beautiful contrast between the... "letter that killeth", the ministration of condemnation and death – and the salvation, the revelation of mercy, the ministration of justification and life'. Yes, it is 'a beautiful contrast'.[31] As William Plumer declared: 'It is right in us to follow the Scriptures and distinguish between the Mosaic and the Christian dispensations. Many and great errors proceed from a neglect to do

---

[31] Brown: *Hebrews* p75.

this'.[32] They certainly do. Infant baptism is one. That is why I have written this book!

The same contrast is underlined in Hebrews 9. The old covenant was done away with at 'the time of reformation' (Heb. 9:10); that is, by the work of Christ. As far as benefits go, the new covenant is on a totally different plane to the old. The first covenant was all outward, it accomplished no salvation and it was done away with. But when we come to the new... What a difference! What a change! The old, 'the blood of bulls and goats', is sharply contrasted with the new, 'the blood of Christ'. What conclusion ought the inspired penman be expected to draw after such a contrast as that? 'How much more shall the blood of Christ... purge your conscience from dead works to serve the living God? And for this reason he is the mediator of the new covenant'. As he said, it was necessary that Christ should redeem from 'the transgressions under the first covenant' because the first covenant was useless to save. And that is the very thing which Christ did (Heb. 9:11-15)! How is it possible for infant baptisers to say these covenants are one and the same?

Hebrews 10:1 keeps up the argument. Omitting the 'and', which is not in the original, the verse reads: 'For the law, having a shadow of the good things to come, not the very image of the things, can never...'. Once again, we have a contrast. Indeed, as Plumer observed: 'In this verse shadow and image are directly opposed to each other'.[33] Colossians 2:17 supports this claim. And the contrast, the opposition, is between the law and the gospel as most commentators agree. John Owen put it this way: 'There is a great difference between the shadow of good things to come, and the good things themselves actually exhibited and granted unto the church. This is the fundamental difference between the two Testaments, the law and the gospel, from whence all others do arise, and into which they are resolved'.[34]

The rest of Hebrews 10 goes on to draw the same contrast between the two covenants, and comes to the same conclusion as earlier

---

[32] Plumer p85.
[33] Plumer p386. The concept of 'shadow' is very important; I will have more to say on it in my forthcoming book on the law. Infant baptisers cling too much to the shadow; the reality has come! See, also, my comments (above and below) on the part played by circumcision in the infant baptiser's argument.
[34] Owen: *Hebrews* Vol.3 Part 1 p429.

passages, but from the opposite point of view; namely, from the point of view of punishment, not mercy. The two covenants both carried punishments, but since the new covenant is so superior to the old, it is only to be expected that the punishments under the new covenant are far more serious than those under the old. And they certainly are. 'Anyone who has rejected Moses' law dies without mercy... Of how much worse punishment, do you suppose, will he be thought worthy who has trampled the Son of God underfoot, counted the blood of the covenant by which he was sanctified a common thing, and insulted the Spirit of grace?' (Heb. 10:28-29). Note the 'of how much worse punishment' under the new covenant. How can the covenants be the same? Their punishments are as different as their benefits.

Hebrews 12:18-29 stresses exactly the same distinction between the covenants. The old covenant was physical; the new is spiritual. The old was full of burning and blackness, darkness and tempest; the new is full of joy and happiness. The old said: 'Stay away, keep off'. The new cries: 'Come and welcome'. The old brought terror, fear and trembling – even for Moses! The new brought peace and salvation. It is impossible that these covenants should be the same covenant. How can anyone say that they are? I prefer the verdict of Isaac Watts:

Curs'd be the man, for ever curs'd,
That does one wilful sin commit;
Death and damnation for the first,
Without relief, and infinite.

Thus Sinai roars, and round the earth
Thunder, and fire, and vengeance flings;
But Jesus, thy dear gasping breath
And Calvary, say gentler things:

'Pardon and grace, and boundless love,
Streaming along a Saviour's blood;
And life, and joy, and crowns above,
Obtained by a dear bleeding God'.

Hark! How he prays (the charming sound
Dwells on his dying lips), 'Forgive!'
And every groan and gaping wound
Cries, 'Father, let the rebels live!'

Go, ye that rest upon the law,
And toil and seek salvation there,
Look to the flame that Moses saw,
And shrink, and tremble, and despair.

But I'll retire beneath the cross;
Saviour, at thy dear feet I'll lie!
And the keen sword that justice draws,
Flaming and red, shall pass me by.[35]

I have spent some time in showing the contrast between the law and the gospel, between the old covenant and the new, because some infant baptisers are very definite in their view that all the covenants – the Abrahamic, the Mosaic and the new – are one and the same. This is manifestly not true.

Unfortunately, as Plumer said, 'many and great errors' come from the misunderstanding – principally as far as the present purpose is concerned, the error of infant baptism. I am well aware of the ways in which infant baptisers explain (or, rather, explain away) the Hebrews passages, for instance. But the contrast is not drawn in Scripture between *certain aspects* of the old covenant and the new. The contrast is *root and branch*. The two covenants themselves are contrasted, the two covenants in their entirety, not only some aspects of the covenants.[36]

What is more, a very serious pastoral question arises at this juncture. What if those who are taught that the two covenants are essentially the same, actually believe it? Does it matter? It certainly does. There is a very real danger that those who think the two covenants are the same might try to find salvation by the old covenant. If so, it would be disastrous. Watts had it right. The gospel is at stake in all this. Personal eternal issues are at stake.

The New Testament is clear. The two covenants are not the same. The Mosaic covenant is abolished in Christ, but the spiritual aspect of

---

[35] *Gospel Hymns* number 394.
[36] The Mosaic covenant was a (I did not say 'the') covenant of works. Christ was born under it, and earned the salvation of his people by keeping its commands and suffering its curse (Gal. 4:4-5). Do covenant theologians who think the covenants are all one and the same, think Christ was born, lived, was cursed and died under what they call the covenant of grace?

the Abrahamic covenant lives on, and lives on with vigour – it is the new covenant.

To that covenant, we must now turn.

4. The new covenant

The terms and promises of the new covenant are to be read in Jeremiah 31:31-34; Hebrews 8:8-12; 10:16-17. They are:

Behold, the days are coming, says the LORD, when I will make a new covenant with the house of Israel and with the house of Judah – not according to the covenant that I made with their fathers in the day that I took them by the hand to bring them out of the land of Egypt, my covenant which they broke, though I was a husband to them, says the LORD. But this is the covenant that I will make with the house of Israel after those days, says the LORD: I will put my law in their minds, and write it on their hearts; and I will be their God, and they shall be my people. No more shall every man teach his neighbour, and every man his brother, saying, 'Know the LORD', for they all shall know me, from the least of them to the greatest of them, says the LORD. For I will forgive their iniquity, and their sin I will remember no more (Jer. 31:31-34).[37]

As we have seen, the covenant has changed dramatically from the old to the new. The Mosaic covenant has been abolished, but the spiritual aspect of the Abrahamic covenant lives on in the new. But, reader, I must remind you once more, Reformed infant-baptisers staunchly disagree. They think the covenants are 'essentially the same'. And consequently they ignore or play down the dramatic changes which have come with the changes in the covenant. But these changes are vital, and cannot be stressed too much. They must not be suppressed or passed over or swamped in a deluge of metaphysics. What are the changes? What do these verses from Jeremiah and Hebrews teach?

In the new covenant, God makes promises to his people. Note, to his people. But, unlike the old, not to his people *and their children*. There is no reference whatsoever to children. The silence about children in the new covenant is deafening, when compared to the old covenant, the physical aspect of the Abrahamic, and the Mosaic. Again, the new covenant is internal; not external, as was the old. In the

---

[37] See end note on p110 for excursus: 'Reformed misunderstandings about the new covenant'.

new covenant, the work is done in the mind and heart; in the old, it was written on tablets of stone, and was in the flesh. Further, in the new covenant, all who are in the covenant receive all its benefits; God says that they all shall know him, from the least to the greatest, and all the sins of all of them shall be forgiven. Not one of them is left out, they all obtain the full benefits of the covenant. There is no exception. But, as has already been shown, in the old covenant many received only the physical benefits, they never did receive the spiritual promises. While they were all of Israel, they were not all true Israelites (Rom. 9:6-8). Jacob was, Esau was not (Rom. 9:10-13). But in the new covenant, all who are in the covenant receive all the benefits of it. This is another staggering contrast to the old.

Lest my argument should be dismissed as Antinomianism, let me hasten to say that under the new covenant, the terms are more strict, more searching, far more penetrating than under the old. 'For sin shall not have dominion over you, for you are not under law but under grace. What then? Shall we sin because we are not under law but under grace? Certainly not! Do you not know...?... Having been set free from sin, you became slaves of righteousness' (Rom. 6:14-18). (See the entire passage, Rom. 5:20 – 8:17). Believers have to 'give the more earnest heed' to the new covenant (Heb. 2:1-4), when compared to the old. The law of God is now written, not on tablets of stone but on the minds and hearts of believers (2 Cor. 3:3; Heb. 8:10). They delight in the law of God, they love it (Ps. 119:77,97) because God has given them a new mind, a new heart, a new will, putting his Spirit within them (Ezek. 36:25-27; 2 Cor. 3:3; 5:17). Thus the believer will keep the law of God – God's Spirit will cause him to do so. 'I will put my Spirit within you and cause you to walk in my statutes, and you will keep my judgements and do them' (Ezek. 36:27). Only the regenerate can keep the commandments of God, but they all will keep them. If men do not, however much they profess they know God, they are liars (1 John 2:3-5).

The difference between the old and the new covenant is not only in the fact that the law is now written on the heart, and not on tablets of stone. A (the?) principal part of the difference in the two covenants lies in this: That law which is written on the heart in the new covenant is not the law of Moses, but the law of Christ (1 Cor. 9:21; Gal. 6:2; see John 13 – 16). And this makes the conditions and terms of obedience far more incisive under the new covenant than under the old.[38] Jesus declared that he had not come to destroy the law; indeed he affirmed that not 'one jot or one tittle' would pass from it. Furthermore, he said that whoever breaks 'one of the least of these commandments, and teaches men so, shall be called least in the kingdom of heaven' (Matt. 5:17-19). That is not all. 'Unless your righteousness exceeds the righteousness of the scribes and Pharisees, you will by no means enter the kingdom of heaven' (Matt. 5:20). Christ took several of the ten commandments, and on each occasion he tightened the screw, saying: 'You have heard that it was said... but I say to you' (Matt. 5:21-22,27-28,31-32,33-34,38-39,43-44). Under the new covenant the laws are far more strict than the old; they deal with the heart, the mind and the motive for obedience, not only a mere outward conformity to a written code. Christ concluded his discourse by stating bluntly: 'Not everyone who says to me, "Lord, Lord," shall enter the kingdom of heaven, but he who does the will of my Father in heaven' (Matt. 7:21). Holiness is essential (Heb. 12:14). See also 1 John 3:7,10,22,24; 5:2-3; 2 John 6.

* * *

Let me sum up this look at the way the practice of infant baptism is based upon the Abrahamic covenant: I have examined this under four headings, and I have tried to show that the physical aspects of the covenant with Abraham do not apply to believers. It is the new covenant – the spiritual aspect of the Abrahamic covenant – which applies to them. Therefore it follows that the children of believers are not included with their parents in the covenant on the grounds that their parents are believers and are in the covenant. The children can only be said to be in the covenant after they have come to faith – not because they are the children of believers. Hence there is no justification for the baptism of infants on the basis that their parents are believers. Until the children demonstrate that they themselves have been brought to saving faith, it is impossible to say that they are in the covenant. It is wrong to baptise them on the assumption that they are – or will be.

---

[38] This is a large subject, upon which, as I explained at the start, my views have clarified since writing *Battle*. Given that I intend to publish on the matter, I will say no more about it now. It has no effect on this book.

End notes to Argument 2: The Abrahamic Covenant

Reformed double-speak

Reader, I remind you of an earlier note: 'Just as these qualifications are commonplace among the Reformers, so also the generality of their baptismal theology conveys a decisively realist message: baptism is God's normal channel for imparting his gifts... to his children' (Wright: *What...?* p99). Take Calvin. Here is the *carte-blanche*: 'Christ by baptism has made us partakers of his death, ingrafting us into it'. Now for the get-out: 'Those who receive baptism with true faith, truly feel the efficacy of Christ's death... and the efficacy of his resurrection in the quickening of the Spirit'. Again, the categorical: 'We are to receive [baptism] as from the hand of its author, being firmly persuaded that it is [Christ] himself who speaks to us by means of the sign; that it is himself who washes and purifies us, and effaces the remembrance of our faults; that it is himself who makes us partakers of his death, destroys the kingdom of Satan, subdues the power of unlawful desire; indeed, makes us one with himself, that being clothed with him we may be accounted the children of God. These things, I say, we ought to feel as truly and certainly in our mind as we see our body washed, immersed and surrounded with water'. Then the qualifier: 'Not that such graces are included and bound in the sacrament, so as to be conferred by its efficacy'. On the other hand, the assurance: 'Nor does he merely feed our eyes with bare show; he leads us to the actual object, and effectually performs what he figures'. Even so, the escape: 'But from this sacrament... we gain nothing, unless in so far as we receive [it] in faith' (Calvin: *Institutes* Vol.2 pp515,520-521). Reader, leaving the question of how a baby can receive all this since it cannot believe, I just cannot keep up with all this double-speak. Can you? Water baptism does not accomplish any of it, of course, but do those who think Calvin is right always keep his caveats in mind? My question is: The large promise or the small print – which predominates? I suspect most infant baptisers, parents – and then the children as they grow up – prefer to believe the 'good' news, whatever theological cautions come their way. And who can blame them?

And the double-speak occurs not only in Calvin. Take Pratt, who spoke of 'the Reformed assertion that there are both connections and separations between baptism and divine grace'. This, of course, enables the Reformed to play fast and loose with the subject and make large promises at the same time as withdrawing them. He went on: 'The New Testament never... speaks of baptism as mere [*sic*] symbol. The language of "sacrament" was sustained by Reformed churches precisely because the New Testament ties baptism so closely to the bestowal of divine grace'. I pause. 'Closely'? Nothing of the sort! If Scripture ties baptism to the bestowal of grace, it does so infallibly and invariably. No nonsense about 'closely' – it does or it does not. 'There is also an antitype which now saves us – baptism' (1 Pet. 3:21). Take: 'This is my body' (Matt. 26:26). Is it – in the sacramentalist's terms? If it is, it is – not closely but absolutely. To let Pratt continue. Having made such claims as: 'Spiritual realities occur in conjunction with baptism' (but see the entire passage), he concluded: 'To sum up: Reformed theology holds that baptism is a sacrament and not a mere [*sic*] symbol. At the same time, it distinguishes itself from traditions that too closely associate the rite and divine grace'. Oh? As Nettles pointed out: 'From [Pratt's] discussion [which, as I say, see] we are led to believe that we really do not know what the sacraments mean, what they convey, when they might transport sacramental grace and when they might not. This appears to communicate [give] a nominalistic [that is, in name only, a question of words, the opposite of 'realistic'] view of divine freedom, so that God might sovereignly decide not to keep any promises "intimately associated" with this sacrament. This is tantamount to an admission that nothing truly congruent with the divine character and reconciliation of sinners to God, nothing necessary to that transaction, is present in the sacraments. Why, then, does Pratt want to reserve an aura of gracious power for what is purely a positive [posited? that is, assumed that it will prove true – see *Concise*] institution and may not operate in accordance with its supposed biblical purpose? The indecision and lack of resolution is powerfully demonstrated in his contentions that "baptism and 'grace and salvation' are not utterly inseparable", that "it is possible for a person to be regenerated or saved without baptism", and that "not everyone who is baptised is certainly regenerated". We are forced to ask: "Is there any other aspect of ostensibly saving grace that operates in such an inconsistent manner or that cannot be relied on to accomplish its stated purpose?"' (John H.Armstrong pp60-64,74-75). In other words, Nettles has exposed the double-speak of the Reformed which leads them, even though they think that God might, or might not, convey grace in baptism, to be prepared to state dogmatically that he does – and then add the qualifiers to let them off the hook. See earlier for the same in Calvin's comments on Eph. 5:26-27.

I repeat the point I made in passing. Why is it that so many sacramentalists cannot seem to stand by their convictions? I refer to talk of a 'close tie' between baptism and the bestowal of grace. This kind of language is very frequent but it is quite wrong. Either baptism and the bestowal of saving grace are linked *absolutely*, or they are not linked at all.

Reformed misunderstandings about the new covenant

The promises of the new covenant are not men's promises to the 'visible church'; they are God's promises given by God to all the elect. Furthermore, these promises do not apply only at the end of the age; they are true of all the elect *now* – contrary to Pratt who thought 'the new-covenant community will consist exclusively of truly regenerate people only when Christ returns... The covenant community [in this present age] in reality consists of two communities... baptised believers and baptised unbelievers... In Rom. 2:28-29... Paul distinguished between the visible and invisible people of God in the

111

Old Testament... The distinction between the visible and invisible church expresses the belief that the visible covenant community of the New Testament remains a mixture of regenerate and unregenerate people who are baptised... When Christ returns in glory, the visible church will be one and the same with the invisible church' (John H.Armstrong pp46,68-69).

This is incredible. Take the question of the time. Are we really to understand that when Jeremiah spoke of, and the writer to the Hebrews quoted, 'the days are coming' (Heb. 8:8), that both men were talking about the *second* coming of Christ? that they were not referring to the *first* coming of Christ, his death and resurrection, and Pentecost? The answer is self-evident. The writer to the Hebrews said these things are true 'now': 'But now', he said, 'but now [Christ] has obtained a more excellent ministry, inasmuch as he is also mediator of a better covenant, which was established on better promises' (Heb. 8:6). Now! Not at the end of this age. 'But now' (not forgetting its equivalents) is one of the most important phrases in the New Testament (see Rom. 3:21; 6:22; 7:6, for instance). Owen: '"Now" is a note of time, of the present time... now the gospel is preached... The accomplishment of these things was in "the fullness of times" (Eph. 1:10)... This time is here intended... the ministry of John the Baptist... the coming in the flesh and personal ministry of our Lord Jesus Christ himself... his death... the resurrection... Pentecost... [and] the apostles, under the infallible conduct of the Holy Ghost' (Owen: *Hebrews* Vol.3 Part 3 pp50,110,141-143). Paul explained what he understood by 'the fullness of the time"; it is the *first* coming of Christ (Gal. 4:4). Lloyd-Jones: 'The whole span of time has been divided by the coming of the Lord Jesus Christ into this world. That is the division [of time] which is emphasised in the New Testament. The times in which we live are called "the last times", "the last days"... and they all refer to the time that follows the [first] coming of the Lord Jesus Christ into this world... [1 Cor. 10:11; Heb. 1:1-2]... The climax of the ages happened at the incarnation. Time has been divided once and for ever by that event' (Lloyd-Jones: *Ephesians 1* pp199-200). Gouge: '"Now"... sets out the time present; namely, the time of our pilgrimage, while... we live on earth... By "these days" he means the time of the gospel, from the time that Christ was exhibited in the flesh to his glorious coming to judgement. They are called "the last days"' (Gouge pp126,552,559). So much for the 'time'.

Furthermore, there is not the slightest hint of a suggestion in Heb. 8:6-13 that the new covenant is made up of two communities – believers and unbelievers, elect and non-elect, all of whom are baptised. The suggestion is incredible. It is true, of course, that the Hebrew people comprised two communities – the physical, non-elect, unbelieving in the old covenant; and, as I have explained, the spiritual, elect, believing in both the old and new covenants. Both communities were in the old covenant, both carried its responsibilities, and both partook of all its benefits. The elect and believing were also in the new covenant, and they partook of all the benefits of both the old covenant *and* the new. And the benefits of the latter are infinitely better than those of the former. We are expressly told that the new covenant is better than the old (Heb. 7:22; 8:6; 12:24). Now, coming to our day, on the Reformed argument we have to believe that while all in the old covenant received all its benefits, some in the new covenant do not receive its benefits. This is ridiculous. It would mean that the new covenant is *worse* – not *better* – than the old! *All* in the old covenant received its benefits; *all* in the new receive its benefits. The New Testament emphasis *is* upon two communities, yes – I agree with Pratt on this – but the two communities in question are the world and the church (John 17:9-11,13-16; Gal. 1:4; Col. 1:13; 1 John 4:5-6; 5:19), not two communities within the new covenant. The New Testament never speaks – as Pratt would like – of *three* communities – two in the new covenant (all baptised; some regenerate, some unregenerate) and one outside. Getting back to Jeremiah and Hebrews, Owen: 'In the promise itself, we may consider... whom it is made unto... The new covenant is made with them alone who effectually and eventually are made partakers of the grace of it... Those with whom the old covenant was made were all of them actual partakers of the benefits of it; and if they are not so with whom the new covenant is made, it comes short of the old in efficacy... The excellency of this [new] covenant... is here declared, that it does effectually communicate all the grace and mercy contained in it unto all and everyone with whom it is made; [to] whomsoever it is made withal, his sins are pardoned' (Owen: *Hebrews* Vol.4 Part 1 pp169-170). And, don't forget, Owen had already explained at large that he understood these things to be in place 'now' – not at the end of the age.

True, the writer to the Hebrews issued many warnings to his readers (Heb. 2:2-3; 3:7-19; 4:1-16; 6:4-8; 10:26-31,35-38; 12:25). Pratt claimed that this means 'even members of the new covenant are now threatened with eternal judgement' (John H.Armstrong pp68-69). But, of course, by this, Pratt meant the unregenerate members of the new covenant, adults who had been baptised as infants but failed to show marks of grace, that *they* are the ones threatened with eternal punishment. This will not stand up. In saying this, Pratt effectively destroyed the warnings. But the warnings are real. And they are not issued to the sort of people Pratt claimed. (In fact, such people did not exist in the New Testament – there is no mention of them whatsoever there – which in itself stands in glaring contrast to infant-baptiser literature. Nor do they exist nowadays). If the warnings were issued to those members of the covenant who, baptised as infants, were unbelieving, I find it passing strange that the writer did not, at least, drop a hint he was referring to such, making full use of the Reformed qualifiers. But if it is still thought that he was addressing such, would Pratt apply Heb. 6:9; 10:39 to *them*? The warnings are, of course, given to all *professing* believers – which is not the same as saying they are actual members of the new covenant. This is no splitting of hairs. 'Examine yourselves as to whether you are in the faith' (2 Cor. 13:5) does not mean: 'All you who are in the new covenant, baptised as infants but showing no signs of grace, examine yourselves'. It is something *all professing believers* must do. The insertion of baptised infants into this discussion is precisely that – an insertion, a novelty, a notion foisted on the text – which would only be thought of by those who have a special interest in trying at all costs to discover the idea of the visible church in Scripture, and so try to justify infant baptism. What is more, such an insertion allows – encourages – those to whom the warnings *are* addressed – professing believers – to avoid self-examination, and to do so on the basis of an unscriptural notion.

Argument 3

Infant Baptisers Claim that the Church Is the Same in Both Testaments

This is a third way in which infant baptisers try to support their practice, and it is closely allied to their flawed view of the covenant arising out of their mistake over the continuity/discontinuity of the Testaments.[1] Contending that the church is the same in both Testaments, they consequently argue that what circumcision was in the Old Testament, baptism is in the New. Baptism, they say, has replaced circumcision. That being so, they go on to argue that since infants were circumcised in the Old Testament church, as they put it, infants ought to be baptised in the New Testament church.

John P.Sartelle actually opened his booklet *What Christian Parents Should Know About Infant Baptism* by saying: 'We begin our study with the Old Testament character Abraham'.[2] What a remarkable opening statement in a booklet to deal with baptism – a New Testament ordinance! Would infant baptisers *begin* a study on the Lord's supper with the Passover? Would they *set about* an examination of church discipline by looking at Moses and the man gathering sticks? Do we *embark* on a discussion of the duties of church elders by considering the hierarchical appointment of the seventy judges to help Moses? Is it not a golden rule of biblical interpretation to start with passages which deal most fully – explicitly – with the subject in hand? Surely the practice of a New Testament ordinance began in the New Testament, did it not? This would seem self-evident. Shouldn't, therefore, the New, not the Old Testament, set the parameters for its practice?[3] And shouldn't the study and explanation

---

[1] As I have pointed out, here is the flaw in much of the defence of infant baptism. Having gone wrong here, much else follows.

[2] Sartelle p3.

[3] In the history of infant baptism, things actually got worse; it wasn't even the Old Testament which set the parameters. It was the stubborn problems raised by the process itself which came to dominate its theology: 'By the

of such an ordinance begin – to say the least – in the New Testament? What did Abraham know about baptism? Of course, Sartelle started with Abraham because he thought that Abraham was in the church, and baptism is the equivalent of circumcision. But that was begging the question!

Warfield wrote of 'the continuity of the church of God... in the Scriptures', and of the inclusion of children in the church 'in its pre-Christian form'. Thus, he argued, the Old Testament practice of circumcision is the basis of the New Testament ordinance of baptism. He even went as far as to assert: 'If the continuity of the church through all ages can be made good, the warrant for infant baptism is not to be sought in the New Testament but in the Old Testament'. This is another remarkable statement, being nothing less than an admission of the non-New-Testament basis for the practice of infant baptism. And since its premise – the continuity of the church in all ages – is false, then it follows that there is no warrant whatsoever for the practice of infant baptism, according to Warfield's own words. Yet he was even prepared to say that this sense of continuity was so strong and so obvious in the apostolic age, he did 'not doubt that children

---

Reformation and its aftermath, the compass of baptismal theology had swung right round, so that *what could sensibly be predicated of infant subjects* came to determine theologies of baptism... If vital contact had been maintained with the New Testament, *the limitations of babies* could never have been allowed to prescribe what was to be taught and believed about baptism... Some devaluation of infant baptism is implicit... [in] consequence of taking with greater seriousness the New Testament, rather than the Old Testament, in considering a theology of baptism'. Under the dominance of infant baptism, 'the New Testament's presentation of baptism became remote' (Wright: *What...?* pp7,15, emphasis mine). If Wright's excellent (though over-cautious) prescription were followed, and we saw a return to the New Testament, it would mean the *end* of infant baptism, not merely its *devaluation*! As Wright pointed out: 'The case for believer's baptism has typically been based on the New Testament alone – which is, after all, the only part of the Bible where we encounter Christian baptism... The mainstream Reformers bequeathed a defence of infant baptism in which even its ablest exponents leaned quite disproportionately on the Old Testament. Believer's Baptists are right to demand that the heirs of the Reformers owe them an apologia for infant baptism which [apologia] unashamedly owns the full-orbed New Testament witness to Christian baptism' (Wright: 'Christian' p168). Wright is to be commended for this statement. I gratefully acknowledge his honesty.

born into the church during this age were both circumcised and baptised'! Indeed the change from circumcision to baptism, he alleged, 'was slow, and never came until it was forced by the actual pressure of circumstances. The instrument for making this change was... Paul. We see the change formally constituted... in Acts 15'.[4] Reader, this is an amazing rewriting of the Acts is it not? Baptism is not even mentioned in Acts 15! Warfield must have had extraordinary powers of sight if in that chapter he could see infant baptism replacing circumcision as its equivalent.

Dabney wrote that the 'church is substantially the same under both dispensations, retaining under the New, the same membership and nature, though with a suitable change of circumstances, which it had under the Old'.[5] Did Dabney really think that the Israelites of the Old Testament, and the saints of the New, were members of the same church, and in the same way, allowing for 'suitable' differences of circumstances? A.A.Hodge went even further than Dabney. He baldly stated that 'the church under the Old dispensation is precisely the same church with the Christian church under the New'.[6] *Precisely* the same?

This entire scheme is based upon a faulty foundation. Actually, it has no foundation at all. The church in the Old Testament is not the same as the church in the New Testament, for the simple reason the church did not even exist in the Old Testament! It is entirely a New Testament body. Hence the deductions of infant baptisers are based on a false premise. In particular, it is useless to argue from this false

---

[4] Warfield pp390,399,404. When Pratt stated that 'the book of Acts reveals that baptism replaced circumcision only through a complex process', he was wrong. Baptism didn't replace circumcision by a complex process; it didn't replace it at all; the non-existent process Pratt spoke of was 'invisible'! And when Pratt said that in Acts 15, 'the... apostles [and the church] determined that circumcision would no longer be required of New Testament believers ['no longer'? – it never was], and that baptism alone would suffice as the initiatory rite for the... church', I should like to know where we can find such a far-reaching statement in Acts 15. As I say, I can discover no mention of baptism in the chapter. And what is this 'alone... suffice'? (John H.Armstrong pp66-67; see Nettles' reply in John H.Armstrong pp75-76). Such shoddy exegesis serves only to prove the weakness of the case.

[5] Dabney p727.

[6] A.A.Hodge p332.

117

premise to say that baptism has replaced circumcision. It has done nothing of the kind.

Pierre Marcel's words may be regarded as typical of the infant baptiser's view. He claimed that 'the church has been and remains one; the nation of Israel was the church; the Christian church, since it also comes under the covenant of grace, is the same church'.[7] Reader, take careful note of Marcel's words. He said that 'the nation of Israel was the church'. This is a staggering statement. It will take some justification. It cannot be done; it is utterly false. The nation of Israel was not the church. Though infant baptisers frequently refer to the 'Jewish church', there was no such thing. When they qualify the church and call it the 'Christian church', or a 'gospel church', and so on, they merely add to this confusion. R.A.Cole, for example, wrote that after Christ's 'breach with the church of Jewry, the Lord began to constitute his own Church'![8] His *own* church as opposed to somebody else's church? The *Christian* church? Is there any other? We ought to do as the New Testament does and speak only of the church, the church of Christ.

Berkhof, writing on the Sinaitic covenant, said: 'In a large measure Church and State became one. To be in the Church was to be in the nation, and *vice-versa*, and to leave the Church was to leave the nation'.[9] What a manifestly false assertion! The nation of Israel the church? Matthew Henry, commenting on Mark 2:23 where it is recorded that the disciples ate the corn on the Sabbath, said: 'What a poor breakfast Christ's disciples had on a Sabbath day morning, when they were going to church'! Going to church? They must have had a remarkably long journey that Sabbath. The church was not even founded at the time. And what a mongrel mix up – the Sabbath and the church! Nevertheless, there is the claim – the church is the same in both Testaments, infant baptisers say. Sadly, some Baptists agree with them; Erroll Hulse, for instance, who said: 'The gospel Church is not a different Church from that which existed in the Old Testament period'![10]

---

[7] Pawson and Buchanan p11.
[8] Cole p79.
[9] Berkhof p298. How much suffering, what appalling torture, how much martyrdom, has come from that principle applied to the church!
[10] Hulse: *Restoration* p26

If so, an interesting question arises. According to infant baptisers, the disciples were members of the church before they met Christ. After all, they were in the covenant, they were circumcised, they belonged to the nation of Israel, hence they were members of the church, according to infant baptisers. Presumably, on regeneration they became members again. But the point is this: If they were members of the church before they met Christ, why did Christ say that he had chosen them 'out of the world' (John 15:19)? According to infant baptisers he had chosen them out of the church! Furthermore, if Jews had been properly admitted to the church by circumcision, why did they have to be admitted to the church all over again by baptism? Why were Jewish converts baptised? Indeed, why, if circumcised, are they today?

At first glance, the Authorised Version of Acts 7:38 appears to justify the idea that the nation of Israel was the church, and therefore supports the claim that the church existed in the Old Testament. The verse speaks of 'the church in the wilderness'. This, however, is a misleading translation of Stephen's words. Instead of 'church', εκκλησια should here be translated 'congregation' or 'assembly'.[11] The Greek word means a gathering of citizens called out to a public place, a gathering or throng.[12] In the Greek version of the Old Testament – the Septuagint – the word is used for the assembly, throng or gathering of the Israelites, and that is how Stephen used it. Unfortunately, the Authorised Version, for reasons of its own,[13] translated it badly by the word 'church', which in the New Testament takes on an altogether different meaning, being used in a technical, specialised sense, peculiar to itself. In these New Testament terms it now means a church, a covenanted body of baptised saints gathered in the name of Christ for the worship of God, and so on. But Stephen did not intend to convey that meaning. He used the word in its Greek Septuagint or Old Testament sense, meaning the throng or assembly of Israel. The Greeks themselves also used exactly the same word to

---

[11] See NKJV, NASB, NIV, NEB.

[12] See Thayer; Arndt.

[13] In the *Preface for the Reader*, the AV translators were quite open about keeping 'the old ecclesiastical words'. This is what King James wanted (Bruce p98). He got his way, but a big price had to be paid for it – one which is still being paid today. The giving of a wrong view of 'the church' to millions is a hefty instalment!

speak of an assembly of citizens convened in a public place to deliberate some particular issue. That is the way the very word translated 'church' in Acts 7:38 is used in Acts 19:39. Nobody would dream of translating Acts 19:39 – 'the lawful assembly', a legally gathered assembly of citizens, or court – as 'the lawful *church*'. Stephen's words, badly mistranslated in the Authorised Version,[14] do not in any way support the claim that the church existed in the Old Testament. It has nothing to do with it.

The church – the word used in the spiritual New Testament or Christian sense – is, as I say, entirely a New Testament body. How could it exist in the Old Testament? The very first time it appears in the Bible is in Matthew 16:18 where Jesus said: 'I will build my church'. Exactly so. That was the founding of the church and it took practical effect on the Day of Pentecost. We know that the church is 'built on the foundation of the apostles and prophets, Jesus Christ himself being the chief cornerstone' (Eph. 2:20). In this verse we have the foundation of the church. What, or who, is the foundation? The apostles and prophets. There is no question or debate over who the apostles were, but who were the prophets? Did Paul mean the Old Testament prophets, or did he mean the New Testament prophets? Clearly, he meant the prophets of the New Testament. Why? For three reasons.

First, if he had intended the Old Testament prophets, he would not have said 'the apostles and prophets', but he would have said 'the prophets and apostles', putting them in their proper chronological order.

Secondly, the immediate context in which Paul wrote makes it abundantly plain that he meant New Testament prophets. A few verses later, he spoke of the mystery of Christ 'which in other ages was not made known to the sons of men, as it has now been revealed by the Spirit to his holy apostles and prophets' (Eph. 3:5). Clearly, the prophets in this verse were the New Testament prophets. The mystery had been fully revealed to them now. This makes it very likely – to put it no stronger – that those spoken of in the earlier passage were those same New Testament prophets. Again, shortly after, when speaking of the church and the gifts Christ gave to the church after his ascension,

---

[14] It would be fair to call it 'loaded'.

Paul said that 'he himself gave some to be apostles, some prophets' (Eph. 4:11). This refers without doubt to the New Testament prophets. Thus the context gives a second reason which makes it extremely likely, to say the least, that Ephesians 2:20 relates to the New Testament prophets. (See also 1 Cor. 12:28).

Thirdly, Paul did not write of 'the apostles and the prophets', but 'the apostles and prophets'. The one definite article qualifies both apostles and prophets; they were, together, the one foundation of the church. They were the joint instrument through which God revealed his truth to found the church, with Christ the chief cornerstone. The apostles were New Testament men; likewise, these prophets.

For these three reasons, we may say – without question – Ephesians 2:20 teaches that the church was founded in the New Testament. And since it was founded in the New Testament, how could it exist in the Old? It did not – it could not – exist before it was founded! Hence, for infant baptisers to maintain that the church is the same in both Testaments, must be completely wrong. It did not even exist in the Old Testament.[15] And consequently, any and every practice which is deduced on that false basis, must itself be false. In particular, infant baptism cannot be justified by this argument of the so-called continuity of the church.

Of course there were true believers in the Old Testament, and they were saved in the same way as believers in the New Testament, they were in the same covenant as New Testament saints, and they will inherit the same eternal glory. In the previous chapter, I spoke of the spiritual aspect of the Abrahamic covenant. This is part of it. The believers of both Testaments are in the same covenant with God – the new covenant – which was the spiritual aspect of the Abrahamic covenant. But while all that was true of the saints of the Old Testament, it is entirely wrong to speak of the church in the Old Testament. There was no church, at that time, in the terms of the New Testament. Therefore, any attempt to apply Old Testament conditions to the church is greatly misguided. Sadly, the fallacious notion that the church existed in the Old Testament is one of the basic arguments of infant baptisers. As a result, they wrongly apply Old Testament practices and conditions, especially about circumcision, to the church.

---

[15] It was prophesied in the Old Testament, but came into existence in the New. I will return to this in my book on the law.

It leads to all sorts of trouble. And it is baseless. When they talk about the *Abrahamic* church, or the *Mosaic* church, they make utterly ridiculous statements. And when they talk of a *gospel* church they simply add to the muddle. In particular, as a consequence of their mistaken view of the continuity of the church in both Testaments, infant baptisers hold that New Testament baptism has replaced Old Testament circumcision. But since the church did not exist in the Old Testament, their appeal for the baptism of infants on that basis falls to the ground.

Warfield summarised the total range of arguments employed by infant baptisers: 'The argument in a nutshell is simply this: God established his church in the days of Abraham and put children into it. They must remain there until he puts them out. He has nowhere put them out. They are still then members of his church and as such entitled to its ordinances. Among these ordinances is baptism'.[16] Reader, this *is* the argument in a nutshell, but the shell is empty! God established his church, not in the days of Abraham, but through Christ in the New Testament (Eph. 2:20). Israel was not the church. Furthermore, God never did put children into his church. God only ever put believers into his church, in the local sense of the word. The church is composed of the elect, not the elect and their children. Warfield's argument falls to the ground because it is based on a false premise. And since, as he said, his argument summarised the entire case of infant baptisers – it is the argument in a nutshell – their whole hypothesis collapses.

---

[16] Warfield p408.

Argument 4

Infant Baptisers Claim that Baptism Has Replaced Circumcision

A fourth claim which infant baptisers make is to say that there is direct New Testament warrant for the change from circumcision to baptism[1] – leaving aside the dispute about the covenant and the so-called continuity of the church.[2] One passage to which they refer is Colossians 2:11-14, which reads:

---

[1] In addition to what I say in the substance of this chapter, if baptism has replaced circumcision, why would Paul not say so at the meeting to discuss whether or not baptised Gentile converts should be circumcised (Acts 15)? Why would he circumcise the baptised Timothy (Acts 16:3)? And why would Peter refuse to eat with converted and baptised Gentiles (Gal. 2:11-12)? See R.E.O.White p211. Peter was wrong, of course, as Paul made clear (Gal. 2:11-21) – but my point is this: If Peter believed, as infant baptisers do, that baptism has replaced circumcision, why did he stop eating with baptised but uncircumcised believers? More important: Why didn't Paul use the argument when confronting Peter?

[2] But as with covenant theology, when the Fathers drifted towards infant baptism, for many years they did not argue for it on the basis of circumcision, and even when they did, it was only a question of analogy. The 4th century, of course, laid the foundations for the theology to develop (Stander and Louw pp37,69,80,183,185), and once that theology was developed, 'traditional defences of infant baptism have leaned heavily on... circumcision' (Wright: *What...?* p15). But it was not always so. Some words of Wright already noted: 'The invocation of circumcision with its covenantal context was generally not an original feature in [the] Reformers' baptismal teaching. It emerges in general terms when, having nailed their colours to the mast of *sola Scriptura*, they had to row back from an initial emphasis on the necessity of faith for beneficial reception of baptism. This re-positioning occurred when the opposition against whom this emphasis was directed, the old Roman Church, was supplanted by the new foe of Anabaptism. We should not underestimate the seriousness of the challenge posed by Anabaptist radicals. More than one of the magisterial Reformers had to overcome early doubts about infant baptism, independently of Anabaptist protests. It can be seriously argued that the baptism of babies was the single most significant constitutive element of

In him you were also circumcised with the circumcision made without hands, by [better, in] putting off the body of the sins of the flesh, by the circumcision of Christ, buried with him in baptism, in which you were also raised with him through faith in the working of God, who raised him from the dead. And you, being dead in your trespasses and the uncircumcision of your flesh, he has made alive together with him, having forgiven you all trespasses.

We may take Hendriksen's comments on the passage as typical. He alleged that 'baptism has taken the place of circumcision. Hence, what is said with reference to circumcision... holds also for baptism'. He meant, of course, that water baptism in the New Testament has taken the place of physical circumcision in the Old. He quoted with approval the *Form for the Baptism of Infants*: 'Since, then, baptism has come in the place of circumcision, the children should be baptised as heirs of the kingdom of God and of his covenant'.[3]

This is wrong. It is based on a poor exposition of the passage. There are four reasons.

In the *first* place, the circumcision spoken of in these verses clearly is not a physical circumcision; it is 'the circumcision made without hands'. In other words, it is spiritual circumcision. Hence it is impossible to use the verses to teach that baptism has replaced the rite of circumcision, since physical circumcision is not even mentioned.

There is a *second* reason why Paul could not have been referring to physical circumcision. The apostle was writing to the Colossians. While this church (possibly) comprised some converted Jews, it (almost) certainly[4] was made up (mostly) of converted Greeks. Yet Paul addressed them all as 'circumcised'. He could not possibly have meant physical circumcision – were the Greeks circumcised?

Thirdly, Colossians 2:11-14 does not say that believers are baptised instead of being circumcised, that baptism has taken the place of

---

church order that the Reformers preserved without explicit biblical warrant' (Wright: 'Children' p30).
[3] Hendriksen: *Colossians* pp86,116.
[4] Internal evidence in the book surely suggests it, to put it no stronger. 'The basic evil with which [this] young church was confronted was the danger of relapse into paganism with its gross immorality... A careful reading of Col. 3:5-11 proves that this peril was basic. The members of the Colossian church were, at least for the most part, rather recent converts from the darkness and coarse sensuality of heathendom' (Hendriksen: *Colossians* p16).

circumcision. It states that all believers have been both circumcised and baptised, the circumcision and the baptism being one and the same. The latter has not superseded the former. Paul declared that the Colossians 'were... circumcised... buried with [Christ] in baptism'. He did not say they were baptised *instead of* being circumcised. He did not say baptism *is the equivalent of* circumcision. He did not say baptism *has replaced* circumcision. He said the Colossians were *both* circumcised *and* baptised. He went further. He did not even use the word *and* between 'circumcision' and 'baptism'. Baptism has not taken the place of circumcision. They were 'circumcised', 'baptised'. In the context, the two are *identical*, one and the same.

Fourthly, the Greek tense which Paul used was the aorist. He said that the Colossians were circumcised, were baptised, were buried, were raised, all at one and the same time in one finished completed act, one with abiding effect. This shows, again, that the circumcision, the baptism, the burial and the resurrection were one and the same thing. It all took place at one and the same time. They all constituted one event. It is clear that the circumcision in the passage is not physical; in the same way, nor is the baptism, nor is the burial, nor the resurrection. None of it is. It is all spiritual. It all speaks of spiritual union with Christ (Rom. 6:1-11).[5] Therefore it is impossible to make the passage teach that water baptism has replaced physical circumcision. Neither of them is even mentioned.

The circumcision in question is not, as Warfield put it, 'the circumcision which Christ ordained'.[6] Paul did not say that Christ *ordained* it; nor did the apostle command believers to be circumcised in order to obey Christ.[7] He declared that the circumcision is something which *Christ did*.[8] Sartelle, too, was mistaken when he

---

[5] Had the believers Paul was writing to been *physically* buried and *physically* raised? Of course not. Paul was not talking about *physical* burial and resurrection. Neither was he talking about *physical* circumcision or *physical* baptism. It was all *spiritual*.

[6] Warfield p405.

[7] The apostles did not command believers to be circumcised, but they did command them to be baptised.

[8] 'The words... are a Hebraism... "Christ-circumcision", that is, circumcision effected for us in Christ, in virtue of our having passed through death into resurrection-life in him' (Newton p11).

alleged that it is 'a symbolic circumcision'.[9] Symbolic? Certainly not! There is nothing symbolic about it; it is an effective, real circumcision. It is, as Hendriksen said, 'that circumcision [which] is yours by virtue of your union with Christ'.[10] In other words, it is spiritual circumcision. Similarly, the baptism in view is not water baptism. It is spiritual baptism. Note also that Christ is the one who circumcises and baptises – not ministers. If Paul had been talking physically, then ministers would play their (vital) part. But he was talking spiritually; ministers do not come into it.[11] The passage has nothing directly to say

---

[9] Sartelle p11. Those who think it is, apparently, want a *symbolic* circumcision, but an *effective* water baptism! Or do they, after all, believe that water baptism is symbolic?

[10] Hendriksen: *Colossians* p117.

[11] But what about 2 Cor. 3:3? 'You are a letter of Christ ministered by us, written not with ink but by the Spirit of the living God... on tablets of flesh; that is... the heart'. Paul was saying that he needed no letter of recommendation to the Corinthians – the Corinthians themselves were all the letter he needed. Christ himself wrote it; that is, by his Spirit he had regenerated the Corinthians and brought them into a living union with himself through their repentance and faith. But, said Paul, Christ had used him as an amanuensis. Christ did the work by his Spirit, but Paul was the hand that he used. This was the proof that he was indeed a minister of Christ. Hence Col. 2:11-12, the argument might go, teaches that as ministers baptise, Christ regenerates.
But such a claim – were it to be made – would be a leap far too far. True, Christ uses his saints as ministers to regenerate his elect under their preaching (using the biblically-wide definition of preaching). There is no quarrel with this. He could, if he wished, regenerate sinners directly, but he generally uses his saints to witness or preach to bring others to himself. As I say, there is no quarrel with this. The issue is, however: What is this amanuensis-work? Is it baptism? Is *this* the hands-on work that ministers – sacramentalists are usually very shy of allowing 'ordinary' believers to get involved (this would hinder the drive to sacerdotalism!) – do in this regard? Is baptism the hands-on work that ministers perform so that Christ regenerates as they baptise? This, indeed, would be a literal hands-on ministry. Is it right?
Not at all. Let us look at the context of 2 Cor. 3:3 – I mean from 2 Cor. 1:1 – 6:2, not forgetting, above all, 1 Cor. 1:10 – 4:21. What do we find? Baptism? The suggestion is ludicrous. I will return to 1 Cor. 1 (where Paul destroys the notion that it is baptism which he is talking about in 2 Cor. 3:3). So, what about the context of 2 Cor. 3:3? Baptism is not mentioned. But preaching is mentioned over and over again – 2 Cor. 1:18-20; 2:12,14-17; 4:2-5,13;

on the subject of water baptism, and when infant baptisers use it to justify their practice, they are making a gross mistake.

What Colossians 2:11-14 does teach is that all believers have been united to Christ, having been regenerated by one sovereign act of God, when they were spiritually circumcised, spiritually baptised, spiritually buried and spiritually raised. The aorist is important! And there is nothing symbolic about any of it. I point out once again, reader, that Paul did not bring in the word 'and'. The circumcision, the baptism in question, are one and the same – they are not separate events. What Paul speaks of has nothing to do with physical circumcision, nothing to do with water baptism. See also John 3:3-8; Romans 2:28-29; 6:1-11; 1 Corinthians 6:11; 12:13;[12] Galatians 3:26-29; Titus 3:5-6; and so on. In not one of these passages is water baptism or physical circumcision in view.[13] If water baptism is forced into any of the passages, the most dire and unscriptural consequences follow.

5:11,18-21; 6:1-2 – and this as the means of bringing sinners to Christ. Ministers are not mentioned in Col. 2:11-12, and baptism is not mentioned in 2 Cor. 3:3. Therefore the objection – namely, that by linking Col. 2:11-12 with 2 Cor. 3:3 we may say that Paul was speaking of baptism by ministers in Col. 2 – if it were to be made, would be baseless. Indeed, the boot is on the other foot. The proper reading of the passages in their context is destructive of sacramentalism.

[12] See end note on p135 for excursus: '1 Cor. 6:11; 12:13'.

[13] Contrary to Beasley-Murray, Wright and many (most?) others. Take Wright: '1 Cor. 6:11... [and] Tit. 3:5-6... show that the baptismal waters spoke prominently of spiritual cleansing'. But the verses do not refer to water baptism. If they did, then all who are baptised with water would be washed from sin and baptised into Christ (1 Cor. 12:13). No qualifiers could prevent it or get round it. It has to be faced; if the verses speak of water baptism, then water baptism saves! There is no talk of a sign in these verses. The baptism actually accomplishes what is being spoken of. And in every case: 'For by one Spirit we were all [not 'some', or even 'most', or 'those who prove to be regenerate', but 'all' were] baptised into one body'. Either water baptism does what is claimed for it, or it does not; a close tie – or a 99.999% success rate – is not good enough. Now we know that Simon (the sorcerer) was baptised but not saved by it (Acts 8:13,21-23). This one 'failure', on its own, proves that saving grace does not come by baptism. Therefore the passages cannot speak of water baptism. Wright thought they do, even though he admitted 'the baptismal interpretation of [Tit. 3:5-6] is not beyond questioning'. Quite! I certainly question it! I do not accept that '"washing" is an unexpected

127

Papists do that very thing and contend for baptismal regeneration on that basis. Likewise the Prayer Book of the Church of England. Reformed infant-baptisers hold that water baptism is in view but they try to fudge the issue. They say – as the Westminster Confession Chapter XXVIII put it – though water baptism is in view 'yet grace and salvation are not so inseparably annexed unto it... that all that are

---

metaphor to use of rebirth if it [baptism] is rejected' as the interpretation; in regeneration, a sinner is spiritually 'washed'. See also Eph. 5:26 where 'washing of water' is connected with 'the word' with no suggestion whatsoever of baptism (see also Jas. 1:18; 1 Pet. 1:23 where 'regeneration' is linked with 'the word' with no mention of baptism). On John 3:5, Wright did not 'attempt to resolve conclusively the meaning of this heavily contested text', but noted 'it was probably second to none in popularity among the post-apostolic generations on baptism'.

I pause to illustrate this last point. Colin Buchanan and Michael Vasey cited an Anglican example of the defence of infant baptism: 'In 1662, the Restoration leaders went for John 3 [instead of Cranmer's use of Mark 10:13-16 – see below]... and that looked much better' (Buchanan and Vasey p7). Or so they thought!

To let Wright continue; he called 1 Pet. 3:21 'a remarkably full-blooded assertion about baptism, and totally unambiguous', but as he said, 'the meaning of "saves" has to be determined rather than assumed'; so for 'baptism', of course. He was sure 1 Cor. 12:13 is water baptism, and seemed to assume the same for Rom. 6:2-11; Gal. 3:27; Col. 2:11-12. In all this, even though, he admitted, 'I have cut many an exegetical corner, but I am not assuming the mantle of a biblical commentator', he nevertheless showed his hand: 'My concern has been simply to convey a sense of the markedly direct terms in which the New Testament documents attribute the multifaceted reception of God's salvation to the instrumentality of baptism'. As he said a little earlier: 'Ask yourself whether [baptism] is an ordinance or sacrament which is merely[!] symbolic rather than truly effective as a means by which Christ or the Holy Spirit works our blessing' (Wright: *What...?* pp88-92). This is not the real question to be asked of the verse (1 Cor. 12:13). But this is: *Which baptism is the verse (and all the other verses cited) talking about?* They do not speak of an ordinance at all, but the sovereign act of the Holy Spirit in regeneration. Wright, of course, is far from alone: 'The most widely held view of 1 Cor. 12:13 is that Paul is referring to water baptism which is the means by which the Spirit is given to the believer and by which they [*sic*] are incorporated into the body of Christ' (Cross: 'Spirit- and Water-' p121). How do we know this is 'the most widely held view'? And even if it is, the minority are not always wrong; sometimes, but not always.

baptised are undoubtedly regenerated'.[14] At least the Papists and the Anglicans have the merit of being consistent! They think that passages like Colossians 2:11-14 and Titus 3:5-6 are to do with water baptism, and they take the promises and statements as they think they stand. They accept the consequences of their assertions. They allege that the baptism in question is water baptism, and that it does regenerate. Reformed infant-baptisers like to claim that the baptism is water baptism, but try to shy away from the odious consequences of their assertions. All three, however – Papists, Anglicans and Reformed – are mistaken.

The passages teach that all who are washed are saved; that all who are baptised are joined to Christ, they are all regenerated and forgiven every trespass. But – and this must be emphasised – the baptism, the washing, is not water baptism; it is spiritual baptism. All who are circumcised spiritually, spiritually baptised, are regenerated, joined to Christ and saved. But beyond all question, water baptism does not accomplish this. It symbolises it, and is to be administered to those who demonstrate they have been regenerated; and only to them.[15] But

---

[14] Westminster p116. Note it well, reader: 'Not... all that are baptised are undoubtedly regenerated'. Not... all... are. This can only mean that some (many) are. Which means that the Westminster documents undoubtedly teach baptismal regeneration (at least for some, if not for many). But where, in these verses we are talking about, is there any suggestion that 'grace and salvation' are not 'inseparably annexed' to the baptism? The question, of course, as always, is: Which baptism do the verses speak of? All the elect, regenerated by the Spirit, are baptised into Christ, and invariably receive grace and salvation, grace and salvation being inseparably annexed to the baptism. Invariably! All who are thus baptised are saved, always. Always! But the baptism in question is spiritual, not water, baptism.

[15] Thomas Goodwin: 'The eminent thing signified and represented in baptism, is not simply the blood of Christ, as it washes us from sin; but there is a further representation therein of Christ's death, burial and resurrection in [our] being first buried under water, and then rising out of it... a representation of a communion with Christ in... his death and resurrection. Therefore it is said: "We are BURIED with him in baptism"; and "wherein you also are RISEN with him". It is not simply said, *like as* he was buried and rose, but *with him*. So that our communion and one-ness with him in his resurrection is [effected by spiritual baptism – regeneration – and is] represented to us therein [that is, in water baptism], and not only our conformity or likeness unto him therein.

129

that is beside the point at this stage, since passages like Colossians 2:11-14 do not refer to water baptism at all. Therefore they give no basis whatsoever for the baptism of infants.

Infant baptisers are mistaken when they say that baptism has replaced circumcision. It has done nothing of the sort. Certainly Colossians 2:11-14 does not teach it. All believers have been spiritually circumcised and spiritually baptised (they are one and the same); they all have been regenerated. And that is how they came to faith. They have all been regenerated and united to Christ. And that is the meaning of Colossians 2:11-14.

* * *

Surprisingly, Romans 4:11 is also used to try to justify the claim that baptism has replaced circumcision. Under the heading: 'What is said of circumcision also goes for baptism', George M.Ella quoted the verse, a remarkable choice for this purpose. Here it is:

And [Abraham] received the sign of circumcision, a seal of the righteousness of the faith which he had while still uncircumcised.

I will have more to say on the verse in the next chapter, but what did Ella say about it? How did he use it to try to justify his claim that baptism has replaced circumcision? In this way:

Paul, in Romans 4:11, identifies what circumcision points to in relation to faith in the very same way as what baptism points to in relation to faith... Given this immediate connection in purpose of circumcision and baptism, it is in keeping with Scripture to hold that what was said of circumcision goes also for baptism. Abraham, as the believing covenant father, had his children circumcised at the command of God. This command is repeated throughout the New Testament with reference to baptism.[16]

And so [water] baptism represents this to us' (Newton p20, emphasis his). Spot on, Mr Goodwin, spot on! Represents – not accomplishes!
[16] Ella p36. Ella mentioned the verse on three more occasions, but added nothing to the point above. But he did speak of what he called Paul's 'long essay on circumcision and baptism starting in Romans 2' (Ella p178). This is another remarkable claim, and a highly idiosyncratic reading of Rom. 2 and on. Baptism does not occur in the book until Rom. 6, and, as I have made clear, even there it is not water baptism but spiritual baptism. Indeed, water baptism is never mentioned in Romans.

What a remarkable statement. We need not spend long on this, surely. May I point out the obvious? A distinction must always be drawn between assertion and proof. Anyone can make an assertion, but what about the proof? Let me illustrate. Anyone can assert the moon is made of green cheese; proving it, however, is altogether something else. In the extract just quoted, note Ella's three assertions: 'What is said of circumcision also goes for baptism... Given this immediate connection in purpose of circumcision and baptism... This command [given to Abraham] is repeated throughout the New Testament with reference to baptism'. Very well. Here we have the assertions. Where are the proofs? May we see them? Reader, note the absence of any corroborating scripture to prove that we can move from circumcision to baptism like this, the absence of any corroborating scripture to prove there is any connection whatever between the two, and the absence of any corroborating scripture to prove that the command to a believing father to baptise his children is repeated throughout the New Testament. In making these three assertions, Ella offered no scriptural proof whatsoever. None.

And taking his last, if there had been the repeated commands as Ella asserted, this debate would never have existed. Or, at least, I wouldn't have taken part in it. Indeed, I would have baptised my children in obedience to God's command. But since I have yet to come across such a command in Scripture to baptise my children – let alone a repeated command to do so – I did not baptise them. And I think it right to challenge Ella's assertion.

Finally, to cap it all, baptism is not even mentioned in Romans 4:11, or in the immediate context. That is why I said it is a remarkable verse to choose to try to establish the interchange between it and circumcision. How can a passage which does not even mention baptism, be used to prove that baptism has replaced circumcision?

* * *

Ephesians 2:11-13 further supports the claim that the New Testament equivalent of circumcision is regeneration and not water baptism. It reads:

Therefore remember that you, once Gentiles in the flesh – who are called Uncircumcision by what is called the Circumcision made in the flesh by hands – that at that time you were without Christ, being aliens from the commonwealth of Israel and strangers from the covenants of promise, having no hope and without God in the world. But now in Christ Jesus you who once were far off have been made near by the blood of Christ.

Paul said that the Ephesians were, at one time, without Christ, totally ignorant of the covenants, hopeless and cut off from God; that is, they were unregenerate. But now all that had changed. They had been brought into a state of grace; they were regenerate and joined to Christ.

It is the way Paul described their state before regeneration which is the point at issue. He reminded the Ephesians that they were 'once Gentiles in the flesh', by which he meant they were uncircumcised. And as he said, the sneering Jews taunted them with this, calling them the Uncircumcision, while bragging of their own physical sign. But of far greater importance – and this is the point – Paul said that while the Gentiles were uncircumcised in the flesh, they were also unregenerate – they were 'without Christ, being aliens from the commonwealth of Israel and strangers from the covenants of promise, having no hope and without God in the world'. *That was their **real** uncircumcision.* Paul was not desperately concerned about their physical uncircumcision. Far from it. 'Circumcision is nothing and uncircumcision is nothing' in this context (1 Cor. 7:19). Nothing! *It was their **spiritual uncircumcision**, or their **unregeneration**, which really mattered.* Thus, when Paul said that the Ephesians were formerly uncircumcised, he meant it in two ways.[17] First, at that time they did not have the physical mark in the flesh; that, however, was now of little importance, except to the bragging Jews. But – and of far greater consequence – at that time, they were also uncircumcised spiritually; they were unregenerate. And that was what counted.

Hence it is clear; to be uncircumcised, in the New Testament sense of the word, is to be unregenerate. Therefore the converse is also true. Spiritual circumcision, the only circumcision which counts, is regeneration. 'For he is not a Jew who is one outwardly, nor is that

---

[17] Paul is engaging in one of his favourite linguistic devices – word play (see Rom. 3:27; 8:1-4; 9:6; 1 Cor. 9:19-23; Gal. 6:2,16; 2 Thess. 3:11 (NIV); Philem. 10-11). James Dunn noted Paul's 'nice word play in the Greek', 'δουλεύετε αλλήλοις... αλλήλους δακνετε' (Gal. 5:13,15), which U.Borse translated as 'serve one another... savage one another' (Dunn p284). God engages in word play (Mic. 1:8-16). Christ does it (Matt. 11:29-30 with Acts 15:10,28; Matt. 16:18).

circumcision which is outward in the flesh; but he is a Jew who is one inwardly, and circumcision is that of the heart, in the Spirit, and not in the letter' (Rom. 2:28-29). There it is; to be *regenerate* is to be *spiritually circumcised.* 'We are the circumcision, who worship God in the Spirit, rejoice in Christ Jesus, and have no confidence in the flesh' (Phil. 3:3). Even in the Old Testament, circumcision pointed to this spiritual aspect (Deut. 10:16; 30:6; Jer. 4:4; 9:26; Ezek. 44:7).

Consequently, baptism is *not* the New Testament equivalent of circumcision, nor has it replaced it, since the equivalent of circumcision is not baptism but regeneration. So, when infant baptisers argue that baptism has taken the place of circumcision, they are wrong. And when they argue that since a Jew and his seed were circumcised, in the same way a Christian and his seed must be baptised, they are even more wrong. The question of water baptism simply does not arise.

* * *

There is another point. We know the old covenant foreshadowed the new (Col. 2:17; Heb. 8:5; 10:1); that is to say, various practices in the old represented the real and living fulfilment in Christ in the new covenant. The sacrifices, for instance. So also circumcision; it was a shadow; it represented a reality in the new covenant. Reformed infant-baptisers argue that circumcision represented or is fulfilled by baptism which now represents washing from sin in the blood of Christ.[18] In other words, one shadow (circumcision) represented another shadow (baptism) which represents the reality of forgiveness; that is, a symbol led to another symbol which, in turn, leads to the reality.

This is wrong. May I make it clear by calling upon a parallel? The old covenant priesthood represented Christ – the true priest – under the new covenant; it did not represent another shadow (another priesthood, say) which in its turn represented Christ.

---

[18] 'Baptism forced circumcision out of the way. When baptism came, circumcision must be discarded... Circumcision belongs to the time of the shadows, and, therefore, must make room for baptism as being the sign of fulfilment' (Hoeksema p17). No! The shadow gives way to the reality. Circumcision gives way to regeneration – not another sign! Of course, the logic of the infant baptiser's argument leads inexorably to the shadow – circumcision – being replaced by baptismal regeneration!

133

But Reformed writers continue to make this mistake of claiming that one symbol or shadow leads to another. Pratt, for instance, criticised Nettles who had rightly argued that the old covenant shadow of circumcision is fulfilled by the new covenant reality of regeneration:

In his [Nettles'] view, circumcision in the Old Testament is seen as a foreshadowing of regeneration in the New Testament rather than a foreshadowing of New Testament baptism. This outlook is unfortunate... In the Old Testament, physical circumcision pointed to the need for inward spiritual circumcision; in the New Testament, physical washing [what now of sprinkling?] in baptism points to the need for inward spiritual washing. The parallels are between two outward acts and the inward realities they represent... Baptism correlates to circumcision, and [just as, he meant or at least implied] the Lord's supper corresponds to Passover.

This is clearly a bad mistake. I should like to see the biblical justification for an old covenant shadow being replaced by another shadow in the new. Significantly, Pratt offered no verse. There is none. But we do have verses – see above – where we are explicitly told that the old covenant shadows led directly to, pointed to, their real and spiritual fulfilment in the new – with no second shadow in between. As Nettles noted: 'Part of the confusion seems to rest in Pratt's view that one symbol is fulfilled by another symbol'.[19] Scripture, of course, teaches that the shadows and symbols in the old covenant are fulfilled by the reality in the new.

In particular, the Passover did not foreshadow the Lord's supper. Certainly not! It foreshadowed *Christ and his sacrifice.* We are expressly told so: Christ is our Passover (1 Cor. 5:7); Christ, not the supper. Similarly, circumcision did not foreshadow baptism.

Can we be shown New Testament proof that baptism is meant to point 'to the *need for* inward spiritual washing'? As far as I am aware, baptism always 'points to the inward spiritual washing' *which has already taken place,* and until that has happened, baptism is completely out of order. Baptism does not represent something which needs to happen; it represents something which has already happened.

* * *

---

[19] John H.Armstrong pp45-46,66,75.

Earlier, when dealing with the covenant, I asked what infant baptisers make of the command found in Genesis 17:14 – the uncircumcised must be cut off from his people. On their reasoning, they must cut off the unbaptised. What, exactly, is this – I asked – in terms of the New Testament? Allowing, for the moment, the infant baptiser's application of the covenant to believers to stand, once we understand that the spiritual equivalent of circumcision is regeneration, we can see that if anyone is uncircumcised, in New Testament terms he is unregenerate; he is indeed cut off from God's people. He cannot be, he must not be, in the church, because he does not belong to Christ. Hence we may say that the church must be composed only of the regenerate. Just as any professing Israelite was cut off from Israel when it was discovered that he was not circumcised, and therefore could not take part in God's ordinances, so no unregenerate, spiritually uncircumcised person should be allowed to join the church; or, if already joined, he should be removed. In the light of this, how can infant baptisers contemplate a church with unregenerate members? But this is what they do, some of them with apparent contentment. It is most improper. Once again, this is getting close to the heart of the practical consequences of infant baptism, consequences which are shocking,[20] consequences which have moved me to write. I will come back to the point.

* * *

This fourth argument of infant baptisers is erroneous. Baptism has not replaced circumcision. The New Testament equivalent of the Old Testament rite of circumcision is regeneration. To link water baptism with Jewish circumcision is to make a very serious mistake.[21]

---

[20] It was, of course, a major bone of contention between the Anabaptists and the Reformers.

[21] Is there any risk that someone reared on the teaching which replaces circumcision by baptism, on hearing of the need to be 'spiritually circumcised' – 'you must be born again' (John 3:7) – might imagine he has been born again in his infant baptism?

End note to Argument 4: Circumcision Has Replaced Baptism

1 Cor. 6:11; 12:13

Gordon D.Fee: In 1 Cor. 6:11, 'it is possible, but not as certain as most interpreters [including sacramental Baptists; Fee cited Beasley-Murray] imply, that the verb "you were washed" is also an allusion to baptism... [But] Paul does not in fact say "you were baptised", which he was perfectly capable of doing if baptism were his concern. This verb [washed] is not used elsewhere in the New Testament to denote baptism (it is joined to baptism in Acts 22:16, but is not the actual verb for baptism itself)... Regeneration, sanctification and justification... for Paul... are the work of the Spirit in the believer's life, not the result of baptism' (Fee: *1 Corinthians* pp246-247).

Fee: In 1 Cor. 12:13, 'it is often assumed that Paul is referring to the sacrament of water baptism, and it is then often argued... [even by sacramental Baptists; Fee cited Beasley-Murray] that this text supports the close tie [see the following note] of the reception of the Spirit with baptism itself. But that assumes more than is actually said'. As Fee observed, water is not mentioned; the baptism is with/in/by *the Spirit*; and, above all, 'one is hard pressed [it is impossible!] to find an equation between baptism and the reception of the Spirit in Paul's letters' (Fee: *1 Corinthians* p604; see also *God's* pp178-182,853-864). Words matter. Little words often matter most. Donald G.Barnhouse: 'In studying the word of God, we must never underestimate the importance of little words' (Barnhouse p157). Paul did not say they received the Spirit *by* baptism; he said they were baptised *by* the Spirit *into* Christ. Fee: 'Paul's usage elsewhere strongly suggests that the prepositions εν and εις should be translated respectively as locative (the Spirit is the "element" into which they were submerged)... The point is that Paul is not referring to water baptism at all' (Fee: *God's* pp861-862). 'The use of εν with βαπτιζω throughout the New Testament is locative, expressing the element into which one is baptised (see on [1 Cor.] 12:13)' (Fee: *1 Corinthians* p445). On the element question, Beasley-Murray agreed, 'suggesting that when Paul uses εν with the verb to baptise, he has in view the element in which baptism takes place... The Spirit... is the element in which one is baptised so as to be in the body'. But, of course, Beasley-Murray was linking this with water baptism, dismissing H.T.Andrews (and E.Best) who 'dared' to query it in 1 Cor. 12:13: 'The question appears naïve from a responsible theologian. The inter-relating of gospel, faith, confession, grace, baptism appears never to have come within the horizon of this writer, nor the idea of baptism as a meeting of God and a penitent sinner on the basis of the Christ event'. 'God's gift to baptism and to faith is one: it is his salvation in Christ' (Beasley-Murray: *Baptism in the New Testament* pp167-168; *Baptism Today and Tomorrow* p37; see also *Baptism Today and Tomorrow* pp27-33). For an assessment of the views of Beasley-Murray, Dunn, Fee, Stott and Lloyd-Jones on 1 Cor. 12:13, see Cross: 'Spirit-

and Water-'; O'Donnell. See also Donald Macleod. Speaking for myself, I hope I am 'responsible', even though I may be 'naive' in the eyes of sacramentalists. Granted that, I do more than question that 'baptism and faith is one' 'gift' and that this 'gift' is 'salvation in Christ'; I deny it absolutely. And I respectfully ask to be shown the biblical proof of it by 'non-naive responsible theologians'.

This discussion needs broadening beyond 1 Cor. 12:13. 'Into', εἰς, denotes the element in which the baptism takes place, and the element determines the outcome of the baptism. Spiritual baptism is baptism in the Spirit which unites to Christ, and water baptism is baptism in water which makes one a professor of Christ. Beasley-Murray, citing Rom. 6:3, raised the sacramentalist view: 'What is meant by baptism to Christ Jesus? Frequently εἰς after the verb βαπτιζειν denotes the goal desired and realised through baptism', citing Matt. 3:11; Acts 2:38; 1 Cor. 12:13. 'It would be possible to view "baptism to Christ Jesus" therefore as baptism in order to be *in* Christ, and so as "baptism *into* Christ". This interpretation is strengthened by the related passage, Gal. 3:26-27'. I pause. Note the muddling of water baptism and spiritual baptism, leading to sacramentalism. The two baptisms must be kept distinct. When talking of spiritual baptism, εἰς means baptism into Christ; that is, spiritual baptism which actually unites to Christ. But when talking of water baptism, εἰς does not carry that weight. Beasley-Murray went on to quote Best on Gal. 3:26-27: 'The implied suggestion is that those who are "in Christ" had come "into him" by [water] baptism, and that therefore εἰς must carry the social and local meaning of εν'. That is to say, according to Best, water baptism actually unites to Christ – a full-blown sacramental position, of course. But, as Beasley-Murray pointed out: 'A difficulty is encountered by this view in that Paul declares the Israelites to have been baptised "to [into] Moses" (εἰς τον Μωσειν, 1 Cor. 10:2), which can scarcely be said to mean "into Moses"'. Best had countered this objection by taking Moses as representative of Christ – so that the baptism into Moses was truly an actual baptism into Christ! The paucity of the argument only serves to show the wrongness of the original claim. As Beasley-Murray said: 'The Israelites were baptised with respect to Moses... for his allegiance' (Beasley-Murray: *Baptism in the New Testament* pp128-129, emphasis his). In other words, in spiritual baptism, baptism εἰς or εν the Spirit actually unites to Christ; in water baptism, baptism εἰς or εν water is profession of Christ, allegiance to Christ, commitment to Christ.

Argument 5

Infant Baptisers Claim that Circumcision Was a Seal of the Covenant to Infants – and Baptism Is the Same

Infant baptisers appeal to Romans 4:11, the verse which speaks of circumcision as the seal which God gave to Abraham – the seal of the justification which he had received by faith, and received long before he was circumcised. The verse reads:

And he received the sign of circumcision, a seal of the righteousness of the faith which he had while still uncircumcised.

From this, infant baptisers argue that their babies should be baptised to seal their interest in the covenant. I have already noted that baptism does not figure in the context of Romans 4:11. Amazing, then, that so many claim so much for a verse which says nothing – nothing – about the subject in hand. With that in mind, let us look at the claim that baptism is a seal for the infants of believers.[1]

Circumcision had a spiritual meaning in the Old Testament, in addition to its national and physical aspects. It was a sign to all the Israelites, a sign of what needed to happen to them spiritually. But, for one man – and one man only – it was more than a sign. It was also a seal. Circumcision served as both a sign and a seal to Abraham. What is more, for Abraham it was not a sign of what he *needed* to experience, but of what he had *already* experienced. Circumcision was an outward rite which brought home to his heart and mind what had happened to him spiritually. Circumcision illustrated it to him, and sealed it to him. He had been justified by faith, and his circumcision sealed this to him in some way; it made his justification real to him, it verified, it confirmed, it guaranteed it to him. The circumcision did not

---

[1] Many Baptists also misuse the verse to talk, wrongly, about baptism as a seal – for believers, of course, not infants. But, as I will show, baptism is not a *seal* for anybody.

138

justify Abraham; it did not contribute to his justification; he was not justified because of or through circumcision. The truth is, *he was circumcised because he was justified.*[2] As John Murray put it: 'If circumcision signified faith, the faith must be conceived of as existing prior to the signification given and, in a way still more apparent, a seal or authentication presupposes the existence of the thing sealed and the seal does not add to the content of the thing sealed'.[3] Let me stress this. Abraham's faith and justification existed before he was sealed by circumcision. It could be no different. Unless he had been already justified, his justification could not have been sealed to him.

There is a difference between a sign and a seal. A sign points to something. We all know the purpose of the signpost on a road or footpath; it marks out the way.[4] A sign is an indicator, an illustration, a source of instruction.[5] But a seal is more, much more. It actually

---

[2] Justification... 'does this blessedness then come upon the circumcised only, or upon the uncircumcised also? For we say that faith was accounted to Abraham for righteousness. How then was it accounted? While he was circumcised, or uncircumcised? Not while circumcised, but while uncircumcised. And he received the sign of circumcision, a seal of the righteousness of the faith which he had while still uncircumcised, that he might be the father of all those who believe, though they are uncircumcised, that righteousness might be imputed to them also, and the father of circumcision to those who not only are of the circumcision, but who also walk in the steps of the faith which our father Abraham had while still uncircumcised' (Rom. 4:9-12). Incidentally, though it is not relevant to the subject in hand, Paul then goes on to show that the law played no more part in Abraham's justification than circumcision (Rom. 4:13-16). And all this applies, as Paul makes very clear, not only to Abraham, but to all who are justified. Infant baptisers, who so strongly link circumcision and baptism, and who attribute so much to both – both are the seal, they say, of justification – not only go further than Scripture in both cases, they risk – to put it no stronger – they risk obscuring the vital point Paul stresses in Rom. 4; namely, nothing we can do, nor any rite we can observe, makes any contribution to justification – circumcision, law, prayers, baptism...
[3] John Murray Vol.1 p137.
[4] Care is needed. A signpost points out the way which has to be taken. Circumcision pointed the Israelites to what needed to happen to them. But baptism is not a sign in this sense. Baptism points to something which has already happened to believers.
[5] Take the stones carried from the Jordan and set up as a sign to the Israelites. Note the question: 'What do these stones *mean* to you?'; not: 'What do these

verifies, it confirms, guarantees and makes real the experience of something. John Murray again:

It is usual [right, essential] to discover a distinction between a sign and a seal; a sign points to the existence of that which it signifies, whereas a seal authenticates, confirms, and guarantees the genuineness of that which is signified... The seal is more than definitive of that in which the sign consisted; it adds the thought of authentication. And the seal is that which God himself appended to assure Abraham that the faith he exercised in God's promise was accepted by God to the end of fulfilling to Abraham the promise which he believed.[6]

---

stones *do* to you?' (Josh. 4:1-9). The stones told, reminded, instructed, informed Israel; they did not convey any grace. But they were not to be despised because they served merely(!) as a reminder, a memorial. The Passover was precisely the same: 'This day shall be to you a memorial' (Ex. 12:14). Christ's command in the supper is: 'Do this in remembrance of me' (Luke 22:19; 1 Cor. 11:24-25). Why the need for such reminders? Because forgetfulness is so common a trait – both among the Israelites and believers (Deut. 8:2-19; Ps. 78:11; 106:13; Matt. 16:9; Luke 22:19; 2 Pet. 1:12-15; 3:1-2).

[6] John Murray Vol.1 p138. A seal is a proof, an evidence, a guarantee, that which brings legal closure to all debate, preventing any addition to, or subtraction from, a transaction. Christ was sealed (John 6:27) by evident signs of the Spirit (Mark 2:10; John 5:20,36-37; 8:18; 10:37-38; 14:11; Acts 2:22). Jeremiah sealed the deed of purchase (Jer. 32:10-14). The Corinthians were the seal of Paul's apostleship, its proof, evidence, certification (1 Cor. 9:2). The stone of Christ's tomb was sealed (Matt. 27:66), as is the bottomless pit (Rev. 20:3). God's elect are sealed; he knows them, they are marked by him, they are protected and kept secure by him (2 Tim. 2:19; Rev. 7:3). Paul's completion of the transfer of the gift of money was a seal (Rom. 15:28). See also Deut. 32:34; Job. 9:7; 14:17; Dan. 8:26; 12:4; Rev. 5:1.

Lloyd-Jones: 'A seal is that which authenticates... establishes the authenticity, the validity, the truth of a document or statement. Another meaning... is that it is a mark of ownership... A seal is also used for the purpose of security... There are three main meanings to this term "sealing" – authenticity and authority, ownership, and security and safety... [which are] authenticated by intelligible signs... confirmed... It means that we can be authenticated, that it can be established by intelligible signs that we are indeed the children of God, heirs of God, and joint-heirs with our blessed Lord and Saviour Jesus Christ... Sealing does not make us Christians, but it authenticates the fact, as a seal always does... It is God's action, in which he bears witness that we are his children, that he is our Father, and that we are "heirs of God and joint-heirs with Christ". It is God's authentication of the fact that we really belong to

So far so good. However, from this, infant baptisers go on to maintain that all the infants who were circumcised, like Abraham they also received not only the sign but the seal. Bannerman: 'As the seal, then, of the covenant according to which Abraham was justified, the ordinance plainly testified that it was the covenant of grace; and, when

---

him' (Lloyd-Jones: *Ephesians 1* pp245-265). Lloyd-Jones was here speaking of the sealing with the Spirit. Without agreeing with him on the baptism of the Spirit, what he said on the nature of a seal – the sealing with the Spirit – is admirable. The Spirit himself is the seal (2 Cor. 1:22; Eph. 1:13-14; 4:30; see also Rom. 8:15,23; 2 Cor. 5:5; Gal. 4:6).

The tragedy is, many (both Baptists and infant baptisers) apply the word 'seal' (and therefore, inevitably, its connotations, however much they try to distance themselves from them) to baptism, and do so without a shred of scripture to support it. By this, they in effect teach that baptism guarantees, authenticates and confirms the one baptised as a true believer. Lloyd-Jones, for instance, himself said baptism is a seal and a sign, the seal being far more important: 'The great thing about baptism is that it is a sealing by God of that which I know has already happened to me... Much more important than the sign is the sealing... The important thing about baptism is the seal'. From this Lloyd-Jones argued the opposite to infant baptisers: Since, as he thought, it is a seal, no infant should be baptised. If it had been only(!) a sign, then infants, he thought, could have been baptised (Lloyd-Jones: *The Church* p43; see also *Romans 3:20 – 4:25* p187). Strange, also, therefore, that he could say: 'Baptism is nothing but a seal' (Lloyd-Jones: *Romans 3:20 – 4:25* p187). Nothing *but* a seal? In light of what he said about a seal, and although he was arguing against baptismal regeneration, how could he use the phrase, 'nothing *but* a seal'? The point will be made clear if the phrase 'nothing but a seal' is used when talking of John 6:27; 1 Cor. 9:2, 2 Tim. 2:19; Rev. 9:4; 20:3. Try it and see, reader! The fact that a seal is so final, definite, dogmatic and far-reaching, is the very reason it *cannot* be applied to baptism.

Finally, to clear up any misunderstanding, leaving aside the talk of a seal, let me return to a point I have already made. Whereas circumcision was a sign to Israel of what needed to happen, this is not so with the two New Testament signs – baptism and the Lord's supper. These point to a reality, something which exists, not an aspiration. Going back to the sign of the stones I mentioned above – the stones commemorated the crossing of the Jordan which had already occurred. Take the Lord's supper. The symbols point to the actual accomplishment of redemption, the finished work of Christ, and the believer's reception of it. As for baptism, the sign is not to be treated as some sort of wish for the person being baptised; nor is it meant to guarantee what is going to happen to him; it is meant to illustrate – not guarantee – what has already happened to him.

administered to infants eight days old, it no less plainly indicated they were interested in that covenant'.[7] Legg: 'This sign and seal of the new birth and of justification was given to infants';[8] to all the infant seed of the Israelites, he meant. Owen alleged that 'the spiritual privilege of a right unto and a participation of the initial seal of the covenant was granted by God unto the infant seed of Abraham'.[9]

Now these statements constitute a huge leap of logic. Is it warranted? Certainly not! Romans 4:11 says that Abraham received circumcision as a sign and a seal. As the above-quoted examples show, infant baptisers argue from this statement to claim that *all* who were circumcised received that same seal. What Scripture gives them the authority to say this? They cannot find a single verse! For which other person does the Bible say circumcision was a seal? It never says it of anyone else other than Abraham. There is no other place in Scripture where it is ever said. To read the books written by infant baptisers, one would think it appeared on every other page! The fact is, we never read that *any* other Israelite viewed his circumcision in this way. And we certainly cannot say that *every* Israelite viewed his circumcision in that way. It is impossible to say that all the circumcised regarded it as a seal. In fact there is a valid – unanswerable – case against it, which I will bring out in the next paragraph. Certainly, infant baptisers cannot say that all circumcised infants were sealed. One thing we do know is – and it is absolutely beyond all doubt – many of the Israelites, even though they were circumcised and born of a father who had been circumcised, were not spiritual Israelites, they were not in the covenant in a spiritual way, they never were justified. Therefore they could not possibly have been sealed; there was nothing to seal in their case! How could justification by faith be assured, authenticated, confirmed and guaranteed to those who never were justified? and never would be justified? Both the argument and its conclusion are nonsensical.[10]

---

[7] Bannerman p73.

[8] Legg p5.

[9] Legg p3; Owen: *Of Infant* in *Works* Vol.16 p259.

[10] Circumcision, as I have repeatedly argued, was a *sign* – a pointer to what *should* happen – to the Israelites. It pointed them to the need for regeneration, faith and repentance, and thence justification. Pratt: 'Physical circumcision pointed to the need for inward spiritual circumcision... [It] expressed externally what was required [quite! – not what had already happened] to be

Circumcision was a seal to Abraham because he was a believer and was justified before he was circumcised.[11] It made his justification real

---

true of the inner person' (John H.Armstrong pp45-46,68). Very well. I agree. How, then, could it serve as a seal? In Abraham's case – and in his case alone – it pointed to what had already happened to him. Hence, it was a *seal* to Abraham – but only to him. Sadly, most, if not all, infant baptisers – and Baptists – simply take it for granted that circumcision was a seal to all. What a massive assumption! Utterly unjustified! And they do the same now for baptism. Newton has offered the only justification for it that I know of, but he failed to deal with the main point. He faced the stricture: 'Some, I scarcely know on what principle, have objected to our speaking of baptism as "a seal" on the part of God'. They say: 'We must beware of exalting baptism... into too high a place... If we say that baptism is to be regarded as a "seal", appointed of God, there is danger of its being supposed that the promise of God is invalid without it, and thus baptism would be made indispensably necessary to salvation'. I agree with them! But it is worse than that. If baptism is a seal – and there is no scripture for it – and Newton certainly made no pretence of offering any – then it *is* a seal, and those who are baptised are invariably sealed, with all connotations of the word. Their baptism guarantees, proves, certifies and secures to them the grace signified. If, as Newton said, 'baptism *is* on the part of God a seal... whereby he visibly pledges his faithfulness and his power *to... effectuate* the results that are in the sign signified' (Newton pp19,126-130, emphasis mine), then baptism does it! For the reasons I have given, this cannot be. Newton did not deal with the point I am making. As for infant baptism being a seal to infants, surely Pratt delivered a fatal blow to his own case when he admitted: ''Furthermore... the sacraments do not guarantee that their recipients will receive the blessings they offer... Those who receive baptism are to be washed not only outwardly but inwardly as well' (John H.Armstrong pp63,68). I cannot see, therefore, how baptism can be a seal to infants – if it shouts from the roof-tops that this infant being baptised *needs to be* washed spiritually. It could be a seal only if the baptism gave the definite and absolute assurance – sealed it – that the infant had already been spiritually washed – or was now being spiritually washed in the baptism. So, this is where infant baptisers end up. On the one hand, they tell the recipients of baptism they are sealed by their baptism. On the other hand, as Pratt stated: 'The sacraments do not guarantee that their recipients will receive the blessings they offer'! If this sentiment formed the last line in all the legal documents and guarantees we depend on in this life, it would make them worthless – worth less than the paper cluttering our deed boxes. How much more serious when we are talking about spiritual – eternal – things.

[11] 'Circumcision... was given to Abraham as a sign [and a seal] to [illustrate and] authenticate the imputation of righteousness to him fourteen years

to him, it guaranteed it – the justification which existed beforehand. This is the point I hinted at above. John Murray put it plainly enough: 'A seal... presupposes the existence of the thing sealed'. Reader, notice this: It 'presupposes the existence of'. Exactly![12] That is the precise doctrine of Romans 4:11. On the basis of this verse – and it is the only verse in the entire Bible which speaks of the subject – it can be properly argued that the sealing could only take place *where the man was already justified by faith*. And there is only one man who was circumcised under those conditions as far as we know – Abraham! To jump from Romans 4:11, and say that the seal aspect of circumcision applied to all who were circumcised, is, to say the least, an audacious speculation. It is totally wrong.[13] All that can be deduced from Romans 4:11 is that Abraham received, viewed and understood his circumcision as a seal to him. His circumcision confirmed to him that he was justified by faith. Quite right, too! After all, he *was* justified! As far as circumcision being a seal, that is as far as anyone can go; that is the end of the matter. Or ought to be!

But, when arguing for baptism as a seal, infant baptisers show no such restraint.[14] In addition to the examples I have already given, take Berkhof: 'If it be said, as it is sometimes in our Reformed literature,

---

before... Circumcision... was that Abraham should have the promise made sure to him... Justification is the basis upon which circumcision is given [to Abraham]' (Lloyd-Jones: *Romans 3:20 – 4:25* p185). All this was true for Abraham – but for nobody else.

[12] As long as 'presuppose' is not reduced to mere assumption or less. Abraham was sealed because he *was* justified; there was no guesswork or vague hope about it. I would use 'works on the basis of'; 'a seal *works on the basis of* the existence of the thing sealed'.

[13] Who was circumcised first? The day Abraham was circumcised, so was Ishmael, and 'all who were born in [Abraham's] house and all who were bought with his money, every male among the men of Abraham's house... that very same day' (Gen. 17:23-27). Were they all sealed that 'very same day'? Indeed, were they all justified by faith? If so, had they been justified, like Abraham, before they were sealed by circumcision? or, unlike Abraham, after they were sealed? The seal was a guarantee, a confirmation, to Abraham, of his justification. Was it the same for all the others?

[14] The points I make here apply equally to Baptists who think baptism is a seal – even if they do not explicitly make the same claims as infant baptisers. The fact is, if baptism is a seal, it is a seal! And this goes for both infant and believer's baptism.

that baptism seals the promise(s) of God, this does not merely mean that it vouches for the truth of the promise, but that it assures the recipients that they are the appointed heirs of the promised blessings'.[15] Really? As I explained above, as one who baptises only believers, and who does so with as much care as he can, and does not regard the ordinance as a seal, I would not dare to 'assure' any person I baptised that he or she was an 'appointed heir of the promised blessings'. I can only say to the person that, on the evidence presented to me, I baptise on the grounds that I believe he or she is regenerate, but this is only certainly known by God. As for infant baptisers, however, they seem able to assure those whom they baptise that they are heirs of the promised blessings, and that the baptism has sealed it. In particular, they seem able to assure infants (and the parents) of this. Really?[16]

Berkhof appreciated that this put him into a quandary. He backed off – or tried to: 'This does not necessarily mean that they are already in principle in possession of the promised good, though this is possible and may even be probable, but certainly means that they are appointed heirs and will receive the heritage, unless they show themselves unworthy of it and refuse it'.[17] Some seal this! Some guarantee! It is guaranteed – said Berkhof – *unless* they show themselves unworthy and refuse it! They are sealed *but...* Where is the New Testament justification for this kind of special pleading? Do infant baptisers believe baptism is a seal, a guarantee, a certification, or do they not? Does it assure the recipient of salvation, or does it not? Of course not, as they admit. I have already quoted Pratt, but it bears repeating: 'The sacraments do not guarantee that their recipients will receive the blessings they [are said, by the Reformed, to] offer'.[18] The truth is, Reformed infant-baptisers have to weaken, and draw back from, their assertions because the consequences are unthinkable.[19] But, in drawing back, in weakening their argument, they are prepared to say that some

---

[15] Berkhof p641.

[16] See end note on p149 for excursus: 'By linking baptism and assurance, many lose contact with reality'.

[17] Berkhof p641.

[18] John H.Armstrong p63. In other words, baptism is a seal – but not always! But a seal is always a seal, or it is no seal at all.

[19] See end note on p150 for excursus: 'Sibbes on infant baptism as a seal'.

of the infants who 'are appointed heirs and will receive the heritage' do not receive it because 'they show themselves unworthy of it and refuse it'. In other words, God may appoint these infants to salvation, and by his authority they receive the seal of assurance that they have it, but they do not actually receive it because they prove themselves unworthy of it! A question suggests itself: Do infant baptisers believe in salvation by divine grace or by human merit? Furthermore, we are told, these infants, although appointed by God to receive salvation, do not receive it because they 'refuse it'. What is this? Calvinism or what? My question is: Has God appointed these infants – who are sealed by their baptism – to salvation, or not? Can we have a clear, unequivocal statement to settle it once and for all? Instead of tinkering with their argument, infant baptisers ought to jettison it. Or else they ought to have the courage of their convictions and say that all baptised infants *are* sealed, guaranteed and confirmed as regenerate. Then, at least, we would all know where we stand.

Let us come to *facts*. In the New Testament, believers are sealed by the Holy Spirit (2 Cor. 1:22; Eph. 1:13-14; 4:30). Infant baptisers like to claim that baptism and the Lord's supper are seals; clearly, it fits in with their defence of infant baptism. But what verse says that baptism and the Lord's supper are seals for believers? Not one! It is pure invention! The only sealing for believers, with the New Testament meaning of the word, is the sealing with the Holy Spirit. And there is none of Berkhof's *unless* about that sealing! It *is* a seal. *That* is the New Testament equivalent to what is said of Abraham in Romans 4:11; not water baptism or the supper. There is no basis whatsoever in that verse for the baptism of infants. It has nothing to do with the subject of baptism. For infant baptisers to use Romans 4:11 in order to sustain their practice is a travesty of scriptural exposition.

David Clarkson, Owen's colleague and successor, argued that just as 'an unbeliever has nothing to do with the promises... and... nothing to do with the covenant, so neither' has he anything to do 'with the seals of it. What right has he to the seals?' he asked. 'The covenant is evidence for heaven, under the hand and seal of God; a deed of gift under the seal of heaven. How does the seal belong to him, who has nothing to do with the deed?' he demanded. Allowing for a moment the mistaken view that the ordinances are a seal, Clarkson was right; a man must be a believer before he can receive the seal of faith. That much is obvious. Clarkson then distinguished between what he called 'the audible promise' – the gospel preached – and 'the visible promise' – the ordinances of baptism and the Lord's supper. He argued:

Now he that [is an unbeliever] has no right to the audible promise, that which offers pardon and life to the ear, has no right to the visible promise, which offers pardon and life to the eye, since the very same thing is tendered in both. As we must not apply the audible promise to an unbeliever, so must we not apply the visible promise; there is the very same reason for both. The promise belongs to believers.

As I say, in his main argument, Clarkson was correct; unbelievers have no interest in Christ, they are not united in covenant to him, the promises of pardon and life do not belong to them.[20] As a consequence, unbelievers have no right whatsoever to the ordinances. Therefore unbelievers cannot be baptised; they cannot take the Lord's supper. Just so. Unfortunately, in the light of what he had declared, Clarkson then made a very odd statement: 'The promise belongs to believers and their seed, both visible and audible promises' belong to them, 'for they' – both sets of promises – 'should never be separated'.[21] He went on quite properly to say, however:

Neither of them belongs to unbelievers, nor their seed, for they are not the heirs of promise. And to make over the inheritance, or the seals and evidences of it to them, would be to give the heir's inheritance, in its sealed evidences, to pretenders and intruders, to those to whom Christ in his will and testament never bequeathed it – an injustice that we should use all our care to avoid. While a man is visibly in unbelief, nothing can be sealed to him but condemnation, because he has no evidence for anything else.[22]

What did Clarkson mean? He was right when he categorically stated that the covenant promises and the ordinances do not belong to unbelievers. (To put it positively, they belong only to believers). But, on the other hand, he was wrong when he asserted they do belong to

---

[20] I am not, of course, saying the commands, invitations and promises of the gospel should not be issued to unbelievers, but the promises *belong* only to believers. They are appropriated by *faith*.
[21] Does this mean the babies of believers can have the Lord's supper in addition to baptism? As we shall see, most – but not all – infant baptisers draw back from this. Why?
[22] Clarkson p93.

believers *and their children*. In particular, he was wrong when he claimed that Christ bequeathed both the promises and the ordinances to the children of believers. He asserted that believers' children are heirs of Christ's will and testament. Did he mean this? Really? In that case, what of those children of believers who prove to be unbelievers at the last – did Christ bequeath the covenant to them? Are they heirs of Christ's promise? They have received its 'sealed evidences'; it is theirs! And yet they, like all other unbelievers, will be damned for ever. Imagine it! Sinners who have received the seal of the covenant, supposedly bequeathed to them by Christ, guaranteed that they are in the covenant, yet separated from him for ever in hell. The idea is incredible![23]

And why are the children of unbelievers to be considered 'visibly in unbelief', while the children of Christians are to be treated as believers? Are not all children – all children – born in sin and unbelief? Now the New Testament teaches us that until a sinner believes in Christ, he has no right whatsoever to the new covenant nor the ordinances. The central theme of Clarkson's own reasoning was correctly based upon it. Sadly, he ruined all when he allowed some, who have not believed, a right to covenant promises and the ordinances. He did this when he included the children of believers in both. But since no child can be considered a believer, it is a gross abuse to allow any child, as any unbeliever, to partake of the ordinances. As Clarkson himself observed, such a step is wrong; we should do all we can to avoid it. In short, children should not be baptised.

Charles Hodge commented on Ephesians 2:4. He rightly said that all children 'are born in a state of condemnation. They need redemption from the moment of their birth'. Reader, what conclusion do you think Hodge drew from this? He wrote – astonishingly – 'and therefore the seal of redemption is applied to them in baptism, which

---

[23] How demeaning to God! In ordinary commerce, if we make a claim under guarantee and the guarantor does not stand by his word and promise, there will be ructions to play. Quite right, too. Well, will God not stand by his seal and guarantee? The very suggestion that he will not is blasphemous. The flaw, of course, is for men to tell all (any!) baptised infants (or their parents!) that they – the infants – are sealed.

otherwise would be a senseless ceremony'.[24] In other words, just because they need redemption, they are to be given the guarantee that they are redeemed! What a contradiction. What utter confusion of thought. If that does not demonstrate that infant baptism is 'a senseless ceremony', nothing will.

But it may be much worse than that. Did Hodge mean something else? Did he mean that the infant needs redemption, and by his baptism he actually gets it? If so, his words were Popish. What now of those who believe such error? And even if Hodge did not intend to say anything of the sort, note the real risk that somebody reading his words on infant baptism might believe it. This is my concern throughout this book; I am not interested in an academic discussion about infant baptism; it is the eternal consequences of the practice which disturb me. And all who teach that baptism is a seal, ought to think about the eternal consequences of their claim.

---

[24] Charles Hodge: *Ephesians* p111.

End notes to Argument 5: Baptism Is a Seal

By linking baptism and assurance, many lose contact with reality

I repeat the note with which I started this paragraph: The points I make here apply equally to Baptists who think baptism is a seal – even if they do not explicitly make the same claims as infant baptisers. The fact is, if baptism is a seal, it is a seal! And this goes for both infant and believer's baptism.

There is a massive point here. By linking baptism and assurance, many lose contact with reality – and it all comes from the false premise that baptism is a seal. Take Lloyd-Jones who, despite all he rightly said about assurance elsewhere, could allege: 'Baptism is an assurance that we are delivered from the guilt of sin and, also, the pollution of sin... Baptism tells me that I am regenerate; it certifies to me that I am born again, that I am united to Christ, and that the Holy Spirit dwells in me... And thus God stoops to our weakness, authenticates our faith, gives us assurance and strengthens and fortifies us when we are attacked by the devil, who tries to tempt us into unbelief' (Lloyd-Jones: *The Church* pp38,46). Really? Where did Lloyd-Jones find such talk in Scripture? Baptism does not do what he said it does. It *reminds* me of the things he listed, and *instructs* me – and others – about them, but it does not *tell* me, *certify* me or *assure* me that they are mine.

How is a believer to be assured? Lloyd-Jones is not the only one to go grievously astray on baptism and assurance. Listen to what Calvin said: 'We ought to consider that at whatever time we are baptised, we are washed and purified once for the whole of life. Wherefore, as often as we fall, we must recall the remembrance of our baptism, and thus fortify our minds, so as to feel certain and secure of the remission of sins. For though, once administered, it seems to have passed, it is not abolished by subsequent sins. For the purity of Christ was therein offered to us, always is in force, and is not destroyed by any stain; it wipes and washes away all our defilements... Believers become assured by baptism, that this condemnation is entirely withdrawn from them' (Calvin: *Institutes* Vol.2 pp514,518). Note the ambiguity (at least in this translation) in Calvin. Those baptised, according to Calvin, are washed and purified from sin. On the other hand, the purity of Christ is only 'offered' in baptism. Which is it? As always, of course, I suspect most of Calvin's followers pay attention to the former and quietly ignore the latter – leaving the theologians to escape, as they think, the consequences, as and when required, by making appropriate use of the get-out clause.

Luther, too, looked to baptism for assurance, as do his modern-day followers: 'As Luther so often emphasised, baptism is a great treasure to which Christians can turn daily for comfort and strength' (taken from the website of the Lutheran Church Missouri Synod answers to question under 'Born Again'). 'When sin and conscience oppress us... you may say: It is a fact that I am baptised, but, being baptised, I have the promise that I shall be saved and obtain eternal life for both soul and body' (Dave Armstrong quoting Luther's

Large Catechism). Pelikan: 'Assurance which the sacrament was intended to provide... Luther could console himself with his baptism in hours of temptation, defying the devil with the cry: "I have been baptised!" precisely because it had been done *to* him, not *by* him' (Pelikan pp94,96, emphasis his). I make two points. *First*, how very different is this to Paul. When a believer needs assurance – when he has to meet 'a charge against God's elect' from one who would 'condemn' him (Rom. 8:33-34) – let him not look to his baptism ('I have been baptised'); let him use the argument of the apostle in Rom. 8:31-39. 'It is Christ who died, and furthermore is also risen, who is even at the right hand of God, who also makes intercession for us'. Baptism indeed! Baptism is significant in the passage only because of its absence! *Secondly*, what if the unregenerate (though baptised as babies) do as Luther and Calvin counselled, and draw, from their baptism, the assurance they were guaranteed by their theologians? This is no idle question. It is precisely what many of them do! See Lusk: 'Paedobaptism' pp111-112 for the kind of practical counsel infant baptisers are supposed to give their children as they grow up. For comfort in a thunderstorm, loneliness at school, facing teenage temptations, to keep them from drugs and immorality, the answer is the same: 'Baptism... baptism... baptism... baptised... baptism'. This, so these growing children are to be told, is the guarantee (and the means) that 'they are not their own, but have been bought with the precious blood of the Son of God. They have been graciously claimed by the triune God and marked with his name'. Yet, sadly, some of these will never be regenerated. Such 'assurance' is nothing but a disgrace! Where, in Scripture, are we encouraged to draw this kind of assurance from baptism? The baptismal silence in Eph. 6:1-4; 2 Tim. 3:14-15 is deafening.

Sibbes on infant baptism as a seal

Sibbes was not afraid to attribute the most enormous benefits to 'every infant that is baptised'; by their baptism they 'have union with the death of Christ', and must think of their baptism when they pray, worship, are tempted... indeed, 'upon all occasions'. As for reading (not excluding the Bible), for those who cannot or will not read, let them 'read their book in their baptism'. Reader, don't take my word for it; listen to Sibbes, and ponder his very own words: 'The means of salvation, and... the seal likewise, which is baptism... As the whole Trinity was at the baptism of Christ, so every infant that is baptised is the child of Christ. And it is a special thing that we should meditate on... There are many that are not book-learned, that cannot read; at least they have no leisure to read. I would they would read their book in their baptism; and if they would consider what it ministers to them upon all occasions, they would be better Christians than they are. Think of your baptism when you go to God, especially when he seems angry... It is the seal of your covenant; you have gone before me by your grace; you brought me into the covenant before I knew my right hand from my left. So when we go to church to offer our

151

service to God, think, by baptism we were consecrated and dedicated to God. We not only receive grace from God, but we give ourselves to God. Therefore it is sacrilege for persons baptised to yield to temptations to sin. We are dedicated to God in baptism. When we are tempted to despair, let us think of our baptism. We are in the covenant of grace, and have received the seal of the covenant, baptism. The devil is an uncircumcised, damned, cursed spirit. He is out of the covenant. But I am in the covenant. Christ is mine; the Holy Ghost is mine; and God is mine. Therefore let us stand against all the temptations of that uncircumcised, unbaptised, damned spirit. The thinking of our baptism thus will help us to "resist the devil" (Jas. 4:7). He is a coward; if he is resisted, he will flee; and what will better resist him than the covenant of grace and the seal of it? When we are tempted to sin, let us think: What have I to do with sin? By baptism I have union with the death of Christ; he died to take away sin, and my end must be his. I must abolish sin in my flesh. Shall I yield to that which in baptism I have sworn against? And then if we be tempted to despair for sin, let us call to mind the promises of grace and forgiveness of sins, and the seal of forgiveness of sins, which is baptism. For as water in baptism washes the body, so the blood of Christ washes the soul. Let us make that use of our baptism, in temptations, not to despair for sin. And in conversing among men, let us labour to maintain the unity of the Spirit (Eph. 4:3,5)... one baptism... They forget their baptism that are... in quarrels... And then for our children... let us make use of baptism. Do they die in their infancy? Make this use of it: I have assured hope that my child is gone to God. He was born in the covenant, and had the seal of the covenant, baptism; why should I doubt of the salvation of my child? If they live to years of discretion, then be of good comfort; he is God's child more than mine; I have dedicated him to God and to Christ, he was baptised in the name of Christ, Christ will care for him as well as for me. If I leave my children behind me, they are God's and Christ's children. They have received the seal of the covenant, baptism. Christ will provide for them. And he that provides heaven for them will provide all things in the way to heaven necessary. God has said: "I will be the God of you and of your children" (Ps. 132:12). They are in the covenant. Yours they were, Lord. A man may commit his children to God on his death bed... as before... by baptism. All this we have by thinking of our baptism' (Sibbes: *Lydia* pp530-531; see also *2 Corinthians 1* pp451,462; *Demand* pp488-490).

Reader, words fail... almost. How much here is given to baptism which belongs to Christ! How many have been misled by the link Sibbes made between water and the blood of Christ? What categorical promises are here heaped upon each other – and all laid at the feet of baptism! Can any infant-baptiser produce an infant who swore anything at his baptism? Do infant baptisers agree with the staggering claims Sibbes made for the baptism of their babies? I have to leave it there; as I say, words fail. I simply cannot understand how such material can be published by evangelicals.

Argument 5: Baptism Is a Seal

I freely admit that Sibbes, in common with so many Reformed infant-baptisers, had his qualifiers – *elsewhere*. I cannot find them *here* in *Lydia*. Qualifiers such as 'we reverse our baptism in some sort'; 'there is [an] outward baptism as well as [an] inward' (this, of course, is perfectly correct – but not as a qualifier for sacramental infant baptism!); 'a man may have all these privileges, and yet notwithstanding be a slave in the bosom of the church'; 'unless now we believe in Christ, and renounce the devil, we renounce our baptism' (Sibbes: *2 Corinthians 1* p451; *Excellency* p219; *Demand* pp478-491; see also *Bowels* p169; *2 Corinthians 1* pp462-463). I know also that Sibbes could speak of baptism as entrance into the church – by which he meant 'the visible church' (Sibbes: *2 Corinthians 1* pp462-463; *Fountain* p511). I also acknowledge that Mark E.Dever made the best case he could when, noting that Sibbes' words in *2 Corinthians 1* p451 'could be taken as assuming baptismal regeneration', he went on: 'Upon careful reading in context, it clearly does not' (Dever p113). I fully accept that, in context, 'with careful reading', Sibbes was talking about the *profession* of Christianity. I note that he warned: 'Let us... try ourselves... whether we are anointed or not... let us not deceive ourselves... If I am a Christian, if I am not only a titular Christian... If I am a real Christian... If I am a Christian' (Sibbes: *2 Corinthians 1* pp442-451). But more needs to be said about this 'careful reading'. Why should such an important issue need 'careful reading'? And what is this 'assuming'? In a sermon, shouldn't Sibbes have made sure he never left the slightest chance – risk – that anyone might 'assume' such a diabolical error as baptismal regeneration? (And in the published volume, shouldn't Thomas Manton, in his 'editorial supervision', have taken greater care?) What is more, as Sibbes himself made clear elsewhere (see above), he knew he was preaching to those who could not or would not read the Bible – let alone give close study to the minutiae of his qualifiers – and he actually capitalised on it. In any case, since he was *preaching*, how could his *hearers* carefully *read* his words? And he *was* preaching! Manton called the volume, 'these discourses' (Sibbes: *2 Corinthians 1* pp2,4), and Dever stated that 'Sibbes published no learned theological treatises except for his sermons' (Dever p98). Finally, let me quote the passage in question: 'So when we are basely tempted to courses unbefitting our dignity, answer them from our baptism: "I am baptised into Christ, and so am become a Christian, and this [behaviour to which I am tempted] is unbecoming to the profession of Christianity. I beseech you, let us remember our calling. We are called to be prophets, kings and priests, and not only here, but in the world to come we shall be so. We must not think to be kings in heaven, except we begin it here. It is with a Christian, as it was with David. He was anointed many years before he was actually a king upon the throne... So we are anointed in this world; in part, we are kings while we are here; kings over ourselves, and over the world. A Christian sees all under him that is worldly, he treads the moon under his feet... We must now carry ourselves as those that shall be kings.

Those that are not kings here, shall never be kings hereafter; those that are not priests here, shall never walk with Christ in heaven... Eternal life is begun here, in all the parts of it. And therefore I beseech you, if our memories are so shallow that we cannot remember other bonds, let us remember our baptism, let us read our duty in our baptism. What are we baptised into? Into Christ; that is, to take the name of Christ upon us, to be Christians; which name implies these three – to be a king, priest and prophet. What do we [do] then when we sin? We reverse our baptism in some sort' (Sibbes: *2 Corinthians 1* p451). Yes, I quite agree, the qualifiers are there – *but so are the massive and dogmatic statements*. I quite agree that by 'careful reading', Sibbes' claims can be seen to be references to the *profession* of Christianity. But, as always, it is not the 'careful reading' of the academic which matters here – *what do the parents with the infant at the font think*? What do they think when they *hear* the words? In Sibbes' day, what did those parents who could not or would not read, think?

Let us hear some more from Sibbes: 'The sacraments are mysteries, because... in [baptism], under water, a visible outward thing, there is signified [if only Sibbes had kept to this and nothing more!] the blood of Christ... The Spirit does not only teach the truths of the gospel, but the application of those truths, that they are ours. This truth of the gospel is mine; the sacrament seals it to me' (Sibbes: *Fountain* pp462-469). Even so: 'To our children, when they come to years, baptism is an obligation to believe; because they have received the seal beforehand, and it is a means to believe' (Sibbes: *Lydia* pp530-531; see also *Demand* pp486-487). An obligation? Sibbes said it was a seal. When did a seal become an obligation? What etymology links the two words? Is baptism a seal or is it not? If it is a seal, it is a seal of the justifying faith which is possessed by the person baptised. How then can a seal be regarded as an obligation to do something, and obtain something, which the seal has already certified and guaranteed as a possession? And what is this about baptism being a *means* to believe? Baptism is only for those who *do* believe!

Elsewhere, Sibbes spoke of *two* seals [where did he find *that* in Scripture?] – 'the common broad seal of God [and] his privy seal'. By 'the common broad seal', Sibbes meant infant baptism; by the 'privy seal', he meant the biblical sealing of the Holy Spirit – 'the sealing of the Spirit after we believe... that our faith is a sound belief, and that we are in the state of grace indeed'. Sibbes went on: 'It is not sufficient that we have the one [infant baptism], that we have admittance into the church by baptism, but we must have this privy seal [the sealing of the Spirit] which Christ sets and stamps upon the soul of a true Christian... When Satan comes to the soul, and shakes the confidence of it, and says: "You are not a Christian, and God does not love you"; why! says the soul, God has loved me, and pardoned my sins; he has given me promises, and particularly sealed them in the sacrament; here is the excellency of the sacrament, it comes more home than the word, it seals the general promise of God particularly to myself. I am sealed in the sacrament, and withal I find the stamp of the Spirit in my heart; and therefore having the inward work of the Spirit, and God having fortified the inward work, and strengthened my faith by the outward seal, I can therefore stand against any temptation whatsoever. They are excellent both together, but the special thing that must comfort, must be the hidden seal of the Spirit. Let us labour therefore to be sealed inwardly' (Sibbes: *2 Corinthians 1* pp456-463).

Let me try to summarise Sibbes. The seal of infant baptism, comes first. This, if the baby dies, proves effective; if, however, the baby lives, it can be ineffective. (In addition to the above, see below; see also Sibbes: *2 Corinthians 1* p462; *Lydia* p531; *Demand* pp486-487). But after coming to faith, a man receives the sealing of the Spirit. Just so! This *is* the biblical position. But then, Sibbes argued, the first seal – his infant baptism, which has now proved effective – fortifies the second seal, the inward work of the Spirit! Indeed, the believer may say: 'I am sealed in the sacrament, and withal [along with it] I find the stamp of the Spirit in my heart'. Even so, all those baptised as infants must labour to be sealed by the Spirit! What an incredible muddle! May I ask how the weaker, 'common', outward seal – being sprinkled in water as a baby, years before – can confirm and fortify the 'privy' inward seal – the work of the Holy Spirit in a believer? According to Sibbes, for anyone reaching the years of discretion, the seal of his infant baptism is ineffective until he comes to saving faith – and yet, said Sibbes, a man receives the inward work of the Spirit along with the baptism! In short, does the Spirit inwardly seal by, through and with the outward baptism, or does he not? What is more, why do we never read any apostle saying such things as Sibbes about two seals to the growing children of believers in the New Testament – children who had, according to infant baptisers, been sprinkled and sealed as a baby? And which verse urges baptised (let alone infant-baptised) believers to 'labour to be sealed inwardly'?

Argument 6

John's Baptism

Infant baptisers insist that when John the Baptist baptised he did so on the same principle as that which governed the Jews when they circumcised infants. Hanko, for instance, said that 'baptism was about to take the place of circumcision', but the change-over was smooth, since this was ensured by the continuity between the two Testaments. We have looked at these claims in previous pages, and found them mistaken; baptism did not replace circumcision, the church did not exist in the Old Testament, and while there is some continuity between the Testaments, the real discontinuity between them must not be glossed over. Nevertheless, based on the faulty foundation he had laid, Hanko proceeded to assert that the principle under which John baptised was 'believers and their seed'. This claim must be measured against Scripture. We know that in:

The beginning of the gospel of Jesus Christ, the Son of God... John came baptising in the wilderness and preaching a baptism of repentance for the remission of sins. And all the land of Judea, and those of Jerusalem, went out to him and were all baptised by him in the Jordan River, confessing their sins... In those days John the Baptist came preaching... saying: 'Repent, for the kingdom of heaven is at hand!'... Then Jerusalem, all Judea, and all the region around the Jordan went out to him and were baptised by him in the Jordan, confessing their sins. But when he saw many of the Pharisees and Sadducees coming to his baptism, he said to them: 'Brood of vipers! Who has warned you to flee from the wrath to come? Therefore bear fruits worthy of repentance...'... I indeed baptise you with water unto repentance, but he who is coming after me... he will baptise you with the Holy Spirit and fire (Mark 1:1-5; Matt. 3:1-12).[1]

John baptised. Whom? He baptised only those who were repentant; he insisted on it. Clearly this excluded infants, not because they were infants, but because they could not repent. They were automatically excluded by John's demands for evidence of repentance before he

---

[1] Hanko: *We* p107.

baptised. But according to the claims of infant baptisers, John was at fault. He should have baptised a man who was repentant, *and his children with him*, 'believers and their seed', as Hanko put it. Indeed, Hanko said that is the principle under which John *did* baptise. Yet John clearly did not. Hanko's claim, therefore, collapses.

John did not baptise those who repented *and their children*. Why not? Whatever the reason, it is clear that John was not operating under the principle of a man and his child. There is only one explanation. John was baptising in a new era; as Mark stated, it was 'the beginning of the gospel of Jesus Christ'. Just so. A new era! A new age! A new law or canon! The Old Testament principle had gone, the New had come (Luke 16:16). In the old covenant, it was a man *and his children*. Not so in the new covenant. John's baptism, far from establishing infant baptism, goes a long way to destroying it.

Hanko admitted that it was 'not likely' that John did baptise children, even though, he alleged, it was the 'background... principle... [and] context' of his ministry. Hanko's suggestion to explain this – which to be fair, he did not press – was that 'in the rugged desert country... it was not likely that people would take their children with them'. But as he rightly said: 'We may not make conclusions on the basis of silence'.[2] Reader, it is a pity that infant baptisers do not remember and act upon that principle when they do argue from silence, as we shall discover in coming pages. What is more, there is no need to reason from silence. We do not have to speak about what is 'likely'. We are told! John baptised those who repented. And only those. That is what it says in the Bible. John did not baptise those who repented, *and their children with them*; this is the point.

May I spend a moment on 'silence'? Although I will have more to say on it, the point here is this: Hanko claimed that John baptised children, working on the basis of the parent and his child, but, as he acknowledged, there is no proof or evidence of this in the scriptural record.[3] Indeed, Scripture, as he recognised, is silent on the matter. Just so. But what does this 'silence' 'prove'? It certainly does *not* prove that John worked on the principle in question. Not at all! The

---

[2] Hanko: *We* pp105-106.
[3] Where is the evidence that the hundreds? thousands? about to be baptised, first went home, fetched their (spouse and) children (and grandchildren and great-grandchildren), and then were all baptised together? Is it at all likely?

silence at best 'proves' neutral – at best! In fact, of course, the silence here means there is no scriptural justification for the claim, and, therefore, that it should never have been made in the first place.[4]

Consider the disciples of Jesus, who were also baptising just after John; indeed, at the same time for a while (John 3:22-26; 4:1-2). Did the disciples of Jesus baptise those who repented, *and their children with them*? Of course not. There is no doubt that the disciples of Jesus baptised in the same way as John did. The alternative is unthinkable; imagine the chaos which would have ensued. Consequently, when the apostles came to baptise in Acts 2:38 – on the basis of repentance – why would they have altered their practice? According to infant baptisers, after Pentecost they baptised believers and their children. But why would the apostles restore the Old Testament system of the children along with the father, when before Pentecost they had already moved to the New Testament basis? Why would they suddenly go back? It is foolish to think it. They baptised only repentant believers; not believers *and their children*. In the light of this, the practice of Philip is very significant. Acts 8:12 reads: 'But when they believed Philip as he preached the things concerning the kingdom of God and the name of Jesus Christ, both men and women were baptised'. Notice, both men and women who believed were baptised – not men and women *and their children*. If only infant baptisers would baptise in the way Philip did! If only they would baptise those who repent and believe; and only those.

John baptised only those who showed signs of repentance. In this, he was completely consistent with the rest of the New Testament. It is not a question of infant or adult baptism. Baptism is always and only the baptism of those who repent (and believe).

---

[4] John Davenant gave good advice: When 'no word [on an important topic] occurs in the holy Scriptures', 'it is rash to assert it' (Davenant p115). There is a world of difference in claiming scriptural warrant for a practice because Scripture does not forbid it, and denying scriptural warrant for a practice because Scripture does not sanction it.

Argument 7

Infant Baptisers Claim that Apostolic Household Baptism Justifies the Baptism of Infants

Infant baptisers appeal to the apostolic practice of baptising households; Lydia's for one: 'And when she and her household were baptised' (Acts 16:15). However, there is no hint whatsoever of what is meant by 'her household'. Whether it included infants is impossible to say, but that it included (or meant) servants and employees is impossible to deny. We just do not know. To build a practice as far-reaching as infant baptism on this verse would seem to be ludicrous.[1]

---

[1] I return to an earlier extract from Sibbes. While I do not say he *built* his case upon Lydia's experience, he did not mind lurching from the clear statement of Scripture to this: Lydia 'had the means of salvation, and she had the seal likewise, which is baptism. [It is not – see earlier]... As the whole Trinity was at the baptism of Christ, so every infant that is baptised is the child of Christ... You see the holy [believing] woman here would be baptised immediately; she would have the seal of the covenant... For our children... let us make use of baptism. Do they die in their infancy? Make this use of it: I have assured hope that my child is gone to God. He was born in the covenant, and had the seal of the covenant, baptism; why should I doubt of the salvation of my child? If they live to years of discretion, then be of good comfort, he is God's child more than mine; I have dedicated him to God and to Christ, he was baptised in the name of Christ, Christ will care for him as well as for me. If I leave my children behind me, they are God's and Christ's children. They have received the seal of the covenant, baptism. Christ will provide for them. And he that provides heaven for them will provide all things in the way to heaven necessary. God has said: "I will be the God of you and of your children" (Ps. 132:12). They are in the covenant. Yours they were, Lord. A man may commit his children to God on his death bed... as before... by baptism. All this we have by thinking of our baptism... And to our children, when they come to years, baptism is an obligation to believe; because they have received the seal beforehand, and it is a means to believe' (Sibbes: *Lydia* pp530-531). I have no doubt that Sibbes, 'after [William] Perkins... was the most significant of the

As far as Lydia's household is concerned, nobody can say that infants were included, and nobody can say that they were not included.[2] There is more evidence in the case of the family of the Philippian jailer: 'And immediately he and all his family were baptised' (Acts 16:33). We know that Paul and Silas included the household with the man when they issued the gospel promise (Acts 16:31), after which 'they spoke the word of the Lord to him and to all who were in his house' (Acts 16:32). Then he and all his family were baptised, and 'he rejoiced, having believed in God with all his household' (Acts 16:34). I frankly admit that I have no idea of the ages of the parties involved. Nor does anybody else. It is irrelevant.[3] But what is very clear is this:

---

great Puritan preachers of Cambridge' (Packer's cover blurb), but judging by the above, when these great Puritan preachers saw the word 'baptism' in a passage, reason, commonsense and – above all – proper biblical exegesis, went out of the window, and sentiment flew in. See earlier for my comments on this extract. All I ask, now, is for some infant-baptiser to write to me and explain how all this talk about babies comes from a passage which does not mention the word. Did Lydia have a husband, let alone a baby?

[2] 'It is not to be doubted but that [Lydia] received and embraced the faith of Christ sincerely... before Paul would admit her unto baptism... Lydia had not in her hand the hearts of all those who were of her household, that she might turn unto Christ whomsoever she would; but the Lord did bless her godly desire, so that she had all her household obedient' (Calvin: *Commentaries* Vol.19 Part 1 pp104-105). Lydia was not baptised until she had believed. Good! Lydia could not make her household believe, although she no doubt desired it. Good! But what did Calvin mean when he said: 'The Lord did bless her godly desire, so that she had all her household obedient'? Did he mean that the Lord granted her wish and answered her prayer so that all her household were obedient to Christ in his gospel? I think so. If so, I agree. But if he meant (I do not think his words can possibly bear the meaning, myself – see also his comments on Acts 16 below) that Lydia got her household servants to obey her command to be baptised even though they were unbelieving, I staunchly disagree. All who believe and are obedient to the gospel must be baptised; and no others. Nobody may be baptised on the faith and obedience of another. And although there is not a suggestion of any baby in the passage – not even a baby may be baptised because of the faith of its parent.

[3] But if infants are involved, we have to believe that they were taken from their beds (cots) in the small hours, listened to the preaching, were baptised, and then sat down to a meal and rejoiced in their father's new-found faith. See Beasley-Murray: *Baptism in the New Testament* p315.

however old or young they were, they all heard the gospel, and they all believed, following which they were all baptised.[4] This is the constant and consistent practice throughout the New Testament. Household baptism is perfectly apostolic – as long as all the above conditions are met. If only infant baptisers would stick to this pattern and order, there would be no need for this discussion. All who hear the gospel and believe must be baptised, and only they – household or no household.[5]

There is another point. The notion that the children were included in the father's faith, proves too much. Acts 16:31 is unequivocal. Paul's promise cannot be limited to baptism. He did not even mention baptism! If the children are included in the father's faith, then the children are *saved*. 'Believe on the Lord Jesus Christ, and you will be *saved*, you and your household'. What Paul meant, of course, when addressing the jailer thus, was that the way of salvation is by faith; only those who believe will be saved; but all who do believe will be saved; *and this is as true as much for your house as for you*. All who believe are saved. Paul certainly did not mean that if the jailer believed he would be saved, and that his family would be swept into Christ on the coat-tails of his faith.[6]

In Acts 11, Peter told the Jews that he had been sent by God to preach the gospel to Cornelius. That this was of God, was confirmed to the apostle by the revelation to Cornelius himself, that Peter would come and 'tell you words by which you and all your household will be saved' (Acts 11:14). This is highly significant. All the household would be saved – not merely baptised. Infant baptisers want to be dogmatic and say that households include infants. If that is the case, then in this instance the promise meant that the infants would be saved with all the rest of the household. And it must have meant saved in

---

[4] 'God... brought all his whole family unto a godly consent' (Calvin: *Commentaries* Vol.19 Part 1 p122). This is all I ask; all who come to 'a godly consent' must be baptised; and no others. Nobody may be baptised on 'the godly consent' of another, whoever he or she may be.

[5] See Lloyd-Jones: *The Church* p41.

[6] See Beasley-Murray: *Baptism in the New Testament* pp319-320; *Baptism Today and Tomorrow* pp116-123. Alford: '"And your house" does not mean that *his* faith would save his household – but that the same way was open to them as to him: "Believe, and you will be saved; and the same of [goes for] your household"' (Alford p764, emphasis his).

such a way that everybody could see it. Reader, we must be very clear about it. Peter was not given a promise that salvation would take place at the time, but would become evident only after several years had passed. Most definitely not! The promise was that the household would be saved under Peter's preaching. And it would take place *at that time*. That was the clear intention of the promise. Infant baptisers must be consistent. If the household included infants, those infants would be saved that very day under Peter's preaching. And their salvation would be clearly evident. If there was an intended delay, why was the salvation of the adults not in the same category? Were the adults to be saved that day, yet the evidence be delayed for several years? Is this what the promise amounted to? The idea is preposterous.

It is certain, is it not, that the promise referred to the members of the household who could believe the gospel and give credible evidence of faith. That is what happened in any event. As Peter preached to the household – and Cornelius' 'relatives and close friends' (Acts 10:24) – 'the Holy Spirit fell on all those who heard the word' (Acts 10:44). On all of them! He then baptised those who gave evidence of having received the Holy Spirit (Acts 10:47-48). But he baptised all of them who clearly had been saved. By God's grace they had repented (Acts 11:18).[7] It is beyond question that households, in this context, are

---

[7] 'This is the... lawful order, that the minister admit those unto the receiving of the outward sign whom God has testified to be his children by the mark and pledge of his Spirit; so that faith and doctrine are first'. So it is! Calvin, however, went on to dismiss, as 'without all reason', 'the unlearned' who 'infer... that infants are not to be baptised'. Calvin was sure 'that God has adopted the children of the faithful before they be born', and therefore they can be baptised. What an 'unlearned' deduction from the passage and his own comments! 'As touching the manifest grace of the Spirit, there is no absurdity' in baptising infants, said Calvin, 'if [the grace of the Spirit] follows [in point of time] after baptism' (Calvin: *Commentaries* Vol.18 Part 2 pp453-454). But this 'if' takes us back to an earlier point; *if* baptised infants do not, in the end, experience grace, then their baptism *was* an absurdity – and worse! And even if they do, Calvin was still putting the cart before the horse.
In any case, there is a far more important point. Did Calvin mean 'since' and not 'if'? Was he teaching that the reality always follows the figure? If so, not only is it an abominable claim, it contradicts what he said elsewhere; namely, that because babies have the reality, they must be given the figure. Which did Calvin believe comes first – the reality or the figure? I ask again: Does

162

those in the family or home who are capable of hearing the gospel preached, who are capable of repenting and believing, and thus capable of being baptised.[8] What is more, even before conversion, Cornelius was said to be 'a devout man and one who feared God with all his household' (Acts 10:2). It would seem very clear that either his household could not have included any infants, or that the infants in the family were not, for this purpose, included in the term 'household'. Can infants be properly said 'to fear God'? If they can, why do infant baptisers agree that infants cannot exercise repentance and faith?

Crispus 'believed on the Lord with all his household. And many of the Corinthians, hearing, believed and were baptised' (Acts 18:8). There is nothing here to support infant baptism, for the reasons given above concerning the households of the jailer and Cornelius. They all believed before they were baptised.[9] Nor can anything be built upon 'the household of Stephanas' (1 Cor. 1:16) except, that since Crispus is mentioned in the context (1 Cor. 1:14), it would appear that the same conditions applied in his case. There is one other thing. We know that 'the household of Stephanas... the firstfruits of Achaia... devoted themselves to the ministry of the saints', and that the church at Corinth had to submit to them (1 Cor. 16:15-16). Would infant baptisers apply *these* words to *infants*?[10]

Infant baptisers cannot support their practice by the baptism of households, which is, on the contrary, entirely consistent with the

---

anybody know Calvin's position? The Bible is clear as to which comes first – the reality! Only those who believe are to be baptised.

[8] Is there any suggestion, in the text, that infants or children were present? Or if they were, that they believingly heard Peter's preaching of the gospel, openly received the Spirit and were baptised? Or if too young to believe, that they were baptised because one or other of their parents (or grandparents or great-grandparents) believed and was baptised? Or if the infants and children were not present, that they were fetched to be baptised with their parents upon *their* profession of faith? And what about the servants? And what about *their* children?

[9] The house believed *with* him – not through or in him.

[10] Ignatius, writing to Polycarp about his wife, spoke of 'the whole of her house and her children', thus clearly distinguishing between the 'house' and the 'children'. S.I.Buse, quoting this, went on to dismiss the attempt to establish infant baptism by reference to 'households', as 'efforts to prop up a tottering edifice' (Buse p124).

baptism of believers only. Despite this, Legg blatantly said: 'The point is that in each case baptism is given to the household because of the faith of the head of the household'.[11] This is manifestly untrue. The evidence of Scripture is that all in the household who were baptised, were baptised because *they all individually believed*, not because the head of the family believed. As Wright said:

In the New Testament documents... the intimate association between being a believer and being baptised is inescapable, both in that faith and its profession are a requirement for baptism... If infants were included in these household baptisms [at Philippi], they were so as believers.[12]

Such a testimony, from such a source, ought to put a stop to the excessive (and nonsensical) claims made by infant baptisers over household baptism. I fear, however, it will not.

What is more, if all the persons in a household are to be baptised when the head of the house is converted, does this mean that all adult children and servants will be baptised, even if they are not converted, make no profession, and are, in fact, totally hostile to the gospel? Will they be forced to be baptised? Or will they be baptised only if they are merely acquiescent and nominally Christian? Legg tackled this very real and practical question: 'We should baptise the children of believers within our churches. This will include the children of new converts. This raises the problem of those who are no longer babies or even little children. At what age does one draw the line?' he asked. But why does Legg want to draw any line? Who gives him the right to draw a line? If a son is living at home, under the authority of the head of the household who has just been converted, why should the son not be baptised, whatever his age, according to the views of infant baptisers? Legg went on to say:

If the father today has authority to bring up his older children in the nurture and admonition of the Lord, to insist that they attend worship or family prayers, then he can have them baptised. However, in these days, when the practice has been virtually unknown and where society and children are not familiar with such authority, this would be very difficult and might be counter-productive, hardly a means of grace! Wisdom is

---

[11] Legg p5.
[12] Wright: *What...?* p36. But since infant baptisers agree that infants cannot exercise faith, how could the infants have been included 'as believers'?

called for and it is hardly wise to insist on something which will probably be misunderstood or resented.[13]

Here we have yet another amazing admission of the breakdown of the infant baptism system. The practice may – to some – sound alright on paper, but when it comes to the practical test then it is found wanting. And how! Apparently the church must now govern its practice by what is acceptable in society, and familiar to present-day children![14] This is an appalling suggestion. Surely infant baptisers realise that the households which were baptised in the New Testament were not households living in times which were amicable to the gospel, for they were living in gross and blatantly pagan societies. The gospel, the church and all its ordinances, worked – and how! – in those hostile circumstances.[15] The early church did not have to wrestle with the peculiar problems which come from the arguments of infant baptisers! No! Whatever the society, however bleak the times, the glory of the gospel is that it works; and it works today. Reader, can you imagine Paul or Peter baptising according to what a pagan society finds acceptable? Infant baptisers, seemingly, need a fairly moderate 'Christian society', a gently benevolent attitude on the part of the world, for its system to work. 'Wisdom is called for', said Legg. It certainly is! The wisdom of the New Testament pattern is called for! As Berkhof put it: 'The New Testament contains no direct evidence for the practice of infant baptism in the days of the apostles'. Astonishingly, he went on to account for this by saying:

Moreover, conditions were not always favourable to infant baptism. Converts would not at once have a proper conception of their covenant duties and responsibilities. Sometimes only one of the parents was

---

[13] Legg p10.

[14] I have already noted how infant baptisers have curtailed what they believe about baptism by the limitations imposed by babies. Here we have limitations imposed by an ungodly society. This is not the last of it! Wright: 'Because fewer requests for baby baptism are now [2005] being made, in many local situations a responsible baptismal discipline is more feasible' (Wright: *What...?* p102). All such talk lets the cat out of the bag. Society, the limitations imposed by babies... these things are not to govern baptism. Scripture is!

[15] Lydia, the jailer and Crispus lived in hostile pagan – Greek and Roman – and Jewish cultures (Acts 16:16-40; 18:1-17).

converted, and it is quite conceivable that the other would oppose the baptism of the children. Frequently there was no reasonable assurance that the parents would educate their children piously and religiously, and yet such an assurance was necessary.[16]

This is a remarkable statement, not least for its frankness. Infant baptisers need favourable conditions for their system to work – when pagans are being converted it runs into insurmountable difficulties, apparently. If so, then it will be of precious little use in pagan England at the beginning of the 21st century![17] What is more, it will never work. Society is *always* ungodly: 'The whole world lies under the sway of the wicked one' (1 John 5:19). This age is 'this present evil age' (Gal. 1:4), and always will be. In any case, where in the New

---

[16] Berkhof p634. As I have noted, Wright saw the problem the other way round, pointing out infant baptisers have had to adjust their belief and practice to cope with 'the limitations of babies' (Wright: *What...?* p7; see also Wright: *What...?* pp20-24). But he also owned recent changes to try to accommodate unbelieving parents; see below.

[17] As for modern developments to cope with a shifting culture, take Wright, commenting on the 1928, 1940 and 1994 changes in the Church of Scotland's *Book of Common Order*: 'The reasons behind these tendencies are not hard to seek. They reflect a desire to accommodate parents... who may not be comfortable confessing their own faith in Christ' (or may not even have one to confess)! The changes are 'altogether less challenging... a pale substitute for professing personal faith in Christ... disappointing features... [which] may be... indicative of a growing emphasis on the way of the Christian as a pilgrimage with no firm starting point, and in this life no attainable goal. So being a Christian [in this modern-day infant baptising system] has no decisive beginning from non-faith in Christ to faith in Christ, but is a quest, a journey within faith, and also within non-faith and doubt'. Other accommodating efforts by other infant baptisers include 'talking of baptism itself as life-long'. Wright properly dismissed this 'strange notion' since it 'runs up against all kinds of objections... [not least] plain common sense. One either has or has not been baptised at any one time'. 'Infant baptism in many churches has to be rescued from being more a family occasion than a church event, and so has to be saved from sentimentality and baby worship'. 'We might conclude that for some who minister in one of these mixed churches the price of continuing to dispense baptism to babies is not believing too much about it' (Wright: *What...?* pp59-62,82,87; see also Wright: *What...?* pp83-88,100-102). Phew! With friends like this, infant baptism in contemporary culture needs no enemies! I shall return to the abomination of regarding conversion as a process started by baptism.

Testament do we find evidence of the parents of infants to be baptised being vetted as to their understanding of 'covenant responsibilities', and all the rest of it? If the conditions Berkhof listed were so important, and since, according to him, their lack of fulfilment practically prevented the baptism of infants in the days of the apostles – there is no direct evidence for the baptism of infants, he said – where is the scriptural evidence for the apostolic concern over the lack? Berkhof's words are pure speculation. Above all, what now of infant baptiser claims? Are infants to be baptised or not? What about the covenant now? What now about the misguided deductions from 1 Corinthians 7:14? – only one parent was converted in that instance. What about their view of household baptism? In theory, infant baptisers are definite; in practice they fudge! Infant baptisers appear to have shot themselves in the foot!

Getting back to 'household baptism', and probing it a little further. If a man is converted, not only should his unbelieving children be baptised, but so should his unbelieving wife, according to the teaching of infant baptisers. She is in the household, she is under the authority of the head of the house, the man. Now if infant baptisers find it difficult to baptise infants in a pagan society – and on their own admission they do – what will they do about the unbelieving spouse? Shall we see an unbelieving wife forced to be baptised on the grounds that her husband has been converted? If not, why not? And if she is baptised, what if she is a Muslim, a Papist, a Jehovah's Witness, or simply a rank pagan? Will she be baptised and become a member of the church, only to be immediately excommunicated? The mind staggers at the very idea.

As one who has no first-hand experience of the attempt to put the theory of household baptism into realistic effect, may I ask if infant baptisers really do believe in household baptism? In a practical way, I mean. What are the rules of household baptism? The Greek word οικος means 'the inmates of a house, all the persons forming one family, a household'. Are infant baptisers prepared to baptise all in the household when its head is converted? Will they baptise the wife, the children, the grandchildren, the great-grandchildren, the servants and their children, of whatever age or in whatever spiritual condition they happen to be? Will they, in the years which follow, demand the baptism of all babies that are born in that household? Will they baptise all adopted and fostered children? Will they baptise all the dependants of a prospective household servant they wish to employ, and will their job adverts make this requirement explicit? Does any infant baptiser do these things? Do infant baptisers actually believe in household baptism or not?

I do! Sadly, I have never had the joy of seeing a whole family converted. But if I had, I should have found it well-nigh impossible to describe my joy at baptising every member of that family – all of whom had come individually to repent and believe, and had given a credible testimony of their experience.

Argument 8

Infant Baptisers Argue from the Words of Jesus to Mothers with Their Children

The verses in question are found in Matthew 19:13-15, with parallel passages in Mark and Luke. Words like:

Let the little children come to me, and do not forbid them; for of such is the kingdom of God. Assuredly, I say to you, whoever does not receive the kingdom of God as a little child will by no means enter it (Mark 10:14-15; see also Matt. 18:1-6).[1]

It will be readily seen that infant baptism and church membership are not spoken of in these passages. This is of the utmost significance.[2] Whatever else is referred to, *baptism – infant or otherwise – is not*. It would seem, however, from an infant baptiser's point of view, that a marvellous opportunity was missed. Infant baptism could have been unequivocally established so easily! It was just the right circumstance. And, if I am not speaking out of turn, if the baptism of infants is what Christ requires, and since he knew what endless controversy there would be over it in the history of the church, it is surprising, to put it no stronger, that he chose not to take the glorious opportunity afforded him at the time, and thus settle the matter once and for all.

That being said, all commentators – infant baptisers and Baptists – find difficulties of interpretation. But certain things stand out. Jesus wants children to come to him, opening his arms to them (Mark 10:16). But he did not say that children are sinless; he did not say that children are regenerate; he did not say that children are in the

---

[1] Are we talking about new-born babies or older children? They brought βρεφη to Jesus in Luke 18:15, but he immediately spoke of παιδια (Luke 18:16-17). παιδια is used in all the other references. βρεφη does mean new-born babies, but παιδια can be older children – see Mark 9:21,24,36. It is not an important question – other than for those who want to argue for *infant* or *baby* baptism from the passage.

[2] 'There is no mention at all of baptism' (Lloyd-Jones: *The Church* p40).

covenant. What Jesus did say is that all who are to be converted must become child-like; that is, they must become totally dependent in their attitude and spirit. No one who is self-sufficient will ever come to Christ, throwing himself absolutely and unreservedly upon his mercy. But that is just what sinners must do; hence, whoever does not receive the kingdom as a little child will never enter it: 'Unless you are converted and become as little children, you will by no means enter the kingdom of heaven' (Matt. 18:3). But all who become like a child in this respect, do belong to the kingdom. Note Christ's words: '*As* little children'; he did not say that children – not even these children – belong to the kingdom of heaven.[3]

Before I look at the way infant baptisers misuse this episode, I ask a question: Reader, when, do you think, men started to use it to justify infant baptism? Judging by the claims made for it today, one would imagine it must have been New Testament times. But, of course, there is not an atom of evidence to indicate that the first disciples ever thought in such terms. What about the next two or three hundred years – the age of the Fathers, when infant baptism arose – did the Fathers turn to these passages? There is scarcely any evidence of it! Wright, after describing the nonsensical procedure for infant baptism in the 7th and 8th centuries, said:

One feature of this infant-dominated descent into unreality deserves special mention. It seems that it was in the course of this regressive

---

[3] 'As a little child'. But 'when [Christ] enjoins his followers to become like a child, this does not extend indiscriminately to all points'. Least of all does it extend to age! 'Comparisons must not be too closely or too exactly carried out, so as to apply at all points... The tender age of little children is distinguished by simplicity to such an extent, that they are unacquainted with... all the incentives to pride... That man is truly humble who neither claims any personal merit in the sight of God, nor proudly despises brethren, or aims at being thought superior to them, but reckons it enough that he is one of the members of Christ, and desires nothing more than that the head alone should be exalted... The term "children" is now applied metaphorically by Christ to those who have laid aside lofty looks, and who conduct themselves with modesty and humility' (Calvin: *Commentaries* Vol.16 Part 2 pp332-334). Pratt, however, showed no such restraint: Christ 'taught... that the kingdom... belonged to the children who were brought to him and to others like them' (John H.Armstrong p71). Not at all. Christ was saying that [the kingdom] belongs to all (men and women) who will become spiritually child-like.

development... that... Jesus' blessing of little children was recruited to justify the laying of hands on infant heads... It is important to stress that there is hardly any trace of this passage being used or interpreted in connection with infant baptism in the patristic period. This should not surprise us, since we have seen that early Christian baptism... focussed on candidates able to answer for themselves.

So it was in the 7th and 8th centuries that these passages were dragooned – note Wright's 'recruited' – into supporting infant baptism. Once this had happened, however, there was no going back:

The 16th-century Reformers... generally include [the episode] as scriptural reading and helpful justification... [of infant baptism]. [In] the *Book of Common Prayer*... 1549 [and its] 1552 revision... this... episode was launched on a new career as a key [so-called] scriptural and indeed dominical support[4] for the practice of baptising babies, a career which would last until the later years of the 20th century.[5]

As an inevitable consequence of the concept of mothers presenting their babies for baptism, the notion arose that those mothers (and others) should act as sponsors for the babies. Why? Because the babies were unable to speak for themselves! The non-speaking babies, not only unable to speak, but unable to have and profess faith – which, infant baptisers admit, is the New Testament requirement for baptism – were said to make 'their' profession of faith – so the theologians argued – through the lips of their sponsors acting as ventriloquists on their behalf! And this 'theology', originating (surprise, surprise!) with Augustine, was reinforced by the Reformers, not excluding Calvin himself![6]

So now we know. The Gospel passages in question were not used to defend infant baptism until the 7th or 8th centuries, and such a use carried with it senseless – utterly daft! – corollaries. So can we hope that infant baptisers in the 21st century will stop using these passages

---

[4] That is, the support of the Lord Jesus Christ himself.
[5] And beyond! Wright: *What...?* pp72-74. Buchanan and Vasey noted that in Thomas Cranmer's justification of infant baptism, 'his weakest points had been his choice and use of Scripture (Mark 10:13-16 – "Suffer the little children...")' (Buchanan and Vasey p7).
[6] See end note on p176 for excursus: 'The madness of Reformed ventriloquism at the baptism of infants'.

171

to try to justify their practice? I doubt it! I fear the love of the sentimental note it has introduced is too deeply ingrained.[7]

How do infant baptisers use these verses to justify their practice? In regard to this, I have already pointed out that baptism is not referred to, but if infant baptisers insist on bringing it into the passages, they prove too much. Let me first demonstrate that they do insist on bringing it in. For instance, Engelsma: 'How important our children's inclusion in the covenant is to God is shown in the New Testament (covenant) by Christ's command: "Suffer little children (infants) to come unto me... for of such (infants of believers) is the kingdom of God (made up)" (Luke 18:15-17)'. Reader, you can see that Engelsma applied a subtle gloss to Christ's words – a gloss which cannot be justified. Could he categorically state that the infants presented to Christ in Luke 18 were 'infants of believers'? Of course not. Yet he said they were, and on the basis of that unwarranted assumption he was prepared to move on to the subject of baptism – which is not mentioned in the passage – and criticise those who do not allow infants to join the church by baptism. 'Every Baptist church denies membership to all children', he complained. He went on to deplore this, saying that such people are engaged in a 'grim teaching and practice' in that they 'will not suffer the little children to come to Christ, but [forbid] them'.[8] Once again, notice the gloss, the subtle adjustment to Christ's words. Christ did not say anything about baptism or joining the church, did he? Yet Engelsma virtually put those words in Christ's mouth. Coming to

---

[7] According to its advocates, infant baptism is often a sentimental social occasion, not far removed from baby-adulation. See, for instance, Carson: *Farewell* pp14-16. But infant baptisers do not stand alone in this particular dock. Many evangelical, not excluding Reformed Baptist, churches have a lot to answer for. The cult of children, so common in the world, has captured large sections of the church – children's church, children's (often toe-curlingly childish) talks, family services, crèches for those well able to remain (and who ought to remain) in the service (and benefit), the inordinate emphasis upon youth work, and such like. I fear that many teenage baptisms in such churches may be little more than social events. Indeed, it is worse. In some cases, they are little removed from a party atmosphere, a kind of half-way house between an English wedding-breakfast and an American high-school graduation, tinged with religion. I speak with sadness of what I know of this growing phenomenon. See Tidball p158 on infant dedication.
[8] Engelsma pp10-11.

Christ is being sprinkled and joining a church as an infant, according to Engelsma! Baptists – who will not baptise infants – are shutting them out from Christ, forbidding them to come to the Saviour, he said. What arrant nonsense. Has Engelsma ever met a Baptist?

Such abuse has a long pedigree. As we have seen, Calvin dismissed the Anabaptists for their refusal to baptise infants, especially because of their argument (the biblical argument) that the only way to be reconciled to God is by faith. He said that this episode in Christ's life proves this is not true for infants; children are reconciled to God and adopted by baptism. Calvin was definite: Christ extended grace to the infants, gave them purity, they were renewed by the Spirit of God to the hope of salvation, and were reckoned by Christ as among his flock. Having made such startling claims, Calvin found no difficulty in thinking it reasonable that infants ought to be baptised. The Anabaptists, he said, were cruel to children, foolishly excluded them, drove them far from Christ's fold, and shut the door.[9] Only eternity will reveal how many have been deluded by Calvin's astonishing claims.

To return to the main point: Since infant baptisers want to support their practice by Luke 18:1-6 and the like, on their logic it follows that all infants should be baptised; at least, all infants who belong to one or both parents who express some general desire that they should be baptised or 'something should be done to them'. Certainly infant baptisers cannot restrict the baptism to the children of parents who are in the covenant; not by arguments from these passages. Were all the mothers in the covenant? How can anyone be sure? Had the mothers been baptised? If so, when? And did any of them have children at the time? If so, why had they not been baptised with their mothers? Why were they being brought separately? And, if the mothers had not been baptised, why weren't they baptised with their babies on this occasion?

---

[9] Calvin: 'Since the whole race of Adam is shut up under the sentence of death, all from the least even to the greatest must perish, except those who are rescued by the only Redeemer. To exclude [infants] from the grace of redemption... would be too cruel; and therefore it is not without reason that we employ this passage as a shield against the Anabaptists [because] they refuse baptism to infants' (Calvin: *Commentaries* Vol.16 Part 2 pp390-391). Calvin's words can only mean that since all infants are ruined in Adam, all infants should be baptised, and thus all infants will be saved. Diabolical!

In any event, as I have pointed out, baptism is not present in the passages. Hence why all this talk about baptism? The verses afford not the slightest ground for baptising anybody, let alone infants.

What is more, why did the disciples, who had been baptising – and, according to infant baptisers, baptising infants in the process – try to stop the mothers bringing their infants to Christ? If they had been used to receiving infants in order to baptise them, why would they now come between Christ and these mothers with their infants? It would have been the most natural thing in the world to welcome children since they had been in the habit of baptising them. Infant baptisers want us to believe that the disciples – who were utterly nonplussed by these mothers bringing their infants to Christ – had been baptising such! This is too much to swallow. Clearly, the disciples were not as sure about what to do with infants as infant baptisers are! They certainly did not look for water.[10]

In 1864, C.H.Spurgeon preached a sermon on this from Mark 10:13-16. It was aptly entitled: 'Children Brought to Christ, Not to the Font'. In his characteristic way he said:

---

[10] And what now about the parent-child principle in the Abrahamic covenant – which infant baptisers make so much of? Robert L.Reymond recognised the point. The best he could come up with was: 'Though the disciples should have known better, their attitude toward children may perhaps be explained from the fact that the status of children under then-current, but totally unbiblical, religious law consistently placed them [the children] in the company of the deaf and dumb, the weak-minded, the blind and crippled, the aged, Gentiles, women and slaves' (Reymond p196). In other words, the parent-child principle had died out at this time. If so, how is it, as infant baptisers claim (I do not agree), John the Baptist used the principle, as did Peter at Pentecost, Paul with the households, and so on? Are we to believe that although John the Baptist used it, the disciples of Christ had forgotten it when the mothers approached them, yet remembered it by the time of Pentecost? How did they recover the principle? When did they recover it? What evidence is there for such a recovery? The argument is utterly flawed, nothing but special pleading. How do we know the Jews had forgotten circumcision and allowed it to lapse at this time? I see no evidence for such a claim. In making his suggestion, Reymond cited Joachim Jeremias who, as one wit remarked, unearthed *at least* all the evidence for infant baptism (see Wright: *What...?* p18; Lane 140). Infant baptisers once again show the desperateness of their position – they seem willing to clutch at any passing flimsy straw.

174

This text has not the shadow of the shade of the ghost of a connection with baptism. There is no line of connection so substantial as a spider's web between this incident and baptism, or at least my imagination is not vivid enough to conceive one. This I will prove to you, if you will follow me for a moment.

It is very clear, dear friends, that these young children were not brought to Jesus Christ by their friends to be baptised... there is not a hint about their being baptised... Surely the parents themselves knew tolerably well what it was they desired, and they would not have expressed themselves so dubiously as to ask (Jesus) to touch them, when they meant that he should baptise them.

In the next place, if they brought the children to Jesus Christ to be baptised, they brought them to the wrong person; for... John, (John 4:2), expressly assures us that Jesus Christ baptised not, but his disciples: this settles the question once for all, and proves beyond all dispute that there is no connection between this incident and baptism.

But you will say: 'Perhaps they brought the children to be baptised by the disciples?' Brethren, the disciples were not in the habit of baptising infants, and this is clear from the case in hand. If they had been in the habit of baptising infants, would they have rebuked the parents for bringing them? If it had been a customary thing for parents to bring children with such an object, would the disciples who had been in the constant habit of performing the ceremony, have rebuked them for attending to it? Would any Church clergyman rebuke parents for bringing their children to be baptised? If he did so, he would act absurdly contrary to his own views and practice; and we cannot therefore imagine that if infant baptism had been the accepted practice, the disciples could have acted so absurdly as to rebuke the parents for bringing their little ones. It is obvious that such could not have been the practice of the disciples who were rebuked [by Christ for hindering the children].

Moreover, and here is an argument which seems to me to have great force in it, when Jesus Christ rebuked his disciples, then was the time if ever in his life, to have openly spoken concerning infant baptism... If he wished to rebuke his disciples most effectually, how could he have done it better than by saying: 'Wherefore keep... these children back? I have ordained that they shall be baptised... how dare you then, in opposition to my will, keep them back?' But no, dear friends, our Saviour never said a word about 'the laver of regeneration'[11]... when he rebuked them – not a single sentence. Had he done so, the season would have been most appropriate if it had been his intention to teach the practice...

---

[11] Reader, please recall the words of Luther, Archibald Alexander, Calvin and others.

To close all, Jesus Christ did not baptise the children... He... dismissed them without a drop of [water]. Now, if this event had any connection with baptism whatever, it was the most appropriate occasion for infant baptism to have been practised. Why, it would have ended for ever the controversy... I, my brethren, would sooner be dumb than speak a single word against an ordinance which Christ himself instituted and practised; and if on this occasion he had but sprinkled one of these infants... then the question would have been settled for ever, and some of us would have been saved a world of abuse, besides escaping no end of mistakes; for which we are condemned, in the judgement of many good people, for whom we have some affection, though for their judgement we have no respect.[12]

I realise that Spurgeon directed his sermon against the advocates of baptismal regeneration,[13] but the arguments he presented are relevant to the case in hand. Indeed, they are more than relevant. They are unanswerable.

---

[12] Spurgeon: 'Children Brought' pp414-415.

[13] But as I have shown, Calvin and many others make statements which amount to it. Many Reformed baptisers are unequivocal sacramentalists – not excluding baptismal regeneration. And, as I have pointed out, increasingly, Baptist scholars are to be included in this stricture. For more on Spurgeon, the baptism of infants and baptismal regeneration, see Grass and Randall pp62-67.

End note to Argument 8: Mothers and Their Children

The madness of Reformed ventriloquism at the baptism of infants

The New Testament demands profession of faith before baptism. As their system evolved, infant baptisers tried to keep to this, but struggled with the impossibility of requiring infants to profess faith – infants who, by definition, cannot speak for themselves. To cope with the dilemma, infant baptisers (by the time of Augustine) had invented the hare-brained scheme of requiring these hapless (non-speaking) babies to 'make a profession' of their (supposed) faith by the ventriloquism of sponsors, the questions and answers being couched in the third person (Bradshaw p114). Wright called this madness 'amazing', 'confusing', a 'flight from reality', 'a failure', 'bizarre', an 'incongruity'. 'To spell it out as simply and starkly as I can', he said, 'for many centuries when virtually all babies born in Europe were baptised soon after birth, the parents or other sponsors declared in baptismal ritual that the babies believed'. Of course, as Clark said: 'From the earliest times infant baptism has been a practice in search of a theology; [and] in many quarters it is still so today' (Cross: 'The Evangelical sacrament' p195); that is, a biblically coherent theology. As a sample of the kind of theology invented to support such a farce – and theologians will always oblige public demand and devise a theology to justify anything the people want (see below) – Wright cited John of Rome (about 500): 'When [babies] are presented by their parents or others, it is necessary that their salvation should come through other people's profession, since their damnation came by another's fault'. What a leap of (il)logic! As Wright said: 'The New Testament's antitype to Adam is not the [parent] but Christ'! What is more, neither sin nor salvation entered the world through the *profession* of anyone; the biblical comparison or contrast is between the *sin* of Adam and the *obedience* of Christ (Rom. 5:12-19). Having referred to Leidrad's 'fullest discussion of the [ventriloquist charade] encountered so far in the history of Christian baptism', concerning which Wright, calling it 'truly a mixed bag', rightly deduced 'the difficulty, even the desperateness, of the position being justified... That so weak a mixture of reasons was resorted to by Leidrad... merely reinforces the deep-seated strength of the traditional and universal procedure'; that is, the biblical procedure of believer's baptism. While 'the English Reformers only marginally improved on late Medieval practice', the Continental Reformers did better. Wright expressed his hope that modern practice will at least correct this obvious and tragic nonsense, but he admitted that 'purging the body ecclesiastical of the detrimental effects of infant baptism's long reign has still some distance to go' (Wright: *What...?* pp8-9,25-26,35,43,47-62). What is needed, of course, is not the correction of some abuses, but the entire abandonment of a practice so far removed from common sense, let alone the New Testament.

Calvin, however, was adamant; in the baptism of infants, sponsors – to be responsible for the spiritual upbringing of the child – are essential: 'It is indispensable for them [the infants being baptised] to have sponsors. For nothing is more preposterous than that persons should be incorporated with Christ, of whom we have no hopes of their ever becoming disciples. Wherefore if none of its relations present himself to pledge his faith to the church that he will undertake the task of instructing the infant, the rite is a mockery, and baptism is prostituted. But we see no reason for rejecting any child for whom a due pledge has been given... If we exclude from baptism those whom we have had proofs of having been domesticated, as it were, in the church, the exclusion would be too rigorous... Let children be admitted to baptism on the condition we have mentioned; namely, that their sponsors engage that they will make it their business to have them brought up in the principles of a pious and uncorrupted religion' (Calvin: *Letters* pp216-217).

A few comments are called for. Does water baptism 'incorporate with Christ'? Allowing it for the moment, notice how Calvin diluted 'incorporation with Christ' into 'domesticated... in the church'. As for sponsors, could we be given the name of one sponsor of one infant (this essential feature of infant baptism) in the New Testament? Where are we given the qualifications and responsibilities of sponsors? We learn about elders, deacons, widows *etc.* Where do we learn about sponsors? And where do we read of apostolic concern over the lack of sponsorship for an infant being baptised?

A moment ago, I noted how theologians will always provide the necessary theology to justify any new practice. Pelikan 'examined the way in which doctrine changed over time, noting that it often had to "catch up" with changes in religious practice' ('Obituary: Jaroslav Pelikan' in *The Daily Telegraph* May 17th 2006). In particular, 'infant baptism was a rite in search of a theology... It was Augustine, of course, who supplied what was for a long time to be the answer to this question' of why? not whether? (Lane p142). The biblical way – does it need to be said – is the other way round; the theology – God's revelation – must lead the practice, and produce it. Paul, for example, in his letters, lays out doctrine at the start, and then calls for the practice on the basis of that doctrine. Infant baptisers tackle the problem the other way about. They have invented a practice and then looked for the doctrine to justify it. This is quite wrong. Indeed, the many tries they have had in search of this elusive theological justification is in itself a sure indication that it cannot be found: they seek it here, they seek it there, they seek it everywhere and anywhere. As my mathematics master at school told us in justification of his teaching the theorems year after year: 'The principle we work on', he said, 'is to keep throwing mud at a wall; the more we throw, the more we might get some to stick'. Likewise here. The more infant baptisers throw their theology at their practice, the more they hope to come up with a justification which sticks.

Argument 9

Infant Baptisers Argue from Silence

Another way the infant baptisers try to justify their practice is to argue from silence, though, as we saw a little earlier, some of them, at least, appreciate the difficulties involved, and are not always so keen on it. The attempt to justify infant baptism from silence is remarkable. Apparently, so we are told, since there is no direct command *not* to baptise infants in the New Testament, infants ought to be baptised. As Marcel put it, and put it very dogmatically: 'The silence of the New Testament regarding the baptism of infants militates in favour of... this practice. To overthrow completely notions so vital, pressed for more than two thousand years... to withdraw from children the sacrament of admission into the covenant, the apostolic church ought to have received from the Lord an explicit prohibition'.[1]

This remarkable argument from silence is of doubtful logic at best, and smacks of stipulating what commands Christ should and should not have given to his church. 'Ought to'? Who said? apart from Marcel and friends, that is.[2] The Holy Spirit has taught us and warned us of many things in Scripture – things which would only come to light centuries later. Yet, apparently, he left us to reason from silence over an issue and a practice as far-reaching as the baptism of infants. Incredible! In addition, the reasoning is absurd. Although infant baptisers admit that Christ and his apostles said nothing about the subject – not a word about it – we are supposed to realise that their very silence is clear proof that we must baptise infants! To my mind at

---

[1] Kingdon p25.

[2] I hope, reader, you can detect the difference between Marcel's 'ought to' and the way I expressed my views on silence in the previous chapter on the mothers and their children. Furthermore, as I have said, there is a right way for arguing from silence – but this means there is also a way which is wrong! Great care is needed. And a greater sense of reverence for Christ than Marcel showed here.

least, the claim seems odd coming from those who so often argue for the Regulative Principle.[3]

And what about the 'two thousand years'? What 'notions so vital', which had been the practice in Israel for 'two thousand years', did Marcel think came over from the Old Testament into the New? Practices such as circumcision, membership of Israel by physical descent, and so on? I have shown that the principles which lay behind those practices, though they had lasted for 'two thousand years', fell with the passing of the old covenant in the death and resurrection of Christ.[4]

Moreover, it must be borne in mind that the silence argument is a game for more than one player. Very strange things have been proposed by its use. What, for instance, of the Presbyterian in 1653 who claimed that since the New Testament does not forbid the maintenance of parish clergy by the 10% levy on all Englishmen (that is, tithes), then this must mean the Church tithe system is the proper way to support ministers?[5] What is more, Papists and others can build their wicked notions on silence. Beware! It *is* possible to use the argument – Spurgeon did it in the sermon quoted earlier – but great care must be taken with it. The scriptural silence on infant baptism can be used to support the case for *not* baptising infants – indeed, infant baptisers have to face the fact that their practice is not even mentioned in the New Testament[6] – but the silence should not be used the other way round, as Marcel did. If Scripture does not command us to do something, we will not claim scriptural authority for it. Is this not the right course? To put it no higher, it is much safer than claiming scriptural warrant for a practice because we are not told it is forbidden.[7]

---

[3] That is, nothing is to be done in the church unless directly sanctioned by Scripture.

[4] Once again I have to ask: Why do infant baptisers cling to the shadows of the old covenant? And as for Marcel's use of old-covenant principles: Should we have the death penalty – stoning – for adultery, blasphemy and witchcraft? Does the New Testament expressly tell us we should not? What about the silence now?

[5] Hill: *Bible* p42.

[6] And *this* is the silence they should be concerned about.

[7] Philpot: 'How are we to know when [omission, arguing from silence] is of importance [valid], and when it is not? By this simple rule: Omission is of

Argument 9: Silence

However, since silence is a weapon infant baptisers like to use, why should females be baptised? Only males were circumcised in the Old Testament, and there is no direct, explicit command to baptise females; so why did the apostles baptise them? Why should they change the practice of, as Marcel put it, 'more than two thousand years'? Silence, it is claimed, means we must carry out Old Testament principles and practices in the church. It was a revolutionary step to baptise women; silence ought to mean – according to infant baptisers – that only males should be baptised.[8]

Again, infant baptisers baptise infants, but in the main they do not allow them to partake of the Lord's supper.[9] As the Westminster

---

great importance when analogy, or the weight of probable evidence, is *against* a thing having occurred; omission is of little importance when analogy is in *favour* of it. To argue from analogy means to argue from what has occurred that the same thing will occur again under similar circumstances... The omission of any example or precept for the baptism of infants in the New Testament is of great weight against that practice. Why? Because both precept and practice in the New Testament are entirely for baptising believing disciples. We therefore argue from analogy (that is, from how we may gather it is most probable that the apostles acted under such and such circumstances), that they *did not* baptise infants. In other words, the stream of analogy is *against* the practice of baptising or sprinkling infants. Now, in this case, the argument from omission is so strong that only one thing can overturn it. And what is that? The producing of an instance of an infant having been baptised in the New Testament, or a precept to baptise them. To argue from "households" [see Argument 7] being baptised, that infants were [baptised], will not do here, as it is to make one omission make up for another omission' (Philpot pp17-18, emphasis his); that is, two silences do not make a stronger argument than one!

[8] The issue of male and female, of course, does not arise in *biblical* baptism. Only believers, and all believers, male and female, must be baptised. There is a question to be asked, and this is it: Is this person a believer?

[9] Calvin: Before the supper, 'examination... must precede, and this it were vain to expect from infants... How, pray, can we require infants to commemorate any event of which they have no understanding; how require them "to show forth the Lord's death", of the nature and benefit of which they have no idea?' Just so! Calvin might bluster: 'Nothing of the kind is prescribed by baptism. Wherefore, there is the greatest difference between the two signs' (Calvin: *Institutes* Vol.2 p550). But, reader, scan the various quotations I have supplied from his writings, and see if this stands up. Above all, read the Bible to see if it does. Where, in Scripture, do we read of any

181

Catechism, question 177, puts it: 'Baptism is to be administered... even to infants; whereas the Lord's supper... only to such as are of years and ability to examine themselves'.[10] But in the Old Testament the (male) children were circumcised, and they and the infant girls, along with their family, partook of the Passover. Why then, on the infant baptiser's logic, can infants not partake of the supper? And since they cannot,[11] why is there no explicit command to say they should not? Surely it would have been a natural development from the Old to the New Testaments, and silence is said to mean that Israelite practice must be taken into the church. So, if the circumcision of infants meant that infants should be baptised, yet the same link does not apply to the supper, why was the early church not told about it? Was there not a very real danger that they might have given them the supper? Why the silence?

In any case, as for infants not partaking of the Lord's supper, if they were baptised on the Day of Pentecost, as infant baptisers mistakenly assert from Acts 2:39, why did they not partake of it? It clearly states that 'those who gladly received his word were baptised; and that day about three thousand souls were added to them. And they continued steadfastly in the apostles' doctrine and fellowship, in the breaking of bread, and in prayers' (Acts 2:41-42). If infants were included in the three thousand of verse 41, why were they excluded from the same group in verse 42? And why is there no explanation of the exclusion? Why the silence? The reality is, no infant was included in the three thousand who were baptised. (I will return to this). But on the infant baptiser's own argument, why is there no explanation to tell us that those infants who were baptised, who joined the church, who

---

person taking the supper who was not baptised, or who was baptised and did not take the supper? What scripture tells us that between baptism and the supper 'there is the greatest difference'?

[10] Westminster p267. Note the difference in the nature and quality of qualification required for the two ordinances. In the Scottish Highlands in the 19th century, all that was required for baptism was absence of 'ignorance and immorality' (in the parent – or the person, if an adult was applying for baptism), whereas 'careful examination of life and experience' was required for the supper (Wright: *What...?* p4). Why? Why this difference in the two ordinances?

[11] But even here there is movement. See end note on p185 for excursus: 'Recent developments in children partaking of the Lord's supper'.

came under the apostles' doctrine, naturally did not partake of the supper? Why the silence?[12]

Having hinted at the proper force of silence in the episode with the mothers who brought their infants to Jesus, I now ask, why, in Acts 15,

---

[12] Infant baptisers argue that since Baptists allow women to partake of the Lord's supper, even though we have no explicit biblical example of it, they are right to baptise infants even though, as they admit, there is no biblical example of it. See, for instance, Calvin: *Institutes* Vol.2 p534. Two things are wrong with this argument. The qualification for partaking of the supper is that the person should be converted, baptised and in fellowship with the church in question. We know that women were converted, baptised and made church members in the New Testament – to cite references would be superfluous. Naturally, therefore, these women took part in the supper – as they did in the prayer meetings, discipline meetings; indeed, in the entire range of church activity. This is the first point. The second is to note the infant baptiser's huge leap of logic – the massive assumption – without any biblical warrant or example – simply to assume that children were baptised. There is no parallel at all with women. Finally, the question I raised above still stands. On the infant-baptiser's argument of silence, why do they not allow – glory in, indeed – allowing infants to break bread? Why are so many of them reticent to follow their own logic? They glory in the baptism of infants, and rebuke Baptists for their denial of it to infants – why not go the whole hog and do the same for the supper? After all, these baptised infants are church members! Andrew Fuller: 'If persons are admitted to baptism without any profession of personal religion, or upon the profession of others on their behalf, their admission to the Lord's supper will in most cases follow as a matter of course. Indeed, it *ought* to follow... Neither Scripture nor the practice of the [New Testament] churches affords a single example of a baptised person, unless his conduct was grossly immoral, being ineligible to communion'. Again, replying to an infant baptiser: 'That the plea for infant communion is equally valid with that of infant baptism, you will not expect me to dispute. If I could be convinced of the one, I see no reason why I should scruple at the other'. The infant baptiser must 'point out the grounds for admitting the former while he rejects the latter'. As for 'households', Fuller asked why the infant baptiser did not '*prove* that some of them at least were infants? If he could have done this, all his other arguments might have been spared'. Dealing with Acts 16:31, Fuller quite rightly remarked that Paul was saying that 'if [the jailer] and his house believed, they should all be saved'. As for passages such as Eph. 6:1-4, Fuller observed that they were 'addressed not to ministers or churches, but to parents. Nor is there... in all that is written in the apostolic letters, to parents or children, a word which implies the latter to have [been] church members' (Fuller: *Practical* p729; *Essays* pp852-853, emphasis his).

when circumcision was under discussion, and was proving so thorny an issue, did nobody state the obvious – 'baptism has replaced circumcision'? Why the silence? It would have solved the problem at once, but nobody said it. Why not? Because it is not true; baptism has not replaced circumcision.

The truth is, the New Testament is not silent on the issue of infant baptism without reason. Since, in the New Testament, there is a great deal of evidence for the change of the covenant, and the spirituality of the new covenant, the fact that there is no explicit command not to baptise infants is not a weakness in the Baptist position at all. With the change of covenant, the old system based on physical descent was abolished. I have supplied plenty of evidence. The silence which ensued indicates that the baptism of infants was never even thought of in the New Testament. Nobody dreamed of it. That is why they were silent about it. Infant baptism was only thought about after the age of the apostles, when it was invented by the Fathers. Of course the New Testament writers said nothing about it! Just as they said nothing about the motor car. It never crossed their mind. Why not? Because it hadn't been invented!

Warfield admitted that the earliest testimony for infant baptism is that of the Fathers, and that this is always linked with baptismal regeneration. Understandably Warfield squirmed; he but feebly addressed the vile and evil error of baptismal regeneration, yet clung to the Fathers' 'testimony to the prevalence of infant baptism in their day', grasping at the straw. Reader, the historical truism is not denied. Among many other errors, infant baptism was invented by the Fathers, yes. Even so, as I have noted, it was not for some time. But listen to Warfield's obvious anxiety as he was forced to own the weakness of his position: 'We admit that their day is not the apostles' day. We could well wish that we had earlier witness'.[13] Yes, but it is not only an earlier witness which is 'wished for'. A biblical, a New Testament, witness, an apostolic witness is *required*! And *that*, infant baptisers do not have! Although they claim that the New Testament silence is a powerful argument in their favour, nothing could be further from the truth. Furthermore, it does not appear that they are quite as convinced as they would like others to believe. Warfield admitted that he would

---

[13] Warfield p402. Yet again, what now of the Regulative Principle?

have been glad of apostolic testimony for the practice of infant baptism! There is no doubt about it – he would have preferred apostolic warrant to apostolic silence! But he didn't have it!

End note to Argument 9: Silence

Recent developments in children partaking of the Lord's supper

Increasingly, children are partaking of the Lord's supper. The 'logic' of infant baptism makes it inevitable, as some of their scholars are openly admitting. Take Wright, for instance: 'Do the infant-baptised become (or are they recognised as already being) members of the church, of the covenant people of God?... Does baptism, or more accurately, the Holy Spirit through baptism, effect anything for babies, or merely mark them out as future recipients? Does baptism... confer specific covenantal blessings on babies, such as new birth or remission of sin, specifically original sin, as Augustine influentially argued?... It may be the case that most evangelical ministers or churches have not endorsed the admission of young children to the communion table. It surely merits more serious consideration than it commonly receives. In its favour is the weighty argument that it takes the baptism of infants genuinely as baptism, as making them truly members of Christ's people. Thus it has the virtue of putting both ordinances of the new covenant on an equal basis, dissolving the anomaly that the infant-baptised have been welcomed into the Christian community, but are debarred for years from its communal meal celebration'. (See below for the notion that infant baptism has to be 'supplemented' by confirmation). Speaking of 'the children of the faithful', Wright raised the question which infant-baptisers (and others – see below) need to answer: Do such 'children [really] belong to the covenant community'? His answer? Yes. 'Whether by baptism, by dedication or by thanksgiving and blessing, we welcome the children of the faithful... and we are right to treat them as new members of God's people, not as no better than little pagans or unbelievers'. But, he said, he drew the line. Where? 'At the possibility of unbaptised children at the communion table' (Wright: 'Children' pp27-28,37,39)!

As one Anglican infant baptiser has admitted: Regarding infants partaking of both baptism and the supper, 'historically [and biblically – DG]... the Baptist has had the better of this argument. The infant baptiser has gone on thinking up reasons for not giving infants and children communion, but they have looked like evasions to the [Baptist]. The necessity of holding both sacraments together in our practice is very strong, and the New Testament is as silent on non-communicating baptised persons as it is on non-baptised believing persons... The time has come to admit the force of the objection. This we can cheerfully do, and then advocate infant and child communion, as the concomitant of infant and child baptism. The two *do* go together, and it is about time we acted accordingly' (Buchanan: *A Case* p19, emphasis his). This is honest. How many will follow his dictum? At what age will it start? Before weaning? In a later booklet, Buchanan and Vasey noted that infant communion had begun in New Zealand in 1970, but it was 1997 before 'the opening of the [flood] gates' in England; even so, a year later they could record 'the practice is spreading fast round the country'. This will continue:

'We do not think the Bible allows a category of the baptised non-communicants, and we suspect that younger brothers and sisters, even without much Bible knowledge, will press their case also as, say, seven-year-olds come on stream' (Buchanan and Vasey pp9,21,24). Innumerable problems suggest themselves. At least, in baptism, a baby is (relatively) passive – but imagine toddlers breaking bread! Buchanan showed how far he was prepared to lower the net in recognising faith: 'If a child can reach the age of two without baptism in a believing household, and then lisps "I love the Lord Jesus", then already we may have an unbaptised believer on our hands' (Buchanan: 'David Wright' p151). Incredible!

On a personal note, I had a conversation with a member of (what used to be known as) the Taylorite section of the Exclusive Brethren. I said I was curious as to how they regarded conversion. Were his infants believers? They were born into the fellowship, I was assured. Do they take the supper? Yes. At what age did they start? When they were baptised. But you baptise them as infants, don't you? Yes. So at what age did your children start to break bread? Four years? Six years? No. Four months. Can a four-month-old child discern the Lord's body? I asked. Yes, I was assured. I cited the solemn warning about not discerning the body. I was told that the Bible tells us that the Lord comes first to the children in the supper. I asked where that was stated. The gentleman said he did not know, but would find out. I told him he wouldn't find it in the Bible. He said he would let me know. I asked him if it came from Darby or the Bible. The Bible, I was assured. Over many months, now going into years, I have heard nothing – even though we live next door to each other. The verse he had in mind, I guess, is Mark 7:27. If so, such exegesis needs no comment from me.

But infant communion is taking place not only among infant baptisers. Again as I write, I hear of a 'modern' Open Brethren assembly which has the supper at the beginning of meetings which are open to all. A warning is given, but even so families partake, *including the children.* (As I go to press, I hear that this service has now been moved to the centre of the service, no warning at all is given, and the overtly unconverted partake!) I also hear of a Baptist church where children are openly welcomed to the table. These things are happening in evangelical churches, sometimes by default, sometimes deliberately, by policy and conviction. In the attempted justification for the practice in the Baptist church, reference has been made to Chris Leach's *Children and the Holy Spirit.* Leach set out three views – the traditional Baptist, the Anglican and the New Church, the latter being 'somewhere between the [other] two'; even so, 'the New Churches have a theology that looks Anglican in all but infant baptism. Children are included in the kingdom... they are not treated as little heathens in need of evangelising'. The Anglican position (which is the New Church position) is: 'Children are basically included rather than excluded, and the prayer and desire of the church is not that they will one day opt in, but rather that they won't one day opt out. A conversion experience is not seen as essential if the child's parents are actively training him or her in the ways of the Lord (although the move from family faith to personal faith does need to be made in later years). A picture often used to explain this is that of the Israelites crossing the Red Sea. No doubt, there were among their number on that day, children of all ages, as well as adults. Some would have toddled through the gap in the waters, some would have been carried in their parents' arms, and some, no doubt, would have slept peacefully through the whole thing, blissfully unaware of the momentous event that God was causing to happen for them. Yet all would have been "saved" as they reached dry land on the other side, free of the Egyptian threat. To suggest that they were not really saved, unless they consciously went through a repeat performance, would simply not be true, although it would presumably be possible for them at any stage to get into a boat, cross back the other way, and hand themselves back into slavery. Thus, the argument goes, those children whose parents have "carried" them into the kingdom, and who are helping them to live out that life of freedom, do not need saving again; they need help and encouragement to live life to the full in the promised land' (Leach pp30-32). What an incredible exposition and application of Scripture, with its muddling of the physical and the spiritual, and its stretching, beyond all reasonable limits, the interpretation of an analogy! Fee: 'All attempts to suggest that Paul saw Israel's experience of the Red Sea, or their eating manna and drinking water from the rock, as something sacramental, are misguided and futile. Paul is not concerned with Israel's experience, but with the analogies they provide... To overload the symbols with a vast array of meanings, some of which are in actual conflict, seems to go far beyond the [apostle's] intent' (Fee: *1 Corinthians* pp445-446). Beasley-Murray: 'The passage... is not intended to be a typological statement of sacramental theology but [an]... exposition of... [events] for the elucidation of Christian ethics'. See his dismissal of such over-stretching of Scripture ('many strange examples of exegesis') as being 'guilty of over-pressing an observation of Paul... to violate the homiletics [the doctrine of preaching]... gratuitous and needs no further consideration... eisegesis [as opposed to exegesis; that is, reading *into* the text rather than *out of* it]... The inference [is]... unreasonable... exegesis run riot... To use a passage like this in justification of infant baptism [and infant participation of the supper] is near to making the word of God of no effect by our tradition... [It] introduces an alien element into Paul's train of thought' (Beasley-Murray: *Baptism in the New Testament* pp181-184). I will return to this interpretation and application of Scripture in Appendix 1. For now, I simply ask its advocates to weigh its appalling consequences. Finally, why did the apostles not use the argument?

Argument 10

Infant Baptisers Argue from the Invented Concept of the Sacraments

This is another way in which infant baptisers develop their system. And yet it is not just 'another way'. It is, as I have said, the root of the trouble. They use the concept of the 'sacraments', a word that has come up from time to time throughout this book. What is more, as I have shown, sacramentalism is on the increase, and in its wake, a growing number are adopting a full-blooded sacramental infant baptism, where words mean what they say. This has consequences.[1] A sacrament? A sacrament is said to be a religious rite which is supposed to be a means of grace.[2] It is not a scriptural term – so where did it come from? Bannerman conceded that 'the term... is of Church origin',[3] by which he meant, dreamed up by the Fathers,[4] who got it from the pagans.[5] Pagan! Let that sink in, reader! Nothing new under the sun (Eccles. 1:9)! Ahaz, you will recall, so much liked the pagan altar he saw at Damascus, he sent the plans back home, had one made – 'the great new altar' – and used it to offer sacrifices to God (2 Kings 16:10-16). Augustine tried to wrap the notion in theologese – by which he certainly confused me, if nobody else. He argued:

The sacrament of a reality takes the name of that reality, so that the sacrament of faith comes to be known as faith... A child is made a believer... by the sacrament of that faith... They are called believers, not by mentally assenting to faith itself, but by receiving the sacrament of it.[6]

---

[1] See end note on p200 for excursus: 'Sacramentalism leads to Rome'.

[2] See end note on p206 for excursus: 'Means of grace'.

[3] Bannerman p4. See Calvin: *Institutes* Vol.2 pp491-511.

[4] How much the Fathers have to answer for – and those who go to the Fathers and not the apostles.

[5] See end note on p208 for excursus: 'Lloyd-Jones on "sacrament"'.

[6] Wright: *What...?* p51. As Wright said: 'This was hardly Augustine at his most impressive, but... scholars and theologians of the [second Frankish dynasty founded about the 9th century] relied heavily on extensive quotations

Have you got it, reader? If so, would you kindly write and explain it to me? Peter Lombard in the twelfth century sharpened Augustine, clearing away much of the fog:

Something can properly be called a sacrament if it is a sign of the grace of God and a form of invisible grace, so that it bears its image and *exists as its cause*. Sacraments were therefore instituted for the sake of sanctifying, as well as of signifying.[7]

Well, that's clear enough. Baptise a baby and you make it a Christian!

So much for the Medieval view of a sacrament. What about the Reformed view? The Westminster Catechisms defined the notion by saying: 'A sacrament is an holy ordinance instituted by Christ; wherein, by sensible signs, Christ, and the benefits of the new covenant, are represented, sealed, and applied to believers'... 'those that are within the covenant of grace... to strengthen and increase their faith, and all other graces'. There are, it is claimed, two parts to a sacrament, 'the one an outward and sensible sign... the other an inward and spiritual grace'. 'The sacraments become effectual means of salvation... only by the blessing of Christ, and the working of his Spirit in them that by faith receive them'.[8]

---

from the Fathers of the early centuries' (Wright: *What...?* p51). Augustine was replying to Boniface who wanted to know whether or not the infant, through its sponsors, could undeniably assert faith, and the sponsors could be sure of it (see Newton pp101-106). See below for Cranmer's use of Augustine's reply.
[7] McGrath: *Christianity* p160, emphasis mine. Note Lombard's 'sanctifying'. He contrasted 'sanctifying' with 'signifying'. In other words, the sacrament causes, effects what it signifies. Baptism saves! Peter J.Leithart: 'If... we begin thinking about baptism by picturing baptism as a "sign", then our main question will be: "What does it signify?" and we may neglect to notice that baptism *accomplishes* something. If we begin with the root picture of "ritual", our questions will be more about what baptism *does*' (Leithart p204, emphasis his). See Appendix 2 for extensive extracts from Augustine.
[8] Westminster pp254-255,313. Horton Davies: 'Does [the Westminster *Directory*] have a high [that is, sacramental] or a low [that is, symbolic] doctrine of the Lord's supper?' Davies argued the case and concluded: 'On all these grounds, it must be adjudged a consistently high doctrine of the real spiritual presence of Christ in the action mediated by the Holy Spirit, and a true means of grace'. I agree. Westminster: 'The word, sacraments and prayer... are made effectual to the elect for their salvation' (Westminster p246). Ames was quite clear; sacraments *represent* and *present* what is

190

And as for an up-to-date statement, of the many I have already cited, let me repeat Lusk:

The infant-baptism question hangs, at least in part, on the question of baptismal efficacy... Without a robust sense of understanding of what *God* does in baptism, the grounds on which infant baptism rested became very tenuous... The logic of infant baptism is tied to its efficacy... A sacrament, by definition, includes the bestowal of the thing signified.[9]

In short, allowing for all their usual caveats – of which I have repeatedly spoken – the Reformed sacramental view, it is fair to say, is that baptism and the Lord's supper are not only signs; they are seals, effective means of grace.[10] In particular, according to this, baptism seals the removal of guilt and pollution and so on, actually conveys or confers grace, assuring those who are baptised that they are heirs of the promised blessings.[11]

---

signified: 'A sacrament of the new covenant... is a divine institution in which the blessings of the new covenant are represented, presented and applied through signs perceptible to the senses'. For more on Ames and the Puritan view in general of sacraments and the covenant, see Davies Vol.2 pp309-323. On the Lord's supper, the Westminster Confession stated: 'Worthy receivers... do... inwardly by faith, *really and indeed*, yet not carnally and corporally, but spiritually, receive... Christ crucified... the body and blood of Christ being... not corporally or carnally, in, with, or under the bread and wine; yet, *as really*, but spiritually, present to the faith of believers in that ordinance, as the elements themselves are to their outward senses' (Westminster p119, emphasis mine).

[9] Lusk: 'Paedobaptism' pp96-100, emphasis his.

[10] See end note on p210 for excursus: 'The Reformed, sacraments and preaching'.

[11] See Lloyd-Jones: *Romans 6* pp30-32 on sacramentalists. 'They claim that it is the act of baptising that, in and of itself, unites the person baptised with the Lord Jesus Christ. It is certainly a clear-cut view, but is it [right]? We need not spend much time on it. One over-riding reason for dismissing it at once is this, that according to the New Testament teaching, it clearly... puts the cart before the horse. The teaching of the New Testament is that the people who are to be baptised are those who have already given evidence that they are regenerate'. By 'sacramentalists', Lloyd-Jones meant Roman Catholics, but, as I have shown, many Reformed are such.

Let me not pussy-foot around the issue. The idea of a sacrament, which is not a biblical term, is obnoxious.[12] As I say, the idea of a sacrament was invented by the Fathers, following which the Papists developed a sacramental theology out of seven sacraments which are supposed to convey grace to those who submit to the rituals. The Reformers reduced the sacraments to two – baptism and the Lord's supper – but trying to qualify their teaching on the two by saying that they are only effective when received by faith.[13] Some Reformers were – quite properly – unhappy about the word 'sacrament' with its horrific associations, and struggled very hard to safeguard against the Papist notions it involved.[14] Even so, at times they were, at best, loose in their statements, as the many quotations I have already supplied have shown. Frankly, some of their statements on the sacraments not only tended towards baptismal regeneration; they actually taught it; they still do.[15]

Let me illustrate the point, by reference to the discussions which took place when the Anglicans and Presbyterians met in the Savoy Conference in 1661. The Presbyterians produced a book of *Exceptions against the Book of Common Prayer*, it being a rehash of the old Puritan complaints, plus some new material, mainly the work of Richard Baxter. One objection the Presbyterians raised concerned the 'sacraments'; the Prayer Book was not sufficiently explicit for the Presbyterians; it did not go far enough. The fact is, the Westminster *Directory*, when dealing with baptism, speaks of the 'sanctifying [of] the water to this spiritual use' by the minister's prayer 'joined with the word of institution'. Similarly, in the supper, it speaks of 'the elements being now sanctified by the word and prayer', after which the minister is directed to take and break the bread, and so on.[16] The point is, the

---

[12] See end note on p211 for excursus: 'But what of Mark (1:4); 16:16; Acts 2:38; 22:16'?

[13] Faith. In baptism, whose faith are sacramentalists talking about? The baby's faith, the parent's, the sponsor's, or...? And when are those benefits conveyed and sealed by faith – at the baptism? or 20 years later?

[14] See end note on p212 for excursus: 'Sacramentalism leads to sacerdotalism'.

[15] This claim, which I have made repeatedly – with evidence – is vigorously disputed by some Reformed teachers. See end note on p215 for excursus: 'Andrew J.Webb's response to the charge of baptismal regeneration'.

[16] Westminster pp383,385.

Presbyterians at the Savoy Conference objected in part to the Prayer Book because it contained no such consecration. *Reader, please let that sink in.* The Presbyterians' demands, and their own *Directory*, make it clear that 'the Prayer Book petition reflects a sacramental doctrine less "high" than the Presbyterian'. Think of that! The Presbyterians demanded a more sacramental view of the ordinances than the Anglicans, who had to go back to the Prayer Book of 1549 to find any such sacramental reference in their rubrics.[17]

On the question of consecration, I realise that I might be referred to 1 Timothy 4:5. Yes, prayer and the word of God do sanctify[18] our food, but this has nothing to do with the ordinances of Christ. Calvin was playing with fire when he wrote that 'we must attend to the distinction between the blessing of the sacramental table and the blessing of a common table... we consecrate, in a more solemn manner, the bread and wine in the Lord's supper'.[19] Regrettably, he was not alone in making such a dangerous statement.[20] Calvin has much to answer for in this matter, even today.[21]

Reformed infant-baptisers, I admit, often stoutly try to avoid the idea that a sacrament conveys grace to the participant simply because of the observance of the ritual;[22] they declare that faith is essential. This is supposed to be a safeguard against Papist notions. Well, in that case how does – how can – an infant benefit from the sacrament of infant baptism? It cannot exercise faith – so how does it benefit from the sacrament? This is most important. In many ways it is the crux of the matter. Great care ought to be taken over the answer by the advocates of the sacrament of infant baptism; precision is essential. What is the status of a baptised infant? How exactly does an infant

---

[17] Nuttall and Chadwick pp116-117. See Davies Vol.1 pp33-34; Vol.2 pp320-322,426-434.

[18] ἁγιαζω – the same word as in 1 Cor. 7:14; see above. This is significant.

[19] Calvin: *Commentaries* Vol.21 Part 3 p106.

[20] See end note on p218 for excursus: 'Dangerous views on "consecration", and their consequences'.

[21] See end note on p220 for excursus: 'Calvin's sacramental view of the Lord's supper'.

[22] See end note on p226 for excursus: 'How the Reformed regard their baptised infants'.

benefit from its baptism, since it cannot believe?[23] One would expect infant baptisers to be very clear. What do they say? Are they precise and lucid? Are their statements free of ambiguity, plain and definite? Far from it!

Luther puzzled over it, changed his mind, and ended up by saying he just did not know. He never rid himself of Papist views on the subject. Indeed, he thought the water itself was holy.[24] The truth is, Luther was completely muddled over the whole matter. He simply did not know how the infant benefited. He said it did, but he did not know

---

[23] Augustine's statement, that 'the sacrament received is judged according to the faith of the recipients', was included by Leidrad in his 'explanation' of how infants benefit from baptism even though they cannot possibly be aware of what it all means. (Does anybody?) As Wright pointed out, Augustine's statement actually destroys the infant baptiser's claim that infants do benefit: It 'is not only beside the point, but even detrimental to it', calling it a 'useless punch line' (Wright: *What?*... pp52-53). Quite! If faith is required in the baby, how can the baby benefit? By the way, in the same statement, Augustine expressly ruled out the faith of the parents, priest or minister, making up the difference: 'The sacrament received is judged according to the faith of the recipients, *and not according to the faith of the giver*' (emphasis mine). Do today's sacramentalists agree?

[24] Following Luther, so do modern-day Lutherans. Luther first of all: 'Baptism is not just plain water, but it is the water included in God's command and combined with God's word'. Now for modern-day Lutherans: 'What's so special about a handful of simple water? Nothing, until God connects his word to it! In baptism, that is exactly what God is doing. He combines his life-creating and life-giving word with the waters of holy baptism, and thereby we are born again of water and spirit (John 3:5)' (taken from the website of the Lutheran Church – Missouri Synod: 'What about Holy Baptism?', an article written by the President, A.L.Barry, quoting Luther's *Small Catechism*). And not just Lutherans. See the complete note, right at the start of my book, of the 2008 article in the *Banner of Truth*, where we read that 'the water of baptism is more than mere water... for the water is so bound to the promise of God that the physical cleansing becomes, if not the instrument, at least the occasion for the spiritual cleansing... As the outer self is washed with water by the minister, the inner self is washed with the blood of the Christ by the Holy Spirit... The two events do coincide and are bound together in the relationship between promise and sign'. I remain amazed that such material can be published in such a magazine.

how.[25] As we have seen, Calvin made dangerous and loose statements; he baptised babies either because they were regenerate already, or because they would be regenerated in the sacrament. Others invented something they called 'presumptive regeneration'; they *presumed* that the infant who is baptised is regenerated and sanctified in Christ. These views still prevail; some Reformed infant-baptisers assume the infant is regenerated at baptism. Berkhof, for instance, quoting the Synod of Utrecht on presumptive regeneration, and quoting it with approval:

Synod declares that, according to the confession of our churches, the seed of the covenant must, in virtue of the promise of God, be presumed to be regenerated and sanctified in Christ, until, as they grow up, the contrary appears from their life or doctrine.[26]

That is *one* of the stances taken by Reformed infant-baptisers when they try to explain the essence of the sacrament of infant baptism. But only one of several. There is strong disagreement among the Reformed about what is going on when they baptise an infant.[27] Listen to Cunningham who, in his defence of the so-called sacrament, fired a broadside at his colleagues. He was prepared to write:

The condition and fate of infants, and the principles by which they are determined, have always been subjects on which men, not unnaturally, have been prone to speculate, but on which Scripture has given us little explicit information... The great difficulty of the whole subject lies in settling, as far as we can, what modifications our conceptions of baptism

---

[25] Berkhof p627. The Lutheran Church has been in this dangerous muddle ever since. But, even though it is muddled about all the ins-and-outs of infant baptism, there is no such muddle about its ultimate resting place; it teaches baptismal regeneration: 'Although we do not claim to understand how this happens, or how it is possible, we believe... that when an infant is baptised, God creates faith in the heart of that infant' (taken from the website of the Lutheran Church – Missouri Synod answers to question under 'Baptism and Its Purpose'). A few moments ago, I noted Calvin's confession that though he claimed Christ's flesh is in the supper, he did not know how.

[26] Berkhof p640.

[27] See end note on p228 for excursus: 'Reformed disagreements about the effect of infant baptism'.

should undergo in the case of infants, as distinguished from that of adults.[28]

Here we have it. To resolve 'the great difficulty of the whole subject', infant baptisers have to go outside Scripture to speculate about 'modifications' and differences between adults and infants in baptism. This one reason alone is sufficient to call a halt to the business! Go outside the Scriptures? True enough that is the only place to find it. The early church was never bothered about 'the great difficulty' of infant baptism – they lost no sleep over it. They had never heard of the nonsensical practice. Where, in the New Testament, is there any example of anyone worrying about these 'modifications'? There were no modifications in the New Testament; they did not baptise infants, therefore they had no need to modify their view of the ordinance. In any case, to 'modify' an ordinance of Christ is sinful disobedience, is it not?[29] Surely the very suggestion proves the wrongness of the practice, does it not?

Cunningham referred to the baptism of believers, describing the scriptural nature of such a baptism. Then he said: 'We' – meaning infant baptisers – 'we are unable to put any such clear and explicit alternative in the case of the baptism of infants, or give any very definite account of the way and manner in which it bears upon or effects them individually... The Scripture really affords no adequate

---

[28] Cunningham p148.

[29] Scores of scriptures tell us of the need strictly to obey God in his word, and of the evil of adding to, or taking away from, any of his commands. See, for instance, Deut. 4:2; 12:32; Prov. 30:6; Isa. 8:20; Rev. 22:18. Christ: 'Laying aside the commandment of God, you hold the tradition of men... You reject the commandment of God, that you may keep your tradition' (Mark 7:8-9). Young: 'More than anything else today, there is need that all our thinking be based upon, and in conformity with, the... Scriptures' (Young p320). *All* of it. And not only our thinking; all our *practice* too must 'be based upon, and in conformity with, the... Scriptures'. Calvin: 'Hence we learn that everything which is added to the word must be condemned and rejected. It is the will of the Lord that we shall depend wholly on his word, and that our knowledge shall be confined within its limits... Everything that is introduced by men on their own authority will be nothing else than a corruption of the word; and consequently, if we wish to obey God, we must reject all other instructors' (Calvin: *Commentaries* Vol.7 Part 1 p290).

materials for doing this'.[30] At least this is honest. But why do infant baptisers persist with a practice when they admit they have no scriptural explanation of what they do? John Hooper's words ring down the centuries:

The Scriptures are the law of God; none may set aside their commands or add to their injunctions... The Scripture and the apostles' churches are solely to be followed, and no man's authority... There is nothing to be done in the church but is commanded... by the word of God.

Reader, if only...

To go on: A.A.Hodge put it this way: 'The children of all such persons as... are received as members of the visible church are to be baptised as members of the visible church, because, presumptively, heirs of the blessings of the covenant of grace. The divinely appointed and guaranteed presumption is, if the parents, then the children'. This is ridiculous. What is a 'guaranteed presumption'?[31] The two words are mutually contradictory, are they not?

The question remains: How do infants – who cannot believe – benefit from baptism since faith is essential? We have a right to expect a clear, unequivocal answer. Papists maintain that the baptism produces the faith; some Reformed infant-baptisers hold that it strengthens faith. But as Berkhof put it: 'This gives rise to a rather difficult question in connection with infant baptism'.[32] It certainly does! But only one question? How can baptism be a means of grace to an infant who cannot exercise saving faith? How, exactly? Does it produce faith? If not, does it strengthen faith? How can it strengthen a faith which is not there? The Papists say it can, by reason of the power of the sacrament. What do Reformed infant-baptisers say about it?[33]

---

[30] Cunningham p150.

[31] A.A.Hodge p329.

[32] Berkhof p641.

[33] Cross: 'There is no single theology or practice of infant baptism'. Paul K.Jewett: 'The thinking of the infant baptisers themselves, from the very beginning of the Reformation, is... split by a difference of opinion... [which] involves the whole theology of the sacrament of initiation' (Cross: 'The Evangelical sacrament' p196). See also Fowler pp211-219. 'Although many infant baptisers utilise both the "priority of grace" argument and the "seal of the covenant" argument, it appears that these two arguments are in fact contradictory. The former logically leads to baptising everyone in the world,

Luther struggled over the problem. Frankly, he was stumped. Eventually the best he could come up with was to refer 'the problem to the doctors of the Church'![34] Cunningham gave an honest reply to the question: 'There is a difficulty felt – a difficulty which Scripture does not afford us materials for altogether removing – in laying down any very distinct and definite doctrine as to the precise bearing and efficacy of baptism in the case of infants'. As I say, this is honest, but that is all that can be said for it! It is a frank admission that the whole system is a muddled charade. As he put it: 'There are undoubtedly some difficulties in the way of applying fully to the baptism of infants the definition usually given of a sacrament'.[35]

The question will not go away. It demands an answer, an answer which is definite and understandable.[36] The Reformed really ought to get their defence of infant baptism sorted out! After all, parents who are not expert in Reformed metaphysics and the ins-and-outs of covenant theology beget children; they ought to understand what is going on when a minister sprinkles their child, shouldn't they? How does infant baptism benefit the infant, since faith is essential and yet the infant cannot believe? Reformed theologians admit the problem and try to cut the knot in three ways. They say that they do not understand how it happens, but it does 'in some mystical way'; that

---

as an offer of the gospel to all for whom Christ died, while the latter leads to the restriction of baptism to those who are called out from the mass of humanity as the holy, covenant people. In terms of infants, the former would imply the baptism of all infants whose parents would allow it, while the second would restrict baptism to the infant children of professed believers. It is possible that one of these arguments might be [logically] valid, but not both simultaneously' (Fowler p218). It could be put more simply, more directly, and more accurately. The first argument demands the baptism of *every* infant; the second, the baptism of *elect* infants. But if the latter, who is going to tell us who these elect infants are? See below for William Perkins, John Preston, infant baptism and the gospel offer.

[34] Berkhof p641.
[35] Cunningham pp126,145.
[36] See end note on p229 for excursus: 'Reformed explanations of infant baptism are incomprehensible'.

198

there is a delay between the sacrament and the grace which is conferred; and that the means of grace is for the parents.[37]

Really! If it were not so serious the whole thing would be laughable.[38] The truth is, as Berkhof made very clear, Reformed infant-baptisers are divided over the reason why infants are baptised at all. Why do they baptise infants? For some, it is because of presumptive regeneration; for others, it is because of the covenant; for others, it is a combination of the two. Some baptise babies because they believe they are regenerate; others, in order to regenerate them.[39] But the New Testament knows of only one reason for baptism. It is obedience to Christ. And it knows of only one basis for baptism. It is

---

[37] Berkhof pp641-642. Riggs: 'The... near-mystical character to baptism was most observable in Calvin, the Reformed Confessions, and especially Schleiermacher' (Riggs p122).

[38] Perry Miller pointed out the irony: 'Cotton... came as near to sentimentality as a Puritan could come: children of the covenant are capable of gracious acts "sooner than we discern", and even in their cradles, "something they have in their hearts which pleases them, though they know not what it is", which they express "in their silent thoughts"'. As Miller went on: 'What thoughts the children of non-members [see below for an explanation of this point] have, Cotton did not enquire, but let himself be persuaded that these particular ones were "professors of the faith parentally, as well as personally"' (Perry Miller pp87-88).

[39] Listen to the testimony of Professor Frank James: 'If I may hazard a generality (a generality, however, based on years of training pastors for Presbyterian ministry), I am quite convinced most Presbyterians, whether in the pulpit or the pew, do not understand clearly why they baptise their infants. If asked to explain why Presbyterians baptise infants... I would expect that many Presbyterians would stumble and blunder the explanation' (Shawn D.Wright p207). Wilkins: 'To many in the [Presbyterian] Church, the covenant is a meaningless, indefinable concept which merely allows infants to be baptised (for some unknown reason)' (Wilkins: 'Introduction' p11). Such devastating testimonies from such sources cannot be ignored – must not be ignored. Beasley-Murray: 'It is not too much to say that there is no argument for infant baptism that is acceptable to all who practice it, even as there is none that is not explicitly rejected by some proponents of infant baptism. It is all very perplexing for the Baptist, who finds himself under the necessity of fighting on a number of fronts at one time; when he discusses the issues separately, he knows quite well that he will be boring at least some of his hearers (or readers) for whom the argument under review has no interest at all' (Beasley-Murray: *Baptism Today and Tomorrow* pp109-112).

faith: 'He who believes and is baptised' (Mark 16:16). 'What hinders me from being baptised?' 'If you believe with all your heart you may' (Acts 8:36-38).[40] No infant can exercise saving faith – so no infant should be baptised.[41]

There is only one thing to do with all this Papist and Reformed mumbo-jumbo of sacraments,[42] for that is what it is. Throw it out. Get away from the Fathers, and get back to the New Testament. Baptism and the Lord's supper are not sacraments. They are not rituals. Christians do not partake of sacraments – they observe Christ's ordinances. There should be no more talk of sacraments. They are an abomination. Grievously, many who should know better, persist in using the wretched word. It ought to stop at once.

* * *

This brings us to the end of our brief glance at the arguments infant baptisers use. Before we leave the subject, however, we must turn to the practical effects of infant baptism.

---

[40] I am not excluding repentance, of course. And while the texts cited above may be contested from a manuscript point of view, nobody, as far as I am aware, contests the doctrine, which is consonant with the rest of the New Testament. In any case, if the words are a gloss, they tell us what the transcriber (and others, presumably) thought about baptism – it is only for those who truly believe.

[41] See end note on p232 for excursus: 'Why, then, did Sibbes, for instance, still want to baptise infants?'

[42] A phrase more apt might be 'hocus-pocus', which almost certainly came from *hoc est corpus meum* (this is my body). In Medieval times, this phrase largely became an incantation gabbled in dog-Latin by a priest who often did not understand it, half-heard by congregations who definitely did not understand it. As for the theology behind it...! Hence hocus-pocus. So much for Rome. But sauce for Rome is sauce for Geneva and Westminster.

End notes to Argument 10: Sacraments

Sacramentalism leads to Rome

I have already remarked on the resurgence of sacramentalism, spreading from the Reformed and Romanist camps, its fingers reaching into places where it would have been abhorred not so long ago – some Baptists, of all people, are now taking a sacramental approach to baptism. Calvin's view of the Lord's supper, and an increasing regard for the Fathers, is part of this spread of sacramentalism; more straws in the rising ecumenical wind. 'The ecumenical movement has... stimulated interest in baptismal and sacramental theology as the various branches of Christendom have attempted to work out a rapprochement' (Douglas p101). Donald Gillies: 'A... distinctive ecumenical principle is the emphasis on sacramental unity. *Ecumenism is sacramental rather than evangelical...* This sacramentalism is not so much the contribution of one segment of the movement as [it] definitely [is] an *ecumenical* phenomenon... The prevailing [Gillies wrote in 1964] emphasis on sacramental unity gives great impetus towards the attainment of a world Church. Indeed, in many ways, the sacrament of the Lord's supper is the real uniting force and hope in ecumenism. In consequence, the strong desire for common participation in the sacrament tends to overrule the consideration of serious differences of interpretation... Why this sacramental emphasis?... The sacramental emphasis... is a force for making unity. It is an outstanding example of a more general trend among nominally Reformed churches towards the acceptance of Roman Catholic doctrines and practices; especially the latter... Sacramentalists are set to establish Catholicism as the faith of ecumenism'. Gillies quoted D.M.Paton from 1962: 'If Catholicism is in a way to becoming biblical, Protestantism is in a way to becoming sacramental'. Gillies concluded his book: 'The Romeward trend is no longer a matter for denial or even debate. It is an established fact. Let us not be deceived. The ecumenical movement is an affront to truth... It is a grievous offence against the God of our salvation. Ecumenism is the enemy of the gospel of regeneration by the Spirit and justification by faith alone' (Gillies pp41-48,106, emphasis his. See the entire volume).
Again, in 1964, David Hedegård argued – and documented (Hedegård) – the ecumenical drive to accommodation with more than Rome, which, unless checked by a return to biblical Christianity, will lead to a world-wide religion embracing the Reformed, the Evangelical, Rome, Islam and all. Who will come out on top remains to be seen. He concluded his book: 'A remarkable fraternisation between Protestants and Roman Catholics is taking place... This fraternisation must promote an amalgamation of Roman Catholics and Protestants' (Hedegård pp90-109,228. See the entire volume). See my book on Baptist sacramentalism for the experience of the Baptist scholar, Michael Walker (1932-1989).

201

As I have also said, one of the grievous aspects of Wright's book – which I have found so helpful in exposing and challenging infant baptism (especially since he was a Reformed infant-baptiser himself) – is his high regard for this notion of the sacrament, and its connection with ecumenicalism. He deplored 'low views of the sacrament of baptism. A certain anti-sacramentalism, or at least disinterest [*sic*] in the sacraments, has characterised too much evangelicalism, often as a reaction against an intolerably high sacramental theology' (Wright: *What...?* p87). He was glad of 'the growing evidence of sacramental thinking among Baptist theologians and... the highly significant developments in the Catholic Church since Vatican II... It is indeed a hopeful and invigorating time to engage in a re-examination of baptismal roots and traditions' (Wright: *What...?* p10; see also Wright: *What...?* pp15-17,102). I agree that we should examine the roots of baptism – that is why I am writing – but I dread the consequences of Wright's overall view. Significantly, he confessed: 'My observation of a mixed mainline Presbyterian church [the Church of Scotland] suggests that increasing lack of confidence among ministers in the truth... is not infrequently compensated for, so to speak, by a heightened concern for the sacraments' (Wright: *What...?* p88).

Reader, there is nothing surprising about this; superstition always rises as truth declines! Wright need have had little fear that the Reformed will not travel the road he desired. Modern-day infant baptisers are already putting the sacramental views of Luther and Calvin into practice, and are far from apologetic about it. After all, as John W.Riggs observed: 'In its own way... the Reformed tradition has a strong priestly theme and a high sacramental character to its worship life. The Reformed idea that the sermon and the sacrament can be the means through which the word of God addresses the people means that both preaching and liturgical language are "priestly"... Even the brief look [that is, as in Riggs' book] at the sacramental and baptismal theology of the Reformed Confessions [has] indicated that word and sacrament had the same office; namely, to present the people with Christ himself... What Calvin said clearly about the eucharistic elements applies, *mutatis mutandis* [making the necessary alterations], to the act of proclamation in preaching and sacrament... Reformed worship [in our day] has undoubtedly become far too didactic and glum, and the *Book of Common Worship* has tried to renew the worship life of the churches in the Presbyterian Church (USA) by renewing their sacramental life. For baptism, [it] drew on the rite of Christian initiation that (supposedly) enlivened the patristic churches, and that the Second Vatican Council hoped would renew the worship life of Roman Catholic Churches. But the Reformed tradition [itself and already] contains within it a vital liturgical theology. The sacraments, and the words proclaimed by the worship leader in preaching, and sacrament, are the very means through which Christ actually encounters us and sets free our joyous gratitude... When baptism is conceived as having two aspects that together form a single event, then Christ is offered, faith clings to Christ, and

God's presence is realised by the one who so trusts. In this way, baptism effects regeneration, as almost the entire Reformed tradition has insisted... Reformed theologians... insisted that baptism effected regeneration because God had entrusted that office to baptism' (Riggs pp116,121). As I say, those who desire more sacramentalism in Reformed churches need lose no sleep over the matter. M.F.Sadler has just been republished for the first time in over a century, for instance. Once again, see my book on Baptist sacramentalism for this sort of thing among Baptists today.

Even as I write, the move towards Rome is gathering pace. Consider the articles by P.Andrew Sandlin ('The Importance of Being Catholic') and Clint LeBruyns ('The Evangelical Advantage: A New Engagement with the Petrine Ministry') in *Act 3 Review*, volume 15, number 2, 2006, pp25-29,53-65. I suggest, reader, that you read these articles in full – coupled with much else in that edition of the quarterly in admiration of N.T.Wright and his work – to fully appreciate the point I am making. Sandlin wrote to promote the recovery of a 'Christian civilization' or 'culture', the 'fatal loss' of which (as established by the Medieval Church) occurred because of the Reformers' break with Rome. In that Reformation, Sandlin was, it seems, relieved that 'the original Reformers' were not averse to much of 'the ecclesiastical developments in the... thirteen centuries' since the Fathers – in whom 'they were steeped'. Although the Reformation was a 'necessity', according to Sandlin it brought with it a 'tragic' loss. Sadly, this loss has been increased, he argued, in the succeeding years, by liberalism among the Protestants, and moral 'scandals in the American priesthood [which] have been a blotch on the faith'. I pause to draw attention to the uneven treatment here. In these past 400 years, Protestants have adopted error; Rome has had moral scandals. That is, according to Sandlin. Really? Have there been no doctrinal developments coming out of Rome, no developments which have taken it further from Scripture, further than it was even in the 16th century? What about the pronouncement of the immaculate conception of Mary (1854), Papal infallibility (1870), and the assumption of Mary (1950)? To let Sandlin continue: Facing 'rampaging secularism and virulent Islamic fundamentalism', we cannot 'afford' the 'luxury' of what he dismissed as 'a division over relatively narrow points of belief and practice', a division which was possible in the time of 'ecclesiastical concensus' in the 16th century. 'Today, the importance of being catholic is perhaps more vital than ever. We must stand with all who truthfully declare "Jesus is Lord", vocally affirm the Apostles' Creed, and visibly work towards Christian culture'. On the basis of such a minimalist measure of agreement, we should, we are told, all unite to establish this 'Christian civilization' to withstand secularism and Islam. Reader, you can have no doubt about my position on this. If Scripture only, and justification by faith alone – to take but two of the 'narrow points' – have to be compromised, count me out! In any case, I should like to see the New Testament justification of a 'Christian civilization' or 'culture'! In my opinion, a resurgent Christendom – see below – will offer no defence against the enemies of Christ. Rather, it has itself been the greatest enemy – not the friend – of biblical Christianity (what a tautology!)

Before I turn to LeBruyns, I think it is worth recalling Lloyd-Jones' view of the minimalist position just outlined: 'We... have to reject... the position of Richard Baxter. He said that all who accept the Apostles' Creed as a summary of belief, the Lord's Prayer as a summary of devotion, and the Decalogue as a summary of duty, are truly Christians and members of the catholic and universal church of Christ. That... would have included Papists and Socinians... and so it was turned down' (Lloyd-Jones: *Puritans* p231). Times are changing. Alister McGrath: 'Modern ecumenical discussions have centred upon identifying which doctrines are essential to Christian belief, and which are open to debate'. He listed some of these 'secondary doctrines, upon which disagreement may be permitted within Christianity' (who has granted this 'permission'?), including: 'Whether, and in what way, Christ is present in the sacraments? Whether baptism signifies or causes believers to be born again?' (McGrath: *Understanding* p66).

I now turn to LeBruyns, and his argument for closer co-operation with, and appreciation of, the Papacy. He started by quoting, with approval, Pope John Paul II who, in 1995, spoke of 'leaving useless controversies behind'. LeBruyns talked of 'a new ecumenical dispensation on the matter of the Papacy' in which we find ourselves, where, he alleged, we cannot afford to elevate 'secondary differences between evangelicals and [Roman] Catholics to the primary level'. He styled the movement amongst evangelicals towards Rome and the Papacy, progress in 'a promising direction'. The Lima publication of 'Baptism, Eucharist and Ministry' in 1982, 'widely regarded as the most significant theological achievement of the ecumenical movement... became the most widely distributed, translated and discussed ecumenical text in modern times', so he informed us. There was one 'unfortunate omission' in the text, he said; namely, 'the ministry of the bishop of Rome'. An 'unfortunate omission', indeed! 'Significant', I should call it. Discussion of the authority and power of the Papacy, would, in my view, be a vital matter to consider in any proposed changes in the Vatican. For a more perceptive (but still not strong enough) view of Lima, see Schrotenboer pp291-313. To go on. LeBruyns thought that those of us who 'start out' by wanting to challenge what he called 'the problematic claims of [Papal] infallibility or jurisdiction or divine institution' are using 'wrong starting points'. This reminds me of the yokel who was asked the way to London. If I was going to London, he replied, I wouldn't start from here. Wrong starting points, indeed! To return to LeBruyns: 'The Papal office should be assessed as a ministry, albeit a different form of ministry against the backdrop of evangelical forms of ministry'. In other words, reader, we should now accept the Papacy. 'This would provide a more helpful and constructive basis from which to tackle an old problem in a new light', we are told. I am sure it would! In other words, the evangelical fly should not only enter the spider's parlour – he could occupy his time before supper no better than by laying the table at which he would be the principal dish. LeBruyns talked of 'many evangelicals [who] have become increasingly cognisant of the nature of the Pope's work as a Petrine ministry, which has phenomenally enhanced their understanding of and relations with Roman Catholicism'. Of course, this tends only to 'close much of the gap between evangelicals and the Pope. To the extent that the Petrine ministry is readily recognised by evangelicals as a ministry of the gospel and mission, evangelicals are nearer the mark of embracing the Papal office as a legitimate structure of the churches'. Quite! Even though 'the Papacy as an institution usually conjures up the wrong images for evangelicals', nevertheless this is being overcome with a suitable 'terminological alteration'. Just so! Fudge is on the menu. Forget the principle – find the 'formula'!

Meanwhile, Rome's position is very clear. Vatican II documents: 'The task of announcing the gospel in the whole world belongs to the body of pastors... [who] are obliged to enter into collaboration with one another and with Peter's successor, to whom, in a special way, the noble task of propagating the Christian name was entrusted'. The Pope himself was generous, as he slipped his iron fist into the velvet glove. Evangelicals make their contribution, of course, but as he stated in his 1995 encyclical: 'Within the college of all the pastors' his (the Pope's) 'mission' 'consists precisely in "keeping watch", like a sentinel, so that through the efforts of the pastors the true voice of Christ... may be heard in all the particular churches... As bishop of Rome... I have a particular responsibility... to find a way of exercising the primacy which, while in no way renouncing what is essential to its mission, is nonetheless open to a new situation'! I don't think this needs translation! The Pope has made his message very clear – to me at least. It reminds of the 1940s. Nobody could complain that Hitler had not made his purpose – to go to war for land in Russia – plain enough twenty years earlier in *Mein Kampf*. But the Russians were content to sleep to the very last and beyond – their locomotives still hauling loads of rubber to Germany even as Hitler was unleashing his barbaric onslaught upon them – and even though Churchill had warned them of the cataclysm which was about to engulf them. Henry Ford, I believe it was, said the one thing we learn from history is that we never learn from history!

According to LeBruyns, if evangelicals study the documents, they will come to see the Papacy as 'a legitimate ministry of the church that seeks sincerely and effectively to proclaim the gospel of Christ and to shepherd the flock of Christ who respond to the gospel'. That morsel having been swallowed, 'at a later stage' they 'could... consider' – consider, I ask you! – 'the issues of infallibility and so forth. In this way... there is juxtaposition in the evangelical and Petrine ministries. Can evangelical Protestants not conceivably accept the Pope as a fellow minister...? I would like to think so, though not without modification[!]... It should be clearer to evangelicals that the Pope can realistically be appreciated as a gift to the evangelical community... as a moral leader, spiritual... voice, guardian of communion'.

LeBruyns concluded: 'Evangelicals must assume a primary responsibility in engaging with the Vatican on how best to renew and reform the Papacy as it presently exists in order that it [may] be seen more visibly as an authentic ministry... Evangelicals now find themselves at a new crossroads – to perpetuate longstanding divisions and fragmentations in the church [which] discredits the ministry of Christ, or to venture into new territory for the sake of Christ and his gospel, so that the world may know him'. I realise, of course, that my book will be placed in the first category – and therefore dismissed – by many. But I think LeBruyns made a mistake in his final sentence. It is not 'new' territory he is asking believers to go into. Not at all. It is just the same old territory; it is the maps which have been re-drawn – without marking the quicksands. See Carson: *New*; *Dawn...*? As I was typing this – and my typing leaves much to be desired – I made a slip. Instead of LeBruyns' 'for the *sake* of Christ', I typed 'for the *sale* of Christ'!

Those who are contemplating a Romeward move should remember Rome's *semper eadem*; they should note the way the wind is blowing, and its gathering strength. Let us recall the history of the past 50 years. Pius XII (1939-1958) had wanted 'a rigid, authoritarian Church whose traditions are sacrosanct... [He] set his face against... ecumenism... re-emphasised the rigidity and authoritarian nature of the Church, at the same time making it more difficult for other Churches to work towards union with the Roman Catholic Church... The Church appeared to be entrenched in the Middle Ages, symbolised by the official declaration of the dogma of the assumption of the Virgin Mary'. John XXIII (1958-1963), with the Second Vatican Council, introduced 'a new ecumenical atmosphere... Paul VI (1963-1978) retained the ecumenical emphasis... [But] John Paul II [1978-2005] turned away from the conversations with the Churches of the Reformation to... the Orthodox Churches and the Church of England. Successive years showed an increasing uneasiness with the effects of the Second Vatican Council'. Cardinal Ratzinger (later to become Benedict XVI), appointed head of Holy Office (the name of which was changed to try to avoid its historical links with the Inquisition) 'to watch vigilantly over [the] purity' of the faith, thought Vatican II had 'been unfavourable for the Catholic Church'. His report, published in 1985, was clear. As Edwin Robertson put it: 'Nothing disguises its reactionary character. This is a return to the Church of Pius XII' (Robertson pp291-294).

So said Robertson in 1986. His words have proved prophetic. Ratzinger, as Benedict XVI, dismantling the 'liberalising' innovations introduced by his predecessor, John Paul II, 'is planning a purification of the Roman liturgy in which decades of trendy innovations will be swept away. This recovery of the sacred is intended to draw Catholics closer to the Orthodox, and ultimately to heal the 1000-year Great Schism. But it is also designed to attract vast numbers of conservative Anglicans, who will be offered the protection of the

Holy Father if they convert... Benedict's pontificate moved into a new phase on July 7th [2007], with the publication of his apostolic letter *Summorum Pontificum*. With a stroke of his pen, the Pope restored the traditional Latin Mass – in effect banned for 40 years – to parity with modern liturgy... The liberation of the Latin liturgy, the rapprochement with Eastern Orthodoxy, the absorption of former Anglicans – all these ambitions reflect Benedict's conviction that the Catholic Church must rediscover the liturgical treasure of Christian history to perform its most important task: worshipping God' (Thompson). As I write, Feb. 2009, Benedict is reinstating four anti-Vatican II bishops who had been excommunicated.

Reformed and evangelical sacramentalists, beware! Look before you leap! Sacramentalism may seem a very tiny seed, but it has within it huge potential which will become apparent to most only after the rampant weed it produces has grown way beyond control. For those who do not know what I am talking about, may I suggest they have a chat with those responsible for trying to eradicate the wild rhododendron of the woodland whose pretty purple flowers seem so innocent – pleasing – in the spring sunshine.

Means of grace

'Means of grace' is not easy to define (see Berkhof pp604-609), but I am writing against the idea that in baptism God conveys that which it symbolises; namely, regeneration, union with Christ, washing from sin, and so on, the very thing which is believed and taught: 'Perkins was the clearest and most popular of the early Puritan theologians; his teaching on the theology of the Lord's supper is typical. Applying his general definition of sacraments... it should be noted that it is a sign representative... a seal confirming God's holy covenant of love with his people, and an instrument conveying Christ and all his benefits, chiefly pardon and eternal life, to the faithful' (Davies Vol.1 p283). Calvin: 'When we speak of sacraments, two things are to be considered; the sign and the thing itself. In baptism, the sign is water, but the thing is the washing of the soul by the blood of Christ and the mortifying of the flesh. The institution of Christ includes these two things' (Calvin: *Commentaries* Vol.22 Part 2 p118). As always, Calvin added the usual qualifiers – but see my earlier comments.

Pratt: 'In its own way, the Reformed understanding of baptism is highly sacramental. That is, Reformed theology views baptism as a mysterious [in truth, a confused and confusing – DG] encounter with God that takes place through a rite involving physical elements and special ceremony... Calling baptism a "means of grace" distinguishes the Reformed tradition from Protestants who conceive... baptism as a mere [*sic*] symbol. Unlike Baptists and Anabaptists who tend to speak of baptism only [*sic*] as an "ordinance" [which is what it is – DG], Calvinists have characteristically spoken of baptism not only as an ordinance, but also as a sacrament or a mystery, a rite through which God applies grace. Although the Reformed vocabulary of "sacrament" was adopted from Roman Catholicism [note the admission – DG], the basis for recognising sacraments as a means of grace was inferred from Scripture... In Reformed theology, the preaching of the word in the power of the Spirit is the primary means by which faith and salvation come to those whom God has chosen. No rite may serve this primary role... [However,] the visible rite of baptism is added to the preaching of the word, in order to confirm what is preached, and what we experience through the inward work of the Holy Spirit in connection with preaching... In the Reformed view, baptism does not normally[!] convey spiritual benefits apart from the preaching and reception of the gospel... Reformed theology's emphasis on God's sovereignty and freedom leaves room for the sacraments to work in unexpected ways, but Scripture establishes the norm that the sacraments work in conjunction with the preaching of the word. Further[more], like the preaching of the word, the sacraments do not guarantee that their recipients will receive the blessings they offer'.

Some comments are called for, both here and below. Note the 'mysterious'. As Nettles pointed out: 'This approach to sacramentalist theology is more confusing than it is spiritually mysterious. Pratt says that "spiritual realities occur in conjunction with baptism", but he lacks certainty as to how or even whether they actually occur. More confusing, and even disturbing, is his contention that "Reformed theology's emphasis on divine sovereignty and freedom leaves room for the sacraments to work in unexpected ways". From his discussion, we are led to believe that we really do not know what the sacraments mean, what they convey, when they might transport sacramental grace, and when they might not'. This is right. Let me prove it. Take Pratt himself: 'When the Scriptures attribute the "names and effects" of God's saving mercy to the rite of baptism, they speak in a sort of theological shorthand by metonymy ["the substitution of the name of an attribute... for that of the thing meant" (*Concise*)], leaving the precise relationship mysterious or unexplained. Reformed theology concurs with Scripture [this is begging the question – DG] that there is more than meets the eye in the rite of baptism. Spiritual realities occur in conjunction with baptism [according to the Reformed], but the Scriptures do not explain in detail how baptism and divine grace are connected'. Pratt quoted Acts 2:38; Rom. 6:3-7; Tit. 3:5; 1 Pet. 3:21. All apart from Acts 2:38, as I have said, refer to spiritual baptism. And if Acts 2:38 *is* saying what Reformed theologians claim, and if the other verses, as the Reformed claim, *do* speak of water baptism, then although Scripture no more explains how baptism saves than it explains how faith saves, there can be no if-or-but about it – baptism saves. Is that a conclusion the Reformed can live with? Note also the 'inferred': 'The basis for recognising sacraments as a means of grace was inferred from Scripture'. How about some *direct* teaching? In any case, with respect it was not 'inferred' from *Scripture*; it was, as I have shown, established by the *Confessions*, which in turn were deduced from the scholastic theory of the covenants invented by the Reformed, and was in fact a classic case of arguing in a circle. I remind you, reader, of what Pratt himself admitted: 'To understand how baptism relates to covenant, we must delve further into'... Into what? Romans? Galatians? NO. 'We must delve further into Westminster's theology' (John H.Armstrong pp59-64,74).

As Anthony Collins, in 1713, observed: 'Priests are not set apart to study divinity, as lawyers and physicians are to study law and medicine. The priests do not study divinity so-called, but only how to maintain a certain *system* of divinity. Thus the Popish, Mohammedan, Lutheran and Presbyterian priests study their several [various] systems'. As Friesen commented: 'Not only have the "Popish, Mohammedan, Lutheran and Presbyterian priests" studied only their own "several systems"; they have also declared these systems to be veritable embodiments of truth, and attacked – indeed, declared to be heretical – all those who would argue otherwise... Rather than return again and again to "search the Scriptures... (John 5:39)", theologians and confessional historians have therefore repeatedly returned to the interpretation of the Scriptures given by their founders, in the process tending only to confirm their various systems of divinity'. Friesen quoted Clarence Bauman who, with penetration (I feel the force of it), noted 'that the various interpretations of the Sermon on the Mount "are for the most part motivated by the dubious aim of restricting the scope of its meaning, qualifying the sense of its validity, and limiting the context of its relevance"' (Friesen pp6-7,141, emphasis mine).

Finally, getting back to the subject in hand, Spurgeon: 'I shall give great offence if I... say, as in the sight of God, that I am persuaded that so long as infant baptism is practised in any... church, Popery will have a door set wide open for its return. It is one of those nests which must come down, or the foul birds will build again in it. We must come to the law and the testimony [that is, Scripture], and any ordinance which is not plainly taught in Scripture must be put away. As long as you give baptism to an unregenerate child, people will imagine that it must do the child good; for they will ask: If it does not do it any good, why is it baptised? The statement that it puts children into the covenant, or renders them members of the visible church, is only a veiled form of the fundamental error of baptismal regeneration. If you keep up the ordinance, you will always have men superstitiously believing that some good comes to the babe thereby, and what is this but sheer Popery? Since the child cannot understand what is done, any good which it receives must come to it after the occult manner so much in vogue with the superstitious; is it a wonder that Popish beliefs grow out of it?' (Spurgeon: *Metropolitan* Vol.19 p556).

Lloyd-Jones on 'sacrament'

I said I would return to Lloyd-Jones on 'sacrament'. 'It is a word that is not found in the Scriptures, but has been introduced into the Church, and her teaching, in subsequent centuries... In pagan religions, [it] was the word used for a secret rite or initiation ceremony... It was certainly true of the mystery pagan religions in the ancient world, and that idea was borrowed by the

Christian Church in order to describe the means of grace which comes to people in this particular way'. Despite this frank admission, Lloyd-Jones played with fire. Dismissing the symbolic view of the ordinances as 'extreme', he plumped for what he called 'the traditional, Reformed Protestant teaching'; namely, that 'the sacraments, so-called, not only signify grace but, as the Westminster Confession puts it, they also seal the grace... The elements are actually a means of conveying grace to us... When we receive any one [either] of these sacraments [baptism or the Lord's supper], we must realise that it is not merely some external representation, but [it] is truly a means of grace, and we should be conscious of receiving something which only comes to us in that special way... [In particular,] when people are baptised they should be conscious that grace is conveyed to them personally in this special way, so that what they have believed in general, they now know to be theirs... It is by this means that God has chosen not only to signify, but also to seal to us our redemption, our forgiveness, the remission of our sins, our union with Christ, our being baptised into him and our receiving the Holy Spirit'. Lloyd-Jones cited Rom. 4:11, but I have already dealt with this misapplication of the verse. I also remind you, reader, that Protestant Churches, not excluding those who hold to the Westminster documents, have taught – and still teach – something far more than baptism being a seal. Baptismal regeneration is rampant, and not only emanating from the Vatican. Why... Lloyd-Jones himself declared that 'the sacraments are not only signs, but are also seals of grace. They confirm the grace that we have already received. Yes, but shall we go further? They even *exhibit* it, says the Westminster Confession, meaning that in a sense they *convey* it'. He tried to distance himself from the Roman Catholic position, but his plea was weak. Speaking about the supper, he denied transubstantiation, and said the grace does not come 'mechanically in the symbols'. Nevertheless, in saying this, he was also talking about baptism and the grace received in it (Lloyd-Jones: *The Church* pp26,28-31,46, emphasis his). But is the notion of baptismal regeneration wrong merely because it is said to happen 'mechanically'? This was Calvin's concern over the Papist view of the supper. See below. There is a lot more wrong with Papist sacramentalism than that! Sacramentalism *itself* is the root trouble!

I have noted the ambiguities, contradictions and caveats used by Reformed teachers, and made the point that non-experts can very easily gloss over the caveats and swallow the best bits. Lloyd-Jones should have been more precise. What grace is conveyed in baptism? What grace is administered to babies in baptism? I acknowledge that he himself came down on the side of baptising only adult believers, but he was not definite enough, even though he knew very well that obscurity is not an option in this matter. He knew that many who talk of baptism as a seal also baptise infants. Have those babies received grace in their baptism? I am sorry that he said 'it ill behoves us to be over-dogmatic and to give the impression that there is only one possible point of view' (Lloyd-Jones: *The Church* pp35-36,39-43). As I have said, I fully accept that good men disagree about the subject, but no useful purpose is served by everybody speaking in muted, vague and tepid terms. Let the 'battle' be fought (in love) and then, like Paul and Barnabas, if we cannot agree, let us go our separate ways. This, I realise, will mean separate churches, but at least all will be out in the open. What is more, as an anti-sacramentalist, I have to accept the consequences of my view – and I do. With respect, sacramentalists must likewise accept the ultimate consequence of their view. And *that*, whatever the Reformed qualifiers, is baptismal regeneration.

The Reformed, sacraments and preaching

Some Reformed infant-baptisers give almost the same weight to the sacraments as they do to preaching. Let me re-quote Pratt, for instance: 'In Reformed theology, the preaching of the word in the power of the Spirit is the primary means by which faith and salvation come to those whom God has chosen. No rite may serve this primary role... [However,] the visible rite of baptism is added to the preaching of the word, in order to confirm what is preached, and what we experience through the inward work of the Holy Spirit in connection with preaching... In the Reformed view, baptism does not normally[!] convey spiritual benefits apart from the preaching and reception of the gospel... Reformed theology's emphasis on God's sovereignty and freedom leaves room for the sacraments to work in unexpected ways, but Scripture establishes the norm that the sacraments work in conjunction with the preaching of the word. Further[more], like the preaching of the word, the sacraments do not guarantee that their recipients will receive the blessings they offer' (John H.Armstrong pp62-63).

I said I would return to this. Note the subtle (assumed) parallel Pratt drew between preaching and the sacraments. Let me probe it a little. In gospel preaching, sinners are offered Christ and salvation. 'The recipients' – those who believe – are promised and assured that they will be saved (Acts 16:31). And they are; they all are; they always are. No 'if' or 'but' or 'maybe'. This is very different to the Reformed view of the sacraments – 'their recipients' are not guaranteed the blessings. What is more, in gospel preaching, Christ is *offered* to sinners. I thought, according to the Reformed view, that Christ is *present* and *presented* in the sacraments; he is actually there. For these two reasons, the assumed parallel does not exist. I can do no better than repeat this from Nettles, quoted earlier: 'Is there any other aspect of ostensibly saving grace that operates in such an inconsistent manner or that cannot be relied on to accomplish its stated purpose?' (John H.Armstrong p75).

But other Reformed infant-baptisers go further than Pratt, and put the sacraments *above* preaching. Yes! It is true. Calvin, after a measured start, took a higher view of the sacraments than Pratt – much higher: 'The Holy Spirit does not ingraft all men into Christ, or endue them with faith... Those whom he does so endue, he... uses for that purpose the preaching of the gospel and the dispensation of the sacraments, together with the administration of all

211

kinds of discipline... The means which the Holy Spirit employs in calling us effectually from spiritual death, and preserving the church... [are] baptism and the Lord's supper. These means are, as it were, the royal sceptre of Christ, by which, through the efficacy of his Spirit, he commences his spiritual reign in the church, advances it from day to day, and after this life, without the use of means, finally perfects it... God purifies his church, so as to be "holy and without blemish" (Eph. 5:26-27)... He promises this cleansing by means of baptism, and performs it in his elect... In regenerating his people... he destroys the dominion of sin, by supplying the agency of the Spirit... [And, quoting Augustine:] "This law of sin is... remitted in spiritual regeneration... because the guilt is forgiven in the sacrament by which believers are regenerated... The law of sin... is forgiven in baptism"... Forgiveness of sins... is dispensed to us by the ministers and pastors of the church, either in the preaching of the gospel or the administration of the sacraments' (Calvin: *Institutes* Vol.1 pp29,517-518; Vol.2 p299). Phew! I fully acknowledge that Calvin can be confusing, at least sometimes muddling 'regeneration', 'repentance', 'faith' and 'sanctification' (Calvin: *Institutes* Vol.1 pp508,515-517; Harrison p34), but this in no way moderates his exorbitant claims for baptism. See below for Calvin on the supper. As for the Puritans, Goodwin certainly seemed to value the sacraments above preaching – preaching is like the moon, he said, variable; the supper, however, is like the sun, constant (Davies Vol.2 pp316-317). Sibbes on baptism: 'Here is the excellency of the sacrament; it comes more home than the word, it seals the general promise of God particularly to myself. I am sealed in the sacrament, and withal I find the stamp of the Spirit in my heart' (Sibbes: *2 Corinthians 1* p462). *More* home! The sacrament comes *more* home than the word. For a full examination of Papists, Anglican and Puritans on the sacraments, see Davies Vol.1 pp30-123; Vol.2 pp286-325). See also Lusk: 'Paedobaptism' p116.

But what of Mark (1:4); 16:16; Acts 2:38; 22:16?

Indeed, what of Mark (1:4); 16:16; Acts 2:38; 22:16? 'He who believes and is baptised will be saved... Repent, and let every one of you be baptised in the name of Jesus Christ for the remission of sins; and you shall receive the gift of the Holy Spirit... Arise and be baptised, and wash away your sins, calling on the name of the Lord'. Water baptism is definitely in view in these verses. On Acts 2:38; 22:16, Wright pulled no punches: 'We should not separate repentance from baptism as what receives the forgiveness of sins', noting how Calvin audaciously 'corrected' Peter in Acts 2:38 (Calvin: *Commentaries* Vol.18 Part 2 pp118-120). As for Mark 16:16, although the Reformers called on the verse, Wright did not, since he thought the passage 'cannot be regarded as part of original Mark' (Wright: *What...?* pp88-90). What, then, of these passages? Do they teach that salvation comes through baptism? that baptism is, after all, a means of saving grace? that it is a sacrament? indeed, that it is *the* sacrament? Not in my opinion. Let me grasp the nettle.

I first note that in all three passages, faith (Mark 16:16), repentance (Acts 2:38) or other evidence of regeneration (Acts 9:5-6,11,18; 22:8,10; 26:15) precedes baptism, and that in Mark 16:16 damnation is expressly ascribed to unbelief, not lack of baptism. All this dovetails perfectly with the rest of the New Testament. So what do the verses teach? Baptism exhibits, symbolises, pictures, represents, illustrates the salvation wrought in believers, and it is administered for their instruction and encouragement, and as a testimony to unbelievers. (Supremely, of course, baptism is obedience to Christ).

The alternative boils down to Luther's conclusion: 'To put it most simply, the power, effect, benefit, fruit and purpose of baptism is to save... To be saved... is nothing else than to be delivered from sin, death and the devil, and to enter into the kingdom of Christ and live with him for ever' (Wright: *What...?* pp96-97).

I do not see any half-way house between these two positions. Baptism cannot be *a* means of conveying saving grace. It is either *the* means of conveying saving grace, or it is a symbol of the saving grace *which has already been conveyed* by the Spirit. The choice has to be made. Huge consequences inevitably follow. It would seem sensible, to say the least, to test any conclusion, drawn from these verses, by the doctrine and practice throughout the rest of the New Testament. And this, I submit, is unequivocal. Faith is the means of salvation, and grace is the cause (Acts 15:11; Rom. 3:21 – 5:11; Eph. 2:5,8).

In passing, although I call baptismal regeneration 'Luther's conclusion', in truth he was only revealing how well he had imbibed Augustine, the head of his order. In any case, as I have shown, Luther was far from being alone; Calvin, the framers of the Belgic and Westminster Confessions, and so on, all took a similar line. See Wright: *What...?* pp94-99. Calvin, typical of the Reformers and the Reformed, of course, wanted it both ways. Even though at times he argued for baptismal regeneration, he could also distance himself from the notion. See Calvin: *Commentaries* Vol.18 Part 2 pp118-120; Vol.19 Part 1 pp302-303; *Institutes* Vol.2 p520. See also Owen: *Psalm 130* in *Works* Vol.6 p466; Gill Vol.5 pp817,976. For more from Augustine, see Appendix 2.

Sacramentalism leads to sacerdotalism

Sacramentalism has consequences – not least sacerdotalism; that is, priestcraft. Modern-day Reformed infant-baptisers still want to avoid the same: 'We can declare the powerful significance and blessings of the sacraments without becoming sacerdotalists' (Wilkins: 'Covenant' p67). From the evidence I have seen, this is very unlikely. History makes it seem inevitable that when sacramentalism begins to rule the roost, can priestcraft be far behind? After all, Calvin was prepared to say: 'What the minister figures and attests by outward action, God performs inwardly'. True, Calvin went on: 'Lest that which God claims for himself alone should be ascribed to mortal man'. But it is the same old story; towering promises qualified by health

213

warnings. Nevertheless, Calvin was quite happy with infant baptism performed by Roman priests, even if they 'were most ignorant of God, and all piety, or were despisers', as long as they were ordained. Ordained! That's the point. Baptism is minister's work: 'It is improper for private individuals to take upon themselves the administration of baptism; for it, as well as the dispensation of the supper, is part of the ministerial office... The practice which has been in use for many ages, and even almost from the very commencement of the church, for laics to baptise, in danger of death, when a minister could not be present in time, cannot, it appears to me, be defended on sufficient grounds'. Here we have it; clergy and laity! An ignorant, ungodly, God-despising 'minister' can baptise; a godly 'layman' cannot. Priestcraft, pure and simple! Sacerdotalism! Sacramentalism *will* lead to sacerdotalism.

And notice the concern about calling in a minister to baptise a baby before it dies. Why the desperate anxiety to baptise a dying infant? Why? It speaks volumes. I have met this precise alarm, personally, in a Roman Catholic midwife. And I know of a believer who, at the time, was a junior nurse on duty in a premature baby unit at University College, London in the 1950s, when, sadly, a baby died in the night. The senior nurse (a Roman Catholic) 'assured' my friend that she had had the baby baptised. This misguided – abominable – panic by Papists, yes, but my point is that here we have it in *Calvin*. His sole concern was that it should be done by a member of the clergy!

There is another point. Talking of Calvin's acceptance of baptism by Roman priests, it was his blind rage against the Anabaptists which drove him to concede not an inch on re-baptism, even for those baptised as infants by Rome – the Anabaptists 'who deny that we are duly [truly] baptised, because we were baptised in the Papacy by wicked men and idolaters; hence they furiously insist on ana-baptism'. Calvin dismissed this as 'absurdities'. This outburst needs setting to rights. Before that, however, let me draw attention to something else – something which, at first glance, seems small but is of huge significance.

Apoplectic over the Anabaptists, Calvin cast common sense to the four winds: 'Against these absurdities, we shall be sufficiently fortified if we reflect that by [Roman] baptism we were initiated not into the name of any man, but into the name of the Father, and the Son, and the Holy Spirit and, therefore, that baptism is not of man, but of God, by whomsoever it may have been administered. Be it that those who baptised us were most ignorant of God and all piety, or were despisers, still they did not baptise us into a fellowship with their ignorance or sacrilege, but into the faith of Jesus Christ, because the name which they invoked was not their own but God's; nor did they baptise into any other name... The objection that baptism ought to be celebrated in the assembly of the godly [which Rome is not!], does not prove that it loses its whole efficacy because it is partly defective'. And, right to the end, in his last and unfinished work, Calvin was still maintaining his stance on the

214

acceptability of Roman baptism, even though performed in so corrupt a system: 'In the Papacy, such declension has grown up through many ages, that they have altogether denied God. Hence they have no connection with him, because they have corrupted his whole worship by their sacrilege, and their religion... differs in nothing from the corruptions of the heathen. And yet it is certain that a portion of God's covenant remains among them, because... God remains faithful... God's covenant with [the Jews] is [was?] not abolished, although the greater part of the people had utterly abandoned God. So also it must be said of the Papists... although with regard to themselves... they are without it [the covenant], and show by their obstinacy that they are the sworn enemies of God. Hence, it arises, that our baptism [which we received from the Papists] does not need renewal, because although the devil has long reigned in the Papacy, yet he could not altogether extinguish God's grace; indeed, a Church is among them... The Church is indeed among them; that is, God has his Church there, but hidden and wonderfully preserved; but it does not follow that they are worthy of any honour; indeed, they are more detestable, because they ought to bear sons and daughters to God, but they bear them for the devil and for idols' (Calvin: *Institutes* Vol. 2 pp504,521,524-525; see also pp313-314; *Commentaries* Vol.12 Part 1 pp120-121). See earlier note of Calvin writing to John Knox (Calvin: *Letters* pp215-216).

Pace Calvin, this is nothing but absurdity! – even though he was here following his mentor, Augustine. (But Calvin, for once, fell out with Augustine over a corollary. The Donatists' view that 'bad ministers' make the sacraments ineffective, Francis J.Beckwith dismissed as the 'error' which 'led Augustine to develop the *ex opere operato* teaching on the sacraments' (Beckwith p92) – which Calvin abhorred). The important point I wish to make is this: in addition to his preoccupation with 'the minister' and 'the formula' – if an ordained man baptises using the right words, the baptism is effective (note the 'efficacy'), even if he does it in the Church of Rome – observe how Calvin here destroyed many of the arguments for infant baptism – a parent being a believer, the covenant, households – unless he was saying Rome comprised believers, men and women in the covenant. Of course he did not think that! 'They are without it... sworn enemies of God', he declared. In other words, by allowing – justifying – Roman baptism by an ordained minister using the right words, Calvin was, in fact, allowing – justifying – the promiscuous baptism of infants, regardless of the state of the parents – even to the extent that 'their religion... differs in nothing from the corruptions of the heathen'! And, of course, by accepting Roman baptism, he was gathering fuel for the ecumenical fire being fed by many of his followers today. I have little doubt they will eagerly latch on to Calvin and Augustine in this!

Now to take up Calvin's outburst against the Anabaptists. The Anabaptists denied they were re-baptising; they denied infant baptism altogether, let alone as administered by Papist priests. As I have already noted, Calvin allowed his hatred of the Anabaptists to warp his judgement. This also accounts for the way he could not allow himself to accept that Paul re-baptised those disciples at Ephesus who had been baptised by John: 'I deny that they were re-baptised (see *Calv. Instruct. adv. Anabapt.*)'; 'I deny that the baptism of water was repeated' (Calvin: *Institutes* Vol.2 p523; *Commentaries* Vol.19 Part 1 p210). I cannot see how this can be maintained in light of Acts 19:5. Please read again the extract from Wright (in the chapter 'Dangerous Statements') on the way infant baptisers have skewed their theology to stop Anabaptists at all costs. This is worthy of further exploration. Acts 19:1-7 clearly teaches that the men in question were re-baptised. The Fathers were unanimous in this obvious deduction. Origen: 'Those persons... are baptised over again by the apostle'. Jerome: 'They who had been baptised by [John] were afterwards baptised with the baptism of Christ'. Augustine: 'Certain who had the baptism of John were commanded by Paul to be baptised, for they had not the baptism of Christ... Paul administered the baptism of Christ to certain persons because they had received the baptism of John only, and not that of Christ'. As Thieleman J.van Braght observed in 1660: 'For more than 1500 years, never [has there] been a single Greek or Latin divine who doubted that those Ephesians were baptised again'. What about the Reformers? In 1521, Melanchthon: 'Those who had been washed in the baptism of John had to be baptised again'. As for Zwingli, in 1524, after his followers had begun to question infant baptism, the Reformer moved. He admitted that Acts 19:1-7 'plainly [bears] witness that twelve men were baptised over again', but, as Friesen commented, 'he sought to get around this apparent conclusion... by arguing that the difficulty was semantic and, therefore, more apparent than real'. 'There could only be one baptism... and therefore the "apparent" differences had to be explained away'. Heinrich Bullinger, Zwingli's successor in Zurich, carried on the fight against the Anabaptists: 'Those twelve men were not baptised again of Paul with water'. Friesen called Bullinger's argument a 'tortuous rationalisation against the apparent [obvious] meaning of the text, and the unanimous opinion of the... Fathers'. Calvin's statement I have already mentioned. Finally, John Whitgift, who let the cat out of the bag: 'It is dangerous to understand... [Acts 19:5] of baptism, lest we should... fall into the heresy of the Anabaptists'. As Friesen justly remarked: 'Here one sees the real reason for the tortured and conflicting interpretations of this passage... From the above Reformation passages one could think that hermeneutics is the art of rationalising your predetermined point of view!' (Friesen pp80,131-136).

Andrew J.Webb's response to the charge of baptismal regeneration
Some Reformed infant-baptisers, stung by what they call the 'Federal Vision' claim – that the Westminster Confession teaches baptismal regeneration – have tried to fend it off; Andrew J.Webb, for one (website of the Providence PCA Mission Church; www.providencepca.com/'Essays'/'Soteriology'/'Is Baptism a Converting Ordinance?', July 23rd 2008). Nevertheless, in my view, the charge still sticks, and its consequences remain.

Webb quoted John 'Rabbi' Duncan's letter to Spurgeon: 'Horrible as the doctrine of baptismal regeneration is, it would be still more so if combined with those scriptural principles which are usually called Calvinism'. Webb deplored the fact that the doctrine of baptismal regeneration *is* being taught today in 'the Reformed community'. He was specific. He noted that 'Norman Shepherd in his book *The Call of Grace*, recently published by P&R, had this to say: "Baptism is the moment when we see the transition from death to life and a person is saved... This covenant sign and seal marks his conversion and his entrance into the church as the body of Christ. From the perspective of the covenant, he is united to Christ when he is baptised... Baptism marks the entrance into the kingdom of God and the beginning of life-long training as kingdom subjects. According to the great commission, conversion without baptism is an anomaly. A sinner is not really 'converted' until he is baptised... Christians are those who have been baptised. Unbelievers are those who have not been baptised"'. Webb also quoted fellow-PCA ministers, Rich Lusk and Jeff Myers, to the same effect. In particular, he quoted David Wright who, as I have shown, convincingly argued that the Westminster 'Confession teaches baptismal regeneration... The Westminster divines viewed baptism as the instrument and occasion of regeneration by the Spirit, of the remission of sins, of ingrafting into Christ (*cf.* 28:1)'.

Webb dismissed this, saying it 'begs the questions'. This, of course, is one way of dealing with the problem! In addition, he went on to cite some well-worn Reformed qualifiers. Even here, however, his extracts included Robert Shaw's statement that infant baptism 'is neither to be called nor accounted christening – that is, making them Christians: for the infants of believing parents are born within the covenant, and so are Christians and visible Church members; and by baptism this right of theirs is acknowledged, and they are solemnly admitted to the privileges of Church membership'. This certainly somewhat lessens the so-called efficacy of infant baptism, but only on the ground that the infant is already a Christian by reason of his birth to a believer! Out of frying pan into the fire!

Above all, for Webb, the solution to the problem lies with 'the teachings of the Southern Presbyterians and Princetonians... The answer to how we deal with and teach infant baptism lies... with a greater appreciation of the work of the Southern Presbyterian theologians'! As always, however, this includes the usual qualifiers. 'While never denuding the sacrament of baptism of its efficacy as a means of grace or reducing it from its rightful place as a sign and seal of the covenant of grace to the status of a "mere symbol" – [they] have sharpened our understanding of the sacrament. By using more careful language, they have safeguarded us from the dire errors of sacramentalism'. In other words, by 'using more careful language', such theologians have explained how infant baptisers can have their cake and eat it.

But what about Calvin? Since he, following Augustine, is the primary theologian of the Reformed system, shouldn't he have sorted it all out? Of course! Yet, as I have shown, Calvin himself has been a major source of the problem. In fact, those Reformed teachers who are trying to fend off the claim that baptismal regeneration is 'kosher' Reformed doctrine, find Calvin an embarrassment in this regard. Webb had to admit that in 'Calvin and some[!] of the continental Reformed theologians, there is indeed an unhappy tendency to use language in regard to infant baptism that would seem to imply that they are regenerated at the time of their baptism... For while I am a great admirer of men like Calvin and Ursinus, they frequently [note the word!] make statements regarding the efficacy of the sacraments that either can be misunderstood or which do indeed, in the case of infants, seem[!] to exceed the bounds of Scripture... We would... be very foolish to suppose that Federal Vision advocates have no statements they can appeal to in the work of Calvin and the continental Reformers in order to support their even more sweeping sacramental theories'. Webb was only admitting the undeniable. I have given plenty of evidence.

But what sort of things did he have in mind? 'For instance, Ursinus in his commentary on the Heidelberg Catechism makes statements such as: "There is in baptism a double washing: an external washing with water and an internal washing with the blood and Spirit of Christ. The internal is signified and sealed by that which is external, and is always joined with it in the proper use of baptism"'. What a remarkable assertion! The most that Webb could salvage from this diabolical statement was to quote the Reformer again in his use of the customary qualifier-technique: 'Ursinus immediately qualifies this by noting that the internal and external washing *"may* take place at the same time"' (emphasis his). I pause. Some sort of qualifier it may be, but in *practical* terms, it's useless. Why? Well, if I believed Ursinus' categorical assertion, I wouldn't be desperately worried whether my baby was regenerated at the time the minister sprinkled him – or later; I would sleep contentedly, knowing that by having my baby sprinkled, I had guaranteed ('always joined' to his baptism!) his regeneration and final salvation! And if that's not baptismal regeneration, words have lost all meaning.

Let Webb continue. In order to stress the customary Reformed qualifiers, he stated, quite categorically, quoting A.A.Hodge, that 'faith and repentance are the fruits of regeneration, [and] faith and repentance are required as conditions prerequisite to baptism'. Just so! And, as I have shown, Calvin: 'But from this sacrament, as from all others, we gain nothing, unless in so far as we receive in faith'. Very well. But here we come up against the perennial problem for infant baptisers – how can a baby exercise saving faith and repentance? 'The problem with the way Ursinus and Calvin occasionally speak of baptism is that they presuppose that this necessary faith exists in the children of believers. Note the language in Ursinus here', said Webb. 'After affirming that adults must first believe and make a profession of faith prior to being baptised, Ursinus writes: "This we admit and would add, that to be born in the Church, is to infants, the same thing as a profession of faith. Faith is, indeed, necessary to the use of baptism with this distinction. Actual faith is required in adults, and an inclination to faith in infants… Infants born of believing parents have faith as to inclination"'. Amazing! What is being 'born in the Church', may I ask? And where in the New Testament do we find that being 'born in the Church, is to infants, the same thing as a profession of faith'? And where in the Bible do we come across this distinction as to 'actual faith' and 'an inclination to faith'? And what is this 'inclination to faith in infants… Infants born of believing parents have faith as to inclination'? Do they? Is every baby born to a believer 'inclined to faith'? Webb, admitting the obvious flaw in Ursinus' assertion, noted the 'numerous infant children of believers [recorded in Scripture] without such an inclination – Esau, Hophni, Phinehas, Ishmael'. And he quoted Charles Hodge with approval: 'Multitudes of the baptised perish'. To get out of the maze, Webb fell back on 'the Southern Presbyterian theologians' and their talk of those baptised as infants as 'minor citizens... ecclesiastical... minors... In the Church, this ecclesiastical minority terminates only when the man is born again of the Spirit of God, it being known that a new and divine life is indispensable to fulfil the obligations of a Christian'. But this, of course, has only fudged the problem – not solved it.

Finally, as I have said, Webb accused Shepherd, Lusk, Myers, Wright and others of 'begging the questions'. Pot and kettle? As one not personally involved in this internal Reformed debate, as far as I can see, the Reformed believers-in-baptismal-regeneration at least have the merit of consistency. They have read the Reformers and their Confessions, and they believe them. All three – Reformed believers-in-baptismal-regeneration, the Reformers and their Confessions – are wrong; they are *biblically* wrong. But at least the modern fully-fledged sacramentalists are *consistently* wrong. What they have found, they do not try to shroud in a metaphysical smokescreen. And above all, as always, what matters most is what 'ordinary' parents believe, standing at the font with their baby in their arms. I have little doubt about what that is! And they have plenty of teachers, some of them giants of covenant theology – past and present – to whom they can appeal!

Dangerous views on "consecration", and their consequences

Others, beside Calvin, have taken too high a view of 'consecration'; Hendriksen, for instance. Leaving aside the Lord's supper, speaking of 'the common table', our ordinary food, he said: 'By means of God's blessing upon [our food] and by means of our confident prayer, it has been consecrated... that is, set apart for holy use, lifted into the spiritual realm. For the Christian, eating and drinking are no secular activities' (Hendriksen: *Timothy and Titus* p148). This is a step too far. Poole was much better: '"Sanctified" in this place signifies made pure, or lawful to be used' (Poole p782). As was Gill: 'Set apart for use, and may be lawfully used at all times... Every creature may be made use of... "Prayer"... being used before eating for a blessing on the food, and after it, in a way of thanksgiving for it, sanctifies every creature of God, or gives men a free use of any, or all of them... Thus our Lord Jesus Christ, at meals, used to take the food and bless it, or ask a blessing on it (Matt. 14:19)' (Gill Vol.6 p606).

But going on to the Lord's supper, what about 1 Cor. 10:16-22? What about 'the cup of blessing which we bless'? Paul, of course, was basing his words on Jewish meal-time practice – the head of the house would pronounce a blessing on the food while holding a piece of bread, after which, the others having said Amen, he would break it and pass it around. But, and this is the point, 'there is no question of blessing the food and transforming it into something different' (Fee: *1 Corinthians* pp467-468, quoting H.W.Beyer).

Taking up this last point, it is objectionable – wrong – for ministers to use the Aaronic priestly blessing as it stands (Num. 6:22-27) when closing a service; worse still is it, as I have witnessed, for a (Reformed Baptist) minister to raise his arms above the congregation, the palms of his hands facing us, as he pronounces the words. It smacks of sacerdotalism; it is sacerdotalism.

Let me give an example of how sinister things can develop. Although it is far removed from mainstream Reformed Christianity, it shows what can happen when people set foot on the slippery slope. I have already referred to the Taylorite Exclusive Brethren. Consider this. At a meeting at Redland, Bristol, March 5th 1932, a certain A.E.M. stated that when believers meet to break bread, Christ is absent. He was challenged: What about Matt. 18:20? A.E.M. replied that he did not think the verse could be tied so definitely, as the questioner was suggesting, to the point he himself was making. When the 'Little Flock' hymn book was re-issued later that year, the words of hymn 233 – 'In thy presence break the bread' – were said to be 'incongruous'. In an explanatory paper, it was stated that from now on the accepted teaching would be that Christ is present at the Lord's supper, and that spiritually, *but only after the bread is broken and not before*. Then, in 1933, the leader, James Taylor, propounded the dogma that although Scripture teaches the priesthood of all believers, not all believers are in a 'priestly' condition; not all believers are spiritually fit enough to be so regarded. Preaching and teaching, and distribution of the elements at the Lord's supper, should be in the hands of those who are recognised as 'priestly'. Such a sequence of events carried large implications. Let G.H.Lang take up the account: 'Putting it all together, the situation arises that certain brethren are priestly in quality; not all believers are so. When one of these "priestly" men has given thanks for the bread and cup, [and broken the bread] then the Lord becomes present in some sense which was not before the case... [Although] the Exclusive view as stated does not attach [Christ's] presence to the elements in particular, [it] carries the... conception that the absent Lord becomes present when the elements have been blessed [and the bread broken] by a "priestly" person. This is close to transforming the breaking of bread into a priestly sacrament, and indeed a ministering brother among them in London, of long and good standing, wrote to me in 1936 using the very word. He said: "How much saints lose by

Argument 10: Sacraments

supposing that the Supper is only commemorative... Surely there is the sacramental aspect, as well as the monumental [memorial]"' (Lang: *Assembly* pp68-70). Sacerdotalism, pure and simple! According to the BBC website, 'Religion and Ethics', updated May 26th 2009, the present leader of the Exclusive Brethren, Bruce Hales, 'The Man of God' or 'The Elect Vessel', appoints 'local priests' in the assemblies. I recognise that this episode may be dismissed as extreme, but it serves, I think, as a timely warning against the slightest step towards sacramentalism.

Calvin's sacramental view of the Lord's supper

I have already referred to increasing interest in Calvin's view of the supper. Naturally! It is all of a piece with the growth of sacramentalism which I have noted. Calvin held that the sacrament of the supper not only *represents* the benefits of Christ's death and resurrection, it also *presents* them – and Christ himself – to the partakers. Mark Horne: 'Calvin and the Presbyterian standards are clear that Christ is really present to believers, so that they partake of his flesh and blood, with all his benefits, at the Lord's table'. Horne quoted Calvin's own words: 'The substance of the sacraments is the Lord Jesus, and the efficacy of them the graces and blessings which we have by his means. Now the efficacy of the supper is to confirm to us the reconciliation... the washing of our souls which we have in the shedding of his blood; the righteousness which we have in his obedience; in short, the hope of salvation which we have in all that he has done for us. It is necessary, then, that the substance should be conjoined with these'. Horne drew attention to Calvin's use of 'conjoined', noting Westminster's claim that 'Christ and the benefits of the new covenant are represented, sealed and applied to believers' in the sacraments (Westminster p313). Horne: 'Calvin is emphatic that we do not simply receive Christ's benefits but that we receive Christ himself in the Lord's supper' (Horne pp143-146,149). That is how some Calvinists see it today. Consider this, taken from a Reformed liturgy for the Lord's supper 'based on... Calvin's Genevan liturgy... (1542) by A.C.Clifford... (2002)': 'As our Lord Jesus Christ, not content with having once offered his body and blood upon the cross... has also supplied them to us as nourishment for eternal life, so grant... that we may... enjoy together his body and blood, even his entire person... We offer you... thanks... for... bringing us to partake of your Son Jesus Christ, whom you... now impart to us...'.

I mentioned 1 Cor. 10:16-22 a few moments ago. Let me return to it. What about the 'communion'? that is, what did Paul mean when he spoke of those who participate in the supper communing with 'the blood' and 'the body of Christ'? κοινωνια means 'fellowship, association, communion, joint participation' (see Thayer), concerning which Paul compared Jewish, pagan and Christian meals. As Fee observed: 'Precisely what [Paul] intended by that term is problematic... The problem has to do with whether Paul's point – or emphasis – is that in sacred meals, one has κοινωνια with the deity (in the

221

Christian's case, with Christ himself), or with fellow participants in the meal as they worship the deity by sacrifice and by eating in his/her honour'. Because of 1 Cor. 10:17, the emphasis would seem to fall on the union between the participants. 'What the evidence does not seem to allow is a sacramental understanding of the meal itself, as if they were "participating in the Lord" by the actual eating of the food, as though the food were the Lord himself. Neither the language and grammar, nor the example of Israel, nor the examples from the pagan meals allow such a meaning. The "fellowship", therefore, was most likely a celebration of their common life in Christ, based on the new covenant in his blood that had previously bound them together in union with Christ by his Spirit... They were thus together in his presence, where, as host at his table, he shared anew with them the benefits of the atonement... There is little evidence that the food of sacred meals was understood to be an eating of the deity... Since... the cup is specifically interpreted by the Lord (*cf.* Mark 14:24), and continued to be so understood in the early church (1 Cor. 11:25), as "my blood of the new covenant", this language almost certainly refers to their sharing in the provisions and benefits of that covenant'. Fee explained: 'They were by faith looking back... and were thus realising again its benefits... In this way, they shared "in the blood of Christ"'... Thus [the apostle] does not mean that by eating the bread believers have some kind of mystical "participation in" the "broken body" of Christ, but, as he clearly interprets in 1 Cor. 10:17, they are herewith affirming that through Christ's death they are "partners" in the redeemed community, the new eschatological people of God... He is not... suggesting that they become that body through this meal; in [1 Cor.] 12:13 he says that happened through their common "immersion" in the Spirit. Rather, by this meal, they affirm what the Spirit has already brought about through the death and resurrection of Christ... Since there is not the remotest hint in Judaism that the sacrificial food represented God in some way, Paul can only mean by "sharers in the altar" that the participants shared together in the food on the altar... The Christian meal was only an analogy of a sacred meal; their sacrifice had been offered once-for-all, and though now celebrated at the meal, was not a part of the meal, as in the Jewish and pagan meals'. 1 Cor. 11:23-24 confirms this. At the last supper, Christ 'invited his disciples to participate in the meaning and benefits of [his] death' (Fee: *1 Corinthians* pp466-471,549-551).

Calvin took a very different line: 'The meaning of the words is: "By participating in the breaking of bread... you shall be participants also in [Christ's own] body"'. True, Calvin went on to say 'the expression is figurative... the term "body" is applied to the bread, as being the sign and symbol of it'. But he quickly began to move: 'The thing signified is not applied to the sign simply as being a representation of it, but rather as being a symbol (that is, an outward token and evidence) of it... The bread is Christ's [own] body because it assuredly testifies that the body which it represents is held forth to us, or because the Lord, by holding out to us that symbol, gives us at the same time his own body... Hence it is regarded by me as beyond all controversy[!], that the reality is here conjoined with the sign; or, in other words, that we do not less truly become participants in Christ's [own] body in respect of spiritual efficacy, than we partake of the bread'. Calvin, 'rejecting... the dream of Papists' as to 'what manner Christ's body is given to us... some explain [I do – DG] that it is given to us when we are made partakers of all the blessings which Christ has procured for us in his body – when... we by faith embrace Christ as crucified for us, and are raised up from the dead, and in this way are effectually made partakers of all his benefits... I have no objection to their holding such a view'. But Calvin wanted to go much further: In the supper, 'Christ does not simply present to us the benefit of his death and resurrection, but the very body in which he suffered and rose again... Christ's body is *really*... that is *truly* given to us in the supper... our souls are nourished by the substance of the body... though it is at a great distance from us [in heaven]'. As Calvin's editor frankly noted: 'In this passage, as, also, in some other parts of his writings, Calvin seems to [he does!] affirm the real presence of Christ in the Lord's supper'. To let Calvin continue. 'You see bread – nothing more – but you learn that it is a symbol (that is, a sign and evidence) of Christ's body. Do not doubt that the Lord accomplishes what his words intimate – that the body, which you do not at all behold, is given to you, as a spiritual repast. It seems incredible that we should be nourished by Christ's flesh, which is at so great a distance from us [in heaven]. Let us bear in mind that it is a secret and wonderful work of the Holy Spirit, which it were criminal to measure by the standard of our understanding... The supper is a mirror which represents to us Christ crucified... Christ is absent from it in the sense that the supper is a commemoration. For Christ is not visibly present, and is not beheld with our eyes, as the symbols are which excite our remembrance by representing him. In short, in order that he may be present with us, he does not change his place, but communicates to us from heaven the virtue of his flesh, as though it were present (that is, he makes the virtue of his flesh pour down upon us from heaven presently and truly)... The supper then is (so to speak) a kind of memorial... that Christ may put us in mind of the benefit of his death, and that we may recognise it before men... This commemoration has been given us... For, as he is not present with us in a visible form, it is necessary for us to have some symbol of his presence, by which our minds may exercise themselves... Christ's body is presented to the wicked no less than the good... God... presents it in reality... the body is presented to them' (Calvin: *Commentaries* Vol.20 Part 1 pp376-389, emphasis his). Again: 'In the sacraments, the reality is given to us along with the sign; for when the Lord holds out a sacrament, he does not feed our eyes with an empty and unmeaning figure, but joins the truth with it... We ought to believe that the truth must never be separated from the signs, though it be distinguished from them... By the hand of the minister, [Christ] presents to us his body, that it may be actually enjoyed by the godly' (Calvin: *Commentaries*

Vol.7 Part 1 p211). In all this, the appalling consequences of sacramentalism (including sacerdotalism – see above) are impossible to miss.

So what did Calvin mean when he said: 'The sacraments... do not of themselves bestow any grace, but they announce and manifest it'? Not what it sounds like! Rather, Calvin was here distancing himself from Rome; the sacraments do not possess an efficacy in themselves, *ex opere operato*; that is, 'by the work that has been worked', accomplishing what is claimed simply by performing the rite. It is the point I made earlier. Calvin was opposing the view that grace is bestowed 'mechanically'. But that is all! As he had said: 'It is not as if I thought that there is a kind of secret efficacy perpetually inherent in them [the sacraments], by which they can of themselves promote or strengthen faith... The sacraments duly perform their office only when accompanied by the Spirit... If he is wanting, the sacraments can avail us no more than the sun shining on the eyeballs of the blind... They confer nothing, and avail nothing, if not received in faith'. Even so: 'What the minister figures and attests by outward action, God performs inwardly'. He quoted Augustine: 'Herein is the whole fruit of visible sacraments; for what do these visible sacraments avail without that sanctification of invisible grace?'

Nevertheless, Calvin had no doubt of the 'presence of the flesh of Christ in the supper'. But how can this be? Not by transubstantiation. But how? Calvin frankly confessed he did not know: 'Should anyone ask me as to the mode [how Christ's flesh is in the supper], I will not be ashamed to confess that it is too high a mystery either for my mind to comprehend or my words to express; and to speak more plainly, I rather feel than understand it. The truth of God, therefore... [is that] in his sacred supper he [Christ] bids me take, eat and drink his body and blood under the symbols of bread and wine. I have no doubt that he will truly give and I receive'. Reader, do not be misled by Calvin's use of 'symbols' here. He was not adopting Zwingli's (the Bible's) position. After all, he had just said: 'They are greatly mistaken in imagining there is no presence of the flesh of Christ in the supper'. Calvin was not watering down his view of the supper; rather, he was striving against transubstantiation. Even so, Calvin *did* believe that the flesh of Christ is in the supper, represented *and presented* to the partakers: 'Though it seems an incredible thing that the flesh of Christ, while at such a distance from us in respect of place [that is, he is in heaven], should be food to us, let us remember how far the secret virtue of the Holy Spirit surpasses all our conceptions, and how foolish it is to wish to measure its immensity by our feeble capacity. Therefore, what our mind does not comprehend, let faith conceive – namely, that the Spirit truly unites things separated by space. That sacred communion of flesh and blood by which Christ transfuses his life into us, just as if it penetrated our bones and marrow, he testifies and seals in the supper, and that not by presenting a vain or empty sign, but by there exerting an efficacy of the Spirit, by which he fulfils what he promises. And truly the thing there signified, he exhibits and offers to all who sit down at that spiritual feast, although it is beneficially received by believers only... I admit, indeed, that the breaking of bread is a symbol, not the reality. But this being admitted, we duly infer from the exhibition of the symbol, the thing itself is exhibited... The rule which the pious ought always to observe is, whenever they see the symbols instituted by the Lord, to think and feel surely persuaded that the truth of the thing signified is also present... I mean Christ, with his death and resurrection. By the effect, I understand redemption, justification, sanctification, eternal life, and all other benefits which Christ bestows upon us' (Calvin: *Institutes* Vol.2 pp497,503-504,563-564,586-587; Davies Vol.2 pp309-317).

Of course, as we have seen over and over again, the qualifiers are in place as usual – but the old question remains: Do any who follow Calvin happily accept the good news and quietly forget the qualifiers? Indeed, do they all understand the qualifiers? Only eternity will show. Note also the clear echoes of Augustine in his equating of the symbol in the sacrament with the things signified. For the part played by Augustine (as well as the Fathers in general), Luther and Bucer in Calvin's view of the supper, see Wendel pp329-355.

So... where did Calvin end up? Wendel: 'Definitely... Calvin did make, side by side, two distinct affirmations that it is difficult to reconcile: on the one hand, he maintained that the body of Christ is present in the supper, and communicates to us "Jesus Christ with his death and resurrection"; that is, the benefits that his merits have won for us. On the other hand, he declares that the body of the Christ has no local or spatial relationship with the material elements of the eucharist. The Christ is corporeally in heaven, and therefore cannot, even invisibly, be present in several places at once at the supper... Whatever may be the value of the arguments that Calvin adduces to justify his particular interpretation of the eucharist, we must acknowledge that his doctrine leaves one with many obscurities, only imperfectly masked by an exegesis that is often peculiar, and by the appeal to mystery. In spite of the function he assigns to the Holy Spirit in establishing contact between Christ and the believer, it is not easy to see how he could maintain that the faithful "really" receive the body and blood of Christ in the communion' (Wendel pp350-355). Although Davies cited Wendel to the effect that Calvin's clashing assertions are in fact compatible, he himself declared that 'the defect of [Calvin's] theory is that it... posits a miracle to cross the abyss between two incompatible statements'. In short: 'Calvin's logic forsakes him' (Davies Vol.1 p84; Vol.2 p310). Consequently I remain convinced that Wendel was right. Ambiguity, obscurity and worse are the hallmarks of Calvin on the supper – but, nevertheless, he was definite in asserting that Christ is *really* present. See John D.Nicholls, writing on Calvin's view of the supper, where, reader, you will meet with: 'Actually made partakers of his flesh and blood', 'union with Christ's body, which is experienced in the supper', 'partakers of Christ's flesh and blood', 'eating... causes us to be united in his body', 'experience of communion with the very body and blood of Christ', 'Christ's presence in the supper can be spoken of as "real" because by the Spirit we are

in personal contact with his flesh', 'Christ's presence is real', 'real
communion with the body and blood of Christ', 'Christ is actually given to
us', 'partaking of Christ's body in the sacrament', 'Christ is truly present in
the supper'. Nicholl's only worry, it seems, was that 'the weakness of
[Calvin's] presentation is chiefly in the tortuous debates... over the mode of
Christ's presence as real but spiritual. Here his use of the scholastic term
"substance" is both confused and confusing. But', said Nicholls, 'this is not a
fundamental flaw in his doctrine' (Nicholls pp35-54). Oh? My point is this,
however: since Calvin is admitted – by his advocates – to be 'confused and
confusing' on the supper, is there any danger that, if his views are adopted (as
I fear they will be), dreadful consequences may be round the corner?

For the historical repercussions – played out in the confrontation at the
Colloquy of Poissy in 1561 between, on the one hand, Theodore Beza
(Calvin's representative), and, on the other, representatives of Rome, the
Cardinal of Lorraine and Claude d'Espence – see Nugent, especially pp85-89,
98-103,110-177,209-219. Nugent: 'd'Espence had explored Calvin's writings
for passages in which the master spoke clearly and unequivocally of a real and
substantial presence [in the supper]. Calvinists generally avoided the term
"substantial presence", preferring "sacramental presence". But d'Espence was
successful in his researches. He proceeded to read aloud to the [Genevan]
ministers, three passages from... a work of Calvin of that same year, wherein a
substantial presence was taught. d'Espence implored the ministers: "Since he
says the body and blood of Jesus Christ to be in the eucharist, to be
substantially exhibited, given and received there, which he puts in a
substantial, but not local, presence, may we not agree here [and now] on the
true presence?' Beza, of course, had his reply; in Nugent's paraphrase: 'Calvin
simply used the term... in contradistinction to an "imaginary" presence. Beza
repeated: "The symbols are on earth, the things in heaven". d'Espence's
researches [according to Beza] had been in vain'. Oh? Peter Martyr, girded by
Aristotle, joined in and complicated the debate, taking a slightly different line
to both Beza and Calvin. In all the seemingly endless scholastic wranglings
and splitting of split-hairs which went on, 'the great fear of the Calvinists was
that the sign might be confused with the reality'. In trying to keep from
foundering on this reef, Beza showed he fully deserved his reputation as 'one
of the founders of Protestant scholasticism' (Nugent pp137,141,152-
153,158,221). See Nugent's note on Augustine's self-contradiction on the
contested point in the supper (Nugent pp111-112) – Augustine on whom
Calvin depended so heavily. Calvinists must not forget Rome's adept use of
its long memory: 'Vatican II avoided the controversial phrase *ex operate
operato* and emphasised rather the presence of Christ in the sacraments'
(Carson: *Dawn...?* p88). For a full discussion of Calvin's effect on the Puritan
view of the supper, including the 'real presence' see Davies Vol.1 pp30-123;
Vol.2 pp286-325.

A final paragraph on the consequences of all this. I remind you, reader, that Calvin frankly confessed he did not know how the real presence of Christ in the supper comes about: 'Should anyone ask me as to the mode [how Christ's flesh is in the supper], I will not be ashamed to confess that it is too high a mystery either for my mind to comprehend or my words to express; and to speak more plainly, I rather feel than understand it'. Reader, may I ask you: since Calvin said the former, who do you think said the following? 'While I believe the consecrated elements to become truly and really [Christ's] body and blood, I learned to withhold my thoughts as to the mode of this great mystery, but as a mystery to adore it'? It was no Calvinist. Far from it! It was the Tractarian, Edward Bouverie Pusey (Rosser p81). Now, if anyone should think I am making a mountain out of a mole-hill in what I have said in this extended end note, he should remember the words of Nathaniel Dimock, writing in the 19th century, when faced with the Tractarian movement. People, he said, used to dismiss 'Puritan objections to some of the Prayer Book ceremonial' (the Puritans called those ceremonies, 'dangerous') as 'unjust and ungenerous'. 'Alas!', Dimock said, 'if anything could justify the apprehensions which we once thought to be unfounded and unfair, it would be the fact that now those who have inherited the fears of their forefathers, can with justice point to spectacles to be seen in some of our prominent places of worship, and ask: "Where now are your assurances that all approaches to the doctrine of the Mass were for ever barred from the Church of England?"' (Rosser p82). And such a warning applies not only to Lambeth. Wherever Calvin's views on the 'real presence', or anything like them, get a grip, the road to Rome is open.

How the Reformed regard their baptised infants

Many Reformed infant-baptisers shy away from the nasty concomitants of sacramentalism. But not all! As I have shown, full-blooded sacramentalism is on the rise among the Reformed. Even so, I admit, many Reformed infant-baptiser theologians still try to avoid the notion that the infant receives grace simply by observance of the ritual; that is, they use the word 'sacrament' in a desiccated way, having sucked virtually all the meaning out of the word to leave the dry husk. Nevertheless, the notion remains! In any case, it is only yet another example of the double-speak rampant in infant baptism circles. Wright's thesis – perfectly rightly, as I have said – is that those who use the term should mean what it says. A growing number, as I have observed, do. Quite right too! We should mean the words we use. This, after all, ought to be axiomatic among believers, should it not?

My suspicion is, however, whatever the professional theologians understand by their metaphysical 'explanations' of it, the vast majority of those who baptise their babies, as I have said, really do believe that, 'if anything should happen to them' after they are baptised, they are now 'all right'. Is this surprising? And is it surprising if vast numbers of those babies, when they grow up, believe the same – even if they are unregenerate? In other words, they really do believe saving grace, somehow or another, has been conveyed to them by the rite. This is what I abhor about a 'sacrament'. As for parents thinking the 'best', their theologians have given them plenty of assurance (with the usual qualifiers, of course). And I mean in Reformed circles. Toon, for example: 'The only possible way to construct a service of holy baptism which seriously reflects the promises of God and the close biblical relationship between faith, baptism and regeneration, is to proceed on the hypothesis that those who are baptised do actually receive the promised blessings from heaven. The assumption must be made that the promised gift is indeed bestowed... [While] there can be no absolute guarantee that at baptism every infant receives the gift of the indwelling Holy Spirit... there can be [however] a total commitment by the parents and church to treat baptised infants as true Christians, and thus to bring them up to be persons of faith, hope and love' (Toon pp114-115). Bad enough, in all conscience. But Luther went further still: 'Little children... are free in every way, secure and saved solely through the glory of their baptism... Through the prayer of the believing church which presents it... the infant is changed, cleansed and renewed by inpoured faith. Nor should I doubt that even a godless adult could be changed, in any of the sacraments, if the same church prayed for, and presented him, as we read of the paralytic in the Gospel, who was healed through the faith of others (Mark 2:3-12). I should be ready to admit that in this sense the sacraments of the New Law are efficacious in conferring grace, not only to those who do not, but even to those who do most obstinately present an obstacle' (Dave Armstrong's quotation of Luther's *Babylonian Captivity*). Luther, arguing from Matt. 28:19-20, claimed that 'Christ commanded us to teach and baptise all heathen, without exception'. Pelikan summarised Luther's application: 'How then could any individual or any nation be excluded from the sign of the covenant, which was baptism? Only those who excluded themselves by refusing to accept the sign and the covenant could be denied baptism. Otherwise, "if we follow his [Christ's] command, and baptise everyone, we leave it to him to be concerned about the faith of those baptised". The gospel was the same for all nations, and therefore for all individuals, including children. Baptism, too, was the same for all, in accordance with the covenant of God, signed in his command to baptise, and sealed in his promise' (Pelikan pp94-96).

As I say, with such teaching to bolster them, one can hardly be surprised if most infant baptisers believe all is well once the baby has been baptised. Those who believe and teach such things, ought to have the courage of their convictions, practice indiscriminate infant baptism, and give a blanket assurance to everybody concerned. Not only so, they should baptise as many 'godless adults' as they can, even if they 'obstinately present an obstacle' to it, and tell them that they have thereby been 'conferred with grace'. And bear the consequences, of course!

This is only one stage better than the practice of Roman Catholic priests in a Japanese internment camp in Hong Kong during the 1939-45 war, who, as I was reliably informed by an inmate of impeccable integrity, who subsequently became an outstanding headmistress, 'baptised' dead infants and claimed them as converts.

Reformed disagreements about the effect of infant baptism
Despite the notion's heavy-weight supporters, some modern infant-baptisers contest the notion of presumptive regeneration. See Reymond p201. Others, however, reject it because it does not go far enough! Presumptive regeneration? *Presumption* is too weak! And they can call on Augustine for support – since 'he asserted most dogmatically that all infants *are* regenerate[d] in baptism' (Sadler p279, emphasis mine)! Lusk: 'Only if we can have confidence that *all* the baptised have received the favour of God, can we have the assurance and gratitude we need to do what we've been called to do'. But, when faced with the question: 'What then of infants? What can a tiny, unreasoning child receive from God in the sacrament of baptism?', Lusk had to admit that there is little agreement among the Reformed, and many (most) simply do not know what to make of the infants. Indeed, noting Calvin's contradictions on the matter, Lusk concluded that infant baptisers 'have plenty of work to do in the future. An entire area of practical theology remains relatively unexplored. We must come to grips with what the baptismal status of covenant children means practically, especially the way their standing should shape the ecclesial and familial [church and family] nurture we give them'. Reader, if after 2000 years of baptism, and about 1700 years of infant baptism, infant baptisers still do not know what to make of baptised infants, words fail! But not quite. If, after so many attempts, infant-baptiser scholars still do not know what to make of baptised infants, think of the many millions of non-theologians who have passed that way. If I was an advocate of the system, this one admission, on its own, would give me pause for serious thought. The possibility that the 'solution' might yet be found seems remote. Nothing seems to have changed since the infant baptiser, Ross, wrote in 1953: 'It is an open secret that among infant baptisers at the present time there is much uncertainty and discussion as to the meaning of baptism and the persons to whom it should be administered. What is the relationship of baptism to grace, to faith, to regeneration, to church membership, to confirmation? Does baptism make any difference to the person baptised, and if so, what?' (Ross p100). And if the definitive 'solution' to the problems *is* found, what of all those millions who lived and died in the system in ignorance of – that is, with the wrong view of – the status of baptised infants? and worse – *who lived and died with a wrong view of their **own** status*? Nevertheless, in the end, Lusk had no doubts himself: 'A baptised person is a Christian until and unless he apostatises. Let us learn to treat our baptised children as the Christians that they are'. In this, he was once again following

229

Augustine – 'if the child turns out ungodly... it has fallen from grace... the child has lost grace, rather than that God has withheld it. Any after-fall into sin is to be laid to the fault of the child, not to any deficiency in the grace of its baptism' (Sadler p279). (What now of election leading to perseverance?) Lusk spelled out the (to him) dreadful alternative: 'Apart from an efficacious view of baptism, the question: "Why baptise infants?" became progressively more and more difficult to answer coherently. The believer-baptists won the day by default' (Lusk: 'Paedobaptism' pp101-120, emphasis his). As to that last, not quite. The 'default' position is the biblical one, but unless those who advocate it are alert, and the present rise in sacramentalism is halted and reversed, it might well be lost in a day rapidly approaching. See my book on Baptist sacramentalism.

But Lusk raised a powerful point. If infants were regenerated by baptism, that would be an excellent reason for baptising them. Indeed, it would make their baptism *essential*. Moreover, it is the *only* reason for baptising them. Anything less than baptismal regeneration proves to be a hindrance, producing confusion at the point of conversion. That is why there are only two stable positions – sacramental baptismal regeneration, or symbolic baptism.

Here is Lord Bernard Manning's reason for baptising infants: 'We do not baptise [children] because we or they have faith. That is sloppy Nonconformist sentimentalism. We do not baptise them in order to make them children of God. That is the false and hideous doctrine of Romanists and Anglo-Catholics. We baptise children because they are already God's. They are not outside his kingdom until it occurs to them to enter it or until it occurs to us to push them into it' (Wright: *What...?* p22). As I have shown, this erroneous teaching is pure Calvinism, and is the position of not a few Calvinists today! Note the use to which James Philip put Manning (Wright: *What...?* p21). And here are Pratt's reasons for baptising infants: 'Reformed churches do not baptise children to regenerate them, or to remove the curse of original sin. Nor do Reformed churches baptise children simply to indicate the parent's dedication of the children to God. We baptise children to initiate them into covenant with God, and to incorporate them into the visible church... Why... should we baptise children of believers?... For two main reasons. First... Rom. 4:11... as... circumcision was a sign and seal of righteousness by faith... even though these same children may not be capable of faith. Second... the covenant promises' (John H.Armstrong pp70-71).

Reformed explanations of infant baptism are incomprehensible

I wonder how many infant baptisers understand the following explanation of Cranmer's view of the baptism of infants? Cranmer called on Augustine's answer to Boniface – which I mentioned earlier: 'Cranmer explains the baptism of infants, who cannot make any profession of faith, and of whom it can never be affirmed, with even a normal degree of human certainty, that they actually have faith. Why then do we baptise infants, and allow the sponsors to make for them a Christian confession [profession]? On this point Cranmer "rehearsed" the answer of Augustine to Boniface, who had asked this same question: "After a certain manner of speech... the sacrament of faith is faith. And to believe, is nothing else but to have faith; and therefore when we answer for young children in their baptism, that they believe, which have not yet the mind to believe, we answer that they have faith because they have the sacrament of faith. And we say also that they turn unto God, because of the sacrament of conversion unto God; for that answer pertains to the celebration of the sacrament". This is the reason why in spite of his refusal to identify the sign and the thing signified, Cranmer can still make a categorical assertion of regeneration in the baptismal office. Even children can be described as regenerate, not because we know that in each individual case there has been an inward operation and renewal, not merely because we look forward in gratitude of faith to a future fulfilment, but because we know that they have the sign and pledge of the grace signified, for which we pray, and to which we bear witness. In literal fact, of course, our external baptism with water is not our regeneration, but it is called this because it is the sacrament of it, and because baptism in the full sense includes the regeneration which is our entry into the baptism of Christ. The external washing with water is the "humanity" of the sacrament to which the "divinity" is conjoined when there is the demonstration of the Spirit and of power, and therefore a baptism in the true and full sense. Objectively, no doubt, it is possible to say that there is always this conjunction, but subjectively – and this is the point and goal of the administration of word and sacrament – it may often enough be the case that there is only an external reception, and therefore only a sacramental regeneration: the sign, but not the thing signified' (Bromiley pp63-64). I repeat my question: How many infant baptisers follow this 'explanation'? I suggest, once again, that most people baptising their infants prefer to believe the good news, and ignore (even if they understand) the metaphysical qualifiers.

Those of us who object to the incomprehensible explanations of the sacraments, as set out by the Reformed, are told by D.Broughton Knox, an advocate of the sacramental system, that we 'have not sufficiently considered... the problem inherent in realistic language'. Take the supper: 'For those who like the Reformers believe that Jesus was speaking sacramentally... there is an ongoing problem of language whenever the bread is spoken of. Thus it is correct to say that we eat with our mouth the body of Christ; and (once the question of realism is raised) it is equally correct to say that we do not eat with our mouth the body of Christ. This dual form of stating the truth must be used by all who believe that Jesus said: "This is my body", with regard to what the disciples were eating and yet do not believe that Jesus implied thereby a real presence of his body in the sacrament'. I pause here, reader. With respect, this is not a 'dual form of stating the truth'; it is a downright contradiction! Black is still black, not white, even after Reformed double-speak! What is more, sacramentalism is not the only alternative to the Papist real presence; symbolism is. 'This is my body' means: 'This represents my body'. No duality, no ambiguity whatsoever. To let Knox go on: 'To deny the logical possibility of this dual form of statement', this sacramentalist tells us, 'is tantamount to affirming that the doctrine of the real presence is the only possible interpretation of our Lord's words'. Scaremongering nonsense! I have already spelled out the biblical alternative to the real presence – symbolism. But to let Knox go on: 'Reformed theologians use one form of words in one context to stress one aspect of the truth, the opposite form of words in another context to correct fatal misunderstanding of the sacrament... Reformed theologians used [and still use] language which has two levels of meaning, for this is scriptural [it is, in fact, begging the question – DG]; but this is not the same as ambiguous language. Reformed exegetes maintain that there is no ambiguity in our Lord's words taken in their context of the last supper'. I pause once again. Of course there is no ambiguity in Christ's words; I am talking about the words of these 'Reformed exegetes'! There is plenty of ambiguity and double-speak 'dual form' there! To let Knox go on: 'Ambiguity is never a virtue; like lying, it is a misuse of language, and is to be eschewed. Theologians, like all who use words, must strive for clarity of expression'. Quite! So, what clarity do we get? 'Realistic language must always be used of the Lord's supper, in order to do justice to the truth of our forgiveness and incorporation in Christ through his death in his human body, but realism, that is, the concept that our Lord's body is present in substance, and not in figure or sacrament only, is rejected without equivocation in all the writings of the English Reformation. Realistic metaphorical language, standing by itself, cannot be distinguished from the language of literal realism, but requires for its true interpretation, qualifying or alternative statements. It follows that the statements about the supper in the English Reformers, and in the church formularies, should be allowed to interpret one another, and not be taken as indications of vacillation or conflict in doctrine; for the Reformers, holding the views that they did about the Lord's supper, could not avoid the use of alterations in language' (Knox pp68-70).

I rest my case. I challenge all non-professional-theologians-and-logicians (the overwhelming majority) who hold to the idea of a sacrament to explain all the ins-an-outs of 'the alterations in language' between 'realistic metaphorical language' and 'the language of literal realism', as interpreted by 'qualifying or alternative statements'. And to do so, not only with regard to the supper, of course, but with regard to infant baptism. And to do so in terms understandable to the average believer. I have already noted Castelein's just observation: 'Reformed and Presbyterian theologies approach baptism and salvation within the framework of an incredibly complex system of Calvinistic theological beliefs' (John H.Armstrong pp83-84); that is, they read Scripture on baptism and salvation through the complications of their own invented covenant theology.

Why, then, did Sibbes, for instance, still want to baptise infants?
Why? After all, he admitted 'that in the ancient [patristic] church... they that were baptised... were questioned: "Do you believe?" "I do believe" "Do you renounce the flesh, and the world and the devil?" "I do renounce them". These two questions were made. Now, *when* they answered this question from a good conscience [1 Pet. 3:21], truly, faithfully and sincerely, *then* they had right in all the good things by Christ'. Very well. So much for the Fathers. Far more important, we know that only believers, only those who professed faith, were baptised in the New Testament. So why baptise infants – who cannot possibly answer these questions? above all, who cannot exercise saving faith? Sibbes: 'Why are children baptised then [since] they cannot make the answer of a good conscience? I answer: [1 Pet. 3:21] must be understood of those of years of discretion'. I pause. What a begging of the question! To let Sibbes go on. He then stated categorically that baptised infants who die are saved – 'they are within the covenant. Have they not received the seal of the covenant, which is baptism? And however they actually answer not the covenant of grace by actual believing, yet they have the seed of believing, the Spirit of God in them, and God comprehends them by his mercy, [they] being not able to comprehend him'. But, of course, if the infant does not die but reaches the 'years of discretion', his baptism changes its nature – it becomes 'an engagement and obligation to them to believe, because they have undertaken, by those who answered for them [see earlier on the madness of sponsors allegedly making vows for the infant], to believe when they are come to years; and if, when they come to years, they answer not the covenant of grace and the answer of a good conscience, if they do not believe, and renounce Satan, all is frustrated. Their baptism does them no good, if they make not good their covenant by believing and renouncing [the devil]... Unless now we believe in Christ, and renounce the devil, we renounce our baptism' (Sibbes *Demand* pp483,486-487, emphasis mine).

Really? Scripture speaks of but one water baptism. Infant baptisers have two – one for infants, the other for believers. Sibbes went further and argued for two *infant* baptisms – a twofold infant baptism. If the infant dies before 'years of discretion', his baptism means all that is claimed for it. If the infant reaches 'years of discretion', his baptism changes its nature – and becomes an obligation, it can be reversed, and becomes meaningless. Worse still, of course, it then increases the sinner's condemnation. See earlier note on the notion that with the passing of time, baptism – which starts as a seal – turns into an obligation.

In any case, what about Sibbes' view of 1 Pet. 3:21? As I have made clear, 1 Pet. 3:21 refers to *spiritual* baptism, not water baptism. Peter was *not* saying that those who are water baptised as infants *must have* the answer of a good conscience when they reach the years of discretion, otherwise their water baptism will be invalid; he was saying that those who are spiritually baptised *do* have a good conscience: 'Baptism (not the removal of the filth of the flesh,

233

but the answer of a good conscience toward God)'. In fact, he *defined* the baptism in question *as* the answer of a good conscience toward God. Whether we take 'answer', επερωτημα, to be 'we have *earnestly sought* a good conscience', 'the *agreement* of a good conscience', 'the *avowal* of a good conscience' (see Thayer), or 'the *expression, confession* or *declaration* of a good conscience toward God' (Brown: *1 Peter* pp251-252), this 'having or exercising a good conscience toward God' is one and the same as spiritual baptism. Of course, those who are spiritually baptised – those who have or exercise this good conscience toward God – must be water baptised. But Peter was not talking about *that*. Nor was he talking about infants! As I said, what a begging of the question!

Part Three

Consequences

Infant baptism is not mere theory. It has practical long-term effects. And those effects are very serious indeed. They lie at the very heart of church life; indeed, of salvation itself. The effect of infant baptism is, in the ultimate, eternal. And that is why I have written this book.

To make my meaning clear, I spell out my concerns in the following two chapters. In Consequence 1, I look at the part played by infant baptism in the formation and development of Christendom and, in its local manifestation, the invented notion of 'visible churches'.

In Consequence 2, I look at the ramifications of infant baptism as played out in three episodes in church history:

1. The New England churches in the 17th century

2. Jonathan Edwards in the 18th century

3. D. Martyn Lloyd-Jones in the 20th century

Consequence 1

Christendom and Visible Churches

Leaving aside all the ins-and-outs of the arguments about infant baptism, all the Reformed assertions and counter-qualifiers, let's get down to the nitty-gritty. What is the practical outcome of infant baptism? What has been its great 'contribution' to the world, its massive legacy? What 'benefit' has it bestowed on humanity?

In a word, Christendom! What is Christendom? It is that grotesque, Satanic invention – that conglomeration of Church and State, in which citizenship and Church membership are one and the same – in which millions of unregenerate babies are 'made' 'Christians' by 'priests' or 'ministers' who exercise sacramental powers through baptism, these babies then being called 'Christians' and Church members, and treated as such (at birth, through life, and at death).[1] Wright:

---

[1] 'Christian', a noun in the Bible, *and only a noun*, has become an adjective – and one of the most (if not *the* most) debased, at that. Those parents who want the full works for their child, start as they mean to go on: the baby is made a 'Christian' at the font, given a 'Christian' name at his 'Christening', is a member of a 'Christian' Church, lives in a 'Christian' country in a 'Christian' continent ruled by 'Christian' kings and princes, attends a 'Christian' school, a 'Christian' university or college, and when old enough (and if the need arises) becomes a 'Christian' soldier to fight in a 'Christian' army for a 'Christian' cause, annually remembering the 'Christian' fallen in battle. Finally, he himself is given a 'Christian' funeral, conducted by a 'Christian' minister, and, supposedly, goes to heaven. And it is all eye-wash! But highly dangerous, even so. Never seeming to learn from history, since 9/11 we are in danger of stirring up the spirit of the Crusades again, and another war between 'Christianity' and Islam is not out of the question. George W.Bush talked about 'a crusade against evil', did he not, and I myself heard an American soldier serving in Iraq claim he was in 'God's army' fighting on behalf of 'God's country', or some-such terminology (Dec. 2005). As in my *Battle*, I urge the principles of Matt. 26:52; John 18:36; 2 Cor. 10:3-5; Eph 6:10-20. I have allowed 'church' to be qualified by 'Christian' in my quotations only because that is what my sources wrote. Above all, the danger is not only temporal. The consequences of Christendom will prove ruinous for millions, eternally speaking. See Stuart Murray: *Post-Christendom* for its legacy.

Universal infant baptism was one of the constitutive elements of the unitary world of Church-State Christianity which is what Christendom commonly denotes... This universal baptising of babies formed one of the building blocks of Christendom,[2] by which I mean that long phase of Christian history during which the Church and the civil order, whether people, nation or empire, were largely co-terminus. Human society consisted of a single population, viewed from one angle as the Christian Church, from another as a State. Characteristic of Christendom was the State Church, the Church legally 'established', or recognised as the privileged Church of the nation or empire. Christendom began to develop under the earliest 'Christian' emperors of Rome, from Constantine in the early 4th century onwards, and survived the disruption of the Reformation largely unscathed. The re-formed Churches which came out of the Reformation, were State Churches or national Churches, whether Lutheran, Reformed or Presbyterian, or Anglican... [In this way,] baptismal development [that is, the introduction of infant baptism] [brought about] a truly massive change in the history of Christ's church. From being a company recruited by intentional response to the gospel imperative to discipleship and baptism, it became a body enrolled from birth. It was arguably one[3] of the greatest sea changes in the story of

---

[2] 'Theologically, [Augustine] came to believe that infant baptism was the sole cure for the guilt of original sin; practically, he came to advocate the universal baptism of infants soon after their birth. The result was a devaluation of baptism in the West, which did much to determine the contours of Christendom' (Wright in Stuart Murray: *Post-Christendom* p91).

[3] *The* greatest, in my opinion. In the New Testament, pagans were converted into Christians by God's grace through faith and repentance; in Christendom, pagans are called Christians and treated as such, by baptising them as babies, either because they are thought to be Christians already, or else claiming to make them so. W. Brock: In the New Testament, 'all who came to believe in Christ with their heart, and to confess... Christ with their tongue, [and were baptised upon profession of faith,] were the members of his church, and no one else. There was no birth-membership, no sacramental membership, no proxy membership. The whole matter was personal' (*Sword* p414). See Brock's entire article for his submission that national Churches, the Church of England in particular, are not the church of Jesus Christ.

Spurgeon: 'We think that our brethren do serious damage to the gospel by baptising children. We do not think their error a little one... Infant baptism is the prop and pillar of Popery, and it being removed, Popery and Puseyism become at once impossible. You have taken away all idea of a national godliness and a national religion, when you have cut away all liberty to administer Christian ordinances to unconverted persons. We cannot see any

239

Christianity. It led... to the formation of Christendom, comprising a 'Christian' empire, 'Christian' nations or peoples. Christianity became a matter of heredity, not decision.[4]

---

evil which would follow, if our brethren would renounce their mistake; but we can see abundant mischief which their mistake has caused, and in all kindness, but with all fidelity, we again enter our solemn protest against their giving baptism to any but disciples... Oh! It is a disastrous thing to call unconverted children Christians, or to do anything which may weaken their apprehension of the great fact that, until they are converted, they have no part or lot in this matter. Brethren, if you differ from me on this point, bear with me, for my conscience will not let me conceal this solemn truth' (Spurgeon: *New Park Street and Metropolitan* Vol.7 p284; see also pp265-272).
[4] Wright: *What...?* pp9,12,74. Lusk: 'Infant baptism and Christendom stand or fall together' (Lusk: 'Paedobaptism' p117). Wright saw the current days, 'the dying days of Christendom', as he put it, as a good time to re-think baptism. As I have explained, he would have liked to have seen a higher status for infant baptism, a more sacramental approach. This, I am convinced is wrong and will lead to a new Christendom replacing the old, but still built on the old foundation – infant baptism. Satan is too wily to let such a powerful weapon slip from his fingers! How will the new Christendom come about? Here is my suggestion: Many Baptists and Reformed infant-baptisers (theologians in the van) will come together as sacramentalists (discussions between both parties have been going on since the late 1970s), and Rome will move just enough to bring them within range and so swallow them alive! 'Recent trends in ecumenical [that is, Romanist and Protestant] reflection on baptism must be regarded as favourable to Baptists' fundamental demand for baptism on profession of faith. Believer's Baptists now have an unprecedented opportunity to promote a theology of baptism which confidently takes the full measure of the New Testament witness and no longer feeds on reaction against the distorting effects of the long reign of infant baptism' (Wright: *What...?* pp9,31; see also Wright: *What...?* p28; see earlier notes on the Romeward movement amongst evangelicals, and Rome's changes, including Wright: *What...?* pp10,15-17,102; see also Jones pp105-129; Beckwith). I am sure Wright would have thought I am doing the latter (reacting against infant baptism) (to which, in this book, I plead guilty), when he would wish the former – a return to sacramentalism. Increasingly, his wish is being fulfilled. See my book on Baptist sacramentalism, where I trace this out in detail with regard to Baptists, the ecumenical movement, the charismatic movement, the New Perspective, conversion regarded as a process, the emphasis upon corporate as opposed to individual salvation, the union of believer's baptism and infant baptism, and inclusivism. In addition to what I say there, take Buchanan and Vasey who recorded a case of an Anglican lady, 'an

Constantine provided the political muscle necessary for this diabolical state of affairs. Who provided the theological logic for it? Augustine, of course. Wright again: 'Augustine of Hippo, who died in 430... It was he who provided the theology that led to infant baptism becoming

---

evangelical charismatic', who, at the 1991 synod, pressed for 'open baptism'; that is, indiscriminate infant baptism. She said: 'The most critical thing for those coming in, is not primarily the grasping of concepts, but the need for them to be networked into a series of relationships within the Body of Christ'. No wonder 'a solid majority' of the synod – in favour of 'open baptism' – 'was uncomfortable... at attempts to sharpen the boundaries of the Church' (Buchanan and Vasey p11; but see their pp23-24). Consider this from N.T.Wright, explaining how he became a sacramentalist: 'In 1981... my view of the eucharist, which had started at a rock-bottom low as an undergraduate, had received an upward jolt through reading Calvin (yes, try it and see)... It finally came together and started to approach that of Paul [which is, of course, to beg the question – DG]'. In a further piece, N.T.Wright went on to set out what he understood by justification: 'Justification... is God's declaration that the person is now in the right, which confers on them the status "righteous". (We may note that, since "righteous" here, within the law-court metaphor, refers to "status", not "character", we correctly say that God's declaration makes the person "righteous", that is, in good standing)... This present declaration constitutes all believers as the single people, the one family, promised to Abraham (Gal. 2:14 – 3:29; Rom. 3:27 – 4:17), the people whose sins have been dealt with as part of the fulfilled promise of covenant renewal (Jer. 31:31-34)'. I pause. Excellent. I agree wholeheartedly. Now – the question is: How does a sinner come into this position? how is he declared righteous by God? on what basis? through what means? N.T.Wright went on: 'The event in the present, which corresponds to Jesus' death and resurrection in the past, and the resurrection of all believers in the future, is baptism into Christ (Gal. 3:26-29; Rom. 6:2-11)'. I pause again. It is the old question: Which baptism was Paul talking about? water baptism or spiritual baptism? N.T.Wright was in no doubt: 'Baptism is not, as some have supposed, a "work" which one "performs" to earn God's favour. It is, for Paul [begging the question again – DG], the sacrament of God's free grace. Paul can speak of those who have believed, and been baptised, as already "saved", albeit "in hope" (Rom. 8:24)' (*Act 3 Review* pp202-204). Quite! But N.T.Wright has mixed up the two baptisms and given the impression – to put it no stronger – that water baptism is a sacrament which produces (or helps to produce) the status of justification. As I have said, I believe all this ties in with the idea of 'initiation' rather than conversion. See Lusk: 'Paedobaptism' p123. Reader: What would Paul have made of this – would it fairly represent his view of conversion?

241

general practice for the first time in the history of the Church',[5] which, as I have explained, was later sharpened by Lombard in the 12th century.

So what is so very bad about this 'Christendom'? C.H.Mackintosh put it like this:

It is a terrible word. It brings before us, at once, that vast mass of baptised profession, which calls itself the church of God, but is not; which calls itself Christianity, but is not. Christendom is dark and a dreadful anomaly. It is neither one thing nor the other... It is a corrupt mysterious mixture, a spiritual malformation, the masterpiece of Satan, the corrupter of the truth of God, and the destroyer of the souls of men, a trap, a snare, a stumbling block, the darkest moral blot in the universe of God. It is the corruption of the very best thing, and therefore, the very worst of corruptions. It is that thing which Satan has made of professing Christianity. It is worse, by far, than... all the darkest forms of Paganism, because it has higher light and richer privileges, makes the very highest profession, and occupies the very loftiest platform. Finally, it is that awful apostasy for which is reserved the very heaviest judgement of God – the most bitter dregs in the cup of his righteous wrath.[6]

Scare mongering? Reformed infant-baptisers, no doubt, will dismiss the above as the *corruption* of infant baptism; their observance of the rite, they would claim, is a million miles away from it. We shall see.

So much for the general picture. What of the local manifestation? Infant baptisers make much of the notion of 'visible churches'.[7] It is a concept which has come up repeatedly. A class of Christians is invented – 'visible' Christians, that is, professed Christians, or those

---

[5] Wright: *What...?* p12; see also Wright: *What...?* pp25-26,94. Luther, it will be remembered, was an Augustinian monk; and Calvin's dependence on Augustine is legendary. As I have noted, theologians always provide the theology required to back up an invented practice. For Augustine's baptismal theology in his own words, see Appendix 2.

[6] C.H.Mackintosh: *Papers on the Lord's Coming*, pp73-74, quoted by Weber pp170-171. See Diprose pp131-135. 'The Anabaptists... opposed... infant baptism, including fundamentally the Church-State alliance, and the use of the coercive powers of State authorities in defence of the new Protestantism. Infant baptism belonged to the complex... called "Christendom", which survived, albeit much transformed, the turmoil of the Reformation' (Wright: *What...?* p29).

[7] As so much in this field, another of Augustine's inventions. See Morgan p3. But not only infant baptisers; sadly, the majority of Baptists use the phrase.

who claim to be Christians; nominal Christians, or those who are not openly non-Christian. Churches composed of this sort of people are visible churches.[8]

---

[8] But even this does not work. 'Of [infant] baptism, it is commonly claimed that its recipients are incorporated into the body of Christ, become members of the church... Now unless this assertion... is given such a spiritual or metaphysical meaning that its truthfulness is wholly inaccessible to the social scientist or historian, it must surely entail membership of the visible church on earth. It would be strange, would it not, if, of hundreds of baptised persons of whom this was predicated over a period of time, none was subsequently found... at worship or engaged in some essential church activity? I am not forgetting that evangelical Christians have traditionally made much of the doctrine of the invisible church, but we should be cautious to summon this into play at this juncture. What this unfortunately-named doctrine really stands for, is the important biblical teaching that only God knows those who are his, and that not all in the visible company of the church thereby truly belong to God. The doctrine of the invisible church is not about a totally different entity from the visible church – except insofar as it embraces those who have died, and joined the heavenly host of God. It is at base, a statement, paradoxically enough, about the visible church, affirming its mixed, imperfect character. I reject its being invoked to accommodate the embarrassing verifiable results of hundreds, thousands, even millions of infant baptisms which have not led to their recipients being verifiably members of the church of Jesus Christ. Let us not beat about the bush... When all the caveats and qualifications have been factored in, there are undoubtedly hordes more people who were baptised as infants in the Church of Scotland [for instance], and are today, to all intents and purposes, wholly unchurched, than there are members of the same church... This paper-membership itself has only a partial purchase on reality; the rule of thumb in the Kirk is that, of the formal membership in any one congregation, a third are active, another third come to special services like communion and Easter, and a third are never seen... [not forgetting the 'hordes' who never make any profession at all]. The state of affairs, thus exposed, confronts infant baptism with some hard questions... [It is worse than useless to try to drive along] escape routes which biblical Christians can scarcely take seriously... We might conclude that for some who minister in one of these mixed churches, the price of continuing to dispense baptism to babies, is not believing too much about it. This is hardly a satisfactory position to find oneself in, but then, the administration of infant baptism has been for some time one of the most conscience-taxing aspects of the work of the ministry for many evangelicals'. In a recent survey, the Church of Scotland discovered that demand for 'baptism for any who wanted [80%], and denying it had any bearing on later church attendance [100%] – starkly illustrates what

243

It goes without saying that all believers must be open (or visible) in their testimony: 'Let your light so shine before men, that they may see your good works and glorify your Father in heaven' (Matt. 5:16). There is no quarrel over that. But the concept of visible churches is not dealing with this command of Christ. Oh no! It is an attempt or invention to cope with the utter disaster of Constantinian and Augustinian practice, in general, and of infant baptism, in particular.[9] Alas, in these days many churches – even among those which ought to understand the folly and mistake of the concept of visible churches – are acting on those very principles. Instead of insisting on clear evidences of regeneration before baptism and church membership, a mere nominal profession is considered enough. It is a dreadful

---

"the long reign of infant baptism" has done to baptism'. Wright spoke of 'the pressure to come to terms – serious conscientious terms – with baptism given so widely to infants, and so infrequently leading to active discipleship. If baptism, administered indiscriminately to babies on request, proves so ineffectual, it cannot retain much doctrinal significance. The logic is simple and unchallengeable... If infant baptism counts for so little, carries so little clout, why bother resisting, often at some emotional cost, requests for it from parents who show next to no sign of genuine commitment to it? Anglican evangelicals, not so long ago, had the habit of talking about such baptismal occasions as "good boats to fish from", that is, welcome evangelistic opportunities. Such is the colour of a baptismally-reductionist church culture' (Wright: *What...?* pp24-25,83-87,100-102). Infant baptisers, not excluding Reformed infant-baptisers, will need a large carpet, a well-bristled broom, and a strong forearm, if they want to hide such testimony. For all the seeming poise of infant baptisers when writing about their practice, and for all their apparent confidence in the covenant theology which buttresses it, in private and in conscience many are wrestling with enormous doubts and difficulties. From time to time these doubts come into the public arena. Take for instance Carson: *Farewell* pp60-77.

[9] Some, at least, of the Reformed, are not apologetic about this; they see it as biblical: 'Baptism is the symbolic linguistic crucible of regeneration and new birth which gives form to the substance of faith in Christ. Therein, regeneration is signified by our being gathered to a people where the Holy Spirit works through our existence in the church to conform us to Christ. Through baptism, we enter this mode of existence, either willingly as adults, or unwillingly as infants... This is the essence of a Reformed understanding of the church' (Harvey p111). Note the word – 'the *essence* of a Reformed understanding of the church'.

mistake. It is worse; it is a contradiction of Scripture. And it will bring havoc in its wake. Indeed it is already doing so.[10]

The notion of visible churches is an idea which is very handy for infant baptisers, but it is entirely foreign to the New Testament. It is more than handy – it is essential for them to think of something to cope with what they find in their churches. As there was an 'Israel after the flesh' (1 Cor. 10:18), so the practice of infant baptism must inevitably produce some 'Christians after the flesh';[11] that is, those who have one or more parents who are Christians, who have been baptised and admitted into the church, who are called holy, members of Christ and Christians, when all the time they are unregenerate. What can infant baptisers do with them?

Listen to the way A.A.Hodge described the practical outworkings of infant baptism in terms of church membership. He quoted *The Directory for Worship* with approval when he wrote:

It is evident that this [baptism of infants] should be supplemented by the rite of confirmation... I refer simply to the historical, universally-practised [universally?] Christian ordinance observed in bringing the Christianly instructed and trained children before the church 'when they come to years of discretion: if they be free from scandal, appear sober and steady, and to have sufficient knowledge to discern the Lord's body, they ought to be informed it is their duty and their privilege to come to the Lord's supper'. Then they who have been members of the church from their birth are admitted to full communion, and are confirmed in their church standing, upon their voluntarily taking upon themselves the vows originally imposed upon them by their parents in baptism. This is the CONFIRMATION, separated from the abortive mask of the so-called

---

[10] I recall a conversation with a Presbyterian minister. He told me there were 400 members in 'his' church. How many at the prayer meeting?, I asked. 40, he replied. The trouble is, he explained, we have an unregenerate elder, and we are waiting for him to die! The overwhelming majority of Baptist churches, too, seem willing to accept such a disproportionate attendance. It is, of course, not the attendance which counts here; it is the attitude which is reflected in such figures. Can it be that 90% of the church are otherwise properly engaged, and to their great disappointment are unable to attend the prayer meeting?

[11] And the disaster occurs not only in infant-baptiser churches. I recall Harry Matthews of Corsham 'fame', some 40 years ago, saying: 'There are too many Ishmaels in the church'. He was talking about evangelical and Baptist churches.

245

sacrament, that John Calvin declared was an ancient and beneficial custom, which he earnestly wished might be continued in the church.[12]

Well, A.A.Hodge and Calvin might have wished this sort of procedure to continue long in the church, but in the light of the New Testament, words fail to describe just how abominable it is. The New Testament churches were composed of saints – nothing at all to do with age.[13] How infant baptisers are infatuated with age! But here it is in black and white; all that infant baptisers demand is for an infant to be baptised, then to be 'Christianly' brought up, 'free from scandal, appear sober and steady, and to have sufficient knowledge', before they become full members of a church. Full members? What is this? The New Testament knows nothing of this *full* membership. Nothing at all! It is a piece of pure invention by infant baptisers, remarkably, as before, often the very people who call loudest for the Regulative Principle![14] Further, where in the New Testament does baptism have to be 'supplemented' as Hodge put it? Church members, according to the New Testament, are saints; they are true believers who give clear evidences and marks of regeneration in their lives. This stands in sharp contrast to the infant baptism system which, apparently, can produce adults who are communicant or full church members but who, nevertheless, are not required to be regenerate, only reasonably decent. Indeed, this is what the Presbyterian Church looks for, according to its *Directory* for worship. They will be steady and sober – or appear to be. But is that *all*? Is that sufficient for church membership? What if some of these steady, sober unregenerate men become preachers, elders and teachers? And they do. Of course they do. It is inevitable. The consequences are horrendous. As Maurice Roberts, the then-editor of the *Banner of Truth*, himself a Presbyterian minister, wrote in his editorial in the April 1994 issue:

---

[12] A.A.Hodge p337. Note how infant baptism – itself an invention – demands a further invention – confirmation – to supplement it.

[13] I have made the point, more than once, that baptism is nothing to do with age. But this does not mean those who baptise believers pay no regard to it whatsoever. The real question, however, is not the age itself, but does the one being baptised give a credible profession of faith?

[14] See above.

Let a man become a church member without the new birth and the probability is he will be secure in his church membership till he wakes up in a lost world. Let a man become a preacher, a divinity professor, a missionary, a church historian, a moderator, an assembly clerk, a printer of Bibles – all without the new birth – and such persons are only twofold more the heirs of hell than they would otherwise have been (Matt. 23:15). However hard it is for us to take in this doctrine, there cannot be the least doubt that it is the plain and obvious teaching of Christ in many places of the Gospels.[15]

All who would be thought a Christian should weigh these words. All elders should, especially. But, in particular, infant baptisers need to pay close attention to them, for the reasons I have given – reasons which arise directly out of their own principles and which have been made abundantly clear by their own writings. To be regenerate is not the same as being 'Christianly' brought up – whatever that may be reckoned to mean – or to 'be free from scandal, appear to be sober and steady'.

How do infant baptisers try to justify this abomination of knowingly accepting unregenerate church members?[16] They grossly abuse the parable of the tares (Matt. 13:24-30), conveniently saying that the field is the church when it is nothing of the sort; the field is *the world*. They expect – and their system produces – churches which are composed of members, some of whom are regenerate and baptised, some of whom are adults who have been baptised but are unregenerate, and some of whom are baptised infants but who give no evidence one way or the other concerning regeneration. What a mixed multitude! This inevitably leads on to the idea of visible churches. The Westminster Confession, Chapter XXV, put it this way: 'The visible church... consists of all those throughout the world that profess the true religion; and of their children'.[17] The main text chosen to serve as a

---

[15] *Banner of Truth* April 1994 p2.

[16] It is more than knowingly. Dabney, without batting an eyelid, was prepared to issue this challenge: 'Cannot that which is worldly, in the true sense, be in the visible church?' (Dabney p785). Of course, as I admit, those of us who want the New Testament basis of church life, and demand regenerate church membership, can be deceived; we do not always get it right! But this is a far cry from virtually *boasting* of carnal members. See Shawn D.Wright pp218-228.

[17] Westminster p107.

proof-text to substantiate this defective and misguided definition is 1 Corinthians 1:2 which reads:

To the church of God which is at Corinth, to those who are sanctified in Christ Jesus, called to be saints, with all who in every place call on the name of Jesus Christ our Lord, both theirs and ours.

It will be readily observed that the text quoted does not support the Confession in the slightest. The Confession speaks of church members as those who profess true religion, whereas the New Testament speaks of church members as those who are sanctified in Christ Jesus, who are called to be saints, and who call upon Christ. Professors, says the one; saints, says the other! Not the same thing at all. The other verses quoted are 1 Corinthians 12:12-13, Psalm 2:8, Revelation 7:9 and Romans 15:9-12, none of which say that church members are mere professors.

The Confession also says that church members are professors *and their children*. The 'proof' text, 1 Corinthians 1:2, says nothing of the sort. 1 Corinthians 7:14 is also quoted. I have already written about that verse, which, in any case, says nothing about church membership. Acts 2:39 is also referred to. Reader, may I suggest that you read the entire passage, Acts 2:37-42? Baptism comes in the verse preceding the proof-text, and church life comes in the verses which follow it. It reads: 'For the promise is to you and to your children, and to all who are afar off, as many as the Lord our God will call'. Let us look at it.

The passage teaches that the gospel invitation, command or promise (which Peter issued in his preaching on the Day of Pentecost) is made to every man, woman and child in the world;[18] invitations, commands or promises such as: 'Look to me, and be saved, all you ends of the earth!' (Isa. 45:22). God's promise – along with his command – is sent to both Jews and non-Jews, both young and old, as long as time shall last. God's mercy is offered in the gospel to all sinners, not only to those who happened to hear it on the Day of Pentecost. The promise is sent to all men, women and children throughout the age. 'God... commands all men everywhere to repent' (Acts 17:30). But surely it does not need to be said, a sinner is saved only when the call is effectual and inward; it being 'as many as the

---

[18] See my *Offer*; my forthcoming book on Septimus Sears; Lloyd-Jones: *The Church* p40.

Lord our God will call'. This caveat qualifies everything which follows. All are called outwardly, but it is only those who are effectually called – and it is all of *them* – who will repent and believe. 'As many as had been appointed to eternal life believed' (Acts 13:48). It is no different today. The elect believe. They are then to be baptised and thus join the church. 'Then those who gladly received his word were baptised' (Acts 2:41).[19] That is what Acts 2:37-42 teaches.

Infant baptisers, however, deny that the qualification, 'as many as the Lord our God will call', applies to all the classes mentioned, and which must be met before any are baptised. In particular, their view is that the children of those who are near do not need to be called before they are baptised and join the church, seeing they are born in the covenant. This is wrong. There are two issues here. *First*, to whom does the proviso – the calling – apply? And, *secondly*, were infants baptised that day?

On the *first*, it is clear that on the Day of Pentecost, the calling applied to all the categories of people, and to all the issues involved. Whether the people were near or far off, adults or children, they all needed to be called. And the believing, the repenting, the being baptised and joining the church, all came under that one stipulation. It was only those who were effectively called – and only those – who repented, believed, were baptised, and so on. The context proves it. That is exactly what happened. It was only those who repented (Acts 2:38) and 'who gladly received his word' – that is those who truly believed (Acts 2:44) – who were baptised and were added to the church to partake in all its life (Acts 2:41-42). In other words, all who were effectively called, were baptised, and only they. It did not matter a scrap whether they were Jews or Gentiles;[20] they had to be called. In this way they joined the church and partook of all the ordinances of Christ including the Lord's supper.

---

[19] Implying that there were some who did not receive his word, and were not baptised – even though they had been outwardly called in the general call of the gospel. See my forthcoming book on Septimus Sears.

[20] True it is, on that day, the vast majority (if not all) who heard and were called were Jews or proselytes. But the principle stands.

Now for the *second* point. There is not the slightest suggestion that infants were involved in any of it.[21] Did they prophesy (Acts 2:17)? No! Did they repent and believe? No! And if infant baptisers persist in saying that infants were involved, and that infants were baptised, then we are forced to conclude that Peter must have exhorted those infants to repent and be baptised. This must be so since we know that he urged all those, whom he later baptised, to 'repent, and let every one of you be baptised' (Acts 2:38). According to infant baptisers, that number included infants. But why ever would Peter exhort infants to repent, when he knew it was an impossibility for them by reason of their age? And why would he exhort the infants to be baptised, in any case? On infant baptism logic, he was wasting his time! As long as one of the parents repented and was baptised, the infants followed automatically. So why would Peter exhort the infants to repent and be baptised? The answer is, of course, he did nothing of the kind. He only exhorted those of sufficient maturity in years, those who could hear, believe and repent; they were the ones whom he exhorted and subsequently baptised upon their profession of faith – not infants. Infants were not baptised on the Day of Pentecost.

On the verse Calvin wrote: 'The promise was first made to the Jews, and then to their children, and last of all, that it is also to be imparted to the Gentiles'.[22] This comment raises an important,

---

[21] But it says 'the promise is to you and to your children' (Acts 2:39). So it does. But this does not have to mean infants. Indeed, it is unlikely to have meant infants. When Paul stated: 'That promise which was made to the fathers... God has fulfilled this for us their children' (Acts 13:32-33), was he talking about *infants*? Of course not! The prophetic promise, given to men long before, had now been fulfilled to their descendants – this present generation. Likewise, Peter might well have been saying that God's promise was not only for those hearing him that day, but for them and for those who would hear in future generations – as many as the Lord our God will call. Compare Deut. 29:29; Josh. 22:24-25; Ps. 78:4-6; 132:12; Matt. 27:25 *etc.*

[22] Calvin: *Commentaries* Vol.18 Part 2 p122. Calvin thought 'this place... abundantly refute[s] the manifest error of the Anabaptists, which will not have infants, which are the children of the faithful, to be baptised, as if they were not members of the church'. If Calvin was right, and the Anabaptists wrong, and all the children of believers (or nominally so) are 'members of the church', we must know what he meant by 'members of the church'. Did Calvin mean 'members of the [visible] church' or 'members of the [biblical]

250

practical question. Why, on this argument, did Peter not tell the Gentiles that their children were included in the promise? You see, reader, accepting for a moment the infant baptiser's argument, the Gentiles would not have realised that their children were included along with the parents – it was a Jewish concept, in their genes under the old covenant, leaving the Gentiles in ignorance of it, 'afar off'. According to Calvin, Peter told the Jews that *their* children were included – Jews, those who were supposed to know all about it – but he omitted to tell the unfortunate Gentiles – Gentiles, the very people who needed to be told, since they didn't have a clue about it! Furthermore, if Calvin was right, the Gentiles could easily have thought their children were not included, since the promise, according to Calvin, was made to the Jews and their offspring, leaving the children of Gentiles high and dry! What makes this even more surprising is, on the basis of the doctrine of infant baptism, all the children of all believers are supposed to be in the covenant. Or is it only the children of Jews who are included? Is the promise made to the Jews because they are Jews? And if the children of believing Gentiles are not included, why do infant baptisers baptise those children today? The truth of the matter is, age and birth are of no consequence; all men, all women and all children – of whatever nationality and age – are included, if they are among the number whom the Lord our God shall call.

What is more, are we to believe that those present, who heard Peter preach, and who repented and believed, but did not have their children (or wife, husband or servant – see Argument 7, 'Household Baptism') with them, went home (or wherever), routed them out, took them back to the apostles, and had them all baptised? Is there the slightest suggestion of this in Acts 2? And what about the resistance put up by some of those so fetched? After all, in such a huge number, it is unthinkable that none of those gathered by the believers would not put up a struggle. Do we get any hint of the scuffles which must have ensued?

---

church'? If the latter, then it takes us back to the point made earlier; namely, all such children are saved, since 'Christ... loved the church and gave himself for her', and will bring all its members to absolute perfection (Eph. 5:25-27). Note also, once again, the infant baptiser's confusion. Are infants baptised to make them church members or because they are?

And when it is all boiled down, church membership is not even in view in Acts 2:38, so how can it be a proof text for church membership? It only arises in Acts 2:41 and on, after the demonstration of faith and repentance, followed by baptism on the part of those who have been called by God's grace. If infant baptisers would restrict church membership to all who have been called and, following faith and repentance, been baptised in obedience to Christ – and to no one else – there would be no need for this discussion. As the infant baptiser Legg quite properly put it: 'The idea of members in the New Testament, that is in the picture of the body of Christ, certainly involves living, spiritual union with Christ and this would militate against saying that the children were members'. When defining church membership, the Savoy Declaration wisely omitted 'and of their children' from their version of the Westminster Confession, but even so the Independents and Congregationalists still wanted their children included in the 'covenant status' in some way. They do to this day. Trying desperately to get round the difficulty, Legg said that 'the church consists of believers with their children'.[23] Reader, did you spot it? To be a Reformed infant-baptiser, one certainly needs to be master of the nuances of the English language; one has to be able to read and digest the small print! 'Believers *and* their children' is it; or 'believers *with* their children'? To the man or woman in the pew, what is the difference? It appears to be a distinction without a difference.

Ezekiel 16:20-21, Romans 11:16, Genesis 3:15 and Genesis 17:7 complete the texts the Westminster Confession produces to 'prove' that churches should be composed of professors and their children. These verses have nothing at all to say upon the subject.[24] Nothing at all! Romans 11:16 gives a principle, namely that if a sample has certain characteristics then the whole batch has the same characteristics; 'if the firstfruit is holy, the lump is also holy; and if the root is holy, so are the branches'. But it has nothing to say about church membership. Nothing! Since infant baptisers quote this verse to support their claim, I presume they understand it to mean that if a parent is a church member, so is his child. Really? Therefore, if a man

---

[23] Legg p13.

[24] In any case, how can *Old* Testament verses be *proof*-texts for the practice of church membership? It is the continuity/discontinuity question again. See above.

is a Christian, his child is, too? If a man is holy, so is his child? The argument is ludicrous.

The blunt fact is the New Testament never speaks of visible churches. It does speak of churches which are found in particular localities – Corinth, Ephesus, and so on. Hence the proper term is *local* churches, not visible churches. Naturally the invented concept of a visible church, where the members are professors and their children, is very acceptable – indeed, it is essential – to infant baptisers, who have to live with the consequences of their mistaken practice. The New Testament churches, however, were composed only of believers who were baptised after profession of faith, and who lived consistently with that profession.

This is the nub of the matter for my purpose in this book. As I said at the start, I have not been interested in an arid study of the assertions for and against infant baptism. I am convinced that infant baptisers are wrong; I think their statements are often dangerous and grossly misleading; I think their arguments are tortuous and complicated, often worked out from a false premise. I also think that, at times, they say highly speculative things about those who die in infancy, and do so with unjustified definiteness. Some of them say things which verge on the maudlin. What is more they have sometimes used highly offensive words about the attitude of Baptists towards these particular infants. On occasion they have used untrue words. What of Engelsma's criticism, for example? I have already referred to his calling the denial of infant baptism a 'grim teaching and practice'. His own full statement makes 'grim' enough reading in its own right:

Among other implications of this grim teaching and practice is that there is no ground for any hope of the election and salvation of the children of believers who die in infancy or in early childhood. Indeed, there is every reason to believe that they perish. They are, according to the Baptists themselves, outside the church and covenant of God; and outside the church and covenant of God [there] is no salvation.[25]

Engelsma's leap of logic is utterly unwarranted and false. What is more, it is offensive. I will repeat what I have said about *all* infants who die very young – *all* infants, not just the infants of believers:

---

[25] Engelsma p11.

'Shall not the judge of all the earth do right?' (Gen. 18:25).[26] Let us draw a veil over what we do not know, and let us trust in God who is 'abundant in mercy, forgiving iniquity and transgression' (Num. 14:18). What God in his sovereign, merciful purposes chooses to do is his own prerogative. Nevertheless, what must govern our practice in the church is not his secret will but his revealed will (Deut. 29:29). Not a few infant baptisers (and some Calvinistic Baptists[27] including, notably, Spurgeon) have been (and are) far too fond of speculating in this very delicate area of infant death. They speak with a glowing confidence and absolute assurance, but they have no scriptural warrant for their over-free statements. They become philosophers and not theologians at this point. It is wrong of them. They should not dogmatise when Scripture is silent. Nor should they belabour those Baptists – those who are not willing to venture where Scripture does not lead – with harsh words in a very sensitive area.[28]

Other criticisms levelled against Baptists by infant baptisers are to the effect that the advance of Baptist teaching has been linked to the growth of Dispensationalism, Arminianism and Modernism. It is freely

---

[26] See my earlier note on this verse.

[27] Not excluding Gospel Standard Strict Baptists. See, for instance, Gadsby pp30-31; *Christian's Monthly Record* 1886 p73.

[28] I am not responding in kind, but simply pointing out what strikes me as the logical conclusion of Engelsma's argument. If every believer's child who dies is guaranteed salvation, is it not preferable for them all to die before they reach the age when they might (and some do!) 'refuse the covenant', turn their back upon Christ, and so perish? This, of course, is nonsense! I am reminded of the parallel wrong-headed argument that the heathen are automatically saved since they have not heard the gospel. If this is true, then we do the heathen the greatest possible disservice by taking the gospel to them!
There is another point. As for the charge of 'grimness', what about the death of the babies of unbelievers, or the babies of Baptists? Speaking for myself, I would apply my line of reasoning to *all* dying infants. But what do those infant baptisers, who take the stance I am criticising, do? Do they agree with Watson's view of those who do not baptise their babies? 'By denying their infants baptism, they exclude them from membership in the visible church, so that their infants are sucking pagans' (Watson Vol.2 p162). We know the Puritans thought their (baptised) infants took in divinity with their mother's milk – so, presumably, they thought of them as 'sucking Christians'. I can see only one logical outcome of this. If a 'sucking Christian' dies, he goes to heaven; if a 'sucking pagan' dies, he goes to hell. This is 'grim' indeed.

granted that the Anabaptists in general, and John Smyth in particular, were Arminians, but it is not essential to be an Arminian to practise believer's baptism. After all, the Particular Baptists arose in the 1630s. Surely Calvinistic Baptists today ought not to be put in the same box as Dispensationalists and all the rest? It is done, however. And it is grossly unfair.

But none of that is my main concern at this time. I deliberately turn away from it. This present publication arises from my book written about the battle to recover the pattern and order and life of the New Testament churches. And it is at this very point that infant baptism is such a disaster. It is the down-to-earth outworking of the practice of infant baptism as it affects day-to-day church life which is my main concern.[29]

I have supplied very many examples to show that infant baptisers regard their children – because they are their children and therefore, they say, in the covenant – as regenerate, as sanctified in Christ, as being the covenant children of God, as having God as their God, as having received the forgiveness of their sins through the blood of Christ, as being heirs of the kingdom of God, and so on. They tell them they are. They treat them accordingly. They make them church members on that basis.[30] Now all this poses a very real, a vital, a

---

[29] It is a fact – which I find very interesting, highly significant – that in the book edited by John H.Armstrong, giving four different views of baptism, the only author of the four who did *not* conclude with a drawing-back from a full-blown application of baptism to church life, was Nettles – who rightly spoke of baptism as a symbol. Nettles saw no need to water down baptism in church life. The advocates of the other views (Reformed, Lutheran and the Churches of Christ) did. In particular, notice Pratt's acknowledgement that several Reformed congregations, while they *encourage* parents to present their babies for baptism, now *require* it only of church officers. As Nettles noted: 'If infant baptism is as important' as has been made out, 'how could a [church] not require it of their membership? Do they have a right to change God's ordinance?... Does this [practice] indicate a deep-seated discomfort as to whether infant baptism can actually be defended as biblical?' While John H.Armstrong observed that 'the contributors to [his] book all seek to keep [the] vital connection [between baptism and church life] in mind', with the exception of Nettles (with believer's baptism), in Armstrong's book, at least, they all signally failed. See John H.Armstrong pp20,72,76,105-109,141-143.

[30] Or else the other way about. They can't seem to make up their mind.

practical question. It is a very simple question. It demands a straight answer. Are those statements true, or are they false? That is the question. They must be one or the other; which is it? Are all such children truly saved, or not?[31]

As a matter of undisputed fact, some Reformed infant-baptisers have actually asserted that it is so, that all their children are undoubtedly saved. Joseph C.Holbrook, for instance, declared that it was 'incredible and impossible' that God should not save all the children of believers according to his promise. No wonder Holbrook said it was 'the most "exceeding great and precious promise" that I know of'. I admit that this is not the commonly held view among Reformed infant-baptisers – Hanko, for example, declared that 'this kind of argument does more harm for the [infant baptism] position than a good argument against it'.[32] Nevertheless, if Holbrook's blanket assertions are rejected by most infant baptisers – and they ought to be – what, exactly, *is* the status of the baptised children of believers? Are the statements which I have quoted true or false? Do infant baptisers believe them, or do they not?

The vast majority of infant baptisers are prepared to admit that not all their children will be saved. Engelsma, for instance, said that it is an 'incontestable fact that not all the children of believers are saved...

---

[31] See end note on p269 for excursus: 'The Reformed and the status of children after baptism'.
[32] Hanko: *We* p49. But Holbrook was not alone. Wilkins: 'What we do not know is whether or not [an unbaptised] man is in covenant with God. If he is not in covenant, he must repent of his sins and believe in Christ Jesus, be joined to the people of God by baptism, and persevere in faithfulness all his days (by the power of the Holy Spirit who works in him to "will and do" for God's good pleasure). If he has been baptised, he *is* in covenant with God, and is obligated to walk in faithfulness' (Wilkins: 'Covenant' pp66-67, emphasis mine). In other words, if he has been baptised as an infant, he has no need to repent and believe, no need of a personal saving experience of Christ. It is obvious how this drastically alters – ruins – the way such people are addressed by preachers who believe such teaching. Far worse, think of the way it affects the eternal state of those concerned. This awful consideration does not seem to stop some infant baptisers. Lusk, for instance, had no time for parents who thought of their children 'instead of "growing up Christian" under continual covenant nurture... expected [them] to undergo their own "conversion experience" at the appropriate age' (Lusk: 'Paedobaptism' pp74-75).

We cannot presume that all our children are regenerate and elect. To presume this is contrary to Scripture and experience'.[33] Quite right! So why do they presume it? Why do they tell them they are heirs of the kingdom of God, and so on? Why did Hanko write that 'the elect children of the covenant are... as a general rule, regenerated and brought to conversion in earliest infancy. The children of the church are covenant children, themselves already regenerated'? Why did he say that the children of believers are 'children of God, God's own elect people... regenerated by the Spirit of Christ'?[34] What did he mean by it? What scriptural grounds did he have for saying these things?

The point I am making is this: When it comes to the theoretical view of children, most infant baptisers claim a very exalted status for their children. They could hardly use more inflated language. They declare that all their children are incorporated into Christ by baptism, they say they are in the covenant, and all the rest of it. They teach their children that it is so. They look upon their children as Christians; they address them as such. They deride Baptists and others who do not view their children as Christians, but treat them as unconverted sinners. Engelsma, for instance, attacked Jonathan Edwards (an infant baptiser himself!) for calling the children of believers, 'Satan's little vipers' – in company with all children, all being born ruined in Adam. Engelsma denounced this view by saying that the children of believers are the children of God, the lambs of the flock of Christ.[35]

---

[33] Engelsma pp11-12. What do those infant baptisers who hold to 'presumptive regeneration' make of this? See above.

[34] Hanko: *Ought* p22; *We* pp55-56.

[35] Engelsma p9. Lusk, speaking of 'the decline of infant baptism' in 19th century America, quoted Lewis Bevens Schenck: 'Uncertainty in regard to the status of children in the Church, was doubtless one great cause of inattention to the ordinance... The question arose in many minds, to what purpose is baptism administered to children? Why bring children to an ordinance in the Church, of which the Church herself makes nothing when it is over?... If the Church had no assurance that the infant children of believers were truly the children of God, if it did not treat them as Christians under her special love and watchfulness, if it ignored practically their baptism, this was reason for the decline of the ordinance' (Lusk: 'Paedobaptism' pp119-120). For the history of this battle in the context of sacramentalism as it developed in 19th century America, including leading protagonists John Williamson Nevin, Philip Schaff, Charles Hodge and James Henley Thornwell, see Lusk:

E.M.B.Green asserted that in a home where there are believing parents, it is not 'necessary or fitting' to evangelise the children. They must be 'treated as being in the Christian fellowship' – Christians, church members, I suppose he meant – 'unless they contract out... And even then they do not need to be converted... rather they need to be corrected by their parents and brought back to the Christian way from which they had strayed'.[36]

This statement is shocking. It is the sort of stance which is taken by many infant baptisers – *in theory*. But what of the practical outworking of that stance? Ah! When it comes to facing up to reality, how the tune changes! To hark back to an earlier figure; how the inflated language is punctured! Listen to Engelsma again: 'Strictly from the point of view of their natural condition', the children of believers are not 'in any better position than the heathens of the world. Our children are by nature dead in sin'. This is simply a flat contradiction of other statements which he made. On the one hand – the theoretical point of view – the children are not ruined in the fall. On the other hand – the practical – they are. Which is it? On the one hand, Engelsma said: 'We do not view them as unsaved heathens ("little vipers")... but we view them as children of God'; on the other hand, they are dead in sin.[37]

Which is it? Are they the children of God, or are they not?

The solution which Engelsma supplied for this conundrum was to say that the position of children in the covenant is *conditional*; that when declarations are made to the effect that the children are sanctified

---

'Paedobaptism' pp71-88; McNeill pp398-401. Schaff's hope for reunion with Rome, and 'Nevin's weighty book: *The Mystical Presence*', with its 'high sacramental doctrine', were potent ingredients in the 'Mercersburg theology' and its challenge to American Calvinism. As can be seen by the above, Nevin's work has not been forgotten! Sacramentalism is on the march!

[36] Kingdon pp99-100. Bushnell argued that the child is 'to grow up a Christian and never know himself as being otherwise' (McNeill p400). See above for an extract from Leach p31 on the same theme. And some words from Wright, already quoted: 'The children of the faithful... we are right to treat them as new members of God's people, not as no better than little pagans or unbelievers' (Wright: 'Children' p37).

[37] Engelsma pp13,16-18.

in Christ, everybody has to understand that this means only 'the elect children'. '*Conditional*'?[38]

---

[38] Engelsma pp14-18. Is the promise, the covenant, conditional or not? Are the children in the covenant or not? Engelsma really admitted that this kind of talk is, in the end, virtually meaningless. He could say 'that *all* children of believers are in the covenant by *conditional* promise', yet immediately limit this to 'the elect children', nevertheless going on to say 'this covenant view is in harmony with the Reformed Confessions. The Westminster Confession [for instance] holds the promise of the covenant of grace to be particular and *unconditional*' (Engelsma pp16-17, emphasis mine). In other words, when it boils down, infant baptisers baptise all their children, assuring them all that they are in the covenant, when all the time they know that for some of them, their words are empty. And what now of his earlier statement: 'The children of believers are included in the covenant *as children*, that is, already at conception and birth. They receive forgiveness of sins through the blood of Jesus, the Holy Spirit of sanctification, and church membership – as children... For they have God as their God, and are his people – as children' (Engelsma p9, emphasis his)? This conditional/unconditional double-speak smacks of Humpty Dumpty who, it will be remembered, told Alice: 'When I use a word, it means just what I choose it to mean; neither more nor less'. The church, however, drawing its principles from Scripture, has to exist in the real world, not in that fantasy-land which is entered only by passing 'through the looking glass'. For more on the misuse of 'conditional', see my *Particular*.
Consider Jonathan D.Moore on Davenant: 'In keeping with his belief in baptismal regeneration, Davenant taught that all baptised infants, without exception, are, by "the goodwill of God", "absolved from the guilt of original sin", and also justified, regenerated and adopted into God's family. However, their justification, regeneration and adoption "is not exactly the same" as that of adult believers, as it can be lost. "The justification, regeneration and adoption of baptised infants, brings them into a state of salvation as far as they are capable", but nevertheless, "the Christian infant who is regenerated in baptism acquires another regeneration when, as an adult, he believes the gospel". Although God is "embracing them with his favour", baptised children "do not continue justified, regenerated or adopted as adults, unless by repentance, faith, and the renunciation promised, they fulfil their vow taken upon them [by others] at baptism"'. Of course, I can hear the response: 'We don't believe that nonsense!' Quite. But what – precisely – *do* modern-day Reformed people believe about the state of their baptised infants? Let us have it out in the open. As Moore went on to point out: 'At the synod of Dort, Samuel Ward, who also held similar controversial views on baptismal regeneration... was counselled by Davenant to keep them quiet so as not to give the Arminians a foothold' (Moore p195).

This is a fatal flaw in the Reformed infant-baptiser's logic. In 1 Corinthians 7:14 – the verse on which so much of the thesis depends[39] – it does not say 'the elect children' are sanctified. Nor does it mean it. The verse teaches that *all* the children of believers are sanctified, whether or not they themselves are elect. That is the point of the verse! The children are sanctified, not because they are elect, but because the parent is a believer. I remind you, it is the meaning of the word 'sanctified' which is crucial.[40] If only Reformed infant-baptisers would pay proper attention to that. God's election is not an escape route in 1 Corinthians 7:14. It is not an escape route at all. It is one of the glorious doctrines of the gospel. It is an abuse to treat the doctrine of election in that cavalier fashion. The election of the child is simply not in the verse – not directly, nor by implication.[41]

It is utterly wrong for infant baptisers to adjust God's declarations to fit in with their interpretation. In theory, infant baptism looks attractive to many. This, I remind you, reader, is why I am writing. I am trying to issue a warning. When they have to face the inevitable, the practical outcome of their system, at that crucial point infant baptisers have to adjust their position. The problem for them is, there are those who are said to be incorporated into Christ by sprinkling, but who later prove they are utterly devoid of saving grace. At that point, some, perhaps nearly all, infant baptisers fall back on to God's election

---

[39] See end note on p270 for excursus: 'Reformed contradictions on 1 Cor. 7:14'.

[40] Please see above for my comments on the verse.

[41] The same point can be made about household baptism. As I have shown, infant baptisers say the children of a man converted to Christ are to be baptised; the practice of the New Testament demands it. So they say. Very well. Do infant baptisers believe Acts 16:31-34 or not? Here is the command and the promise: 'Believe on the Lord Jesus Christ, and you will be saved, you and your household'. Here is the obedience: 'Immediately he and all his family were baptised'. Infant baptisers argue for the obedience. Do they believe the promise? Or is it *conditional*? is it *presumptive*? I fail to detect such qualifying adjectives in the apostle's words: 'You will be saved, you and your household', is what he said. He issued the command and the promise and got the obedience, to and from all of the family, *on the same basis*. If infant baptisers really do think the apostle baptised the children on the basis of their father's (or mother's) faith, why do they not do the same – *and tell them they are saved – on that same basis*? And stick with it!

as an escape clause. And in doing that, they have thrown out of the window all their swelling claims for their children. They may deride Baptists and others for their approach to children, but when it comes to it, the children of infant baptisers are ruined in the fall as much as any children. They will be saved, if they are saved, like all who are saved – including the children of Baptists! – they will be saved because God the Father elected them, Christ died for them, and the Holy Spirit works in them.

Reader, this is our only hope. Men ought not to treat God's electing decree as a loop-hole, bringing it in at the end of their case in order to evade all the disasters they have produced. What is more, God's election is our *hope*, for us and our children; it is not a *hindrance*. God's election produces salvation; it does not stand in the way of it! Election produces saved sinners; it does not produce damned sinners.[42] We are to look upon God's gracious decree to save sinners as something to rejoice in, not something to dread. God hated Esau, it is true, yet he loved Jacob (Mal. 1:2-3; Rom. 9:13). But which half of the text is the more amazing, the more wonderful? Which do you emphasise? The fact that God hated Esau is not as amazing as that he loved Jacob! Esau was not kept out – Jacob was brought in – by God's election. Some infant baptisers give the impression that they look upon God's electing decree as a barrier to their children being saved. From birth, they themselves treat them as saints, they bring them up in that way, they tell them they are Christians – and then they tell them, after all is said and done, it is God who, with his decrees, keeps some of them out! Their parents and elders said they were Christians; God said they were not! I dare say I shall be accused of a caricature – but that is the way I am forced to read their words.

Speaking for myself, God's election is my only hope in this matter. My children were born ruined in Adam and under the curse of God, as all children are. My wife and I dared not tell them they were Christians, nor treat them as if they were. Our only hope was that God in time would show that in eternity he had chosen them to salvation, if indeed he had, by calling them to repentance and faith.[43] Whatever the

---

[42] See my earlier note on Rom. 9:21.

[43] See earlier extracts from Wilkins and Lusk. I repeat the latter. Lusk had no time for parents who thought of their children 'instead of "growing up Christian" under continual covenant nurture... expected [them] to undergo

claims of infant baptisers, that is the reality. Sinners are saved only through faith, only by being redeemed by the blood of Christ, only and entirely because God elected them to salvation. Not because they were born to believing parents!

In stark contrast to the notions of infant baptisers when they come to the reality of dealing with their children, listen to some more words of Spurgeon, found in his sermon entitled 'Jesus and the Children', another sermon on Mark 10:13-16. Oh! that infant baptisers would heed them. Oh! that all my readers would. Spurgeon addressed himself to the ignorance of the apostles concerning the children's need, when the mothers brought their children to Christ: 'But these little ones with bright eyes, and prattling tongues, and leaping limbs, why should they come to Jesus? Ah, friends! they [the apostles] forgot that in those children, with all their joy, their health, and their apparent innocence, there was a great and grievous need for the blessing of a Saviour's grace'. Spurgeon went straight on to apply this point to his hearers, saying:

If you indulge in the novel idea that *your* children do not need conversion, that children born of Christian parents are somewhat superior to others, and have good within them which only needs development, one great motive for your devout earnestness will be gone. Believe me, brethren, your children need the Spirit of God to give them new hearts and right spirits, or else they will go astray as other children do. Remember that however young they are, there is a stone within the youngest breast; and that stone must be taken away, or be the ruin of the child. There is a tendency to evil even where as yet it has not developed into act, and that tendency needs to be overcome by the divine power of the Holy Spirit, causing the child to be born again. Oh that the church of God would cast off the old Jewish idea which still has such force around us, namely, that natural birth brings with it covenant privileges! Now, even under the Old dispensation, there were hints that the true seed was not born after the flesh, but after the spirit, as in the case of Ishmael and Isaac, and Esau and Jacob. Will not even the church of God know that 'that which is born of

---

their own "conversion experience" at the appropriate age' (Lusk: 'Paedobaptism' pp74-75). Speaking for myself, I plead 'guilty', and unashamedly so. If I may speak for my children, I am sure they are glad my wife and I did not treat them as believers before they professed faith, but were looking for and praying for their 'conversion experience'. At least, that is how they are dealing with their own children.

flesh is flesh; and that which is born of the Spirit is spirit'? 'Who can bring a clean thing out of an unclean?' The natural birth communicates nature's filthiness, but it cannot convey grace. Under the new covenant we are expressly told that the sons of God are 'born, not of blood, nor of the will of the flesh, nor of the will of man, but of God'. Under the old covenant, which was typical, the birth according to the flesh yielded privilege; but to come at all under the covenant of grace you must be born again. The first birth brings you nothing but an inheritance with the first Adam; you must be born again to come under the headship of the second Adam.

But it is written, says one, 'that the promise is to you, and to your children'. Dear friends, there never was a grosser piece of knavery committed under heaven than the quotation of that text as it is usually quoted. I have heard it quoted many times to prove a doctrine which is very far removed from that which it clearly teaches. If you take one half of any sentence which any man utters, and leave out the rest, you may make him say the opposite of what he means. What do you think that text really is? See Acts 2:39: 'The promise is unto you, and your children, and to all that are afar off, even as many as the Lord our God shall call'. This grandly wide statement is the argument on which is founded the exhortation, 'Repent, and be baptised every one of you'. It is not a declaration of privilege special to anyone, but a presentation of grace as much to all that are afar off as to them and their children. There is not a word in the New Testament to show that the benefits of divine grace are in any degree transmitted by natural descent: they come 'to as many as the Lord our God shall call', whether their parents are saints or sinners. How can people have the impudence to tear off half a text to make it teach what is not true? No, brethren; you must look sorrowfully upon your children as born in sin, and shapen in iniquity, 'heirs of wrath, even as others'; and though you may yourself belong to the line of saints, and trace your pedigree from minister to minister, all eminent in the church of God, yet your children occupy precisely the same position by their birth as other people's children do; so that they must be redeemed from under the curse of the law by the precious blood of Jesus, and they must receive a new [heart] by the work of the Holy Ghost. They are favoured by being placed under godly training, and under the hearing of the gospel; but their need and their sinfulness are the same as in the rest of the race. If you think of this, you will see the reason why they should be brought to Jesus Christ – a reason why they should be brought as speedily as possible in the arms of your prayer and faith to him who is able to renew them.[44]

---

[44] Spurgeon: *Metropolitan* Vol.32 pp569-570.

As Spurgeon entitled another sermon already quoted, 'Children (must be) brought to Christ, not the Font'.

Just over a year later than 'Jesus and the Children', Spurgeon preached a sermon entitled 'The Blood of Sprinkling and the Children', in which he spoke of the need to instruct children in the great themes of the gospel by arousing their curiosity, by taking them to witness the carrying out of Christ's ordinances. Spurgeon said that we must get our children to:

Know and trust in the finished sacrifice... This will necessitate your teaching the child his need of a Saviour. You must not hold back from this needful task. Do not flatter the child with delusive rubbish about his nature being good and needing to be developed. Tell him he must be born again. Don't bolster him up with the fancy of his own innocence, but show him his sin. Mention the childish sins to which he is prone, and pray the Holy Spirit to work conviction in his heart and conscience. Deal with the young in much the same way as you would with the old. Be thorough and honest with them. Flimsy religion is neither good for young nor old. These boys and girls need pardon through the precious blood as surely as any of us. Do not hesitate to tell the child his ruin; he will not else desire the remedy. Tell him also of the punishment of his sin, and warn him of its terror. Be tender, but be true. Do not hide from the youthful sinner the truth, however terrible it may be. Now that he has come to years of responsibility, if he believes not in Christ, it will go ill with him at the last great day. Set before him the judgement-seat, and remind him that he will have to give an account of the things done in the body. Labour to arouse the conscience; and pray God the Holy Spirit to work by you till the heart becomes tender and the mind perceives the need of the great salvation.
Children need to learn the doctrine of the cross that they may find immediate salvation... The most fundamental truth should be made most prominent; and what is this but the cross? Some talk to children about being good boys and girls, and so on; that is to say, they preach the law to the children, though they would preach the gospel to grown-up people! Is this honest? Is this wise? Children need the gospel, the whole gospel, the unadulterated gospel.[45]

Reader, all children need all of that – all children, including the children of believers. I put it to you, that you have been presented with two very distinct ways of dealing with children. One way is that used by infant baptisers; the other is that used by those who reject infant

---

[45] Spurgeon: *Metropolitan* Vol.33 pp587-588.

baptism. They cannot both be right. One of the two is clearly wrong; the other is clearly scriptural. Which is which?

Reader, the subject is so important, I trespass on your patience for just one more quotation from Spurgeon. I also point out that, contrary to the opinions of some infant baptisers, many of us who reject their practice still have strong views on the spiritual state of children and their upbringing. Such matters are not the monopoly of those who talk of 'covenant children'. I quote from Spurgeon's sermon 'A Promise For Us and For Our Children' preached from Isaiah 44:1-5 during the year 1864. Having, in the first place, addressed the parents, he went on to say:

Here comes a blessed promise for our children – 'I will pour my Spirit upon thy seed', in which observe first of all, the need. Our children want the Spirit of God. They are not like children educated in the street, the tavern, or the low theatre; they have not heard from our lips words of lust or profanity; they have been hushed to sleep by the name of Jesus as their lullaby; they breathe the air of religion, but for all that they need the Spirit of God. We love to see the children of godly parents brought into church membership, but we would avoid above all things anything like hereditary profession or inherited religion; it must be personal in each individual or it is not worth a groat... We must not adulterate our membership by the reception of the children of godly parents, unless we have clear proof that they themselves are converted to God. Your children need the Holy Spirit quite as much as the offspring of the Hottentot or the Kaffir. They are born in sin and shapen in iniquity: in sin do the best of mothers conceive their children, and, however well you may train them, you cannot take the stone out of the heart nor turn it into flesh. To give a new heart and a right spirit is the work of the Holy Spirit, and of the Holy Spirit alone...

It was the work of the Spirit which transformed their fathers – it is that which must transform them. The Word may come to them and not be blessed; we may be silly enough to take them to baby-baptism and they would not be blessed... I do not know that the parent needs to say much to his child about baptism... except, sometimes, a gentle word as to the duty of the believer, and a clear explanation of the meaning... Tell the child that he is dead in trespasses and sins, let there be no doubt about his natural condition... I think that in some Sunday School addresses there is not always the gospel so clearly and decidedly proclaimed as it should be. It is not very easy, I know, to preach Christ to little children, but there is nothing else worth preaching. To stand up and say, 'Be good boys and girls, and you will get to heaven', is preaching the old covenant of works, and it is no more right to preach salvation by works to little children than to those who are of a mature age. We are all dead, and as the Spirit of God can alone renew us, so he alone can renew them.[46]

I leave the matter there. But have you noticed that when children are addressed by preachers,[47] they are frequently asked if they *love* Jesus? Do please remember that a sinner is justified by faith, and not by love. However young or old the sinner is, saving faith is essential (Acts 16:31; Eph. 2:8). Little acts of kindness do not justify, at whatever age they are done (Eph. 2:8-9). The point is, the children of saints have exactly the same need of justifying faith as the children of pagans, whatever some infant baptisers may say to the contrary.

The problem is getting worse. In recent days, I have noticed a growing trend in some evangelical churches which do not baptise infants; namely, in their children's 'talks', to address the children as 'Christians', to call them 'Christians', and to pray for help for them in 'their Christian lives'.[48] What are we coming to?[49]

So, to return to my earlier question to infant baptisers: Are all the children of believers in the covenant, or not? It is all very well making enormous theoretical claims for the children – what of the practical outcome? The fact remains that infant baptisers produce men and women who have been told they are Christians when they are not. That is the issue which must be faced.

Interestingly, Marcel solved the conundrum – of why some 'covenant children' are not converted – by taking a totally different escape route to Engelsma who, it will be recalled, hid behind God's election. Indeed, what Marcel alleged flatly contradicted Engelsma's suggested solution. Marcel said that not all 'the children of believers [will be blessed]... with saving faith. A certain number of them will voluntarily choose unbelief or rebellion despite the work of God in

---

[46] Spurgeon: 'A Promise' pp212-213.

[47] In children's talks – how few address them at all during the sermon.

[48] If the parents (and the church), who do *not* baptise babies, nevertheless are *dogmatic* that their infants 'under the age of responsibility' are saved, and treat them as 'little Christians' as they are growing up, and submit them to 'children's talks' where they are addressed as believers – even if they do not allow them to partake of the Lord's supper, which a growing number are now doing (see below) – is it any wonder if these infants, when they become adults, think themselves true believers – even if they are not?

[49] See end note on p271 for excursus: 'Reformed inclusivism gone mad'.

266

their hearts by the Holy Spirit'.[50] In other words, Marcel declared that the promise of the covenant said one thing according to infant baptisers, but in the course of time some growing children will say the opposite, when they will resist the work of the Holy Spirit in their hearts. This is an amazing statement. It is breathtaking! Marcel went further than the Arminians. At least they only go as far as to say that sinners can resist the external call of the gospel, whereas Marcel was prepared to state that sinners can resist the internal working of the Spirit in the heart.

The fact remains, however they explain it, infant baptisers inevitably produce at least some young people and adults who are unregenerate, but who have been assured they are Christians. There is no getting round this unpalatable truth. Apparently we are to believe that these unfortunate people get into this horrific condition either by God's electing decree, or by their own choice in that their rebellion successfully resists the work of the Holy Spirit in their hearts. Which is it – God's choice, or theirs? How many infant baptisers agree with Charles Hodge who said that 'little ones have their names written in the Lamb's book of life [by baptism], even if they afterwards choose to erase them'?[51]

But the stubborn question remains – it will not go away.[52] Whatever the reason for it, infant baptisers produce some unregenerate sinners who are told they are Christians. What will they do with them? Do any of them concur with the highly influential Puritan, John Cotton? He tackled this question of church members who have no

---

[50] Hanko: *We* p73.

[51] Kingdon p65.

[52] 'What, then, is the position of our children? Are the children of believers within the covenant of grace, but nevertheless to be regarded as the children of wrath until they give clear evidence of being savingly converted? Or are they within the covenant, and presumptively elect or regenerate until they give clear evidence to the contrary? Or are they outside the covenant altogether, and standing desperately in need of regeneration? Or, if they are elect and within the covenant, has it anything to do with the fact that they are children of believers? Or, to widen the question, what is the ground of covenant interest?' (Boorman pp98-99). I have set out my answer to these questions – clearly enough, I hope. But how do infant baptisers answer them? Answer them, they must! See Buchanan: 'David Wright' pp151-152; Buchanan and Vasey p23.

grace in them. Some left the church, thereby proving they were not true members, he said. But he had to face up to the certainty that 'there are some who continue faithful friends to the church, and never fall off'. Although they 'have no truth of grace in them', nevertheless they remain church members – what of *them*? Cotton was prepared to assert that 'they have the place of members, but they are not true members', and he was willing to keep them. To make his reasoning clear(!), he gave an illustration. He likened the church to a man with a glass eye or a wooden leg. Unconverted church members play the part of that glass eye or wooden leg, Cotton maintained! 'So such may be ornaments and supports of the church, but yet not true members', he declared.[53] Reader, is this not a fantasy world? Frankly, it is madness. What is more, think for a moment of the spiritual state, the spiritual danger, of those wretched unregenerate glass-eye-or-wooden-leg church members. Speaking spiritually: Allowing for a moment that they may be a benefit to the church – though I stoutly deny it – think of the curse the church has been to them! Some church 'ornaments' end up in hell! Who helped to send them there? Where is the Scripture for all this?

However, some have plumbed even greater depths than Cotton. In 18th century New England, Solomon Stoddard 'and many other great divines', no doubt because of their views on infant baptism, came to

---

[53] Cotton p225. And how about this? On the premise 'that one and the same covenant, which was made to Abraham in the Old Testament, is for substance the same with that in the New; and this, under the New Testament, the very same with that of Abraham's under the Old', Shepard wrote of what he called the double covenant – the parent's and God's, the external and the internal covenant, the elect and the church seed. He saw nothing wrong in all the members of a believer's household – whether 'visibly godly or the children of such', the children, both 'good and bad' – being church members. Federal holiness covered it all, according to Shepard; the children may be unbelievers, of course, but even so be 'federally holy'. What if these children grow up profane? They are still church members 'until they are cast out', but for this they must 'positively reject the gospel', otherwise 'they are to be accounted of God's church'. As I say, all was based on the covenant with Abraham. Shepard admitted such churches would be 'mixed with many chaffy hypocrites, and often profane persons', but he thought all is well since 'ordinarily God gathers out his elect' from such 'profane and corrupt churches'. And so on, and on (Iain Murray: *Reformation* pp379-405). Shepard's entire treatise should be read. *That*, in itself, should give infant baptisers pause for thought.

the remarkable conclusion that 'even excommunicated persons are still members of the church of God; and some suppose, the worshippers of Baal in Israel, even those who were bred up such from their infancy, remained still members of the church of God'. So wrote Jonathan Edwards. He even added that some held that Papists who continue to practise their idolatry and superstitions 'still are in the visible church of Christ'.[54] It takes one's breath away!

Even where men draw back at that, it is almost inevitable that infant baptisers end up with mongrel churches that have a partly regenerate and a partly unregenerate membership. They invent a variety of ways to try to cope with it, but they are left with a diabolical confusion.[55] It is even worse than that. Their system tends to produce – it actually does produce – some men and women who, though unregenerate, think they are children of God. And it can produce more than 'some' who are deluded; as I have shown, it can produce many. Now since this is so important, I want to illustrate the point further. I do so from three well-documented testimonies.[56]

---

[54] Edwards p434.

[55] 'In the 16th century some of the leading Reformers went through phases of extreme frustration at trying to promote a godly faithful church on the basis of universal infant baptism. Some of them resorted, for a time, to working with small groups of true believers [who were] pledged to a committed evangelical devotion and discipline incapable of being expected from the whole population' (Wright: *What...?* p100). The former concern, mission impossible, is still being attempted; the latter is an admission of the New Testament position. Note the hypocrisy in all this. The Reformers lambasted the Anabaptists for their views on baptism, yet secretly (and not so secretly) envied them, and wanted their discipline and spirituality. See my *Battle*. The phrase for the invented escape-route is 'a church within a Church'.

[56] See also Wright: *What...?* See end note on p275 for excursus: 'William Perkins and John Preston, and the complications and consequences of sacramentalism'.

End notes to Consequence 1: Christendom and Visible Churches

The Reformed and the status of children after baptism

David Boorman: 'For the Reformers and Puritans... children of believers... were included in the covenant of grace. But just what did that mean? It was at this point that fundamental differences began to appear. Calvin had little doubt as to the status of these children. "The offspring of believers are born holy because their children, while yet in the womb, before they breathe the vital air, have been adopted into the covenant of eternal life. Nor are they brought into the church by baptism on any other ground than because they belonged to the body of the church before they were born". "The children of believers are not baptised, that they may thereby be made the children of God... but, on the contrary, they are received into the church by a solemn sign, because they already belong to the body of Christ by virtue of the promise"'. Boorman went on to say that 'not all the Reformers would go as far as Calvin'; even so, 'although it was recognised that not all those who had received baptism in infancy would manifest saving grace in their adult life, it was believed that the baptised children before reaching maturity should be regarded... as recipients of God's saving grace, until the contrary became plainly evident'. 'This stood in contrast to the Anabaptist view that "the personal response to the gospel of salvation was all-determinative"'. For a modern view, take Lusk: 'While covenant children must manifest a growing, dynamic faith, in accord with their increasing mental abilities, there is no reason to doubt they have faith in some sense even from the womb' (Lusk: 'Paedobaptism' p116).

Take 17th century New England; how did they handle the business? Thomas Shepard: 'The good by children's [church] membership especially when sealed [by baptism], is... [as follows:] God shows hereby the riches of his grace towards them, in taking them to be his people; in adopting them to be his children... Parents hereby may see, and wonder at, the riches of God's grace, to become a God, not only to themselves, but to take in their seed also... Hereby God gives parents some comfortable hope of their children's salvation, because they may be within the pale of the visible church... Hereby they may not only hope and pray, but are encouraged to believe, concerning their children and the rest of those that are in covenant among them, that God will do them good'. Since Shepard meant far more than a general good, Boorman rightly called these 'stupendous claims', immediately adding: 'The New England ministers at once began to qualify and to limit them'; then the logical niceties were wheeled out! It was all a case of 'external covenant'/'internal covenant', 'outward covenant'/'inward covenant', and so on. As Boorman observed, in all this 'the tensions in early New England theology are revealed'. The Puritans, making full use of the double-speak qualifiers already noted, were 'ambidextrous theologians; what the right hand took away, the left hand could retrieve'; 'equally, what the left hand gave, the

270

right hand snatched away. Having preached a comforting doctrine of the covenant, and of the blessings of being within that covenant, and having the seals of covenant, the ministers then took away that encouragement, by preaching sermons which, instead of urging men and women and boys and girls to look away from themselves to the covenant grace of God [better expressed, to look to Christ], insisted that they should look deep into their hearts to discern those signs of regeneration which alone would entitle them to communicant membership of a visible church'. In their approach to growing children, these ministers 'mixed' their 'teachings painfully and paradoxically'. 'Consequently, parents and ministers were kept in a state of suspense and doubt as to the spiritual standing of children'. 'In the children's catechisms [which this system produced] very little, if any, of the joy in Christ was found. The preachers thought it their God-given responsibility to frighten children, supposedly in gracious covenant with God, into religious enthusiasm' (Boorman pp77-82).

Though lack of space forbids any further exploration of these dreadful consequences here, they are well documented (see Bremer p113; Perry Miller pp57-67,214; Pettit pp139,164,176-177,189,205,210-211,221; Stout pp35-41,325, for instance). But what do modern-day infant baptisers think of such things? And how do they run their churches? How do they regard their baptised babies as they grow up? Those who are thinking of adopting infant baptism would do well to face these things now – before they take up the practice and have to cope with inevitable consequences.

Reformed contradictions on 1 Cor. 7:14

Contradictions seem to abound in statements made by infant baptisers on the verse. Take Reymond. He was prepared to quote another author with approval: 'It is God's will and declared purpose that his saving grace runs in the lines of generations', citing 1 Cor. 7:14 as one of the 'proof texts'. Yet a few pages earlier, commenting on the same verse, he had said: 'Paul... cannot mean by the word "holy" that these children are actually saved by virtue of the relation that they sustain to their parents'. And in between the two statements, he spoke of the effect of baptising an infant according to the rubric of the Westminster Confession, saying (by quoting) it is a 'great sin' not to do so: 'This is not to suggest that Reformed infant-baptiser Christians regard the infant so baptised as a saved individual by virtue of his baptism *per se*, any more [than] that they believe that the infant of Christian parents is saved by virtue of his relation to his parents'. But Reymond was whistling in the dark, for he immediately added: 'They in fact do not or, at least, should not believe so!' Yet he closed his chapter by saying that he and his wife had publicly affirmed that their babies were 'holy in Christ, and, as members of his church, ought to be baptised' (Reymond pp197-206). I am making the same point I have made repeatedly. Which of the two sets of contradictory statements should the rank-and-file believe? The theologians, deep down, recognise that many do 'get hold of the wrong end' of the stick. If, however, such theologians still doubt my assertion about the way most parents (and their growing children) think of these things, I suggest they ask those who have pastoral responsibilities in infant-baptist circles – those at the pew-face around the font. *They* know what many (if not most) people standing there believe about these things.

Reformed inclusivism gone mad

I hope to write something on what I consider to be one of the great curses in the churches today, something I have already noted in this chapter; namely, inclusivism. Everybody – including the unbeliever – has to be made to feel at home, nothing must be said to give the slightest cause to make them concerned, preachers continually talking of 'us' and 'we', and so on. This, in my experience, is commonplace. It applies not only to children but to all and sundry. How many churches have in their congregations old people who have attended for years, been treated as virtual believers, addressed as such, feel totally at ease, and who are yet unconverted! This is, as I say, commonplace in my experience. And, to avoid misunderstanding, my experience is almost entirely limited to Reformed and evangelical churches which baptise believers.

But some infant baptisers today are going much further. They actually advocate that all in the congregation (baptised as infants, in the covenant) should be treated and addressed as elect – told that they are – told that everything written to the New Testament churches applies to them; Rom. 8:29-39; Eph. 1:1-6; 2 Thess. 2:13; 1 Pet. 1:1-2; 2:9-10, for example. According to John Barach, all such people – whether believers or not – as long as they were baptised as infants – are to be told: 'God chose you to be in his covenant, to have that bond with him in Christ. That choice, worked out in history when you were baptised, is grounded in God's eternal predestination. He had you baptised, according to his eternal plan... In eternity, God chose to have you baptised, engrafted into the Church, joined to Christ, the Elect One, joined to Christ's body, the Church, made a member of his chosen nation. That's glorious good news. That is privilege'. Omitting the reference to baptism, so it is – for those for whom it is true. But what of those so addressed who prove, finally, not to be saved? 'Yet in God's wisdom, he has decreed that some of those whom he has chosen to bring into a covenant relationship with him, will enjoy that relationship only for a time. God truly brings those people into his covenant, into union with Christ. They are "in him", to use Jesus' words in John 15... [But] God chooses not to work in these people so that they persevere... Using our traditional theological and confessional language [but, reader, not *biblical* language, please note], we would say that these were non-elect members of the covenant. Using Calvin's terminology, these people were "generally elect", but not "specially elect". Using the language of Scripture, they were among God's chosen people'. I pause. Note

272

the wording. A moment ago, they *were* chosen – now they are *among* the chosen. This may be a question of semantics. By 'among', I think Barach meant 'one of', but if he meant 'sitting among but not really one of' – and made this clear in his addresses to the congregation – this particular debate would be over. To let Barach continue: These non-elect, generally but not specially elect, covenant members, 'were the people that God addresses as elect. They were joined covenantally to Christ, the Elect Cornerstone, but they have been cut off from Christ. They have stumbled and fallen... just as they were appointed to do (1 Pet. 2:8)'. Even so, Barach concluded: 'Pastors must tell their congregations that he chose them' (Barach pp15-44). Wilkins: 'All who are baptised may be truthfully addressed as the "elect of God"... If they later reject the Saviour, they are no longer elect... and... lose their elect standing. But their falling away doesn't negate the reality of their standing prior to their apostasy. They were really and truly the elect of God because of their relationship with Christ [biblically, this is the wrong way round, of course!]... Those who ultimately prove to be reprobate may be in covenant with God... Here, then, we have those who are joined to Christ in a vital union... and yet who end up cursed and condemned' (Wilkins: 'Covenant' pp56-64). Lusk, quoting E.V.Gerhart: 'A man is born into the kingdom of heaven by the sacrament of holy baptism, endowed with divine grace, which is new life in Christ Jesus. He is a babe in Christ... [But] it does not follow that a person must be saved because he is born of the Spirit in holy baptism' (Lusk: 'Paedobaptism' p121). Lusk again: 'In one sense, all those in the covenant are "saved"... [But] even today, there are "Hams" in the ark of the Church. They were "saved" by God in baptism, but fail to persevere in that salvation, and fall away... God mysteriously has chosen to draw many into the covenant community who are not elect in the ultimate sense, and who are not destined to receive final salvation. These non-elect covenant members are actually brought to Christ, united to him and the Church in baptism... They become members of Christ's kingdom... The sacraments they received had objective force and efficacy. But God withholds from them the gift of perseverance, and all is lost. They break the gracious new covenant they entered into at baptism'. I pause. Did the infants enter into any covenant? If they did, was it consciously? How did they do this? If they entered it unconsciously, how can they be guilty of breaking vows they never actually made? Lusk again: 'They fail to inherit the promises and are excommunicated from the family of God... [Even so,] all covenant members are invited to attain to a full and robust confidence that they are God's eternally elect ones. Starting with their baptism... baptism marks them out as God's elect people... We should not hesitate to speak to our fellow covenant members the way Paul addressed his churches. We can say to our fellow churchmen: "You're elect! God loves you, and Christ died for you! You're forgiven and regenerated!" Covenantally, these things are true of them. Until and unless they apostatise, their covenant membership must be taken as a sign of their eternal election...

273

A pronouncement to the congregation: "Your sins are forgiven!" is very powerful, much more so than: "Whoever here is elect and regenerated and [repentant] is forgiven!" The conditions and qualifications are true enough, but they all too easily point us in the wrong direction... We need to learn to use terms such as "elect", "regenerate" *etc.*, not just in a narrow decretal [God-ordained, legal?] sense, but also in a broader covenantal sense, as they so often function in Scripture [which is, of course, to beg the question! – DG]' (Lusk: 'New' pp284,287-289,293). See also Douglas Wilson pp268-269.

I must be brief – and restrained – in my comments. I grant that the apostles addressed their readers in the terms they did, but they often included obvious riders and conditions. For instance, Paul wrote 'to the saints... and faithful in Christ Jesus', those who had been regenerated and brought to saving faith (Eph. 1:1,12-13; 2:1-3,8). He did not write 'to those who are covenantally in Christ by baptism, including the non-elect'! He wrote to the elect who were proving their election *by their faith in Christ and consequent obedience.* They were the ones – and only they – who had been blessed with every spiritual blessing listed in Eph. 1. To apply these words to all who have been baptised as infants, and to do so by inventing an unbiblical class – non-elect covenant members of Christ – is a travesty of Scripture; it does not take account of its own clearly expressed presuppositions. Take another case – 2 Thess. 2:13. Paul wrote this to those who he knew were elect *by the evidence of their faith in Christ and consequent obedience to the gospel* (1 Thess. 1:2-10; 2:10,13-14; 2 Thess. 1:3). Furthermore, it is not only the explicit suppositions; the implicit suppositions of Scripture are important. Let me illustrate. Paul commands believers to give thanks 'always for all things' (Eph. 5:20). Clearly, he does not mean 'all things whatever they might be'. If a believer's daughter is raped, is the believer supposed to thank God for it? Job showed the right spirit. When disasters struck, he was resigned, he did not rebel against God but blessed him for his sovereignty – but did he rejoice, and thank God that his children had been smitten down and were dead? Surely not. Likewise, the terms used in addresses to New Testament churches must be understood in the light of the obvious implications. When we read Scripture to a mixed congregation, the personal terms used – elect, predestined, redeemed *etc.* – apply only to those who are such.

Finally, it is all based on a misreading of John 15. Was Christ teaching what the above writers say; namely, that the elect, those in him, can be cut out of Christ, cast away and burned? Certainly not! Calvin: 'Can anyone who is engrafted into Christ be without fruit? I answer, many are supposed to be in the vine, *according to the opinion of men*, who actually have no root in the vine. Thus, in the... prophets, the Lord calls... Israel his vine, because, by outward profession, they had the name... Those who are cut off from Christ are said to wither like a dead branch... not that it ever happens that anyone of the elect is dried up, but because there are many hypocrites who, in outward appearance, flourish and are green for a time' (Calvin: *Commentaries* Vol.18

Part 1 pp108,110, emphasis mine). This, of course, is true. The right course, therefore, is to act upon this fact. That is, instead of telling all the congregation that they are elect, they should be told that mere profession is not enough. If they are in Christ, then all that is said about the elect is true of them; but if they are not in him, but merely profess that they are, none of it is! They should be told that when they hear the reading of Scripture as it speaks to believers, they are overhearing the reading of somebody else's correspondence.

Sadly, infant baptism based on covenant theology leads to the sort of confusion set out above. Many Reformed writers, though not coming to the same ridiculous conclusions as the above writers, get close. Hendriksen, for instance. True, he rightly argued that those cast away had no 'spiritual, saving union with Christ'. Nevertheless, they were in the covenant: 'Not all those who are in the covenant are of the covenant' (Hendriksen: *John* Vol.2 p295). As before, note the subtle semantics – '*in* the covenant', not '*of* the covenant'. Hutcheson: 'Professors... some being only in [Christ] by external and visible communion, as being in the visible church, and externally covenanting and professing relation to him; others being also in him by faith, as having spiritual inward communion with his person' (Hutcheson p314).

All this goes to show the dreadful consequences of not keeping to the scriptural basis of church membership – regeneration with the evidence to go with it. And, as I have already noted, surely the right way to address a congregation is to warn them that mere profession is not enough, that they should examine themselves (2 Cor. 13:5; 1 John). Surely it must be wrong to address a congregation the way the above writers say. Such addresses are bound to mislead many, delude many, giving them a false assurance. The responsibility of such teachers and their teaching is immense. Barach quoted Dort. Very well. Let Dort sum it up: 'As... election... is clearly revealed in the Scriptures... so it is still to be published in due time and place in the church of God, for which it was peculiarly designed, provided it is done with reverence, in the spirit of discretion' (*Three* p40; Barach p16). Quite! Again: These writers do not seem to mention the fact that, in part using their own terms, there might be three classes (with subdivisions) of people in a congregation: True believers (some of whom have not been baptised as infants and reject covenant theology), infant-baptised non-elect covenant-members, and rank unbelievers (some of whom have been baptised as infants and hold to covenant theology, and some who have not been baptised as infants and do not hold to covenant theology). In their addresses, how will they distinguish these? Will they concentrate on baptism and covenant membership? If so, is there no danger that the hearers might well get the impression that baptism is the all-important thing? How very different this rigmarole is to Scripture, how complicated. There are only two fundamental classes – believers and unbelievers.

William Perkins and John Preston, and the complications and consequences of sacramentalism

To set the scene for what is to come concerning the ridiculous complications and dangerous consequences of sacramentalism leading to visible churches – including the gospel offer (see earlier note) – consider the views and practices of two Puritans, William Perkins and John Preston.

First, Perkins. As I have already noted, Perkins was the leading early Puritan who was highly influential in the development of 17th century Puritanism and beyond. In particular, he laid the ground-work for much of what I spell out in the next chapter.

As Moore explained, Perkins declared that 'the reprobate do not have any title to the death of Christ' – that is, since Christ did not die for the reprobate, they have no right to be told or to believe that he did: 'The universal gospel call does *not* consist in being called upon to believe that one "is effectually redeemed by Christ"'. Quite right. It is no part of the gospel offer to tell sinners that Christ died for them (see my *Offer*; *Particular*). Nevertheless, because of his 'judicial ecclesiology [concept of 'church'] and high sacramentology', Perkins went on to argue that this is only true for reprobates *as reprobates*. Those reprobates who are in the covenant – 'those whom God has made outward members of [the] Church' – 'they do have such a title'; that is, they can be told that Christ died for them: 'However, "everyone in the Church, by God's commandment – [that is,] 'believe the gospel' – is bound to believe that he is redeemed by Christ; indeed, even the reprobate as well as the elect"'. I pause. According to Perkins, if they have been baptised as infants and are members of the visible Church, the reprobate are bound to be told and believe a lie (that Christ died for them) – and *that* by God's command in the gospel! To let Moore continue: 'So', according to Perkins, 'all Church members [even though they might be reprobate!] are to work out their own salvation in fear and trembling *as Christians*, and not in order that they might *become Christians*. They work out their salvation from *within* the covenant, not in order to enter it, and do so on the basis of their very real judicial standing and sacramental privileges... "God the Father has made an evangelical covenant with his [visible] Church". This results in a relaxing of his [Perkins'] particularist provisos [that is, limiting the gospel offer, and so on, to the elect] within [that is, when addressing] the visible Church, since this is, after all, to be considered as the company of God's elect... It is to the [visible] Church that Perkins acknowledges Christ makes "offers". To the world of the lost, Christ makes no offers. To them the gospel is presented as a divine command, and the particular promise [of the gospel] is generally proclaimed' (Moore pp53-54, emphasis his). Reader, is it not amazing that such an accomplished theologian as Perkins could end up with such a farrago of nonsense? And it all stemmed from his sacramental view of infant baptism!

Now for Preston. He also thought the universal call of the gospel was structured in terms of the visible Church. He justified this by speaking of a double covenant – one that 'belongs to all men... a general covenant propounded without exception', and 'another covenant of grace, which belongs peculiarly to the elect'. Those 'outside the [particular] covenant', though in the general covenant, are 'unregenerate', even though they are Church members. 'The reprobate are only baptised into "a general covenant propounded without exception"'. 'The proof that Preston gives for this assertion that "none are excluded out of this general covenant", is that "baptism, the seal of the covenant, is to be administered to all within the [visible] Church, to infants though afterwards they do not actually and visibly believe"' (Moore pp124-125). Words fail. But not quite. As Moore said: 'Yet this leads Preston into an unstated dilemma. He states that "the great match is made in baptism" [that is, Christ offers himself to sinners in the visible Church in baptism], but through infant baptism [which took place in the visible Church and made them members], all his hearers are thus married to Christ already[!] Yet, his evangelical theology tells him that this is not truly the case with most Englishmen' – 'Preston was convinced that "the greatest part of... common Protestants neglect the gospel"' – 'thus Preston shifts the focus of the gospel call from baptism to the Lord's supper. The result is that the gospel call is sometimes seen in terms of an offer to the visible Church' (Moore pp135-136). In the following chapter, I will delineate the noxious weeds which grew from these seeds.

Consequence 2

Three Testimonies

The three testimonies I have chosen to illustrate the points I have been making are: The experience of the New England churches in the 17th century,[1] and the published accounts of the experiences of Jonathan Edwards and D.Martyn Lloyd-Jones. In other words, examples from the 17th, 18th and 20th centuries. Although, in passing, I have mentioned some of these records, and quoted from them, I now return to them in a little more detail in order to underscore the grievous consequences of infant baptism.

The New England churches of the 17th century

I have already referred to men such as John Cotton and Thomas Shepard, and their defences of infant baptism and justification of non-regenerate church membership. But if I left it there I would give an entirely false impression. The New England Puritan settlers did not start out with such views. Far from it! Let me go back to the beginning. Their experience is particularly relevant to any today who are thinking of taking up infant baptism, and yet hope to avoid its nasty side-effects. It should serve as a salutary warning.

In the 1630s, the settlers were determined to set up pure churches in their new land; they had had more than enough of the mixed churches in England.[2] On reaching the New World, they rightly

---

[1] In what follows, when I speak of the churches of New England, I am thinking in the main of the churches in the Bay. I exclude the two outer wings; that is, I exclude not only the Baptists banished to Rhode Island (which goes without saying), but the churches at Plymouth which were more lax over church membership than those in the Bay (see Middlekauff pp48-49). In addition to the references below, see Bauckham.

[2] By 'mixed churches', I mean so-called 'visible' churches, knowingly comprised of believers and unbelievers, this mixture being regarded as acceptable, even right and advantageous. I fully accept, as I have explained, that those who insist on a totally regenerate membership do not always attain

278

demanded marks of regeneration in prospective church members. They would only receive those who were, in their terms, visible saints; that is, those who could give good evidence of an experience of saving grace and a life consistent with that profession; any who later proved hypocrites were to be removed. Shepard, for instance, though he admitted 'that there is and will be a mixture of close hypocrites with the wise-hearted virgins in the purest churches', nevertheless was clear. He urged 'all the churches of the Lord Jesus, here planted in these western parts of the world, to maintain your church chastity and virginity; you have a name of it abroad, pure, chaste, virgin churches, not polluted with the mixtures of men's inventions, not defiled with the company of evil men; pure ordinances, pure people, pure churches... Look you maintain it'. But he had a warning: 'Few churches retain their purity long... In the last days, carnal security either is, or will be, the universal sign of virgin churches... This is the temper [spirit, state] of the body [bulk] of the churches'. Even so, this did not mean the New England churches should accept it. He spoke of 'that diligent and narrow search and trial, churches here do, or should, make of all those whom they receive to be fellow-members with them... None have [a] right to Christ and his ordinances but such as shall have communion with Christ at his coming to judge the world; hence, if we could be so eagle-eyed as to discern them now that are hypocrites, we should exclude them now; as Christ will [when he comes], because they have no right [to be members]; but [although] that we cannot do [that is, we cannot find every hypocrite]... Yet let the churches learn from this to do what they can for the Lord now'. For the fact is, 'the ruin of a church may be the letting in of... one ill member'.

---

it – but they deplore the fact, and do all they can to put it right. Not all the churches in Old England were mixed – the Anabaptists, for instance – but, it goes without saying, the would-be settlers, while still in Old England would never have dreamed of touching them or their ilk with a barge-pole! Once in New England, however, they wanted to form *infant-baptising* churches composed only of those who were regenerate. They had had more than they could take of 'mixed churches'. *This* is what I am referring to. See the note on Perkins and Preston at the close of the previous chapter.

'One man or woman secretly vile, which the church has not used all means to discover [uncover, expose], may defile a whole church'.[3]

So far, excellent. But these Puritans, for all their desire for pure churches, established a built-in contradiction right at the start; they baptised babies, accepting them as members![4] Of course, in their zeal for purity,[5] they would baptise only babies born to church members; they had had more than enough of that promiscuous infant baptism they had left behind in Old England![6] Naturally, since they had large families, many baptisms followed, and thus the churches grew. True, these baptised infants, although church members, were barred from the supper until they gave evidence of a saving experience for themselves; even so, they were members.

But time has a habit of passing. Men and women grow old and die, even the godly. Baptised babies who are church members grow up, and, whether or not they prove to be elect, in turn they marry and have children. Thus, grandchildren were born to the original settlers in New England; in their turn, they had children; and so on. Now it is a sad but undeniable fact – whatever claims men make about the covenant and infant baptism – not all who are baptised as infants prove to be elect when they reach adulthood. So it turned out in New England. However

---

[3] Shepard pp32,78,144,241; Morgan p114. Shepard preached *The Ten Virgins* from 1636 to 1640. The dates, I remind you, reader, are all-important.

[4] It was (and is), as I have explained, more complicated than that. Richard Mather: 'We do not believe that baptism makes men [babies] members of the church, nor that it is to be administered to them that are outside the church, as the way and means to bring them in, but to them that are within the church, as a seal to confirm the covenant of God unto them' (Perry Miller p87; but see Middlekauff p75).

[5] I do not intend any note of scorn. I think I have made it clear that I am a stickler for pure churches myself.

[6] The Presbyterians in Old England who, if they had gained power, would have baptised babies virtually indiscriminately, were shocked by the (initial – see below) exclusiveness of their friends across the ocean. In New England, Hooker felt the force of their arguments, and would have liked to have baptised more widely, but could not break free from the covenant theology in which he was trapped. See Perry Miller pp84,87,89; Morgan pp119-120. As for Old England, in the Westminster debates, as Edmund Calamy reported, 'many of the Assembly' showed their hand when it was reported that they 'will baptise the children of those they will not admit [to the Lord's supper]' (Paul p439).

pure the original church, however sound and powerful the preaching and teaching, however rigorous the catechising, however strongly the parents pressed upon the growing children the profession they had 'made' as babies at the font, not all baptised babies came to saving faith in adulthood; no, not even in New England in the days of Thomas Hooker, John Cotton and Thomas Shepard!

The question was as I have spelled out: what to do with them? In particular, what to do with *their* children? After all, the young adults in question had been baptised as infants and become church members, but now, when they were having children, they themselves could not give evidence of saving grace; therefore, they were barred from the supper. But what about their babies? Should they be baptised and become church members? Indeed, should the unregenerate adults be allowed to remain as church members? If not, when should they be expelled? Were they, after all, in the covenant? And what about their infants? If the parents were expelled, should the babies still be baptised, or expelled? Were they in the covenant, or what? And what now of the teaching they all had received and imbibed – concerning the purity of the church and its maintenance? To keep a pure church, expulsion ought to take place. But when, and who, and on what grounds?[7]

The second generation of New Englanders were forced to wrestle with such problems. Morgan:

Given both infant baptism and the restriction [broadening!] of church membership to visible saints, it was impossible for the Puritans, either to evade the questions..., or to answer them without an elaborate casuistry that bred dissatisfaction and disagreement. The history of the New England churches during the 17th and 18th centuries was in large measure a history of these dissatisfactions and disagreements.[8]

---

[7] The trouble arose because promises made to Abraham and the nation of Israel were applied to the church. The churches of New England were not nations; they certainly were not the nation of Israel. In Israel, a circumcised boy was an Israelite – whether he was good or bad – he was an Israelite. The folly of infant baptism and the covenant is to say a baptised baby is regenerate, or will be, or to work on that basis.

[8] Morgan pp128-129. Perry Miller, speaking of the way the Presbyterians in England viewed the goings-on in New England: 'The system pretended to admit none but saints... but if they retained the children and grandchildren, will they not have to embrace the doctrine of "baptismal regeneration"? And if

The New Englanders needed to sort it out, but failed to do so. True, the Cambridge Platform of 1648 properly denied the idea that the citizens of a parish are church members – quite right! It is unscriptural.[9] But that synod, although it had been asked to deal with the issues raised above, left them unresolved, pretending there was no problem, and so abandoned the churches without a chart upon a rising sea. Most churches shut their eyes to the predicament, allowed the non-regenerate adults to remain as members, and baptised their babies. The problem was compounded in 1657 when some Connecticut churches relaxed their stress on purity of membership, and recognised the parish churches of England as true churches, saying that members of such churches, 'coming into New England, had a right to all church privileges, though they made no profession of a work of faith and holiness upon their hearts'. Meanwhile, their home-grown problem did not go away; rather, it naturally increased.[10]

It could not go on; it had to be resolved; and, at last, it 'was'. In 1662, the New England synod declared that parents could have their infants baptised even though they themselves were unconverted – as long as they themselves had been baptised as infants, were not scandalously wicked, and were prepared to assent to certain statements of fact they were supposed to have believed when they were babies. These parents were to be regarded as church members – but without full rights, of course. It was nothing but a fudge; the membership

---

they cut them off, will they not have to acknowledge that saints do not persevere...? New England had walked into a trap [of its own making]; could it get out?' (Perry Miller p89). For Samuel Rutherford's sneer, see Perry Miller p78. I give credit, of course, to these misguided Puritans for trying to discipline. What a contrast to the foolish notion – not unheard of today – based on a misguided interpretation of Matt. 7:1 – that it is wrong to 'judge' in this matter. But I am commenting on the folly of trying to discipline so-called '*visible*' saints according to biblical principles set out for true believers. It is a mistake – it is impossible – to apply spiritual principles to carnal men. My advice for those who are tempted to repeat the mistake is: When in a hole, stop digging!

[9] It comes from Constantine.

[10] Let me state the obvious: The numbers produced by natural generation can never be fewer than the numbers produced by spiritual regeneration.

afforded to these parents was a kind of half-way membership – and came to be known as the half-way covenant, mentioned earlier.[11]

This fudge having been adopted – not without some disagreement – much work was now done by the theologians to argue the case,[12] and to drum up evidence[13] from the works of the founding fathers (many of whom had by this time died) to 'prove' that they would have supported such a resolution. But this, of course, involved a 180 degree shift![14] The now-dead Shepard, as I quoted a moment ago, had once strongly argued for the removal of hypocrites. Now another manuscript of his was dug out and published – to argue the contrary! This is the work I quoted previously – to show that despite all Shepard had said at an earlier time – when the churches were starting out on their course – he had later argued that a true church could have 'many chaffy hypocrites and often profane persons', and that this was no bad thing, he thought; good could come of it. I have also quoted Cotton to the same effect.

The controversy over the half-way covenant was 'ended' by Increase Mather's change of mind – he was at first against it, but in 1675 produced, in addition to a work of his own, manuscripts from the founders, including his father and father-in-law (Richard Mather and

---

[11] See end note on p298 for excursus: 'Tortuous times under the half-way covenant'.

[12] But, as I have already observed, theologians will always provide the theology (or at least some logic or formula) required to 'justify' the practice. The logic in this case, however, as always with infant baptism, was mind-boggling. Consider the following. On the question of applying 'the seal of baptism' to babies of parents who were unfit for the supper, one of the 'solutions' was to talk of *jus ad rem* ('right to the thing') as opposed to *jus in re* ('a right in the thing')! (Cotton Mather p303). See also Cotton Mather pp304-305 for talk of an 'explicit' covenant and an 'implicit' covenant. I wonder how many parents at the time really comprehended the difference between *jus ad rem* and *jus in re*? I wonder how many of the growing children got it?

[13] Which was not lacking. Naturally, with the passing of time (*the* great test!), the founders had themselves seen the warning signs – but, as I have noted, the dates must be watched.

[14] This explains the glaring contradictions in the works of these New England teachers, some of which I have quoted. In their early days they were dogmatic for purity in the churches; later, they were all for compromise and tolerance of the unregenerate as members. The dates, as I keep repeating, are all-important in works of this period.

John Cotton), to show that they too would have been half-way covenant men; indeed, that they all had anticipated some such scheme to get round the problem.[15] The capitulation of such a large and important figure, gave the ὁι πολλοι (hoi polloi) all the sanction they needed to settle down, easy in conscience, to a life of respectable carnality, and still be church members and have their babies baptised. Naturally – literally so – they gratefully accepted Increase Mather's pronouncement. The consequences for thousands will only be known at the day of judgement.

This invention was the only way the New England churches could 'reconcile' infant baptism and the attempt to preserve a godly church membership. But the fact is, churches – which started out by wanting at all costs to have a pure membership – after about twenty years, found themselves stocked with an increasing number of hypocrites and non-regenerate members, and having to agree that this was right!

---

[15] For the part played by Increase Mather, see Middlekauff pp85-86,113-138; Perry Miller pp94-109,227. Increase Mather wanted a pure church, and at the 1662 synod argued for the restriction of baptism to the babies of members in full communion. But five or six years later, he accepted the idea of the half-way covenant, because he felt he could still hold to church purity, and because he was forced to recognise that if the children of the unregenerate were not baptised, the churches would decline in membership. Increase had come to see one of the fundamental flaws in the practice of infant baptism. It is, so its advocates maintain, a seal. I have dealt with this. A seal of what? For the believer it is a seal, so it is said, of his initiation into Christ; for the child, it is a seal, so it is said, of what? Of his initiation into Christ, or into the *promise* of his initiation into Christ, or of the *desperate hope* of his initiation into Christ? These were the conundrums Increase Mather wrestled with in New England three centuries ago. But they need to be faced by infant baptisers today. Whichever solution is adopted, large consequences are inevitable for church life and beyond. The dates are significant. As I noted above, Increase's father, Richard, dying in 1669, urged his son to baptise the infants of New England. As I asked: Was this promiscuous baptism?
When Increase Mather recognised that if there was any slowing in the rate of infant baptism then the churches would inevitably decline in numbers, he was facing up to the obvious – and the well-known. Oecolampadius, in 1527, trying to counter the Anabaptists: 'If anyone no longer baptises children... then the number of visible Christians will immediately decline. That is a very important consideration' (Friesen pp67-68). The love of numbers, and the justification of practices to keep them up, is not merely a *modern* god!

284

Indeed, they found themselves baptising babies belonging to unbelieving members – who were members because of their own baptism as infants twenty or thirty years before – but who, if they had presented themselves for membership as an adult, would have been refused![16]

The following generations, of course, felt little of such qualms. Being born under the system to parents who were inured to it, they themselves had been baptised as infants, grown up, married, had children, had them baptised... all the while being taught by prestigious ministers to think this was genuine Christianity. No wonder they were lulled into a carnal stupor, careless of their spiritual condition – but vehemently jealous of their church privileges and the social standing this gave them – sleep-walking into eternity.

I raise this episode as a clear warning to those who are setting out on the same course as the early settlers in New England. As I said at the start of this book, I am concerned that such people should look before they leap. For those who believe the New Testament demands a regenerate church membership – and only a regenerate membership – and yet are thinking of adopting infant baptism, I say this: It may seem a very easy matter to reconcile the two – *at the start*, where you are now. But take a glance twenty or thirty years down the road. By then the infants being baptised today will be producing their own children. What if those parents are not regenerate? Will they be church members? Will the church baptise their babies? Will *they* be members? Glance a further twenty or thirty years; your grandchildren will be bearing children. What then? The events in New England tell us of the

---

[16] What now of the argument, based on 1 Cor. 7:14, that the baby is baptised because one of the parents is a believer? New England ended up baptising babies where neither parent was a believer! The Puritans of Old England attacked the whole affair, as might be expected. But both sets of Puritans vented their spite on the Anabaptists, the Puritans of New England being the more vitriolic. There seems to be a principle here. The Anabaptists wanted pure churches; the Puritans of New England wanted pure churches but had to live with, and try to justify, the failure of their system; the Puritans of Old England accepted mixed churches as the norm and right. The principle? The closer somebody gets to what he wants – but fails because of a systemic fault in his approach – the more critical he gets of those who more nearly get the desired result by using the right system. 'Attack', seems to be the watchword, rather than think about changing – jettisoning – the failed system.

in-built contradiction between infant baptism and the striving after a regenerate church membership. Reader, you may feel it does work in your present circumstances. But the start of the process – and it is a process – is not the time to test the *effects* of infant baptism.[17] You have to wait twenty, forty years and beyond. Are you prepared to contemplate your grandchildren in churches with many 'chaffy hypocrite' members, some of whom may well be elders and ministers? Are you content to think of them as 'glass-eye-or-wooden leg ornaments and supports of the church'? Whatever you do, do not adopt Hezekiah's policy.[18] Hezekiah? Yes. Amazingly, Hezekiah was relieved that the disaster he was told of would come only after his time: 'At least there will be peace and truth in my days' (Isa. 39:8), he said. But what about the days – and not so far off, at that – when what you are doing now will lead inevitably[19] to what I have described here?[20]

---

[17] *Now* is the time, of course, to test the *principles* of infant baptism, and to test them by Scripture. But the grievous *effects* of infant baptism will take *time* for them increasingly to impose themselves on *experience*. Which they will do.

[18] Nor Pilate's (Matt. 27:24). Pilate, of course, was working on a very different principle to Deut. 21:6-8.

[19] Of course, in your case all the babies baptised now, and in every following generation, may be elect, and so will be regenerated. Or, it may be, the churches will expel the unregenerate – though how and whom and when has to be thought about long before the time arrives – and preserve a regenerate membership – and the people may accept perhaps many such expulsions without too much fuss, and without wanting their babies baptised. But these are large 'hopes'. What if those who were once in the covenant do not accept that they are no longer? And what if they want their babies baptised? Which New Testament passage will you turn to in order to discover how the apostles dealt with this problem?

[20] 'By confining church membership to those believers giving evidence of their conversions, the founders of New England had strongly endorsed experimental religion. After them, their sons had striven valiantly to maintain their fathers' faith, yielding only to half-way membership when the people proved incapable of undergoing any but the most perfunctory religious experience. And the grandsons, addressing churches empty of believers, but full of hypocrites, felt themselves standing on the edge of the abyss as their generation spurned gracious experience in favour of carnal experience' (Middlekauff p279). The Mathers illustrate the impasse. Richard Mather

Things could only get worse in New England. And they did. Let us move on a couple of generations.

The testimony of Jonathan Edwards

In passing, I have referred to Edwards' difficulties at Northampton, New England, in the 1740s. He tried to bring the church away from the unscriptural position it had adopted down the years over its procedures for taking in members and administering the Lord's supper. Members were received without evidence of personal, saving faith; baptism when an infant, lack of scandal, and a measure of head knowledge of the Christian religion was considered sufficient. Thus the inevitable 'church within a Church' was established.

It was no new problem. By 1707, the aforementioned 'venerable Stoddard' had published his view that the non-sanctified could take the Lord's supper; two years later he declared that the table is open to those who 'be destitute of a saving work of God's Spirit on their hearts'.[21] These downward steps, of course, ruined church life. From then on, the unconverted would have their say in the discipline of the church, including that of the converted members! Not only was this a spiritual impossibility, it confirmed many in their carnal ways, and contributed directly to their damnation. Naturally – as night follows day – the next step was to allow unconverted men into the ministry. Indeed, Stoddard argued that unconverted ministers could perform certain duties lawfully. As a result of all this:

The difference between the church and the world was vanishing away. Church discipline was neglected, and the growing laxness of morals was invading the churches. And yet never, perhaps, had the expectation of reaching heaven at last been more general, or more confident... The hold

---

started out all for purity but had to compromise. His son, Increase Mather, was against his father's change, but he too had to accept the compromise. And Cotton Mather criticised his father's (Increase's) resistance to his grandfather's (Richards's) change. For more on this history, see Perry Miller pp68-104; Morgan pp113-138; Middlekauff pp35-57,113-161,191-368; Cotton Mather pp276-315.

[21] Stoddard and the Mathers (Increase and Cotton) were at daggers drawn over these matters, although a kind of peace was patched up. See Middlekauff pp115-138; Perry Miller pp226-289,467.

of truth on the consciences of men was sadly diminished. The young were abandoning themselves to frivolity, and to amusements of dangerous tendency.[22]

Reader, that was written of the churches of New England in the early 18th century; could the same not be written about not a few churches of Old England in this generation?[23] And, let me remind you, even though 'occasional revivals... and the preaching of sound doctrine' had slowed the pace of decline in New England, they did not stop it. Those today who admit the problem exists in our churches, but cling to the hope that revival or sound preaching will sort it all out for us, are grievously mistaken. We need sound preaching and revival, yes, but nothing will replace the proper ordering of our churches, proper – biblical – discipline. Nothing! And while we cannot organise a revival, we can and must put our house in order. I do not appeal for one or the other – we need both. Let us do our duty before it is too late.

It is a sad catalogue I have put before you, is it not? I do not say that those who hold to infant baptism must inevitably come to such a pitiful state, and I have admitted that many so-called Baptist churches are rotten at the core, and are no churches at all.[24] But I do say – it is undeniable! – that the unscriptural doctrine and practice of infant baptism was at or near the root of the troubles in New England. Nor can it be gainsaid that infant baptism *per se* did nothing to put a stop to the wicked fandango.

And so to Edwards. Coming to see that the church was in a shocking condition, Edwards deplored that 'a considerable number... have woefully deceived themselves'. And they had not been unaided in this self-deception. Their theologians had given them the tools with which to destroy themselves. Edwards recognised it and admitted he was responsible. But he had now woken up! By 1744, he was convinced that something had to be done; the Northampton church must return to the New Testament order. Mere sincerity and

---

[22] Tracy pp3-8.

[23] In this comment, and the ones like it which follow, I am speaking of evangelical churches whatever their practice on baptism.

[24] Increasingly, such churches are becoming little more than social clubs. I challenge all such: get rid of the extra-scriptural social activities you have introduced to boost attendance, to 'evangelise' and produce 'fellowship', and return to Acts 2:42, and see how many attenders remain.

acknowledgement of general Christian principles were not enough; he wanted a credible profession of saving faith, and he proposed that the church should stop the knowing admission of the unregenerate. He acknowledged, of course, that some unconverted people would get in – they did in New Testament days – but not knowingly (Jude 4).[25]

Even so, Edwards' view still fell short of the New Testament. He continued to allow baptised infants 'to be in some sort members of the Christian church', and he continued to divide the church into those members who are 'in complete standing', as opposed to those who are not. This unscriptural notion of 'full' membership had not yet died; indeed, it is alive and kicking today. Edwards also failed to comprehend how infant baptism impinges upon church life, and he side-stepped it when he wrote on the qualifications for membership and participation in the Lord's supper. He did not seem to appreciate that infant baptism was an integral part of the problem he was dealing with. He ought to have done. After all, he had admitted that baptised infants might easily grow up destitute of grace, but even so he thought it was 'generally allowed' that they should 'not be cast out of the church'.[26] It may be that Edwards was correct in speaking for the general view of infant baptisers, but he was most decidedly out of step with the New Testament, which knows nothing of infant membership.

Despite the compromises, Edwards still failed in his attempt to reform the Northampton church. It is hard to imagine how the result could have been different; at least a majority of the members were unconverted. To ask them to vote for the introduction of New Testament principles was like asking turkeys to vote for Christmas (or, rather, Thanksgiving)! Edwards was forced to admit defeat, painfully confessing in his farewell sermon: 'I have reason to fear I leave multitudes in this large congregation [it was more than seven hundred] in a Christless state'.[27] Edwards' biographer made a terrible but true comment when he remarked: To expect the unregenerate to return to the New Testament was asking them 'to relinquish the only resting place which human ingenuity had discovered, in which an unconverted person might – for a time at least – remain unconverted, both securely

---

[25] Edwards lxi, p453; Iain Murray: *Edwards* pp274-275,335-336.

[26] Edwards p434.

[27] Edwards ccv; Iain Murray: *Edwards* p338.

and lawfully'.[28] I have only one quarrel with that last statement. I object to the word 'had'. I am writing this book because, sadly – horrifically – this sort of thing is no quirk of history. Human ingenuity continues to devise and use these methods to find resting places for unconverted men and women. The appalling truth is, these resting places are churches so-called, and the human ingenuity is being used by the leaders of those churches.

Edwards belatedly came to the view that when churches knowingly admit the unconverted to membership and the Lord's supper, the church is exposed to the gravest danger. But it is far worse than that. When churches move away from the New Testament, eventually the gospel testimony is ruined, and this will lead to the damnation of sinners. Above all, the glory of God is tarnished. Credit is to be given to Edwards for the stand he made, and for the price he was willing to pay. Oh! that all who read these pages were willing to face the issues squarely and answer the questions which they pose – answer them now as they will one day have to answer before God. I agree with Edwards when he said that the devil knows how important this matter is: 'I believe the devil is greatly alarmed by the opposition made to the lax doctrine of admission to the Christian church'.[29] He is indeed. My readers, let us arise and greatly alarm the devil in our generation!

So much for the 17th and 18th centuries. Now for the 20th.

The testimony of Martyn Lloyd-Jones

When Lloyd-Jones became a minister in Aberavon in the 1920s, the Presbyterian Church Secretary was E.T.Rees. Although Mr Rees was a member of the church and a church officer, he was unconverted. He knew absolutely nothing of regeneration, nothing at all – neither in theory nor in practice. It is said that he 'believed in a type of evangelical religion, but he was later to feel that he had been as ignorant of the doctrine of regeneration as Nicodemus'.[30]

I say this is an example of the inevitable outcome of the practice of infant baptisers. I fully acknowledge that Baptist churches can have unregenerate members and officers. I unreservedly accept that. I

---

[28] Iain Murray: *Edwards* p339.
[29] Edwards cxxxiii; Iain Murray: *Edwards* p347.
[30] Iain Murray: *Lloyd-Jones* Vol.1 p164.

deplore it, but I cannot, I do not, I dare not, deny it. I do not claim that Baptist churches are completely pure. Not at all! I go further. I say again that even the New Testament churches were not perfect in this respect; I know that even the apostles were deceived at times. Jude complained of those who 'crept in unnoticed' (Jude 4), but there is a world of difference between that and the knowing connivance at unregenerate members. I hope I have made myself clear – I am not throwing stones at infant baptisers from the vantage of a Baptist position which supposedly produces flawless churches. Not for a minute. But – and this is the point – the practice of infant baptism itself actually encourages and produces and justifies churches which have unregenerate members. Surely I have quoted enough words of infant baptisers to prove it. Infant baptisers fully expect to have unregenerate church members and try to cope with it. Dabney was quite prepared to own it when he asked this rhetorical question: 'Cannot that which is worldly, in the true sense, be in the visible church?'[31]

Mr Rees must have been one among hundreds, must he not? The church at Aberavon was not the only Presbyterian Church that had unregenerate members in the 1920s, was it? Reader, I put it to you, his experience was a direct result of the system. But, and in stark contrast, the New Testament churches did not cope with this sort of membership. They disciplined, they excommunicated in order to keep a regenerate membership, a membership which behaved consistently with that regeneration. Churches must not *expect* to have unregenerate members. They must not even tolerate them. 'By their fruits you will know them' (Matt. 7:20). There should be no unregenerate church members. It is a contradiction in terms.

To proceed with the experiences of Lloyd-Jones. As I have implied, E.T.Rees was not alone; Mrs Lloyd-Jones was in exactly the same spiritual condition. She, too, was a member of the Presbyterian Church, but she was unregenerate. What is more, she did not understand that she needed to be regenerated! What a condemnation of the system. It is said:

Having attended church and prayer meetings from childhood, Bethan Lloyd-Jones had always believed that she was a Christian... in a sense she had always feared God; her life was upright, and yet she knew that she had

---

[31] Dabney p785.

no personal consciousness of the forgiveness of sins, no sense of inward joyful communion with Christ.[32]

That is a tragic though honest statement. But it should cause no surprise. It is not to be wondered at if Mrs Lloyd-Jones always believed she was a Christian. Notice the words 'from a child'. Have we not seen that this is exactly what the Presbyterian Church is supposed to do – to tell the children that they are Christians from birth? Reader, you see it was no idle question I asked earlier – what if baptised children actually do believe what their teachers and parents keep telling them? What is more, for membership, the Church merely demands an appearance of soberness, and so on. Can infant baptisers wonder if sober, steady and respectable but unregenerate people do become church members, church officers, or even ministers themselves? Their very own system has produced it.

But as if these cases were not enough to prove what I am trying to say, what of Lloyd-Jones himself? When he reached his teens, his minister in the Calvinistic Methodist (Presbyterian) Church suggested – *suggested* mark you! – that the young man and his two brothers might like to join the church. So that is what he did. He professed faith and became a communicant member of the church. Then at the age of eighteen he became Sunday School Superintendent at the Charing Cross Road Church. In what spiritual condition was he? He had been baptised as an infant. He had been brought up in 'the pale of the Church'. He had professed faith. He was outwardly decent and respectable. He was developing into a useful Church officer, showing signs of promise. In short, he was an ideal member of the Presbyterian Church. It has been written that 'he was certainly conditioned to think of himself as a Christian... [seeing it] as a God-appointed process in virtue of which we become Christians by family ties and by church connections'. The truth is, however, 'he had never been a Christian at all'.[33]

I pause at this point just to emphasise the words, 'at the suggestion of the minister', 'certainly conditioned', 'in virtue of', and 'family ties and by church connections'. I repeat the point I am making. No church can infallibly claim to be free of deceivers and the deceived, but

---

[32] Iain Murray: *Lloyd-Jones* Vol.1 p166.
[33] Iain Murray: *Lloyd-Jones* Vol.1 p57

admitting that is a far cry from what I am criticising. The Presbyterian infant baptism system encourages church membership for unregenerate men and women who are conditioned to think of themselves as Christians by virtue of their birth – their family or church connections. It is actually part of the deceiving process, deceiving unregenerate sinners. And this is wicked.

To proceed. Many years later, when he was giving a series of lectures on preaching, Lloyd-Jones referred to this time in his experience and said:

For many years I thought I was a Christian when in fact I was not. It was only later that I came to see that I had never been a Christian and became one. But I was a member of a church and attended my church and its services regularly. So anybody assuming, as most preachers did, that I was a Christian was making a false assumption. It was not a true assessment of my condition. What I needed was preaching that would convict me of sin and make me see my need, and bring me to true repentance and tell me something about regeneration. But I never heard that. The preaching we had was always based on the assumption that we were all Christians, that we would not have been there in the congregation unless we were Christians. This, I think, has been one of the cardinal errors of the church especially in this present century.[34]

These words carry far more weight than any of mine. Their criticism is far more powerful. Some may dismiss my criticisms of the infant baptism system as coming from one who stands aloof. Be that as it

---

[34] Lloyd-Jones: *Preaching* p146. That bewitching preoccupation, yet again – inclusivism! Today, as I have already remarked, inclusivism seems to be the determining policy of most evangelical churches. Everything has to bow down at its altar. Nothing must be said and done in any way to cause the slightest offence to the unregenerate. Quite the opposite! From the opening remarks – bright and breezy – after the 'leader' has bounced onto the dais, or into the pulpit (if there still *is* a pulpit) – to the closing chat (often about yesterday's football, the latest shopping bargain, or last week's holiday; rarely over spiritual matters) over a cup of tea, what used to be called 'divine service' has been reduced, in many cases, to little more than 'man service', a cheery social gathering tinged with religion. And if anybody dares to question it...!!! 'Don't you believe in evangelism?'! 'Evangelism' – a non-biblical word – has become the god of the age. Reader, if you should think that by expressing such sentiments I have no concern over sinners and have no interest in seeing them converted, read my *Offer* and *Particular*.

may, the words I have just quoted come from one who was right at the heart of it. Look at what it did for him. It would seem fair to say that he was converted in spite of the system, not by means of it. This is what 'presumptive regeneration' comes to. He was presumed to be a Christian – by his family, by the church and by his ministers; above all, by himself! It was tragic. But he was not an isolated case. I urge you, reader, to give due weight to his criticisms. For Lloyd-Jones went on to say that it was not his experience alone, but he had met it many, many times in his ministry. In truth, it was the 'most common experience in conversation with people' who approached him after hearing him preach, he said. He had discussed this, and other associated matters, with an old man many years before – how had the church in Wales got like it? How had the spirituality of the church become so poor? The old man referred to the 1859 revival and said:

Before that there had been a distinction between 'the church' and 'the world'. The tests of admission to membership had been very strict, with the result that prior to 1859 there were always a number of people attending public worship and preaching who were listeners and adherents only and had not become members of the church.

As Lloyd-Jones put it:

This is a most interesting and important point. How rarely does one find this in the church today... The change took place partly as the result of the great movement of the Spirit in revival, and the increasing tendency to regard the baptised children of church members as Christians. The result was that the preachers regarded all the listeners as Christians and stopped preaching evangelistically... It was assumed that everyone was a Christian, and the ministry was devoted entirely to edification, with the result that a generation grew up that had never known the power of the gospel, and never really heard preaching which was likely to convict of sin. As I have said I personally belong to that generation... I was received into the church because I could give the right answers to various set questions; but I was never questioned or examined in an experimental sense. I cannot reprobate too strongly this tendency to assume that because people come to church that they therefore must be Christian, or that the children of Christians are of necessity Christians.[35]

Lloyd-Jones clearly – and rightly – looked back upon his experience with horror. When preaching on Ephesians 4:4-6, he said:

---

[35] Lloyd-Jones: *Preaching* pp147,151-152.

A work of preparation is absolutely essential in us before we can be parts of the church. Much has to be done to the natural man before he can become a member of the body of Christ... Failure to realise this and to remember it accounts for most of the problems in the life of the Christian church today, as it has always done throughout the centuries. The visible church, alas, is composed of many who have never undergone this work of regeneration... There are many and varied ways in which people become members of the visible church. It is sometimes a pure accident of nationality... In other instances it is often a pure accident of belonging to a certain family or to a certain tradition. These are the factors that so frequently operate. Many of us have known what it is to be made a member of a church, not because the Holy Spirit had done anything in us, or to us, but simply because of one of these accidents. When I was personally received as a full member of the Christian church in which I was brought up, I was asked one question only. I was asked to name the brook which our Lord and his disciples had to cross while going from the upper room to the place of trial. I could not remember the answer to that question; nevertheless I was received into full membership of the church. That literally is what happened to me at the age of fourteen. And similar things have happened to many others. Perhaps at a given age the minister or clergyman had a conversation with your parents, suggesting it was time for you as an adolescent to become a full member of the church. You may in addition have attended an instruction or preparation class, or confirmation class. You had no living experience; you did not really know what it was about fundamentally; it was 'the thing to do'. That is what so often happens in the visible church... You can become a member of the visible church in that way; you will never become a member of the body of Christ in that way. Before we can become members of the body of Christ the Holy Spirit has to do a work of definite preparation.[36] As you are by nature you cannot be bound to the Lord in all his glory and his purity, because by nature you are 'a child of wrath, even as others', 'dead in trespasses and sins'.[37]

If ever there was a condemnation of visible churches, this is it. But even so, Lloyd-Jones persisted in thinking and speaking in terms of the 'visible' church. There is nothing of the sort in Scripture. Grievously, many today think and speak in terms of visible churches when they actually belong to churches which are supposed to be based upon the New Testament pattern of church membership. This loose talk must be

---

[36] I would express this differently – bearing in mind 'preparationism'. You have to be born again. But Lloyd-Jones' thrust was right.
[37] Lloyd-Jones: *Ephesians* pp60-61.

stopped. If we use wrong words based on mistaken notions today, we shall have the wrong practice itself tomorrow.

These quotations from the experience of Lloyd-Jones express what I have tried to say and they have put it far more eloquently. Reader, please do not dismiss my words as coming from a man with an arrogant, critical spirit – I realise that Baptist churches have their faults; indeed they badly need reform in many of these very areas, including preaching. The discipline, too, in many churches which practise believer's baptism is unspeakably weak or non-existent in these days, and it must be put right as a matter of the utmost urgency. But my contention is that the infant baptism system itself tends to produce the terrible results you have just read about. And do not forget, the one who made the assertions was a minister of the Presbyterian Church. I urge all my readers to ponder what he said.

* * *

I realise I have used strong language. But not as strong as some infant baptisers have used about Anabaptists and others. I have not set out to offend, but the issues involved are so important I have had to speak frankly. If I have caused needless offence, I sincerely apologise. It was not my intention. But I am afraid the views of Reformed infant-baptisers do lead to very dangerous consequences. They must face up to them. I fully acknowledge that many infant-baptiser churches are far better than their creed, and I do not say that in any patronising manner. Those churches which take steps to discipline and remove from their membership those who demonstrate that they are not regenerate, even though they were born to Christian parents, were baptised as infants and were 'Christianly brought up within the pale of the Church', certainly have moved a great deal closer to the New Testament; but, I am bound to add, still not close enough. Nevertheless, it is obvious that such churches are not included in many of my strictures. And I admit that what God has done through individual infant baptisers is breathtaking – my own accomplishments are minuscule in comparison. A huge number of infant baptisers have been – and are – among the godliest men and women the world has ever seen. Just because I condemn their views, it does not mean I attack their person, character or spirituality. Nevertheless, the tendency of the doctrine and practice of infant baptism I unrepentantly assert is dangerous and wrong.

But what gives me the right to criticise? Only this, that I am a believer and a minister of the gospel. I do not claim perfection. In any case, if perfection is demanded in a critic before he speaks, then that is the end of all honest critical study. I admit that I have not tackled the points thoroughly enough; I can only plead my desire to keep my book within bounds.

Legg wrote – in 1982 – that the case for infant baptism had gone by default over the years. He offered an explanation for this, saying that 'in the interests of peace and unity we have, by and large, kept silent while the Baptists have made hay'.[38] Whatever the truth of that statement in 1982, I am convinced the pendulum has now swung the other way. Sacramentalism, as I have made plain, is on the march, and there has been a large amount of infant baptism material published in recent years. The Banner of Truth Trust, for instance, has brought out several volumes which contain teaching on church order and practice, and the overwhelming bulk of this publication has been in favour of infant baptism. As a simple statement of fact, a great many of the quotations I have supplied from infant baptisers have come from Banner of Truth books. I regard this as a serious development. I am tempted to say, a sinister development. Let me hasten to remind you that by saying that I do not, of course, intend any slur on the character or spirituality of those I disagree with over this issue. Not for a second! It is their *system* which I deplore. In the light of previous pages, it can be no surprise to anyone to read that I regard the *system* of infant baptism as dangerous and wrong. I believe the early Baptists rediscovered New Testament teaching, and threw off the shackles which had been fastened on the church for centuries.

Sadly, I am convinced that this process is going in reverse these days. Indeed we are fastening the shackles on ourselves. It is not unknown for Reformed Baptist churches to base their practice of the Lord's supper on the possibility that so-and-so (usually a household name in infant baptist circles) might be in the congregation. For fear of offence, some base their church order and discipline at the Lord's supper on the grounds of this remote possibility. This is not the way to go on. I realise I will be called divisive and unloving for these statements, but we must all remain faithful and true to what we

---

[38] Legg p15.

believe, whatever the cost. I do not expect infant baptisers to adjust their practice to suit me, just because I am convinced they are mistaken. Nor do I think infant baptisers expect me to change my views for them. Love for one another we must have. But allegiance to Christ comes first, beyond everything else. Where sincere love is, the truth can be spoken frankly. If things go on as at present, Reformed Baptists might well wake up to find that the old battles to recover the New Testament order have to be fought all over again. Finally, I have written out of love for the souls of men and women who might, by default, adopt infant baptism for themselves and their children. As I said at the beginning, I ask them to 'look before they leap'.

One seemingly small point. I have had enormous difficulty in deciding when to use 'Church' as opposed to 'church' throughout this book. Although this may appear to be a trivial matter, it actually illustrates much of what I have been trying to say and is a fair description of the point of my writing. The New Testament knows only 'church'. It is men who have invented 'Church'. I realise the Greek has no distinguishing mark, but the New Testament gives no warrant for all that is meant by 'Church'. If only men had stuck to the New Testament! As for sticking to the New Testament, Cunningham wrote:

Justification and regeneration... must *already* exist before even [ever?] baptism can be lawfully or safely received. The general tenor of Scripture language upon the subject of baptism... proceeds upon the assumption, that the profession implied in the reception of baptism by adults – the profession, that is, that they had already been led to believe in Christ, and to receive him as their Saviour and their Master – was sincere, or corresponded with the real state of their minds and hearts... And that thus a profession of faith is ordinarily associated with the Scripture notices of the administration of baptism; so that, as has been explained, we are to regard baptism upon a profession of faith, as exhibiting the proper type and full development of the ordinance.[39]

If the word *universally* replaced *ordinarily*, we could ask for no better statement on the subject of baptism. As I said above, if only men would stick to the New Testament.

---

[39] Cunningham Vol.2 pp144,151.

End note to Consequence 2: Three Testimonies

Tortuous times under the half-way covenant

As Perry Miller pointed out, 'half-way covenant' was a misnomer. The unregenerate *were* church members, but the covenant was now split into two, the external and the internal, the covenant of the church and the covenant of God. Instead of a 'half-way covenant', it was a 'double-covenant way'. In other words, the unregenerate were in one covenant but not the other (Perry Miller p96); in short, it was a 'two-sort membership' – two sets of qualifications leading to two sorts of members (Middlekauff pp55-56). It could be argued that it was in fact a 'three-sort membership' – regenerate adults, baptised as babies, taking the supper, in both covenants; unregenerate adults, baptised as babies, not taking the supper, in one covenant; and baptised babies, not taking the supper, whose regenerate/unregenerate state was as yet undetermined, in one/two covenants! The tortuous change of mind of Richard Mather, who lived through the crisis – having reached New England in 1635, and dying in 1669 – will illustrate the point. Its ins-and-outs are, for me at least, very difficult to unravel, but as I understand it, this is the road he travelled: In 1636, Richard Mather was uncertain about baptising the infants of unregenerate members, and was convinced hypocrites should be removed from the church. By 1645, however, he had changed his mind about infants; from now on, it was not the fitness of the parents – that is, their evident spirituality – which qualified the infants for baptism, but it was the fact that they, the parents, (and the children themselves?) were in the covenant, even though they gave no evidence of it in their lives. So Richard Mather argued. But which covenant was he talking about? On the question of unbelieving adults who applied for membership, Mather refused to budge, differing from Shepard, who now thought it better to include ten hypocrites and not exclude one believer (despite what he had written earlier. I remind you, reader: 'The ruin of a church may be the letting in of... one ill member'. 'One man or woman secretly vile, which the church has not used all means to discover, may defile a whole church'). Mather thought it better to keep out many believers rather than admit one hypocrite; he would never adopt Cotton's (and others') view that hypocrites have their uses in the church. Even so, as time passed, he had to compromise; he wanted a pure church, but the system itself produced unregenerate members. And so he ended up accepting what at one time he would never have dreamed of: 'The church must remain as pure as possible, but it must also recognise that while some of its members would be able to demonstrate their graciousness, others would not. Some would possess qualifications for the Lord's supper; others would not. Some would be truly holy, though men would never be able to identify them with absolute certainty; others, whatever evidence they gave or withheld, would be unregenerate' (Middlekauff pp35-57; see also Perry Miller pp87-100). But Richard Mather was uncomfortable: 'Late in his career, he conceded that grace did not inevitably show itself. He made this sad concession to reality in the defence he made of the half-way covenant. But his preaching to his flock does not seem ever to have accommodated this reality'. And: 'Among his last words to [his son] Increase was a plea that the children of New England should be baptised and brought into the church' (Middlekauff pp74-75). How did this differ from promiscuous baptism?

I return to a question I have raised before. Where is there any such weaving and wavering in the New Testament? I quite understand the lack of discussion about the motor car in the New Testament; it wasn't invented! But sinners were converted in those days; they married and had children; and so on; and we know that not all who professed faith and became church members proved to be true believers. In other words, the people of the New Testament were very much like 17th century New Englanders (and us), and met the same problems as they did (and we do). *But where in all the New Testament is there any discussion of the logic of covenant theology and its application to the problem of babies and their baptism?* The silence says far more than a thousand words from me. I can think of only one reason for the silence.

Appendices

In Appendix 1, I show that dipping is the only way baptism was administered in the New Testament, and that this is essential. And Appendix 2 comprises lengthy extracts from Augustine.

Appendix 1

Sprinkling or Dipping?

Very few would quarrel with the assertion that baptism in the New Testament was by immersion, and never in any other way; or at least, if they do quarrel with it, they find themselves opposed by theological giants, many of them infant baptisers. Men like Calvin, for instance, were quite clear that New Testament baptism was by immersion.[1] Of

---

[1] Zwingli spoke of 'John's dipping' (Friesen p133). Calvin: 'We see our body washed, immersed and surrounded with water... dipped in water... immersing... in water' (Calvin: *Institutes* Vol.2 pp520,525-526). Lloyd-Jones: 'For the first thousand years of the Christian Church, the common mode of baptism was immersion'. He noted that the Westminster Assembly in the 1640s excluded immersion only by a vote of 25-24. Even so, he was yet again obscure, allowing both immersion and sprinkling: 'I am not able to give you all the evidence, obviously, but in the writings of the various Fathers there is a great deal to suggest that' descending into the stream and sprinkling was the apostolic way. He thought 'the mode of baptism is not the vital thing... To say that complete immersion is absolutely essential is not only to go beyond the Scriptures, but is to verge upon heresy, if not to be actually heretical' (Lloyd-Jones: *The Church* pp43-45; see also Iain Murray: *Lloyd-Jones* Vol.2 pp790-791). With respect, I repeat my earlier point. Would Lloyd-Jones have allowed such a woolly difference of opinion, based upon the Fathers, to colour his view of church government, inter-church relations, the Lord's supper, and so on, not to mention original sin, substitutionary atonement and justification? Is it heretical to seek to copy the New Testament over *those* questions? Is the boot not on the other foot – did not the Fathers introduce heresy in all these areas? Moses was commended for making everything according to the pattern he had been given (Heb. 8:5). Should not we seek the same commendation? Immersion is the only mode in the New Testament. Immersion is essential to the ordinance. As to whether or not my saying so makes me a heretic, I leave it to God to pronounce at the last day.
For the long history of immersion, see Wright: *What...?* pp40,76-78,91-92. For immersion and the Fathers, see Stander and Louw pp37,41,49,79,112,181, 185; Bradshaw pp110-111. See also Newton pp94-100. When drawing up the Westminster Confession, 'most of the divines seem to have recognised the legitimacy of [immersion, 'dipping'] and wanted it to be acknowledged in the

course it was. We know that baptism is a symbol of the washing away of sins, the total cleansing from all pollution by the blood of Christ. It further symbolises union with Christ in his death, burial and resurrection. For these reasons, immersion is essential if a proper outward sign of the inward spiritual reality is to be demonstrated by water baptism (John 13:10; Acts 2:38; 22:16; Rom. 6:1-14; 1 Cor. 6:11; 2 Cor. 5:17; Gal. 3:27; Col. 2:11-13; 1 John 1:7 *etc.*). Water baptism does not accomplish any of this, of course, but it is meant to symbolise it fully, and do so in a simple and clear manner.[2] New Testament immersion meets all these criteria; no wonder it was the universal practice of the apostolic church. Sprinkling or pouring are not sufficient; both fall woefully short of a full demonstration of what needs to be represented in baptism.[3]

But immersion is essential for other reasons. The New Testament has a word for 'sprinkle' – ῥαντίζω – it is used in Hebrews 9:13. But it is never used of water baptism. Never once. Why not? Because it is not

---

Directory, but others, including the Scots, were anxious to exclude anything that might throw doubt on the practice of sprinkling' (Paul pp374-375,394). For a present-day Anglican argument for 'submersion', 'immersion' or 'dipping', see Buchanan and Vasey pp26-27.

[2] Ross made an interesting point: As for the 'early Arminian Baptists... immersion is not mentioned until... 1660, and this may have helped to retard the [re-]discovery of the symbolic importance of baptism. The Calvinistic Baptists, on the other hand, were, from the first, more interested in the symbolic... [They] practised immersion as early as about 1640, and the Confessions of 1644, 1646, 1656, 1677 and 1689 all declare [baptism's] symbolic [nature]' (Ross p102).

[3] I fully accept that burial in biblical times was not necessarily a downward action in the earth. Lazarus and Christ, we know, were buried in caves. But this does not militate against the point above. The only way, by water, to symbolise burial – putting the body out of sight – is by immersion. Sprinkling or pouring cannot possibly symbolise *that*. 'Paul likens baptism to a burial by which the former sinfulness is buried; that is, utterly taken away' (Thayer, commenting on συνθάπτω). John Murray was wrong to say that 'the burial of Jesus was the proof of the reality of his death' (John Murray Vol.1 p215). Not at all! What a ridiculous remark! Burial disposes of the body, removes it completely from sight; it does not prove the person was dead! Proof of death has to precede burial. No undertaker could or would bury a corpse without first seeing the death certificate. Likewise, credible evidence of faith has to precede baptism.

right to baptise by sprinkling. Again, the New Testament has several words for 'pour' – βαλλω, καταχεω, εκχεω, εκχυνω and επιχεω (John 13:5; Matt. 26:7; John 2:15; Rev. 16:1-4; Luke 22:20; 10:34 *etc.*). But they are never used of water baptism. Why not? Because it is not right to baptise by pouring. The two words which *are* used for 'baptise' are βαπτω and βαπτιζω. The first means 'to dip, to dip in, to immerse'. Then it means 'to dip into dye, to dye or to colour'. But the root meaning is 'to dip' (see Luke 16:24; John 13:26). The first word for 'baptise' leads on to the second which means 'to dip repeatedly, to immerse, to submerge'. In Classical Greek the root meaning is applied to the sinking of vessels or ships, the dipping of sheep, and to drowning and the like. Vessels disappear beneath the waves when they sink, and sheep are thoroughly immersed when they are dipped, it is essential to the process. The word then means 'to cleanse by dipping or submerging, to overwhelm'. The early Baptists were called 'dippers'.

The translators of the English Bible failed miserably at this point; their efforts were abject in the extreme. They should not have converted the Greek word for 'baptise' into an Anglicised word, which is what they did; the truth is, sadly, they did not attempt to translate, which is what they ought to have done. Instead, they transliterated or refashioned the Greek letters into English.[4] This can be verified by the explanation given in the Oxford English Dictionary; this respected authority asserts that the word for baptism in English came into existence through being 'refashioned after Latin and Greek'. In short, the translators of the English Bible did not translate the Greek words, but refashioned or invented a word in English instead. As the Dictionary goes on to explain, the verb in Greek means 'to dip, immerse'. The English word the translators should have used was 'dip', a perfectly good word, and one which meets every requirement

---

[4] In the AV, it fitted in with the use of ecclesiastical words which I noted earlier. 'Baptise' sounds much more 'churchy' than 'dip', and adds specious weight to the ideas of ritualism and sacramentalism. Compare the earlier note about the use of 'infant' instead of 'baby'. I agree, of course, that when the word 'dip' is used to speak of spiritual baptism (as in Rom. 6:3-4; 1 Cor. 12:13; Col. 2:12-13), it takes on a metaphorical sense and becomes a 'technical' word used by believers. But this is no different to εκκλησια – see above. In both cases, the original, basic, use of the word is paramount. For baptism, 'dipping' is the word.

of translation. That is exactly what the Greek means – to dip. The sorry failure of the translators to translate caused harm to the church of God. As an example of what the English translators should have done, take the Septuagint, the Greek version of the Old Testament. 2 Kings 5:14 in the Greek has βαπτιζω. The English version is, quite properly, 'so he went down and *dipped* seven times in the Jordan'. Exactly so, since βαπτιζω is to dip. If only that same, correct, approach had been adopted in the New Testament – as it ought to have been – the issue would have been clear for all to see.[5]

I admit, of course, that on two occasions in the New Testament, the word βαπτιζω is translated by 'washing'; in Mark 7:4 and Luke 11:38. However, in neither case is the question of baptism involved. Nevertheless we need to look at those verses. Take Mark 7:4 first of all. There is some manuscript doubt about the Greek word in the original; it could be βαπτιζω, 'to dip', or it could be ραντιζω, 'to sprinkle'. If the latter, there is no case to answer. According to M.R.Vincent, two of the most important manuscripts have ραντιζω.[6] But in any event, as Hendriksen said in his comments on the passage: 'Merely sprinkling the hands would probably not have satisfied the rabbis. Nothing less than a thorough rinsing or ceremonial washing seems to have been required'. Reader, note that. As Hendriksen (an infant baptiser) pointed out, even if βαπτιζω was used in the original, it cannot mean 'to sprinkle'; it has to mean, at the very least, 'a thorough rinsing or ceremonial washing'. Therefore, even though the verse in question does not deal with baptism, we can say that 'to sprinkle' will never adequately translate the word for 'baptise'.[7]

Hendriksen then referred to Luke 11:38, where Jesus was criticised for not washing himself – βαπτιζω – before dinner. Hendriksen

---

[5] 'I know not why it is that we yield to the superstitions of our Christian brethren, so much as to use the word "baptise" at all. It is not an English, but a Greek word. It has but one meaning, and cannot bear another. Throughout all the classics, without exception, it is not possible to translate it correctly, except with the idea of immersion; and believing this, and knowing this, if the translation [of Matt. 28:18-19] is not complete, we will complete it... "Go, therefore, and teach all nations, *immersing* them in the name of the Father, and of the Son, and of the Holy Ghost"' (Spurgeon: *New Park Street and Metropolitan* Vol.7 p284, emphasis his; see also pp265-272).

[6] Vincent Vol.1 p108.

[7] See end note on p316 for excursus: 'βαπτισμα'.

suggested that total immersion is not in view in the verse.[8] I totally agree; in both verses, Mark 7:4 and Luke 11:38, I am very happy to concur that total immersion is not the issue. But I also go on to remind you, reader, that in neither verse is water baptism the issue. More to the point, however, *dipping* or plunging is in view in them both, and *sprinkling* is most definitely not. Translate both verses by 'dipping', and you have the sense of the Greek.

But some authorities actually go further, much further; they think that the complaint of Luke 11:38 is that Jesus had not completely bathed himself. But I do not categorically state it myself. I am content to come back to the undeniable; in both the verses in question, where the word βαπτιζω is used, it is best translated 'dipping', as indeed it ought to be. If only the word had been properly translated out of the Greek, the English New Testament would speak, as does the original Greek Testament, of dipping or plunging. The argument would be virtually at an end. In Mark 10:38 (compare Ps. 42:7; 69:2; 124:4) the word must be 'plunged'; by no stretch of the imagination can it be 'sprinkled'.

As for those who ask how couches could be dipped or plunged (Mark 7:4), the truth is the relevant words και κλινων are disputed from a manuscript point of view. Vincent said they are omitted in some of the best texts. Hendriksen left them out.[9] But one thing is certain, sprinkling would have been totally inadequate. The pots, jugs and pans – as the hands – were not cleansed by a few drops of water, nor by a rub with a damp cloth. They were plunged or dipped.

Furthermore, when Jesus was baptised by John in the Jordan, he went 'into' the water. The Greek word is εις (Mark 1:9). It is used in such phrases as 'into a house' or 'into a hollow', a place 'in which an object can be hidden'. Literally it speaks of entering into something. I freely grant that the word has other senses, and several shades of emphasis within those senses, but its root meaning is 'entrance into, or direction and limit: into, among'. Jesus went into the Jordan. He entered the river, and he was baptised. He was dipped. Then he came up out of the Jordan; or came away from the Jordan, depending on the manuscript used (Matt. 3:16; Mark 1:10). As the Greek lexicon puts it,

---

[8] Hendriksen: *Mark* p273.
[9] Vincent Vol.1 p109; Hendriksen: *Mark* p272.

'εις marks the element into which the immersion is made'.[10] Jesus entered into the river and was dipped in it.

Despite this obvious fact, some infant baptisers simply will not or cannot face up to the consequences. In his comments on Mark 1:9, Hendriksen, for instance, posed a most ridiculous question – a question I suggest which could only be asked because centuries of baptism by sprinkling have conditioned some men's thinking. Jesus went into the river – right into it. Then he was dipped in the river. That is what the Greek says. The river was not sprinkled on him; he was dipped in it. I repeat, that is what the Bible says. Hendriksen, however, felt it necessary to ask: 'Did Jesus step down Jordan's bank into the water, so that his feet were covered with water, and did the Baptist then pour or sprinkle water on the Master's head?'[11] What an absurd question! The answer, if it is required, is very simple. Jesus did step into the river; he went right into it – he got very wet indeed – far more than his feet were covered; after which he was plunged or dipped in the river.

Even so, take another infant baptiser, J.A.Alexander. In his comments on the preceding verse, Mark 1:8, he said the meaning is 'bathe'; he certainly did not try to argue that it is 'sprinkle'.[12] But on verse 9, he went on to make a comment which is fatuous in the extreme. He spoke against the idea of submerging, and said if immersion is essential, it ought to be done naked for, he maintained, 'the two things naturally go together, and immersion without stripping seems to rob the rite in part of its supposed significance'.[13] What a stupid comment! If this is the best argument against immersion, don't show me the worst. John went into the Jordan with Jesus. It is recorded that John dipped Jesus in the river. The Jordan was certainly not sprinkled or poured on the head of Jesus.

---

[10] Thayer (on βαπτιζω and εις). See earlier note on 1 Cor. 12:13.

[11] Hendriksen: *Mark* p42.

[12] J.A.Alexander pp10-11. Having given 'bathe' as the right translation, Alexander went on to claim that the reference to baptism with the Spirit is 'proof that primitive baptism was not exclusively or necessarily immersion'! From one of those who depend so heavily upon logic, such illogical statements are incredible.

[13] Why? Owen seemed to use the absurdity introduced by the Fathers – baptising naked – to smear believers who want to follow, not the Fathers, but the apostles (Owen: *Of Infant* in *Works* Vol.16 p267). Any stick will do!

It is highly significant that the one nation on earth who ought to understand the meaning of the Greek words used – the Greeks themselves – have always baptised by immersion. This is conceded even by those who sprinkle. The infant baptiser A.A.Hodge acknowledged that 'the Greek church has always insisted on immersion'. Despite the obvious and only construction to be placed on this frank admission, Hodge went on to say:

During all the more modern freer and more evangelical ages the tendency toward baptising by sprinkling has increased and become more general. The general body of Christians have always felt... they were free to do in the matter as convenience or local custom suggested.[14]

This last statement is a very important admission on the part of a staunch defender of the practice of sprinkling. It is a fatal admission. Are we to accept the view of 'the general body of Christians', and try to obey Christ as 'convenience or local custom suggests', because we are supposed to live in a 'freer and more evangelical' age? Isn't it the New Testament which matters, and only the New Testament? 'Let God be true but every man a liar' (Rom. 3:4), must be our position. We are not 'free to do' what we or others think convenient. Oh no! Let us be captive to the word of God. This one simple and unanswerable argument, an argument put forward by so many faithful men and women time and time again when challenged about their doctrine and practice, is the only argument for Christians; all other claims are worth less than a brass farthing between them. The Scriptures, and the Scriptures only, are our guide in all things. Some believers have sealed their testimony with their blood. 'To the law and to the testimony! If they do not speak according to this word, it is because there is no light in them' (Isa. 8:20). Whenever men go outside of Scripture to invent their own schemes, or whenever they speak contrary to God's word – however good they may be in other areas, on that issue they are at fault. They have no light in them at that juncture. Imagine what would be said, quite properly, by Reformed believers if Hodge's words had been written by a Liberal. To my mind at least, they sound no better – they are worse – coming from a Calvinist.

One last point. In the New Testament, they needed more than a cupful or basinful of water in order to baptise. They needed 'much

---

[14] A.A.Hodge p324.

water' (John 3:23). Our attention is expressly drawn to this. Why? If they wanted to sprinkle, a cupful or less would have been sufficient for each baptism. Do those who practise sprinkling or affusion need 'much water'? Clearly the apostolic church did. Why? Listen to Calvin who said, 'From these words, we may infer that John and Christ administered baptism by plunging the whole body beneath the water'. In spite of this, A.A.Hodge tried to argue, 'in all probability' – please note, 'in all probability' – 'the original manner of applying water in Christian baptism was by pouring the water out of the hollow of the hand, or out of a shell or small vessel'.[15] Reader, this statement is completely unjustified; it flies in the face of all the facts, and is pure speculation; it is special pleading.

Did the eunuch not have a supply of water with him when he was passing through the desert? Even allowing the unthinkable – that he did not – why did he point out an oasis when he raised the issue of baptism (Acts 8:36), following which both he and Philip went down into the water (Acts 8:38)? Do those who sprinkle or pour go down into the water with those they baptise? On this verse Calvin said: 'Here we see the rite used among the men of old time in baptism; for they put all the body into the water'. But for all that he was prepared to state that in his opinion sprinkling is perfectly acceptable, and that 'we ought not to stand so much about such a small difference of a ceremony... the Church did grant liberty to herself... to change the rites somewhat'.[16]

This hypothesis enjoys the merit of honesty; but that is all that can be said for it. Christians have no right or authority to change the least of God's commands and ordinances. None whatsoever. Not even the great John Calvin can sanction it.[17] The Particular Baptists of the 1640s, among others, saw this principle very clearly, and despite massive opposition they had the grace and the courage to take the necessary steps back to the New Testament in order to adopt the

---

[15] A.A.Hodge p322.

[16] Calvin: *Commentaries* Vol.18 Part 2 p364.

[17] Imagine, reader, what Calvin would have said if a Romanist had defended the Mass – the adulteration of the Lord's supper – in his own words: 'We ought not to stand so much about such a small difference of a ceremony... the Church did grant liberty to herself... to change the rites somewhat'. His reply would rightly have been blistering! See below.

practice of the early church in every respect. In every respect! All
honour to them. Would that Calvin had done the same.

Calvin made the same mistake on John 3:23 as on Acts 8:38, when
he showed a similar willingness to fly in the face of Scripture. On John
3:23 he was very clear. The baptism of the New Testament was 'by
plunging the whole body beneath the water', he said. Nevertheless he
immediately proceeded to state that we have no need 'to give ourselves
any great uneasiness about the outward rite'.[18] Reader, if that principle
is applied to all Scripture doctrine and practice, we shall end up...

---

[18] 'John and Christ administered baptism by plunging the whole body beneath
the water... Christ did this by his disciples' (Calvin: *Commentaries* Vol.17
Part 2 pp130-131). Quite! So why would his disciples change the practice
taught them by their Master? If, as Calvin said, they did change their Master's
practice, did they also tinker with the supper, not giving themselves 'any great
uneasiness about' making such a change? If so, why didn't Paul make this
clear in 1 Cor. 11:17-34? And why did he so precisely repeat the details of
what Christ did, and what Christ said, at the institution of the supper – if he
felt no 'uneasiness' about tinkering with Christ's command? As Calvin said
on the supper (1 Cor. 11:23-29): 'The institution of Christ is a sure rule, so
that if you turn aside from it but a very little, you are out of the right course.
Hence, as the Corinthians had deviated from this rule, [the apostle] calls them
back to it. It is a passage that ought to be carefully observed, as showing that
there is no remedy for correcting and purging out abuses, short of a return to
God's pure institution'. Calvin went on to challenge the Papists about the
Mass – 'that it is full of wicked abominations; hence there is need of
reformation. We demand – what it appears Paul had recourse to – that our
Lord's institution be the common rule' (Calvin: *Commentaries* Vol.20 Part 1
pp372-373). What Calvin said to the Papists about the supper, I say to infant
baptisers about baptism; let us 'return to God's pure institution', and 'our
Lord's institution be the common rule'. To use Calvin's words, 'we demand'
it. The Puritans, after all, were called Precisians. Richard Rogers, accused of
being 'too precise' replied: 'I serve a precise God' (Brook p234). Quite right!
So let's have some 'precision' and consistency in *this* matter. See my earlier
note on the strange fact that though the Reformers quarrelled vehemently with
the Papists over the supper, they had little disagreement with them over
baptism. Both of Christ's ordinances were corrupted by the Fathers and the
Papacy – why did the Reformers fail to make an equal – a consistent – stand
on both issues? Significantly, for infant baptism, Bucer – who had such a large
influence on Calvin – and Calvin himself, relied heavily upon the Fathers. See
Wendel p326. How much the Fathers – and those who depend on them – have
to answer for.

where? My words about A.A.Hodge apply to Calvin too. Owen would certainly have disagreed with both men. He wrote: 'What men have a right to do in the church... they have a command to do'. Quite! And since there is no command to meddle with baptism by immersion only, men have no warrant for sprinkling or pouring.

Matthew Poole also commented on John 3:23. He pointed out that John did not baptise in Aenon because the water was holy; the sole reason was that there was plenty of water in the area. This was a rarity in Judea, said Poole. He rightly observed: 'It is from this apparent that both Christ and John baptised by dipping the body in the water, else they need not have sought places where there had been a great plenty of water'. Thus far his observations were excellent; they were right. But the Puritan spoiled his admirable comments by a ridiculous remark, saying 'it is probable that they did not constantly dip'![19] Why not?

Poole said a similar thing on Acts 8:38. He declared that in Scripture it 'was usual to baptise by dipping the body in the water', but he qualified his statement – totally without justification – by limiting the dipping to 'hot countries'.[20] Hot countries indeed! As before, is it not amazing that those who contend vehemently for the Regulative Principle – or something like it – can be so cavalier with God's ordinances? Calvin, Poole and many others, have all admitted that the New Testament method of baptising was by dipping the whole body into water, but they have found all sorts of reasons – excuses – to tinker with the revelation of God's mind in Scripture. It is a great wrong. No Christian has any right to tamper with the least aspect of God's ordinances. We must be 'obedient in all things' (2 Cor. 2:9). That is what God requires of us.

A few testimonies from some other infant baptisers might be helpful. W.J.Conybeare: '(Rom. 6:4) cannot be understood unless it be

---

[19] Poole p293.

[20] Poole p412. Another infant baptiser, Hutcheson, argued the other way about: 'In these hot countries – water being so scarce... it need not seem strange that John was not permitted to make use of wells, even for sprinkling... but... rivers and brooks, where the water was copious' (Hutcheson p51). Note the gloss; John did not baptise *from* wells or brooks, but *in* the Jordan, where there was plenty of water. Baptism requires water deep enough to plunge and immerse the entire body.

borne in mind that the primitive baptism was by immersion'. Dr Bloomfield on the same text affirmed 'there is here... plainly a reference to the ancient mode of baptism by immersion'. Handley C.G.Moule wrote of the 'plunge' and an 'entire immersion'. Dean Stanley contended 'baptism was not only a bath but a plunge, an entire submersion in the deep water'. Thomas Chalmers declared: 'The original meaning of the word baptism is immersion... we doubt not that the prevalent style of the administrations in the apostles' days was an actual submersion of the whole body under water'. Dr Wall, himself 'a staunch defender of infant baptism', said 'immersion is so plain and clear by an infinite number of passages, that one cannot but pity the weak endeavour of such as would maintain the negative of it'. On the reference to the quantity of water in John 3:23, John Albert Bengel wrote: 'So the rite of immersion required'. On the same point A.Plummer declared that it was 'for immersion'. Calvin maintained: 'Baptise means to immerse entirely, and it is certain that the custom of thus entirely immersing was anciently observed in the church'.[21]

All this would seem clear enough. The question I ask is: Why not stick to it? Why try to baptise by pouring or sprinkling?

---

[21] Frank White pp86,89; Moule p164; Cramp pp7-8; Lang: *Churches* p49; Bengel p282; Plummer p108; Calvin: *Institutes* Vol.2 p524. As above, how Calvin, with his high view of Scripture could also, in the same breath, say: 'Whether the person baptised is to be wholly immersed... or whether he is only to be sprinkled with water, is not of the least consequence; churches should be at liberty to adopt either, according to the diversity of climates', I simply cannot fathom. But it is going on still. Pratt: 'The mode of baptism in Reformed theology is largely a matter of indifference' (John H.Armstrong p66). Who said? It may be – in 'Reformed theology'. But is it in the Bible? 'The amount of water and the precise mode in which [baptism] is administered are surely matters of indifference' (Marshall p23). No, they are not! Who has the right to tell us what is, and what is not, indifferent? In particular, the biblical use of the word, and the significance and graphic imagery of the ordinance, are all jettisoned by dismissing immersion as a thing indifferent. The *visibility* of the sign is crucial. See the earlier note on the need for scrupulous obedience to Christ – and how Calvin so strenuously argued (rightly) for it in the supper. Well, as for the supper, so for baptism. Consistency is required. Consistency!

The scriptural mode was corrupted very soon after the apostolic period, certainly by the beginning of the 2nd century,[22] and baptism by sprinkling or pouring had probably replaced immersion altogether by about the 12th century. The Anabaptists, when they recovered the New Testament ordinance of believer's baptism, failed to immerse as a general rule, at least in the beginning. The Reformed Churches and the Presbyterians under Calvin's influence kept to sprinkling, although immersion was not entirely abandoned; it was allowed in the Church of England, but it had fallen into practical disuse by about 1600. It was the Particular Baptists of the early 1640s who came to a definite, clear position on baptism by immersion, as they returned to the New Testament practice which had been discontinued for so long. And once established, the baptism of believers by immersion rapidly gained much ground, not only among the Particular Baptists, for the General Baptists also adopted it. The Particular Baptist Confession of faith of 1644 stated:

The way and manner of the dispensing of this ordinance the Scripture holds out to be dipping or plunging the whole body under water: it being a sign, must answer the thing signified, which are these: first, the washing of the whole soul in the blood of Christ: secondly, that interest the saints have in the death, burial and resurrection; thirdly, together with a confirmation of our faith, that as certainly as the body is buried under water, and rises again, so certainly shall the bodies of the saints be raised by the power of Christ, in the day of resurrection, to reign with Christ.[23]

But does it matter? Is the amount of water to be used in baptism, worth all this ink? The question can be linked to another: Does the age of the person baptised matter?

The answer to both is, in one sense, the same. If it had not been for the Church's corruption of New Testament practice, neither question would have arisen. Only believers would have been baptised, and they, all of them, would have been immersed upon profession of faith.

Does it matter? Only if the church matters. What is the church? Who can be a member? How do you come to be a member? Do *those* questions matter? Infant baptism has consequences – far beyond

---

[22] But see Wright: *What...?* pp40,76-78,91-92. The plunging pools of the 4th century and later can be seen in North Africa today.

[23] Lumpkin p167; Ramsbottom p30.

baptism. Infant baptism is fundamental to a sacramental institution, that institution divided into clergy and laity, the clergy having sacramental rights and powers. Does *that* matter? Let me not mince words. It is nothing other than priestcraft.

Does it matter? Only if the deluding of millions into thinking they are saved by their baptism matters.

Does it matter? Only if obedience to God in his word matters. But, reader, if *that* matters to you, then you will only be involved with a system which baptises believers upon profession, baptises *all* believers on profession, baptises *only* believers upon profession, and does so by immersion. I recognise that many whom I have had in my sights claim to be following Scripture, and doing so on principle – a principle which they defend as vehemently as I.[24] But, although I respect their claim to be following Scripture, I disagree with their conclusions. And I hope that any who might be thinking of adopting infant baptism will give serious regard to the arguments I have tried to put forward. If they still disagree, perhaps they would be kind enough to write to me and show me where, in their opinion, I have gone astray.

---

[24] Having said that, as I have noted, at least some of them admit they have to go outside Scripture, turn to the complex logic of their covenant theology, and rely upon the Confessions, to make their case – and, without biblical warrant, are willing to dismiss biblical practice as 'indifferent'.

End note to Appendix 1: Sprinkling or Dipping

βαπτισμα

Take Jesus' figurative reference to baptism in: 'I have a baptism to be baptised with, and how distressed I am till it is accomplished' (Luke 12:50). Clearly, he was speaking of his impending sufferings and death. Baptism, βαπτισμα. 'Jesus certainly makes an allusion to his baptism at the hands of [John the Baptist]... The figure is as follows: Jesus sees himself about to be *plunged* into a bath of flame' (Godet Vol.2 p113, emphasis mine). 'The words "baptism" and "to be baptised" are here probably [definitely!] used in a figurative sense: Jesus is going to be "overwhelmed" by agony. He will be *plunged* into the flood of horrible distress' (Hendriksen: *Luke* p682, emphasis mine). Hendriksen cited Ps. 42:7; 124:4; Isa. 21:4; Mark 10:38. '[Christ] compares death – as in other passages – to baptism (Rom. 6:4), because the children of God, after having been *immersed* for a time by the death of the body, shortly afterwards rise again to life, so that death is nothing else than a passage through the midst of the waters' (Calvin: *Commentaries* Vol.17 Part 1 p169, emphasis mine; see also Vol.5 Part 1 pp138-139). Baptism, βαπτισμα, plunged, overwhelmed, immersed, passage through the waters. Sprinkled? Certainly not! In addition to other verses cited, see Ps. 88:7; Jonah 2:2-6. Gill: 'The baptism of his sufferings is meant, which are compared to a baptism, because of the largeness and abundance of them; he was, as it were, *immersed*, or *plunged* into them; and which almost all interpreters observe on the text, and by which they confess the true import and primary signification of the word used; as in baptism, performed by *immersion*, the person is *plunged* into water, is *covered* with it, and continues a while *under* it, and then is raised *out* of it' (Gill Vol.5 p496, emphasis mine).

But what about: 'All our fathers [Israel]... all were baptised into Moses in the cloud and in the sea' (1 Cor. 10:1-2)? Opinions are divided. Some see no reference or allusion to the mode of baptism: 'There is no allusion to the mode of baptism' (Charles Hodge: *1 Corinthians* p172). Others do, and some of them use the 'all' to argue for infants to be included in baptism. If so, of course, they have to give them the supper – since 'all' ate and drank (1 Cor. 10:3-4). Others argue for baptismal sacramentalism. But Paul was concerned with analogy, and drawing on baptism and using the word in the way the believers at Corinth would understand. I myself would not push the analogy, but if pressed, I would take Gill's line: Having left Egypt through the Passover, the Israelites gave themselves up to Moses, signally in their 'baptism' in the cloud and sea; likewise, sinners upon conversion, repentance and faith in Christ, profess and follow Christ in baptism. And while I would not build my case for immersion from this passage, I am glad I don't have to try to establish sprinkling or pouring a few drops from it. I cannot see how such a practice could be deduced from Ex. 15:4-5,8,10; Josh. 24:7; Ps. 78:53; 106:9,11; Isa. 51:10; 63:11-13. See Gill Vol.6 pp211-212; Fee: *1 Corinthians* pp443-446; Beasley-Murray: *Baptism in the New Testament* pp181-185. The most ingenious interpretation I have come across is that cited by John Macleod (and by Leach). Macleod quoted a man who argued that all the Israelites (including the infants) were baptised in the Red Sea; the Israelites were not immersed but, even so, were saved; the Egyptians were immersed but, even so, were drowned (John Macleod p254). For my part, I wonder what conclusions he drew. Are all the baptised, including infants, saved? Even in the exodus, the argument breaks down. All the Israelites (including their infants) left Egypt. How many entered the promised land? We know the significance of this (Heb. 3:7 − 4:11; see also 1 Cor. 10:5). Does the same ratio apply to the practice of infant baptism? As I say, it is an ingenious interpretation, but one which leaves its advocates with insuperable problems. See my earlier note (in Argument 9) on this episode in Israel's history, and the way it is grievously misused today with regard to children.

Appendix 2

Augustine on Baptism

As I have shown, Augustine is *the* theologian of infant baptism, the one upon whom the Reformers – principally, for my purpose, Calvin – drew heavily.[1] So that you, reader, can weigh Augustine's words on

---

[1] In addition to what I have already said, consider this from Lusk: 'Augustine, Anselm, Aquinas, Luther, Calvin, Bucer, and so on, held to both the sovereignty of God in salvation, and to the sacraments as effectual means of salvation'. Lusk rejected Warfield's claim (which 'has become commonplace') that 'Augustine bequeathed to the Church for solution [a problem – the conflict between predestination and sacramental efficacy – which] the Church required a thousand years to solve'; that is, according to Warfield, Augustine's bequeathed problem was solved by the Reformers at the Reformation. Lusk explained: 'But the problem is really no problem at all, unless we have already assumed that predestination and sacramental grace are incompatible. The early Reformers identified no such problem, as a close reading of Calvin's *Institutes* bears out. Thus, we must strongly disagree with Warfield's conclusion [which was]: "For the Reformation, inwardly considered, was just the ultimate triumph of Augustine's doctrine of grace over Augustine's doctrine of the Church". In reality, it was the Anabaptists, not Calvin or Luther, who felt pressure to pit Augustine's ecclesiology [doctrine of the Church, including his sacramentalism] against his soteriology [doctrine of salvation]. Calvin, Luther, Bucer, Cranmer and the other leading Reformers, unlike Warfield, did not think a high doctrine of the Church and sacraments presented "great obstacles" to a doctrine of salvation by sovereign grace. We need the "whole Augustine", so to speak – his teaching on both predestination and sacramental efficacy' (Lusk : 'Introduction' iii). So said Lusk.
Although I disagree with Lusk's final claim, he was making an important point – and the abundant evidence I have supplied has done nothing to challenge it. Which is? Augustine, and his theology of effective sacramental infant-baptism, set in train, what I can only describe as a massive departure from Scripture, and that the Reformers took their stand upon – and promulgated – his doctrine of the sacraments. And the stark fact is, a growing number of today's Reformed writers and teachers are calling for the 'whole Augustine', and justly claiming Calvin, in particular, and the other Reformers, in support. I deplore this, as I have made clear. Those to whom I have been speaking throughout this book – in the main, those who are thinking of

319

baptism, the use of 'the formula', priestcraft, and his arguments against the re-baptising of schismatics who returned to the Catholic Church,[2] plus a little on the Lord's supper, I have taken the following from his full works as found on the Roman Catholic website, www.newadvent.org, under 'Fathers' then 'Augustine'. Although Augustine intended the opposite – and many of his followers down the centuries have thought he was right! – to my mind, most of his 'reasoning' and expositions of Scripture – see the full works! – form one of the best arguments *against* sacramental baptism in general, and infant baptism in particular. Let Augustine speak for himself:

First, his *On Baptism, Against the Donatists*, in which Augustine argued against re-baptising schismatics (Donatists) on their return to the Catholic Church. In passing, he sets out his sacramental view of baptism. It is this to which I draw attention:

The sacrament of baptism is what the person possesses who is baptised; and the sacrament of conferring baptism is what he possesses who is ordained. And as the baptised person, if he depart from the unity of the Church, does not thereby lose the sacrament of baptism, so also he who is ordained, if he depart from the unity of the Church, does not lose the sacrament of conferring baptism... For as those who return to the Church, if they had been baptised before their secession, are not re-baptised, so those who return, having been ordained before their secession, are certainly not ordained again... They retain the sacrament of their ordination... (1.1.2).
The Church, the mother which could give birth to sons in the baptism of Christ... (1.10.13).

---

adopting infant-baptism, not least because of the weight of those who have held the practice – need seriously to think about these facts. They can read Augustine for themselves in what follows in this Appendix, on the website, and in Sadler pp269-274. And they should bear in mind that Luther, Calvin, and so many others, depended heavily on the kind of material which they read.
[2] In Augustine's time, it must be remembered, 'Catholic' did not mean '*Roman* Catholic'; rather, it meant 'Universal'. Those who left (such as the Donatists) were called 'heretics' or 'schismatics' by the Catholics. (Here I am making no comment as to the rightness or otherwise of the Catholic claim that those who left were heretical). In time, the Catholic Church split into the Eastern, 'Orthodox' or 'Ecumenical' Church, and the Western, 'Roman Catholic' Church. Augustine's theology became Rome's (and the Reformers') theology.

There is one Church which alone is called Catholic; and... [re]generation... proceeds from the Church, whose sacraments are retained, from which any such [re-]birth can alone in any case proceed... (1.10.14).

When by the breathing of our Lord the Holy Spirit was given to the disciples, he then went on to say: 'Baptise all nations in the name of the Father, and of the Son, and of the Holy Ghost' (Matt. 28:19). 'Whose soever sins ye remit, they are remitted unto them; and whose soever sins ye retain, they are retained' (John 20:23)... (1.11.15).

What is regeneration in baptism, except the being renovated from the corruption of the old man? And how can he be so renovated whose past sins are not remitted? But if he be not regenerate, neither does he put on Christ... For the apostle says: 'For as many of you as have been baptised into Christ have put on Christ' (Gal. 3:27); and if he has not so put on Christ, neither should he be considered to have been baptised in Christ. Further, since we say that he has been baptised in Christ, we confess that he has put on Christ; and if we confess this, we confess that he is regenerate... (1.11.16).

So the grace of baptism is not prevented from giving remission of all sins, even if he to whom they are forgiven continues to cherish hatred towards his brother in his heart. For the guilt of yesterday is remitted, and all that was before it, nay, even the guilt of the very hour and moment previous to baptism, and during baptism itself... (1.12.20).

For what does it matter to him who lacks charity, whether he be carried away outside the Church at once by some blast of temptation, or remain within the Lord's harvest, so as to be separated only at the final winnowing? And yet even such, if they have once been born [again] in baptism, need not be born again... (1.14.22).

If the water is not sanctified, when through want of skill the priest who prays utters some words of error, many, not only of the bad, but of the good brethren in the Church itself, fail to sanctify the water. For the prayers of many are corrected every day on being recited to men of greater learning, and many things are found in them contrary to the Catholic faith. Supposing, then, that it were shown that some persons were baptised when these prayers had been uttered over the water, will they be bidden to be baptised afresh? Why not? Because generally the fault in the prayer is more than counterbalanced by the intent of him who offers it; and those fixed words of the gospel, without which baptism cannot be consecrated, are of such efficacy, that, by their virtue, anything faulty that is uttered in the prayer contrary to the rule of faith is made of no effect... And if over some, he offer an erroneous prayer, God is present to uphold the words of his gospel, without which the baptism of Christ cannot be consecrated, and he himself consecrates his sacrament, that in the recipient, either before he is baptised, or when he is baptised, or at some future time when he turns in truth to God, that very sacrament may be profitable to salvation, which, were he not to be converted, would be powerful to his destruction. But who is there who does not know that there is no baptism of Christ, if the words of the gospel in which consists the outward visible sign be not forthcoming?... The baptism of Christ, that is, every baptism consecrated in the words of the gospel, is everywhere the same, and cannot be vitiated by any perversity on the part of any men... (6.25.47).

I... have no hesitation in saying that all men possess baptism who have received it in any place, from any sort of men, provided that it were consecrated in the words of the gospel, and received without deceit on their part with some degree of faith; although it would be of no profit to them for the salvation of their souls if they were without charity, by which they might be grafted into the Catholic Church... (7.53.102).

Now for Augustine's *On the Creed: A Sermon to Catechumens* (15 & 16) – (those receiving instruction before baptism), in which he speaks of the 'forgiveness of sins':

You have [this article of] the Creed perfectly in you when you receive baptism. Let none say: 'I have done this or that sin: perchance that is not forgiven me'. What have you done? How great a sin have you done? Name any heinous thing you have committed, heavy, horrible, which you shudder even to think of; have done what you will, have you killed Christ? There is not than that deed any worse, because also than Christ there is nothing better. What a dreadful thing is it to kill Christ! Yet the Jews killed him, and many afterwards believed on him and drank his blood: they are forgiven the sin which they committed. When you have been baptised, hold fast a good life in the commandments of God, that you may guard your baptism even unto the end. I do not tell you that you will live here without sin; but they are venial, without which this life is not. For the sake of all sins was baptism provided; for the sake of light sins, without which we cannot be, was prayer provided. What [is] the prayer? 'Forgive us our debts, as we also forgive our debtors'. Once for all we have washing in baptism, every day we have washing in prayer...

In three ways then are sins remitted in the Church; by baptism, by prayer, by the greater humility of penance; yet God does not remit sins but to the baptised. The very sins which he remits first, he remits not but to the baptised. When? When they are baptised. The sins which are after remitted upon prayer, upon penance, to whom he remits, it is to the baptised that he remits...

Now for Augustine's *Merits and Remission of Sin, and Infant Baptism*:

It may therefore be correctly affirmed, that such infants as quit the body without being baptised will be involved in the mildest condemnation of all. That person, therefore, greatly deceives both himself and others, who teaches that they will not be involved in condemnation; whereas the apostle says: 'Judgement from one offence to condemnation' (Rom. 5:16), and again a little after: 'By the offence of one upon all persons to condemnation' (Rom. 5:18)... Thus, then, was fulfilled what God had spoken: 'In the day that you eat thereof, you shall surely die' (Gen. 2:17). As a consequence, then, of this disobedience of the flesh, and this law of sin and death, whoever is born of the flesh has need of spiritual regeneration – not only that he may reach the kingdom of God, but also that he may be freed from the damnation of sin. Hence, men are, on the one hand, born in the flesh liable to sin and death from the first Adam, and, on the other hand, are born again in baptism associated with the righteousness and eternal life of the second Adam... (1.21).

But those persons raise a question, and appear to adduce an argument deserving of consideration and discussion, who say that new-born infants receive baptism not for the remission of sin, but that, since their procreation is not spiritual, they may be created in Christ, and become partakers of the kingdom of heaven, and by the same means children and heirs of God, and joint-heirs with Christ. And yet, when you ask them, whether those that are not baptised, and are not made joint-heirs with Christ and partakers of the kingdom of heaven, have at any rate the blessing of eternal life in the resurrection of the dead, they are extremely perplexed, and find no way out of their difficulty. For what Christian is there who would allow it to be said, that anyone could attain to eternal salvation without being born again in Christ – [a result] which he [Christ] meant to be effected through baptism, at the very time when such a sacrament was purposely instituted for regenerating in the hope of eternal salvation? Whence the apostle says: 'Not by works of righteousness which we have done, but according to his mercy he saved us by the laver of regeneration' (Tit. 3:5)... (1.23).

And let no one suppose that infants ought to be brought to baptism, on the ground that, as they are not sinners, so they are not righteous. How then do some remind us that the Lord commends this tender age as meritorious, saying: 'Suffer the little children to come unto me, and forbid them not, for of such is the kingdom of heaven' (Matt. 19:14)? For if this is not said [of such] because of likeness in humility (since humility makes [us] children), but because of the laudable life of children, then of course infants must be righteous persons; otherwise, it could not be correctly said: 'Of such is the kingdom of heaven', for heaven can only belong to the righteous. But perhaps, after all, it is not a right opinion of the meaning of the Lord's words, to make him commend the life of infants when he says: 'Of such is the kingdom of heaven'; inasmuch as *that* may be their true sense, which makes Christ adduce the tender age of infancy as a likeness of humility. Even so, however, perhaps we must revert to the tenet which I mentioned just now, that infants ought to be baptised, because, although they are not sinners, they are yet not righteous... Now, inasmuch as infants are not held bound by any sins of their own actual life, it is the guilt of original sin which is healed in them by the grace of him who saves them by the laver of regeneration... (1.24).

Hence also that other statement: 'The Father loves the Son, and has given all things into his hand. He that believes in the Son has everlasting life; while he that believes not the Son shall not see life, but the wrath of God abides on him' (John 3:35-36). Now in which of these classes must we place infants – among those who believe in the Son, or among those who believe not the Son? In neither, say some, because, as they are not yet able to believe, so must they not be deemed unbelievers. This, however, the rule of the Church does not indicate, for it joins baptised infants to the number of the faithful. Now if they who are baptised are, by virtue of the excellence and administration of so great a sacrament, nevertheless reckoned in the number of the faithful, although by their own heart and mouth they do not literally perform what appertains to the action of faith and confession, surely they who have lacked the sacrament must be classed among those who do not believe in the Son, and therefore, if they shall depart this life without this grace, they will have to encounter what is written concerning such – they shall not have life, but the wrath of God abides on them. Whence could this result to those who clearly have no sins of their own, if they are not held to be obnoxious to [because of?] original sin?... (1.28).

Now those very persons, who think it unjust that infants which depart this life without the grace of Christ should be deprived not only of the kingdom of God, into which they themselves admit that none but such as are regenerated through baptism can enter, but also of eternal life and salvation – when they ask how it can be just that one man should be freed from original sin and another not, although the condition of both of them is the same, might answer their own question, in accordance with their own opinion of how it can be so frequently just and right that one should have baptism administered to him whereby to enter into the kingdom of God, and another not be so favoured, although the case of both is alike. For if the question disturbs him, why, of the two persons, who are both equally sinners by nature, the one is loosed from that bond, on whom baptism is conferred, and the other is not released, on whom such grace is not bestowed; why is he not similarly disturbed by the fact that of two persons, innocent by nature, one receives baptism, whereby he is able to enter into the kingdom of God, and the other does not receive it, so that he is incapable of approaching the kingdom of God? Now in both cases one recurs to the apostle's outburst of wonder: 'O the depth of the riches!'... (1.30).

The Christians of Carthage have an excellent name for the sacraments, when they say that baptism is nothing else than salvation, and the sacrament of the body of Christ nothing else than life. Whence, however, was this derived, but from that primitive, as I suppose, and apostolic tradition, by which the Churches of Christ maintain it to be an inherent principle, that without baptism and partaking of the supper of the Lord it is impossible for any man to attain either to the kingdom of God or to salvation and everlasting life? So much also does Scripture testify, according to the words which we already quoted. For wherein does their opinion, who designate baptism by the term 'salvation', differ from what is written: 'He saved us by the washing of regeneration' (Tit. 3:5), or from Peter's statement: 'The like figure whereunto even baptism does also now save us' (1 Pet. 3:21)? And what else do they say who call the sacrament of the Lord's supper life, than that which is written: 'I am the living bread which came down from heaven' (John 6:51); and: 'The bread that I shall give is my flesh, for the life of the world' (John 6:51); and: 'Except ye eat the flesh of the Son of man, and drink his blood, you shall have no life in you' (John 6:53)?[3] If, therefore, as so many and such divine witnesses

---

[3] Augustine again: 'For [Christ] took upon him earth from earth; because flesh is from earth, and he received flesh from the flesh of Mary. And because he walked here in very flesh, and gave that very flesh to us to eat for our salvation – and no one eats that flesh, unless he has first worshipped – we have found out in what sense such a footstool of our Lord's may be worshipped, and not only that we sin not in worshipping it, but that we sin in not worshipping [it]. But does the flesh give life? Our Lord himself, when he was speaking in praise of this same earth, said: "It is the Spirit that quickens, the flesh profits nothing"... But when our Lord praised it, he was speaking of his own flesh, and he had said: "Except a man eat my flesh, he shall have no life in him" (John 6:54). Some disciples of his, about seventy, were offended, and said: "This is an hard saying, who can hear it? And they went back, and walked no more with him". It seemed unto them hard that he said: "Except ye eat the flesh of the Son of Man, you have no life in you". They received it foolishly, they thought of it carnally, and imagined that the Lord would cut off parts from his body, and give unto them; and they said: "This is a hard saying". [But] it was they who were hard, not the saying; for unless they had been hard, and not meek, they would have said unto themselves, he says not this without reason, but there must be some latent mystery herein. They would have remained with him, softened, not hard: and would have learned that from him [that] which they who remained, when the others departed, learned. For when twelve disciples had remained with him, on their [the others'] departure, these remaining followers suggested to him, as if in grief for the death of the former, that they were offended by his words, and turned back. But he

325

agree, neither salvation nor eternal life can be hoped for by any man without baptism and the Lord's body and blood, it is vain to promise these blessings to infants without them. Moreover, if it be only sins that separate man from salvation and eternal life, there is nothing else in infants which these sacraments can be the means of removing, but the guilt of sin – respecting which guilty nature it is written, that no one is clean, not even if his life be only that of a day (Job 14:4). Whence also that exclamation of the Psalmist: 'Behold, I was shapen in iniquity; and in sin did my mother conceive me' [Ps. 51:5]! This is either said in the person of our common humanity, or if of himself only David speaks, it does not imply that he was born of fornication, but in lawful wedlock. We therefore ought not to doubt that even for infants yet to be baptised was that precious blood shed, which previous to its actual effusion was so given, and applied in the sacrament, that it was said: 'This is my blood, which shall be shed for many for the remission of sins' (Matt. 26:28)... (1.34).

Infants, unless they pass into the number of believers through the sacrament which was divinely instituted for this purpose, will undoubtedly remain in this darkness (1.35).

Some, however, understand that as soon as children are born they are enlightened; and they derive this opinion from the passage: 'That was the true Light, which lights every one that comes into the world' (John 1:9). Well, if this be the case, it is quite astonishing how it can be that those who are thus enlightened by the only-begotten Son, who was in the beginning the Word with God, and [himself] God, are not admitted into the kingdom of God, nor are heirs of God and joint-heirs with Christ. For that such an inheritance is not bestowed upon them except through baptism, even they who hold the opinion in question do acknowledge. Then, again, if they are (though already illuminated) thus unfit for entrance into the kingdom of God, they at all events ought gladly to receive the baptism, by which they are fitted for it; but, strange to say, we see how reluctant infants are to submit to baptism, resisting even with

---

instructed them, and says unto them: "It is the Spirit that quickens, but the flesh profits nothing; the words that I have spoken unto you, they are spirit, and they are life" (John 6:63). Understand spiritually what I have said; you are not to eat this body which you see; nor to drink that blood which they who will crucify me shall pour forth. I have commended unto you a certain mystery; spiritually understood, it will quicken. Although it is needful that this be visibly celebrated, yet it must be spiritually understood' (Augustine: *The Ennerations, or Expositions on the Psalms*, Psalm 99 section 8). By 'visibly celebrated', Augustine meant what he called 'the sacrament of the Lord's supper'. It doesn't take a rocket scientist to see how this led to the doctrine of the 'real presence'.

strong crying. And this ignorance of theirs we think lightly of at their time of life, so that we fully administer the sacraments, which we know to be serviceable to them, even although they struggle against them. And why, too, does the apostle say: 'Be not children in understanding' (1 Cor. 14:20), if their minds have been already enlightened with that true Light, which is the Word of God?... (1.36).

In such circumstances, no man of those who have come to Christ by baptism has ever been regarded, according to sound faith and the true doctrine, as excepted from the grace of forgiveness of sins; nor has eternal life been ever thought possible to any man apart from his kingdom... Now none who shall partake of this life shall be made alive except in Christ, even as all die in Adam (1 Cor. 15:22)... Accordingly, also the Lord himself (wishing to remove from the hearts of wrong-believers that vague and indefinite middle condition, which some would provide for unbaptised infants – as if, by reason of their innocence, they were embraced in eternal life, but were not, because of their unbaptised state, with Christ in his kingdom) uttered that definitive sentence of his, which shuts their mouths: he that is not with me is against me (Matt. 12:30). Take then the case of any infant you please: If he is already in Christ, why is he baptised? If, however, as the truth has it, he is baptised just that he may be with Christ, it certainly follows that he who is not baptised is not with Christ; and because he is not with Christ, he is against Christ; for he has pronounced his own sentence, which is so explicit that we ought not, and indeed cannot, impair it or change it... (1.55).

Let us now examine more carefully, so far as the Lord enables us, that very chapter [John 3] where he says: ' Except a man be born again – of water and the Spirit – he shall not enter into the kingdom of God'. If it were not for the authority which this sentence has with them, they would not be of opinion that infants ought to be baptised at all. This is their comment on the passage: Because he does not say: 'Except a man be born again of water and the Spirit, he shall not have salvation or eternal life', but he merely said: 'He shall not enter into the kingdom of God', therefore [those in error say] infants are to be baptised, in order that they [the infants] may be with Christ in the kingdom of God, where they will not be unless they are baptised. Should infants die, however, even without baptism, they will have salvation and eternal life, seeing [those in error say] that they [the infants] are bound with no fetter of sin. Now in such a statement as this, the first thing that strikes one is, that they [in error] never explain where the justice is of separating from the kingdom of God that image of God which has no sin. Next, we ought to see whether the Lord Jesus, the one only good teacher, has not in this very passage of [John] intimated, and indeed shown us, that it only comes to pass through the remission of their sins that baptised persons reach the kingdom of God; although to persons of a right understanding, the words, as they

327

stand in the passage, ought to be sufficiently explicit: 'Except a man be born again, he cannot see the kingdom of God' (John 3:3), and: 'Except a man be born of water and of the Spirit, he cannot enter into the kingdom of God' (John 3:5). For why should he be born again, unless to be renewed? From what is he to be renewed, if not from some old condition? From what old condition, but that in which our old man is crucified with him, that the body of sin might be destroyed (Rom. 6:6)? Or whence comes it to pass that the image of God enters not into the kingdom of God, unless it be that the impediment of sin prevents it? However, let us (as we said before) see, as earnestly and diligently as we are able, what is the entire context of this passage of [John], on the point in question... (1.58).

Since this great and wonderful dignity can only be attained by the remission of sins, [Christ] goes on to say: 'And as Moses lifted up the serpent in the wilderness, even so must the Son of man be lifted up; that whosoever believes in him should not perish, but have eternal life' (John 3:14-15)... As, therefore, it then came to pass that whoever looked at the raised serpent was both healed of the poison and freed from death, so also now, whosoever is conformed to the likeness of the death of Christ by faith in him and his baptism, is freed both from sin by justification, and from death by resurrection. For this is what he says: 'That whosoever believes in him should not perish, but have eternal life' (John 3:15). What necessity then could there be for an infant's being conformed to the death of Christ by baptism, if he were not altogether poisoned by the bite of the serpent? (1.61).

He then proceeds thus, saying: 'God so loved the world, that he gave his only-begotten Son, that whosoever believes in him should not perish, but have everlasting life' (John 3:16). Every infant, therefore, was destined to perish, and to lose everlasting life, if through the sacrament of baptism he believed not in the only-begotten Son of God; while nevertheless, [Christ] comes not so that he may judge the world, but that the world through him may be saved. This especially appears in the following clause, wherein he says: 'He that believes in him is not condemned; but he that believes not is condemned already, because he has not believed in the name of the only-begotten Son of God' (John 3:18). In what class, then, do we place baptised infants but among believers, as the authority of the Catholic Church everywhere asserts? They belong, therefore, among those who have believed; for this is obtained for them by virtue of the sacrament and the answer of their sponsors. And from this it follows that such as are not baptised are reckoned among those who have not believed. Now if they who are baptised are not condemned, these last, as not being baptised, are condemned. He adds, indeed: 'But this is the condemnation, that light is come into the world, and men loved darkness rather than light' (John 3:19). Of what does he say: 'Light is come into the world', if not of his own advent? And without the sacrament of his advent, how are infants said to be in the light? And why should we not include this fact also in men's love of darkness, that as they do not themselves believe, so they refuse to think that their infants ought to be baptised, although they are afraid of their incurring the death of the body? However, [Christ] declares the works of him who comes to the light are wrought in God (John 3:21), because he [the man who comes] is quite aware that his justification results from no merits of his own, but from the grace of God. 'For it is God, says the apostle, who works in you both to will and to do of his own good pleasure' (Phil. 2:13). This then is the way in which spiritual regeneration is effected in all who come to Christ from their carnal generation. He explained it himself, and pointed it out, when he was asked: 'How these things could be?' He left it open to no man to settle such a question by human reasoning, lest infants should be deprived of the grace of the remission of sins. There is no other passage leading to Christ; no man can be reconciled to God, or can come to God otherwise, than through Christ (1.62).

What shall I say of the actual form of this sacrament? I only wish some one of those who espouse the contrary side would bring me an infant to be baptised. What does my exorcism work in that babe, if he be not held in the devil's family? The man who brought the infant would certainly have had to act as sponsor for him, for [the infant] could not answer for himself. How would it be possible then for him to declare that he renounced the devil, if there was no devil in him? that he was converted to God, if he had never been averted from him? that he believed, besides other articles, in the forgiveness of sins, if no sins were attributable to him? For my own part, indeed, if I thought that his opinions were opposed to this faith, I could not permit him to bring the infant to the sacraments. Nor can I imagine with what countenance before men, or what mind before God, he can conduct himself in this. But I do not wish to say anything too severe. That a false or fallacious form of baptism should be administered to infants, in which there might be the sound and semblance of something being done, but yet no remission of sins actually ensue, has been seen by some among them to be as abominable and hateful a thing as it was possible to mention or conceive. Then, again, in respect of the necessity of baptism to infants, they admit that even infants stand in need of redemption – a concession which is made in a short treatise written by one of their party – but yet there is not found in this work any open admission of the forgiveness of a single sin. According, however, to an intimation dropped in your letter to me, they now acknowledge, as you say, that a remission of sins takes place even in infants through baptism. No wonder; for it is impossible that redemption should be understood in any other way. Their own words are these: 'It is, however, not originally, but in their own actual life, after they have been born, that they have begun to have sin' (1.63).

You see how great a difference there is among those whom I have been opposing at such length and persistency in this work – one of whom has written the book which contains the points I have refuted to the best of my ability. You see, as I was saying, the important difference existing between such of them as maintain that infants are absolutely pure and free from all sin, whether original or actual; and those who suppose that so soon as [they are] born, infants have contracted actual sins of their own, from which they need cleansing by baptism. The latter class, indeed, by examining the Scriptures, and considering the authority of the whole Church as well as the form of the sacrament itself, have clearly seen that by baptism remission of sins accrues to infants; but they are either unwilling or unable to allow that the sin which infants have is original sin. The former class, however, have clearly seen (as they easily might) that in the very nature of man, which is open to the consideration of all men, the tender age of which we speak could not possibly commit any sin whatever in its own proper conduct; but, to avoid acknowledging original sin, they assert that there is no sin at all in infants. Now in the truths which they thus severally maintain, it so happens that they first of all mutually agree with each other, and subsequently differ from us in material aspect. For if the one party concede to the other that remission of sins takes place in all infants which are baptised, while the other concedes to their opponents that infants (as infant nature itself in its silence loudly proclaims) have as yet contracted no sin in their own living, then both sides must agree in conceding to us, that nothing remains but original sin, which can be remitted in baptism to infants... (1.64).

In infants it is certain that, by the grace of God, through *his* [Christ's] baptism who came in the likeness of sinful flesh, it is brought to pass that the sinful flesh is done away. This result, however, is so effected, that the unlawful desire [lust] which is diffused over and innate in the living flesh itself is not removed all at once, so as to exist in it no longer; but only that that might not be injurious to a man at his death, which was inherent at his birth. For should an infant live after baptism, and arrive at an age capable of obedience to a law, he finds there somewhat to fight against, and, by God's help, to overcome, if he has not received his grace in vain, and if he is not willing to be a reprobate. For not even to those who are of riper years is it given in baptism (except, perhaps, by an unspeakable miracle of the almighty Creator), that the law of sin which is in their members, warring against the law of their mind, should be entirely extinguished, and cease to exist... (1.70).

We have, my dearest Marcellinus, discussed at sufficient length, I think, in the former book the baptism of infants – how that it is given to them not only for entrance into the kingdom of God, but also for attaining salvation and eternal life, which none can have without the kingdom of God, or without that union with the Saviour Christ, wherein he has redeemed us by his blood. I undertake in the present book to discuss and explain the question: 'Whether there lives in this world, or has yet lived, or ever will live, any one without any sin whatever, except the one mediator between God and man, the man Christ Jesus, who gave himself a ransom for all (1 Tim. 2:5-6)' – with as much care and ability as he may himself vouchsafe to me. And should there occasionally arise in this discussion, either inevitably or casually from the argument, any question about the baptism or the sin of infants, I must neither be surprised nor must I shrink from giving the best answer I can, at such emergencies, to whatever point challenges my attention... (2.1).

Unlawful desire, therefore, as the law of sin which remains in the members of this body of death, is born with infants. In baptised infants, it is deprived of guilt, is left for the struggle [of life], but pursues with no condemnation, such as die before the struggle. Unbaptised infants it implicates as guilty, and, as children of wrath, even if they die in infancy, draws [them] into condemnation. In baptised adults, however, endowed with reason, whatever consent their mind gives to this unlawful desire for the commission of sin is an act of their own will. After all sins have been blotted out, and that guilt has been cancelled which by nature bound men in a conquered condition, it still remains – but not to hurt in any way those who yield no consent to it for unlawful deeds – until death is swallowed up in victory (1 Cor. 15:54) and, in that perfection of peace, nothing is left to be conquered... (2.4).

The apostle indeed says: 'Else were your children unclean, but now are they holy' (1 Cor. 7:14); and therefore they infer there was no necessity for the children of believers to be baptised. I am surprised at the use of such language by persons who deny that original sin has been transmitted from Adam. For, if they take this passage of the apostle to mean that the children of believers are born in a state of holiness, how is it that even they have no doubt about the necessity of their being baptised? Why, in short, do they refuse to admit that any original sin is derived from a sinful parent, if some holiness is received from a holy parent? Now it certainly does not contravene our assertion, even if from the faithful holy children are propagated, when we hold that unless they are baptised those go into damnation, to whom our opponents themselves shut the kingdom of heaven, although they insist that they are without sin, whether actual or original. Or, if they think it an unbecoming thing for holy ones to be damned, how can it be a becoming thing to exclude holy ones from the kingdom of God? They should rather pay special attention to this point: 'How can something sinful help being derived from sinful parents, if something holy is derived from holy parents, and uncleanness from unclean parents?' For the twofold principle was affirmed when he said: 'Else were your children unclean, but now are they holy'. They should also explain to us how it is right that the holy children of believers and the unclean children of unbelievers are, notwithstanding their different circumstances, equally prohibited from entering the kingdom of God, if they have not been baptised. What avails that sanctity of theirs to the one? Now if they were to maintain that the unclean children of unbelievers are damned, but that the holy children of believers are unable to enter the kingdom of heaven unless they are baptised – but nevertheless are not damned, because they are holy – that would be some sort of a distinction; but as it is, they equally declare respecting the holy children of holy parents and the unclean offspring of unclean parents, that they are not damned, since they have not any sin; and that they are excluded from the kingdom of God because they are unbaptised. What an absurdity! Who can suppose that such splendid geniuses do not perceive it? (2.41).

Our opinions on this point are strictly in unison with the apostle's himself, who said: 'From one all to condemnation, and from one all to justification of life'. Now how consistent these statements are with what he elsewhere says, when treating of another point: 'Else were your children unclean, but now are they holy', consider a while. Sanctification is not of merely one measure; for even catechumens, I take it, are sanctified in their own measure by the sign of Christ [the Lord's supper?], and the prayer of imposition of hands; and what they receive [that is, the supper] is holy, although it is not the body of Christ – holier than any food which constitutes our ordinary nourishment, because it is a sacrament. However... the sanctification [that is, taking the Lord's supper] of the catechumen, if he is not baptised, does not avail for his entrance into the kingdom of heaven, nor for the remission of his sins. And, by parity of reasoning, that sanctification likewise, of whatever measure it be, which, according to the apostle, is in the children of believers, has nothing whatever to do with the question of baptism and of the origin or the remission of sin. The apostle, in this very passage which has occupied our attention, says that the unbeliever of a married couple is sanctified by a believing partner: 'For the unbelieving husband is sanctified by the wife, and the unbelieving wife is sanctified by the husband. Else were your children unclean, but now are they holy' (1 Cor. 7:14). Now, I should say, there is not a man whose mind is so warped by unbelief, as to suppose that, whatever sense he gives to these words, they can possibly mean that a husband who is not a Christian should not be baptised, because his wife is a Christian, and that he has already obtained remission of his sins, with the certain prospect of entering the kingdom of heaven, because he is described as being sanctified by his wife (2.42).

If any man, however, is still perplexed by the question why the children of baptised persons are baptised, let him briefly consider this: Inasmuch as the generation of sinful flesh through the one man, Adam, draws into condemnation all who are born of such generation, so the generation of the Spirit of grace through the one man Jesus Christ, draws to the justification of eternal life all who, because predestinated, partake of this regeneration. But the sacrament of baptism is undoubtedly the sacrament of regeneration: Wherefore, as the man who has never lived cannot die, and he who has never died cannot rise again, so he who has never been born cannot be born again. From which the conclusion arises, that no one who has not been born could possibly have been born again in his father. Born again, however, a man must be, after he has been born; because: 'Except a man be born again, he cannot see the kingdom of God' (John 3:3). Even an infant, therefore, must be imbued with the sacrament of regeneration, lest without it his would be an unhappy exit out of this life; and this baptism is not administered except for the remission of sins. And so much does Christ show us in this very passage; for when asked: 'How could such things be?', he reminded his questioner of what Moses did when he lifted up the serpent. Inasmuch, then, as infants are by the sacrament of baptism conformed to the death of Christ, it must be admitted that they are also freed from the serpent's poisonous bite, unless we wilfully wander from the rule of the Christian faith. This bite, however, they did not receive in their own actual life, but in him on whom the wound was primarily inflicted... (2.43).

This law of sin, however, which the apostle also designates sin, when he says: 'Let not sin therefore reign in your mortal body, that you should obey it in the lusts thereof' (Rom. 6:12), does not so remain in the members of those who are born again of water and the Spirit, as if no remission thereof has been made, because there is a full and perfect remission of our sins, all the enmity being slain, which separated us from God; but it remains in our old carnal nature, as if overcome and destroyed, if it does not, by consenting to unlawful objects, somehow revive, and recover its own reign and dominion. There is, however, so clear a distinction to be seen between this old carnal nature, in which the law of sin, or sin, is already repealed, and that life of the Spirit, in the newness of which they who are baptised are through God's grace born again, that the apostle deemed it too little to say of such that they were not in sin... And yet these very persons, because they still carry about Adam's old nature, mortally generate children to be immortally regenerated, with that propagation of sin, in which such as are born again are not held bound, and from which such as are born are released by being born again. As long, then, as the law by unlawful desire dwells in the members, although it remains, the guilt of it is released; but it is released only to him who has received the sacrament of regeneration, and has already begun to be renewed. But whatsoever is born of the old nature, which still abides with its unlawful desire, requires to be born again in order to be healed. Seeing that believing parents, who have been both carnally born and spiritually born again, have themselves begotten children in a carnal manner, how could their children by any possibility, previous to their first birth, have been born again? (2.45).

You must not be surprised at what I have said, that although the law of sin remains with its unlawful desire, the guilt thereof is done away through the grace of the sacrament... (2.46).

And therefore, if there is an ambiguity in the apostle's words when he says: 'By one man sin entered into the world, and death by sin; and so it passed upon all men' (Rom. 5:12); and if it is possible for them to be drawn aside, and applied to some other sense – is there anything ambiguous in this statement: 'Except a man be born again of water and of the Spirit, he cannot enter into the kingdom of God' (John 3:5)? Is this, again, ambiguous: 'You shall call his name Jesus, for he shall save his people from their sins' (Matt. 1:21)? Is there any doubt of what this means: 'The whole need not a physician, but they that are sick' (Matt. 9:12)? – that is, Jesus is not needed by those who have no sin, but by those who are to be saved from sin. Is there anything, again, ambiguous in this: 'Except men eat the flesh of the Son of man, that is, become partakers of his body, they shall not have life'? By these and similar statements, which I now pass over – absolutely clear in the light of God, and absolutely certain by his authority – does not truth proclaim without ambiguity, that unbaptised infants not only cannot enter into the kingdom of God, but cannot have everlasting life, except in the body of Christ, in order that they may be incorporated into which they are washed in the sacrament of baptism? Does not truth, without any dubiety, testify that for no other reason are they carried by pious hands to Jesus (that is, to Christ, the Saviour and Physician), than that they may be healed of the plague of their sin by the medicine of his sacraments? Why then do we delay so to understand the apostle's very words, of which we perhaps used to have some doubt, that they may agree with these statements of which we can have no manner of doubt?... (3.8).

With these and such like palpable arguments, should I endeavour, as I best could, to convince those persons who believed that sacraments of cleansing were superfluously applied to the children of the cleansed, how right is the judgement of baptising the infants of baptised parents, and how it may happen that to a man who has within him the twofold seed – of death in the flesh, and of immortality in the spirit – that may prove no obstacle, regenerated as he is by the Spirit, which is an obstacle to his son, who is generated by the flesh; and that that may be cleansed in the one by remission, which in the other still requires cleansing by like remission, just as in the case supposed of circumcision, and as in the case of the winnowing and thrashing. But now, when we are contending with those who allow that the children of the baptised ought to be baptised, we may much more conveniently conduct our discussion, and can say: You who assert that the children of such persons as have been cleansed from the pollution of sin ought to have been born without sin, why do you not perceive that by the same rule you might just as well say that the children of Christian parents ought to have been born Christians? Why, therefore, do you rather maintain that they ought to become Christians? Was there not in their parents, to whom it is said: 'Do you not know that your bodies are the members of Christ' (1 Cor. 6:15) – a Christian body? Perhaps you suppose that a Christian body may be born of Christian parents, without having received a Christian soul? Well, this would render the case much more wonderful still. For you would think of the soul one of two things as you pleased – because, of course, you hold with the apostle, that before birth it had done nothing good or evil (Rom. 9:11) – either that it was derived by transmission, and just as the body of Christians is Christian, so should also their soul be Christian; or else that it was created by Christ, either in the Christian body, or for the sake of the Christian body, and it ought therefore to have been created or given in a Christian condition. Unless perchance you shall pretend that, although Christian parents had it in their power to beget a Christian body, yet Christ himself was not able to produce a Christian soul. Believe then the truth, and see that, as it has been possible (as you yourselves admit) for one who is not a Christian to be born of Christian parents, for one who is not a member of Christ to be born of members of Christ, and (that we may answer all, who, however falsely, are yet in some sense possessed with a sense of religion) for a man who is not consecrated to be born of parents who are consecrated; so also it is quite possible for one who is not cleansed to be born of parents who are cleansed. Now what account will you give us, of why from Christian parents is born one who is not a Christian, unless it be that not generation, but regeneration makes Christians? Resolve therefore your own question with a like reason, that cleansing from sin comes to no one by being born, but to all by being born again. And thus any child who is born of parents who are cleansed, because born again, must himself be born again, in order that he too may be cleansed. For it has been quite possible for parents to transmit to their children that which they did not possess themselves – thus resembling not only the wheat which yielded the chaff, and the circumcised the foreskin, but also the instance which you yourselves adduce, even that of believers who convey unbelief to their posterity; which, however, does not accrue to the faithful as regenerated by the Spirit, but it is owing to the fault of the mortal seed by which they have been born of the flesh. For in respect of the infants whom you judge it necessary to make believers by the sacrament of the faithful, you do not deny that they were born in unbelief although of believing parents... (3.17).

Nevertheless, whatever be the sanctification meant, this must be steadily held: that there is no other valid means of making Christians and remitting sins, except by men becoming believers through the sacrament according to the institution of Christ and the Church. For neither are unbelieving husbands and wives, notwithstanding their intimate union with holy and righteous spouses, cleansed of the sin which separates men from the kingdom of God and drives them into condemnation, nor are the children who are born of parents, however just and holy, absolved from the guilt of original sin, unless they have been baptised into Christ; and in behalf of these our plea should be the more earnest, the less able they are to urge one themselves (3.21).

For this is the point aimed at by the controversy, against the novelty of which we have to struggle by the aid of ancient truth; [namely,] that it is clearly altogether superfluous for infants to be baptised. Not that this opinion is avowed in so many words, lest so firmly established a custom of the Church should be unable to endure its assailants. But if we are taught to render help to orphans, how much more ought we to labour in behalf of those children who, though under the protection of parents, will still be left more destitute and wretched than orphans, should that grace of Christ be denied them, which they are all unable to demand for themselves? (3.22).

As I have explained, in his *On Baptism, Against the Donatists*, Augustine wrote extensively on the question of whether a Donatist, wanting to join (or rejoin) the Catholic Church, should be re-baptised. Although some Fathers thought they should – principally Cyprian – Augustine thought not. Twelve hundred years later, Calvin, as I have shown, when faced with a similar question – converts leaving Rome and joining the Reformed Church – was prepared to accept infant baptism performed in the Church of Rome. Echoes of Augustine can be clearly heard in Calvin. In what follows, I summarise Augustine's 'reasoning' and conclusions – although, I have to confess, I have not always found it easy to unravel his meaning, and his conclusions seem, to me at least, to be self-contradictory:

If a person is baptised in the Catholic Church, he does not lose its benefit by leaving the Church, and is not to be re-baptised on rejoining. Indeed, the priest who possesses the power to baptise because of his ordination in the Catholic Church, does not lose that power by his defection. Once a man has been ordained by the Catholic Church as a priest with the power of sacramental baptism, he always retains that power (1.1.2).

Although the schismatics' baptism is a defective baptism (1.3.4), if in doubt, it is better to be baptised by the schismatics than not at all (1.5.6). Nevertheless, it is the Catholic Church alone which has the power to regenerate by the sacrament of baptism. If the schismatics retain the essence of the Catholic Church, their baptism can regenerate (1.10.13; 1.10.14).

The reason why the schismatics have lost the power to regenerate by baptism is because they hate their brothers (showing this by their leaving the Catholic Church) (1.11.15; 1.15.16).

Even so, the baptism practised by the schismatics is a true baptism (1.11.17).

But those baptised by baptism in the Catholic Church are regenerated, and once regenerated by baptism need not be re-baptised, even if they defect to the schismatics or fall by temptation. The same goes for the schismatics – their baptism is effective because of its derivation from the Catholic Church, even though their system is false (1.12.19; 1.14.22; 1.19.29).

Cyprian got it wrong. He thought there could no baptism among the heretics and schismatics. But in saying this, he failed to distinguish 'the sacrament from the effect or use of the sacrament'. He failed to recognise that even in the Catholic Church many who are baptised prove to be chaff. Further, he did not realise that even though the schismatics' baptism failed to stop them sinning, nevertheless they had the sacrament itself (6.1.1)

Bad people (that is, bad priests) who have been baptised may confer true baptism – whether or not the baptism is saving or damning to the one being baptised depends on the one being baptised, not the baptiser (6.3.5; 6.4.6).

Baptised heretics, even though baptised by heretics, should not be re-baptised when coming back to the Catholic Church (6.16.27).

Although only the Catholic Church possesses the real baptism, every baptism which is performed with the right formula – by heretics or schismatics – is true baptism (6.25.47).

Heretics have the same baptism as the Catholic Church in the outward form but not the inward reality (7.15.29; 7.19.37).

Heretics who were baptised in the Catholic Church, did not lose its benefit when they defected – nor do they need to be re-baptised when they return (7.29.57).

Catholic baptism alone is saving (7.39.77).

The right formula makes baptism right whatever the circumstances of the baptism, even among heretics (7.47.93).

The right formula makes baptism right whatever the circumstances of the baptism, but unless they return to the Catholic Church (that is, have and show charity) heretics will not be saved (7.53.102).

The schismatics' baptism is ineffective, but when they return to the Catholic Church, they do not need to re-baptised – they are already baptised – but upon their return to the Catholic Church, their baptism becomes effective (7.54.103).

Indices

Source List

Act 3 Review, Vol.15, number 2, 2006, Carol Stream.

Alexander, Archibald: *Thoughts on Religious Experience*, The Banner of Truth Trust, Edinburgh, reprinted 1978.

Alexander, J.A.: *A Commentary on the Gospel of Mark*, The Banner of Truth Trust, London, 1960.

Alford, Henry: *The New Testament for English Readers...*, Vol.1 Part 2, Rivingtons, London, 1863.

Armstrong, Dave: *Baptismal Regeneration: Luther, Wesley, and Anglicanism*, internet 1996.

Armstrong, John H. (ed.): *Understanding Four Views On Baptism*, Zondervan, Grand Rapids, 2007.

Anderson, Robert: 'Christian Baptism and Baptismal Regeneration', being an Appendix to *The Bible or the Church?*, London, 1908.

Arndt, William F. and Gingrich, F.Wilbur: *A Greek-English Lexicon of the New Testament and Other Early Christian Literature*, The University of Chicago Press, Chicago... and The Syndics of the Cambridge University Press, London, 1957.

Bannerman, James: *The Church of Christ*, Vol.2, The Banner of Truth Trust, London, 1960.

Banner of Truth, The Banner of Truth Trust, Edinburgh.

Barach, John: 'Covenant and Election', in Wilkins, Steve and Garner, Duane (eds.): *The Federal Vision*, Athanasius Press, Monroe, 2004.

Barnhouse, Donald G.: 'The Meaning of the Term "Baptism"', in Stevenson, Herbert F. (ed.): *The Ministry of Keswick*, Second series, Marshall, Morgan and Scott, London, 1964.

Bauckham, Richard J.: 'Adding to the Church – During the Early American Period', being a paper given at The Westminster Conference 1973: *Adding to the Church*.

Beasley-Murray, G.R.: *Baptism Today and Tomorrow*, Macmillan, London, 1966.

Beasley-Murray, G.R.: *Baptism in the New Testament*, The Paternoster Press, Exeter, 1972.

Beckwith, Francis J.: *Return to Rome: Confessions of an Evangelical Catholic*, Brazos Press, Grand Rapids, 2009.

Bengel, John Albert: *Gnomon of the New Testament*, Vol.2, T.&T.Clark, Edinburgh, 1859.

Berkhof, L.: *Systematic Theology*, The Banner of Truth Trust, London, 1959.

Boorman, David: 'The Halfway Covenant', being a paper given at The Westminster Conference 1976: *The Puritan Experiment in the New World*.

Bradshaw, Paul F.: 'The profession of faith in early Christian baptism', in *Evangelical Quarterly*, April 2006.

Bremer, Francis J.: *Congregational Communion: Clerical Friendship in the Anglo-American Puritan Community, 1610-1692*, Northeastern University Press, Boston, 1994.

Bromiley, G.W.: *Thomas Cranmer: Theologian*, Lutterworth Press, London, 1956.

Brook, Benjamin: *The Lives of the Puritans*, Vol.2, Soli Deo Gloria Publications, Morgan, reprinted 1994.

Brown, John: *An Exposition of Hebrews*, The Banner of Truth Trust, London, 1961.

Brown, John: *Expository Discourses on 1 Peter*, Vol.2, The Banner of Truth Trust, Edinburgh, 1975.

Bruce, F.F.: *The English Bible...*, University Paperbacks, Methuen, London, 1963.

Buchanan, Colin: *A Case for Infant Baptism*, Grove Books Limited, Bramcote, 1990.

Buchanan, Colin and Vasey, Michael: *New Initiation Rites...*, Grove Books Limited, Cambridge, 1998.

Buchanan, Colin: 'David Wright: *What has Infant Baptism done to Baptism?...*: A response by an English Anglican Evangelical', in *Evangelical Quarterly*, April 2006.

Buse, S.I: 'Baptism in the Acts of the Apostles', in Gilmore, A. (ed.): *Christian Baptism...*, Lutterworth, London, 1959.

Calvin, John: *Institutes of the Christian Religion*, James Clarke and Co., Limited, London, 1957.

Calvin, John: *Commentaries*, Baker Book House, Grand Rapids, reprinted 1979.

Calvin, John: *Letters of John Calvin...*, The Banner of Truth Trust, Edinburgh, 1980.

Carson, H.M.: *Farewell to Anglicanism*, Henry E.Walter Ltd., Worthing, 1969.

Carson, H.M.: *The New Catholicism*, The Banner of Truth Trust, London.

Carson, H.M.: *Dawn or Twilight? A study of contemporary Roman Catholicism*, Inter-Varsity Press, Leicester, 1976.

Castelein, John D., in Armstrong, John H. (ed.): *Understanding Four Views on Baptism*, Zondervan, Grand Rapids, 2007.

Clark, Neville: 'The Theology of Baptism', in Gilmore, A. (ed.): *Christian Baptism...*, Lutterworth, London, 1959.

Clarkson, David: *Works*, Vol.1, The Banner of Truth Trust, Edinburgh, 1988.

Clifford, A.C.: *Reformed Liturgy...*, Norwich Reformed Church, 2002.

Cole, R.A.: *The Gospel According to... Mark*, The Tyndale Press, London, 1961.

Cotton, John: *An Exposition of First John*, Sovereign Grace Publishers, Evansville, 1962.

Cramp, J.M.: *Baptist History*, Elliot Stock, London, 1875.

Cross, Anthony R.: 'Spirit- and Water-Baptism in 1 Corinthians 12:13', in Porter, Stanley E. and Cross, Anthony R. (eds.): *Dimensions of Baptism*, Sheffield Academic Press, Sheffield, 2003.

Cross, Anthony R.: 'The Evangelical sacrament: *baptisma semper reformandum*', in *Evangelical Quarterly*, July 2008.

Cunningham, William: *Historical Theology*, The Banner of Truth Trust, London, 1960.

Dabney, R.L.: *Systematic Theology*, The Banner of Truth Trust, Edinburgh, 1985.

Davenant, John: *Dissertation on the Death of Christ*, Quinta Press, Weston Rhyn, 2006.

Davies, Horton: *Worship and Theology in England...*, Book 1, William B.Eerdmans, Grand Rapids, 1996.

Dever, Mark E.: *Richard Sibbes: Puritanism and Calvinism in Late Elizabethan and Early Stuart England*, Mercer University Press, Macon, 2000.

Diprose, Ronald E.: *Israel in the Development of Christian Thought*, Instituto Biblico Evangelico Italiano, Rome, 2000.

Douglas, J.D. (gen. ed.): *The New International Dictionary of the Christian Church*, The Paternoster Press, Exeter, 1974.

Dunn, James D.G.: *The Epistle to the Galatians*, A&C Black, London, 1993.

Edwards, Jonathan: *The Works of Jonathan Edwards*, Vol.1, The Banner of Truth Trust, Edinburgh, reprinted 1976.

Edwards, Mark U.: *Luther's Last Battles... 1531-46*, Cornell University Press, Ithaca, 1983.

Ella, George Melvyn: *The Covenant of Grace and Christian Baptism*, VKW/RVB, 2007.

Engelsma, David J.: *The Covenant of God and the Children of Believers*, Protestant Reformed Church, South Holland, Illinois, third printing, 1993.

Evangelical Quarterly..., Paternoster, Milton Keynes.

Fee, Gordon D.: *The First Epistle to the Corinthians*, William B.Eerdmans Publishing Company, Grand Rapids, reprinted 1991.

Fee, Gordon D.: *God's Empowering Presence: The Holy Spirit in the Letters of Paul*, Hendrickson Publishers, Peabody, Massachusetts, 1994.

Fowler, Stanley K.: *More than a Symbol: The British Baptist Recovery of Baptismal Sacramentalism*, Wipf and Stock Publishers, Eugene, 2006.

Friesen, Abraham: *Erasmus, the Anabaptists, and the Great Commission*, Wm. B.Eerdmans Publishing Co., Grand Rapids, 1998.

Fuller, Andrew: *The Practical Uses of Christian Baptism*, in *The Complete Works of... Andrew Fuller...*, Henry G.Bohn, London, 1866.

Fuller, Andrew: *Essays, Letters, &c., on Ecclesiastical Polity*, in *The Complete Works of... Andrew Fuller...*, Henry G.Bohn, London, 1866.

Gadsby, William: *Sermons by William Gadsby...*, Gospel Standard Trust Publications, Harpenden, 1991.

Gay, David: *Battle for the Church*, Brachus, Lowestoft, 1997.

Gay, David H.J.: *The Gospel Offer is Free*, Brachus, Biggleswade, 2004.

Gay, David H.J.: *Particular Redemption and the Free Offer*, Brachus, Biggleswade, 2008.

Gill, John: *The Cause of God and Truth*, W.H.Collingridge, London, 1855.

Gill, John: *Gill's Commentary*, Baker Book House, Grand Rapids, 1980.

Gillies, Donald: *Unity in the Dark*, The Banner of Truth Trust, London, 1964.

Godet, Frederick Louis: *A Commentary on the Gospel of Luke*, Two Volumes in One, Zondervan Publishing House, Grand Rapids.

Gospel Hymns, compiled by The Strict and Particular Baptist Society, London, 1915. Third Edition 1935.

Gouge, William: *Commentary on Hebrews*, Kregel Publications, Grand Rapids, 1980.

Grass, Tim, and Randall, Ian: 'C.H.Spurgeon on the Sacraments', in Cross, Anthony R. and Thompson, Philip E. (eds.): *Baptist Sacramentalism*, Wipf and Stock Publishers, Eugene, 2003.

Grimm-Thayer: *A Greek-English Lexicon of the New Testament*, Baker Book House, Grand Rapids, 1991.

Haldane, J.A.: *The Doctrine of the Atonement...*, Old Paths Gospel Press, Choteau.

Hanko, Herman: *We and Our Children*, Reformed Free Publishing Association, Grand Rapids, 1981.

Hanko, Herman: *Ought the Church to Pray for Revival?*, The Covenant Reformed Fellowship, Larne, 1990.

Harrison, Graham: 'Becoming A Christian – in the Teaching of John Calvin', being a paper given at The Westminster Conference 1972: *'Becoming A Christian'*.

Harvey, Thomas: 'Baptism as a Means of Grace: A Response to John Stott's "The Evangelical Doctrine of Baptism"', in *Churchman* Vol.113 number 2 ,1999.

Hedegård, David: *Ecumenism and the Bible*, The Banner of Truth Trust, London, 1964.

Hendriksen, William: *The Gospel of Mark*, The Banner of Truth Trust, Edinburgh, 1975.

Hendriksen, William: *The Gospel of Luke*, The Banner of Truth Trust, Edinburgh, 1979.

Hendriksen, William: *The Gospel of John*, The Banner of Truth Trust, London, 1959.

Hendriksen, William: *Galatians*, The Banner of Truth Trust, Edinburgh, 1974.

Hendriksen, William: *Colossians and Philemon*, The Banner of Truth Trust, Edinburgh, reprinted 1974.

Hendriksen, William: *Commentary on I and II Timothy and Titus*, The Banner of Truth Trust, London, 1959.

Hill, Christopher: *The English Bible and the Seventeenth-Century Revolution*, Penguin Books, London, 1994.

Hill, Christopher: *The Experience of Defeat: Milton and Some Contemporaries*, Bookmarks, London, 1994.

Hodge, A.A.: *Evangelical Theology*, The Banner of Truth Trust, Edinburgh, 1976.

Hodge, Charles: *A Commentary on Romans*, The Banner of Truth Trust, London, 1972.

Hodge, Charles: *An Exposition of the First Epistle to the Corinthians*, The Banner of Truth Trust, London, reprinted 1964.

Hodge, Charles: *A Commentary on the Epistle to the Ephesians*, The Banner of Truth Trust, London, 1964.

Hoeksema, Herman: *The Biblical Ground for the Baptism of Infants*, Sunday School of the First Protestant Reformed Church, Grand Rapids, 1990.

Holland, Bernard G.: *Baptism in Early Methodism*, Epworth Press, London, 1970.

Horne, Mark: 'What's for Dinner? Calvin's Continuity with the Bible's and the Ancient Church's Eucharistic Faith', in Wilkins, Steve and Garner, Duane (eds.): *The Federal Vision*, Athanasius Press, Monroe, 2004.

Hulse, Erroll: *The Restoration of Israel*, Henry E. Walter, Ltd., Worthing, 1968.

Hutcheson, George: *The Gospel of John*, The Banner of Truth Trust, London, 1972.

Hyde, Daniel R.: 'A Catechism on the Holy Spirit – 4: The Work of the Holy Spirit upon the Church', in *Banner Of Truth*, May 2008.

Jones, Hywel R.: *Gospel and Church: An evangelical evaluation of ecumenical documents on church unity*, Evangelical Press of Wales, Bryntirion, 1989.

Kendall, R.T.: *Calvin and English Calvinism to 1649*, Paternoster Press, Carlisle, 1997.

Kingdon, David: *Children of Abraham*, Henry E. Walter Ltd., Worthing, 1973.

Knox, D.Broughton: *The Lord's Supper from Wycliffe to Cranmer*, The Paternoster Press, Exeter, 1983.

Lane, Anthony N.S.: 'Baptism in the thought of David Wright', in *Evangelical Quarterly*, April 2006.

Lang, G.H.: *The Local Assembly...*, Raven Publishing Company, Belfast, 1955.

Lang, G.H.: *The Churches of God*, The Paternoster Press, London, 1959.

Leach, Chris: *Children and the Holy Spirit*, Kingsway Publications, Eastbourne, 2001.

LeBruyns, Clint: 'The Evangelical Advantage: A New Engagement with the Petrine Ministry', in *Act 3 Review*, Vol.15, number 2, 2006, Carol Stream.

Legg, John: 'Children of the Covenant', being a paper given at the 1982 Congregational Studies Conference, The Evangelical Fellowship of Congregational Churches.

Leithart, Peter J.: '"Judge Me, O God": Biblical Perspectives on Justification', in Wilkins, Steve and Garner, Duane (eds.): *The Federal Vision*, Athanasius Press, Monroe, 2004.

Lloyd-Jones, D.Martyn: *An Exposition of Romans 3:20 – 4:25. Atonement and Justification*, The Banner of Truth Trust, Edinburgh, 1970.

Lloyd-Jones, D.Martyn: *An Exposition of Romans 6. The New Man*, The Banner of Truth Trust, Edinburgh, 1975.

Lloyd-Jones, D.Martyn: *Romans: An Exposition of Chapter 8:5-17. The Sons of God*, The Banner of Truth Trust, Edinburgh, 1974.

Lloyd-Jones, D.Martyn: *An Exposition of Romans 9. God's Sovereign Purpose*, The Banner of Truth Trust, Edinburgh, 1991.

Lloyd-Jones, D.Martyn: *An Exposition of Ephesians 1:1-23. God's Ultimate Purpose*, The Banner of Truth Trust, Edinburgh, 1978.

Lloyd-Jones, D.Martyn: *An Exposition of Ephesians 4:1-16. Christian Unity*, The Banner of Truth Trust, Edinburgh, 1980.

Lloyd-Jones, D.Martyn: *Preaching and Preachers*, Hodder and Stoughton, London, reprinted 1973.

Lloyd-Jones, D.Martyn: *The Puritans: Their Origins and Successors*, The Banner of Truth Trust, Edinburgh, 1987.

Lloyd-Jones, D.Martyn: *The Church and the Last Things*, Hodder and Stoughton, London, 1998.

Lumpkin, William L.: *Baptist Confessions of Faith*, Judson Press, Valley Forge, Sixth Printing, 1989.

Lusk, Rich: 'Paedobaptism and Baptismal Efficacy: Historic Trends and Current Controversies', in Wilkins, Steve and Garner, Duane (eds.): *The Federal Vision*, Athanasius Press, Monroe, 2004.

Lusk, Rich: 'New Life and Apostasy: Hebrews 6:4-8 as Test Case', in Wilkins, Steve and Garner, Duane (eds.): *The Federal Vision*, Athanasius Press, Monroe, 2004.

Lusk, Rich: 'Introduction', in Sadler, M.F.: *The Second Adam and The New Birth; or, The Doctrine of Baptism as Contained in Holy Scripture*, Athanasius Press, Monroe, 2004.

Luther, Martin: *A Commentary on Paul's Epistle to the Galatians*, James Clarke and Co., Ltd., London, reprinted 1961.

Macleod, Donald: *The Spirit of Promise*, Christian Focus Publications, Fearn, 1986.

Macleod, John: *Scottish Theology...*, The Banner of Truth Trust, Edinburgh, 1974.

Marshall, Howard: 'The Meaning of the Verb "Baptise"', in Porter, Stanley E. and Cross, Anthony R. (eds.): *Dimensions of Baptism*, Sheffield Academic Press, Sheffield, 2003.

Mather, Cotton: *The Great Works of Christ in America...*, Vol.2, The Banner of Truth Trust, Edinburgh, 1979.

McGrath, Alister E.: *Understanding Doctrine: Its Purpose and Relevance Today*, Hodder and Stoughton, 1990.

McGrath, Alister E.: *Christianity: An Introduction*, Blackwell Publishing, Malden, 2006.

McNeill, John T.: *The History and Character of Calvinism*, Oxford University Press, New York, 1967.

Middlekauff, Robert: *The Mathers: Three Generations of Puritan Intellectuals, 1596-1728*, Oxford University Press, London, 1971.

Miller, Graham: *Calvin's Wisdom*, The Banner of Truth Trust, Edinburgh, 1992.

Miller, Perry: *The New England Mind: From Colony to Province*, Beacon Press, Boston, 1961.

Milton, John: *Areopagitica and Other Prose Works*, J.M.Dent & Sons Ltd., London, 1927.

Moore, Jonathan D.: *English Hypothetical Universalism: John Preston and the Softening of Reformed Theology*, William B.Eerdmans Publishing Company, Grand Rapids, 2007.

Morgan, Edmund S.: *Visible Saints: The History of a Puritan Idea*, Cornell University Press, Ithaca, 1963.

Moule, Handley C.G.: *The Epistle to the Romans*, Pickering & Inglis Ltd., London.

Murray, Iain: *The Reformation of the Church: A collection of Reformed and Puritan documents on Church issues*, selected with introductory notes, The Banner of Truth Trust, London, 1965.

Murray, Iain H.: *The Forgotten Spurgeon*, The Banner of Truth Trust, London, 1966.

Murray, Iain H.: *D.Martyn Lloyd-Jones*, Vols. 1 & 2, The Banner of Truth Trust, Edinburgh, 1982/1990.

Murray, Iain H.: *Jonathan Edwards*, The Banner of Truth Trust, Edinburgh, reprinted 1992.

Murray, John: *The Epistle to the Romans*, Two Volumes in One, Marshall, Morgan and Scott, London, 1974.

Murray, Stuart: *Biblical Interpretation in the Anabaptist Tradition*, Pandora Press, Kitchener, 2000.

Murray, Stuart: *Post-Christendom*, Paternoster Press, Milton Keynes, 2004.

Nettles, Thomas J., in Armstrong, John H. (ed.): *Understanding Four Views on Baptism*, Zondervan, Grand Rapids, 2007.

Newton, Benjamin Wills: *The Doctrine of Scripture Respecting Baptism Briefly Considered*, Lucas Collins, London, 1907.

Nicholls, John D.: '"Union with Christ": John Calvin on the Lord's Supper', being a paper given at The Westminster Conference 1979: *Union and Communion: 1529-1979*.

Nugent, Donald: *Ecumenism in the Age of the Reformation: The Colloquy of Poissy*, Harvard University Press, Cambridge, 1974.

Nuttall, Geoffrey F. and Chadwick, Owen (eds.): *From Uniformity to Unity, 1662-1962*, S.P.C.K., London, 1962.

'Obituary: Jaroslav Pelikan', in *The Daily Telegraph* May 17th 2006.

O'Donnell, Matthew Brook: 'Two Opposing Views on Baptism with/by the Holy Spirit and of 1 Corinthians 12:13. Can Grammatical Investigation Bring Clarity?', in Porter, Stanley E. and Cross, Anthony R. (eds.): *Baptism, the New Testament and the Church*, Sheffield Academic Press, Sheffield, 1999.

Owen, John: *An Exposition of Hebrews*, 7 Volumes in 4, Sovereign Grace Publishers, Evansville 13, Indiana, 1960.

Owen, John: *A Practical Exposition upon Psalm 130*, in *The Works of John Owen*, Vol.6, edited by William H.Goold, The Banner of Truth Trust, London, 1966.

Owen, John: *Of Infant Baptism and Dipping*, in *The Works of John Owen*, Vol.16, edited by William H.Goold, The Banner of Truth Trust, London, 1968.

Packer, J.I.: *Keep in Step with the Spirit*, Inter-Varsity Press, Leicester, 1984.

Paul, Robert S.: *The Assembly of the Lord...*, T.&T.Clark, Edinburgh, 1985.

Pawson, David, and Buchanan, Colin: *Infant Baptism under Cross-Examination*, Grove Books, Bramcote, 1974.

Pelikan, Jaroslav: *Spirit versus Structure: Luther and the Institutions of the Church*, Collins, London, 1968.

Pettit, Norman: *The Heart Prepared: Grace and Conversion in Puritan Spiritual Life*, Yale University Press, New Haven and London, 1966.

Philpot, J.C.: *Two Letters... Strict Communion... Were Christ's Disciples Baptised?... Extracted, with Corrections from the Gospel Standard for 1840*, Gospel Standard Publications, London, 1967.

Plumb, J.H.: 'The Historian', in Taylor, A.J.P., James, Robert Rhodes, Plumb, J.H., Hart, Basil Liddell and Storr, Anthony: *Churchill: Four Faces and the Man*, Book Club Associates, London, 1969.

Plumer, William S.: *Commentary on... Hebrews*, Baker Book House, Grand Rapids, 1980.

Plummer, A.: *The Gospel according to... John...*, Cambridge University Press, Cambridge, 1891.

Poole, Matthew: *A Commentary on The Holy Bible*, Vol.3, The Banner of Truth Trust, Edinburgh, reprinted 1975.

Pratt, Richard L., in Armstrong, John H. (ed.): *Understanding Four Views on Baptism*, Zondervan, Grand Rapids, 2007.

Rainbow, Jonathan H.: '"Confessor Baptism": The Baptismal Doctrine of the Early Anabaptists', in Schreiner, Thomas R. & Wright, Shawn D. (eds.): *Believer's Baptism: Sign of the New Covenant in Christ*, B&H Academic, Nashville, 2006.

Ramsbottom, B.A.: *Stranger than Fiction: The Life of William Kiffin*, Gospel Standard Trust Publications, Harpenden, 1989.

Reymond, Robert L.: *Contending for the Faith...*, Mentor, Fearn, 2005.

Riggs, John W.: *Baptism in the Reformed Tradition: A Historical and Practical Theology*, Westminster John Knox Press, Louisville and London, 2002.

Robertson, Edwin: 'A Personal Odyssey', being a review article in *Theology*, Vol. LXXXIX July 1986 no.730, SPCK, Holy Trinity Church, Marylebone Road, London NW1 4DU.

Ross, J.M.: 'The Theology of Baptism in Baptist History', in *The Baptist Quarterly*, Vol.XV no.3, July 1953.

Rosser, John: 'The Anglican Position: "Concensus Communion" (from the first Prayer Book to Series 3)', being a paper given at The Westminster Conference 1979: *Union and Communion: 1529-1979*.

Sadler, M.F.: *The Second Adam and the New Birth; or, The Doctrine of Baptism as Contained in Holy Scripture*, Athanasius Press, Monroe, 2004.

Sandlin, P.Andrew: 'The Importance of Being Catholic', in *Act 3 Review*, Vol.15, number 2, 2006, Carol Stream.

Sartelle, John P.: *Infant Baptism, What Christian Parents Should Know*, Presbyterian and Reformed, Phillipsburg, 1985.

Schrotenboer, Paul (ed.): 'An Evangelical Response to "Baptism, Eucharist and Ministry"', in *Evangelical Review of Theology*, Vol.13 no.4, The Paternoster Press, Exeter, October 1989.

Shaw, Robert: *The Reformed Faith*, Christian Focus Publications, Inverness, reprinted 1974.

Shepard, Thomas: *The Ten Virgins*, Tyndale Bible Society, Florida.

Sibbes, Richard: *Bowels Opened*, in *Works of Richard Sibbes*, Vol.2, The Banner of Truth Trust, Edinburgh, 1983.

Sibbes, Richard: *Exposition of 2 Corinthians 1*, in *Works of Richard Sibbes*, Vol.3, The Banner of Truth Trust, Edinburgh, 1981.

Sibbes, Richard: *The Excellency of the Gospel above the Law*, in *Works of Richard Sibbes*, Vol.4, The Banner of Truth Trust, Edinburgh, 1983.

Sibbes, Richard: *A Fountain Sealed*, in *Works of Richard Sibbes*, Vol.5, The Banner of Truth Trust, Edinburgh, 1977.

Sibbes, Richard: *Lydia's Conversion*, in *Works of Richard Sibbes*, Vol.6, The Banner of Truth Trust, Edinburgh, 1983.

Sibbes, Richard: *The Demand of a Good Conscience*, in *Works of Richard Sibbes*, Vol.7, The Banner of Truth Trust, Edinburgh, 1982.

Spurgeon, C.H.: *The Sword & Trowel...*, Passmore & Alabaster, London, 1867.

Spurgeon, C.H.: *The New Park Street and Metropolitan Tabernacle Pulpit... 1861*, Vol.7, Passmore and Alabaster, London, 1862.

Spurgeon, C.H.: *The Metropolitan Tabernacle Pulpit*, Vol.19, Passmore and Alabaster, London, 1874.

Spurgeon, C.H.: *The Metropolitan Tabernacle Pulpit*, Vol.31, The Banner of Truth Trust, London, 1971.

Spurgeon, C.H.: A sermon on Mark 10:13-16, entitled: 'Jesus and the Children', preached and revised in 1886, *The Metropolitan Tabernacle Pulpit*, Vol.32, The Banner of Truth Trust, London, 1969.

Spurgeon, C.H.: A sermon on Exodus 12:21-27, entitled: 'The Blood of Sprinkling and the Children', preached and revised in 1887, *The Metropolitan Tabernacle Pulpit*, Vol.33, The Banner of Truth Trust, London, 1969.

Spurgeon, C.H.: A sermon on Isaiah 44:1-5, entitled: 'A Promise For Us and For Our Children', preached and revised in 1864, Pilgrim Publications, Pasadena, 1976.

Spurgeon, C.H.: A sermon on Mark 10:13-16, entitled, 'Children Brought To Christ, Not To The Font', preached and revised in 1864, Pilgrim Publications, Pasadena, 1976.

Spurgeon, C.H.: *The Early Years 1834-1859*, The Banner of Truth Trust, London, 1967.

Stander, H.F., and Louw, J.P.: *Baptism in the Early Church*, Carey Publications, Leeds, 2004.

Stout, Harry S.: *The New England Soul: Preaching and Religious Culture in Colonial New England*, Oxford University Press, 1986.

Thayer, Joseph Henry: *A Greek-English Lexicon of the New Testament*, Baker Book House, Grand Rapids, Ninth Printing 1991.

The Confession of Faith and other documents of the Westminster Assembly, The Publication Committee of the Free Presbyterian Church of Scotland, 1967.

The Three Forms of Unity..., Protestant Reformed Churches of America, 1991.

Thompson, Damian: 'Pope gets radical and woos the Anglicans', being an article in *The Daily Telegraph*, November 16th 2007.

Tidball, Derek: 'A Baptist perspective on David Wright, *What has Infant Baptism done to Baptism?...*, in *Evangelical Quarterly*, April 2006.

Toon, Peter: *Born Again: A Biblical and Theological Study of Regeneration*, Baker Book House, Grand Rapids, 1987.

Tracy, Joseph: *The Great Awakening*, The Banner of Truth Trust, Edinburgh, 1976.

Tuttle, George M.: *John Mcleod Campbell on Christian Atonement: So Rich A Soil*, The Handsel Press, Edinburgh, 1986.

Underwood, A.C.: *A History of the English Baptists*, The Carey Kingsgate Press Limited, London, 1947.

Verduin, Leonard: *The Reformers and Their Stepchildren*, The Paternoster Press, Exeter, 1964; reprinted, Baker Book House, Grand Rapids, 1980.

Vincent, M.R.: *Word Studies in the New Testament*, Macdonald Publishing Company, Florida.

Walker, Michael J.: *Baptists at the Table: The Theology of the Lord's Supper amongst English Baptists in the Nineteenth Century*, Baptist Historical Society, Didcot, 1992.

Warfield, Benjamin B.: *Studies in Theology*, The Banner of Truth Trust, Edinburgh, 1988.

Watson, Thomas: *A Body of Divinity...*, The Banner of Truth Trust, London, 1958-1960.

Weber, Timothy P.: *Living in the Shadow of the Second Coming: American Premillennialism, 1875-1982*, The University of Chicago Press, Chicago and London, 1987.

Website (www.bbc.co.uk/religion) of the BBC.

Website (www.providencepca.com) of the Providence PCA Mission Church.

Website (www.newadvent.org) of the Roman Catholic Church.

Website of The Lutheran Church – Missouri Synod.

Wellum, Stephen J.: 'Baptism and the Relationship between the Covenants', in Schreiner, Thomas R. & Wright, Shawn D. (eds.): *Believer's Baptism: Sign of the New Covenant in Christ*, B&H Academic, Nashville, 2006.

Wendel, François: *Calvin: The Origins and Development of his Religious Thought*, Collins, London, 1973.

White, Frank H.: *Christian Baptism*, S.W.Partridge & Co., London.

White, R.E.O.: *The Biblical Doctrine of Initiation*, Hodder and Stoughton, London, 1960.

Wilkins, Steve and Garner, Duane (eds.): *The Federal Vision*, Athanasius Press, Monroe, 2004.

Wilkins, Steve: 'Introduction', in Wilkins, Steve and Garner, Duane (eds.): *The Federal Vision*, Athanasius Press, Monroe, 2004.

Wilkins, Steve: 'Covenant, Baptism, and Salvation', in Wilkins, Steve and Garner, Duane (eds.): *The Federal Vision*, Athanasius Press, Monroe, 2004.

Wilson, A.N.: *The Victorians*, Arrow Books, London, 2003.

Wilson, Douglas: 'The Church: Visible or Invisible', in Wilkins, Steve and Garner, Duane (eds.): *The Federal Vision*, Athanasius Press, Monroe, 2004.

Winstanley, Gerrard: *Selections from his Works*, edited by Hamilton, Leonard, The Cresset Press, London, 1944.

Wright, David. F.: 'Infant Dedication in the Early Church', in Porter, Stanley E. and Cross, Anthony R. (eds.): *Baptism, the New Testament and the Church*, Sheffield Academic Press, Sheffield, 1999.

Wright, David F.: 'Children, Covenant and the Church', in *Themelios*, RTSF, Leicester, Spring 2004.

Wright, David.F.: *What has Infant Baptism done to Baptism? An enquiry at the end of Christendom*, Paternoster Press, Milton Keynes, 2005.

Wright, David: 'Christian baptism: where do we go from here?', in *Evangelical Quarterly...*, April 2006.

Wright, N.T.: *The Challenge of Jesus*, SPCK, London, 2000.

Wright, Shawn D.: 'Baptism and the Logic of Reformed Paedobaptists', in Schreiner, Thomas R. & Wright, Shawn D. (eds.): *Believer's Baptism: Sign of the New Covenant in Christ*, B&H Academic, Nashville, 2006.

Yoder, John Howard: 'The Recovery of the Anabaptist Vision', in *Radical Reformation Reader: Concern No.18*, Scottdale, 1971.

Young, Edward J.: *The Book of Isaiah*, Vol.1, William B.Eerdmans Publishing Company, Grand Rapids, 1976.

Zins, Robert M.: *On the Edge of Apostasy: The Evangelical Romance with Rome*, White Horse Publications, Huntsville, 1998.

Index of Scripture References

Made in the USA
Monee, IL
06 July 2021